The Fathers of the Towns

The Johns Hopkins Studies in Historical and Political Science

Ninety-Fourth Series (1976)

Edward M. Cook, Jr.

THE FATHERS OF
THE TOWNS

Leadership and Community Structure
in Eighteenth-Century New England

The Johns Hopkins University Press
Baltimore and London

This book has been brought to publication with the generous assistance
of the Andrew W. Mellon Foundation.

Edward M. Cook, Jr., is an assistant professor of history at the University of Chicago.

Manufactured in the United States of America

The Johns Hopkins University Press, Baltimore, Maryland 21218
The Johns Hopkins University Press Ltd., London

Library of Congress Catalog Card Number 75-36937
ISBN 0-8018-1741-2

Library of Congress Cataloging in Publication data
will be found on the last printed page of this book.

FOR

LEE

CONTENTS

LIST OF TABLES

PREFACE

In recent decades the colonial New England towns have attracted scholarly interest from several directions. One group of historians, drawing inspiration from sources as diverse as the ancient debate about the Germanic origins of the towns, the stimulating essays of Bernard Bailyn on colonial education and of Edmund Morgan on *The Puritan Family*, recent achievements in urban history, and the attempts of French scholars to seek out local roots of social change before the French Revolution, has produced a series of studies of local communities that seek to understand family organization and behavior, social structure, community ethos, and political behavior in early New England by examining society in one town in elaborate detail. By drawing heavily on modern social science for approaches to research, and on the demographic techniques developed by English and French social historians, members of this group have brought fresh precision to the study of local history.[1] A second, closely related group of historians has focused primarily on religion and the relationship of Puritan religion to the social order, in response to the challenge presented by Perry Miller's hypotheses about the social dimensions of religion in New England. This line of inquiry, which has stimulated both studies of individual communities and studies drawing on traditional literary sources, has partially merged with the one first mentioned in both method and interpretation.[2] Finally, scholars interested in the political process in colonial America have extracted large amounts of information about the numbers, the background, and the apparent motivations of voters and politicians from town and colony records.[3]

The studies produced by scholars of New England local history would now fill a sizable shelf, but the interpretive advances hardly seem proportional to the effort invested. Part of the deficiency undoubtedly stems from the natural contentiousness of scholars, but the diverse aims, methods, and techniques embodied in the studies also contribute to the confusion that has arisen. Conflicting conclusions reached in local studies employing similar methodologies have demonstrated the danger of assuming that any one town was typical of a colony or of the whole region, and have pointed up the need for some kind of conceptual framework for explaining how the experience of one town might relate to that of another. The absence of comparative information on a large number of communities also has hampered the interpretation of statistical data within individual towns. Statistics on population and family structure can often be compared with similar statistics in European studies to provide perspective on their meaning. When New England local studies propose measures of social and political behavior, however, they usually break new ground, leaving the probable range of variation from community to community very much in doubt. Until a scale of numerical variation is established, the behavioral correlates of any particular value remain extremely unclear.

The problem just mentioned and several others plague the students of early American politics. Political studies have included data from several towns at once in an effort to avoid the problem of typicality that faces the investigator of a single town, but they have never succeeded in constructing a sample large enough or diverse enough to expose the whole range of variation possible in the statistical measures used. In the absence of a satisfactory understanding of measures, rival historians have been able to associate similar figures with diametrically opposed explanations of social and political behavior. In the face of the supposed certainty of "the numbers," therefore, a substantial debate has raged over the nature of the political system, specifically as to whether the system was democratic, oligarchic, "deferential," or as most recently proposed, dominated by the need for communal consensus.

Merely discovering the range of a measure such as the percentage of adult males able to vote, of course, would not resolve the debate over the nature of the political process. Part of the dispute hinges on definitions alone, and substantive investigation can never settle a dispute about what a given pattern of behavior should be called. But more is involved than a question of labels. To be significant, any single measure of behavior must appear in a context that clarifies its relationship with other aspects of individual and community life, as well as in a context of numerical associations. In their attempt to establish the broad existence of such factors as a high rate of voter eligibility or a pattern of consensual town politics, historians dealing with many communities have often sacrificed the deep understanding of many aspects of town political and social life that is the principal advantage of single community studies. Clearly, investigations dealing with multiple communities must attempt to bridge the gap.

It is in an awareness of the problems outlined above that the present study undertakes to throw new light on the social assumptions underlying political behavior, to create a frame of reference for the interpretation of statistical data on the political behavior of the towns, and to suggest a typology within which the variations among single community studies are intelligible. Because the relationships among the inhabitants and voters of a town, the men who filled the principal town offices, and the men who held offices in county and colonial governments seem central to an understanding of the political system, the study focuses on the composition and selection of groups of local leaders in towns throughout New England, their length of service, their family relationships with other leaders, and their economic positions. Inevitably, the study deals with all strata of society in the towns and in the colonies as well, discussing the political roles of non-leaders, and the general social, political, religious, and economic structure of the society.

The necessity of dealing with enough towns to insure the inclusion of major differences in local behavior and the necessity of looking at each town in some detail have dictated the sampling techniques employed and the kinds of data selected for analysis. Technically speaking, the method used to select the seventy-four towns studied most closely is called "disproportional stratified sampling."[4] First a number of criteria according to which towns might vary were isolated. These criteria included geographical location, size of town, rate of population growth, age of town, religious complexion of the population, number of parishes within the town, the land system (gradual division among proprietors, complete division upon first settlement, or speculative sale), and origin of the town as a new settlement or division of an existing community. The criteria then served as a basis for constructing a list of towns that would reflect the widest possible range of variation, while at the same time including communities with well-preserved and accessible records. Finally, individual towns of special interest, such as provincial capitals, college towns, and towns that have been studied extensively, were added to the list. Because the study proposes to place in perspective towns like Dedham and Andover, such towns have been used extensively as examples of behavior and trends.

It is important to emphasize that the sample is designed to reflect the presence or absence of variations and not their proportionate strength. Because statistical generalizations must allow for a certain amount of purely random variation, the sample includes several examples of each suspected variational type. County seats, for example, made up a very small percentage of the towns in New England, but several are included in the sample because to generalize from a single example would risk attributing that town's unique aberrations to an entire class of communities. Conversely, the large number of towns founded after 1760, especially in Maine and New Hampshire, are underrepresented in proportion to their numbers because inclusion of more towns would not have provided much further information.

The sample, nevertheless, is designed to include roughly proportionate numbers of towns from each of the four colonies. Despite institutional differences among the several colonies, towns in New England were more similar to each other than to local institutions anywhere else in America, and in fact they behaved more consistently than studies focused on the unique qualities of individual colonies have suggested. In this respect the present study has borne out the assumptions made by such scholars as Kenneth Lockridge and Michael Zuckerman, who have undertaken to discuss "the New England town" on the basis of research conducted exclusively in Massachusetts. Before such a conclusion could be formed, however, it was necessary to examine towns in every colony. Accordingly, the sample included towns from each colony roughly in proportion to that colony's share in the whole number of towns in New England.*

In addition to a description of the method by which towns were selected, a word about the sources of data on each town seems to be in order here. Although towns were chosen partially because of the quality of surviving records, sources were not uniformly available. Every town studied has surviving town meeting records, which record the names of men elected to both major and minor town offices, as well as the details of much of the town's business.[5] In some cases local historians have collected rosters of major town officials from the records and have included them in town histories. Because of their wide availability in one source or the other, lists of town leaders and the generalizations about length of service and distribution of power derived from them constitute important sources of information for the comparative study of the towns.

Basic biographical information about town leaders, at least to the extent of vital statistics and family relationships, is also widely available, although not as consistently as information found in town meeting records. Moreover, the variety of forms in which this information appears is confusing. Fundamental are the vital records kept by town clerks and often now published by those interested in genealogy. Equally valuable are lists of deaths, especially those from church and cemetery records, since they often reveal the age at which a person died, and often include the honorific titles like "deacon" or "captain" that link a man with the leader in the meeting records and provide the means for discriminating among the several men with identical names born in a town. Because they often rely on memory and estimation for ages, church and tombstone records must be used with some risk of error, but careful cross-checking reduces the risk, and in any case, a recent study has suggested grounds for believing that

*Towns in New England:

Colony	Year	Towns	% of All Towns	Sample Towns	% of Sample
Massachusetts	1776	306	55.0	43	58.1
Connecticut	1774	75	13.5	10	13.5
New Hampshire	1773	147	26.4	15	20.3
Rhode Island	1774	28	5.0	6	8.1

Evarts B. Greene and Virginia D. Harrington, *American Population Before the Federal Census of 1790* (New York, 1932), 31–40, 58–61, 68. Jeremy Belknap, *History of New-Hampshire*, 3 vols. (Philadelphia, 1784–92), 2: 375.

such records are about as accurate as the official vital statistics.[6] Genealogies of New England families are abundant, and offer a rich source of information unobtainable anywhere else. As with any document, these
works must be approached with care. Some genealogists are both careless
and credulous, attributing children to parents who were either in infancy or
extreme old age at the date of birth and attempting to trace ancestry back
to Adam and Eve, usually through lines of mythical kings and queens. Most,
however, are more accurate, and this is usually true of the comprehensive
and invaluable genealogies of leading local families included in many
nineteenth-century town histories. In using local historical and genealogical sources of information to determine the official service and vital statistics of each local official mentioned in the text or in the compilation of
tables, I have not attempted the unmanageable and unproductive task of
giving exact citations in each instance. The main sources for each town are
grouped in the first section of the bibliography, and the main genealogical
sources are listed in the second section with a note on how I have used them.
Throughout the study, I have cited public records in the form "(town) Town
Records," and have underlined the citation when the source is available
in published form. I have omitted town record citations in instances where
the text refers to general conclusions based on the town records rather than
to specific events or actions.

In addition to information about the town leaders, this study has relied
on a number of sources that provide other kinds of data on the towns. Tax
lists provide invaluable information on the social structure in the towns,
and in the decades before censuses became common they form the only reliable basis for estimating population short of total family reconstitution.
Tax lists occur in an enormous variety of forms, as Chapter 3 will reveal.
Church records reveal the nature of religious life in the towns, as well as
providing the basis for determining the religious affiliations of individual
leaders. Colony records also constitute a major source of data, informing
the study of internal town behavior by revealing how deeply the towns and
their inhabitants were involved in the politics and economy of the entire
region. Together the sources mentioned, and others as well, provide the
basis for a broad understanding of who local leaders were, and how their
identity and behavior reflected the nature of and variations in the political
order in eighteenth-century New England.

Because this study aspires to present data for comparison with that
gathered by others, some procedural comments are appropriate. The lists
of officeholders used in preparing the tables are based on reports of annual
elections in the town records, and contain occasional missing years because
of lacunae in the records. I have tried to include officials elected in midyear
to replace men who died or resigned. I have calculated service years from
election meeting to election meeting, and have credited them to the calen-
dar year in which most service occurred. For example, officers listed for

1750 were elected in December 1749 in Connecticut, in March 1750 in Massachusetts and New Hampshire, and in June 1750 in Rhode Island. In all other uses, years are standardized to begin in January. Moderators involve a further complication to the tabulations, because a new one was elected at each town meeting. I have credited each moderator elected during the course of the year with one term of service, regardless of the number of meetings (or adjournments) at which he presided, and have omitted moderators elected at meetings held solely to draw the names of jurors from the jury box because available evidence suggests that such gatherings were town meetings in name only, with no more than half a dozen men present. Tax lists also present some technical problems beyond those discussed in Chapter 3. In calculating distributions of wealth, I have counted all men named in the lists, even if they paid only poll taxes (and hence a property tax of zero), because my reference group was the entire community rather than just the property holders. Odd numbers of taxpayers were assigned to deciles by placing the first one-tenth plus one persons in the first category, the next one-tenth plus one in the second category, and so forth until the remainder resulting from division by ten was exhausted. Such a procedure seemed preferable to omitting the last few taxpayers. When tax lists identified a sum taxed to a man's "faculty," I have included it in the personal property assessment.

In closing these introductory remarks I would like to make mention of a few of the many persons and institutions who have helped to make this study possible. The clerks of many towns have assisted me well beyond their statutory obligations to make the public records available, and the staffs of the several state and local libraries and historical societies have been generous with their time. Leo Flaherty of the Massachusetts Archives has been especially helpful. Albert T. Klyberg and his staff at the Rhode Island Historical Society made me so much at home during the nearly two years that I spent with them that in the end, I am sure, they almost forgot that I did not work there too. The John Carter Brown Library in Providence made much of the research possible by granting me a dissertation fellowship for 1970–71, by providing computer funds, and by making their facilities and collections available to me; and the Social Science Research Committee at the University of Chicago provided support for the later stages of research. I am indebted to Curtis A. Ermer for computer programming assistance. I owe special thanks to Jack P. Greene of The Johns Hopkins University, who directed the study ably when it was a dissertation, offering assistance when it was needed, and leaving me with the records when that was necessary; and to Robert Forster, who read and criticized the dissertation manuscript. I have also profited from the discussion of a preliminary report on the project at the Brandeis Conference on New England Community Studies in February 1970, from the comments of Robert Zemsky and Michael Zuckerman on the paper "Local Leadership and the Typology

of New England Towns, 1700–1785" at the December 1970 American Historical Association Convention, and from the suggestions of my colleagues
at Chicago, especially Arthur Mann and Neil Harris. Peter J. Reilly assisted
with proofreading. Finally, my wife, Lee, has typed and edited more drafts
than she cares to remember and has provided advice and encouragement
from beginning to end.

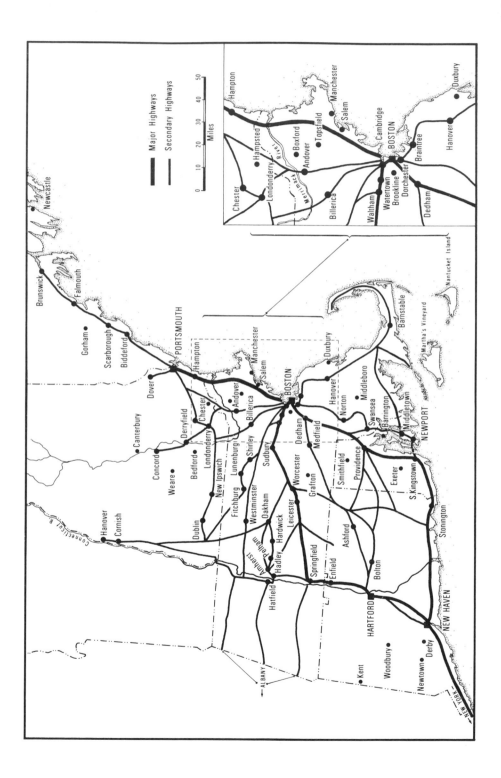

Major Highways
Secondary Highways

Miles
0 10 20 30 40 50

Inset (Boston area): Hampton, Manchester, Duxbury, Hampsted, Boxford, Topsfield, Salem, Cambridge, BOSTON, Hanover, Chester, Londonderry, Andover, Billerica, Waltham, Watertown, Brookline, Dorchester, Braintree, Dedham, Merrimack River

Newcastle, Brunswick, Falmouth, Gorham, Scarborough, Biddeford, Dover, Canterbury, Concord, Weare, Bedford, Londonderry, Derryfield, Chester, New Ipswich, Lunenburg, Fitchburg, Shirley, Andover, Billerica, Manchester, Salem, Hampton, PORTSMOUTH, BOSTON, Hanover, Middleboro, Duxbury, Barnstable, Martha's Vineyard, Nantucket Island, Westminster, Oakham, Sudbury, Dedham, Medfield, Norton, Swansea, Barrington, Middletown, NEWPORT, Worcester, Grafton, Smithfield, Providence, Exeter, S. Kingstown, Stonington, Hanover, Cornish, Dublin, Amherst, Pelham, Hatfield, Hadley, Hardwick, Leicester, Ashford, Bolton, Springfield, Enfield, HARTFORD, NEW HAVEN, Kent, Woodbury, Derby, Newtown, Connecticut R., ALBANY, NEW YORK

·1·

THE CHOICE OF THE TOWN MEETING

An account of local leadership in eighteenth-century New England must begin with the ultimate testing ground of a town leader, the annual town meeting of election. Every March in Massachusetts and New Hampshire towns, every June in Rhode Island, and every December in Connecticut, the freeholders gathered to elect some of their number to lead them for the next year, and others to fill lesser and more menial positions. In each colony, the rules under which the elections were held were remarkably imprecise. The law specified the month in which the meeting was to be held; established qualifications that were supposed to determine who voted; named some, though not all, of the officials to be elected; prescribed oaths to bind officials to their duty; and beyond that said surprisingly little.[1] How the meeting should be called, how nominating and voting should be conducted, and for a time even how order was to be maintained in the proceedings were left to local arrangements. With more than 550 towns in New England exercising their own initiative, local electoral practice was understandably varied; but the most remarkable and revealing aspect of local practice was not its variety, but its underlying similarity. As the century progressed, the towns quite uniformly adopted a set of standardized electoral practices that emphasized not only the growing sophistication of the electorate, but also the continuing ability of the townsmen to recognize clearly bounded groups of leaders among them and their universal willingness to fill their major offices of trust with those leaders.

In the middle of the eighteenth century a town's "annual meeting for the election of town officers" commonly opened with the previous year's selectmen presiding, and turned immediately to the election of its permanent presiding officer, the moderator.[2] This position called for a man of both commanding presence and universal respect within the community who could not only maintain order in the meeting, but also keep its attention directly on the business at hand. Men of suitable stature were not numerous, and the election was accomplished quickly, either by a summary tabulation of paper ballots or more commonly by nomination and acclamation. Now safely in the hands of the moderator, the meeting would turn directly to the election of the chief town officers. First of all, the town needed a clerk to

1

record the business of the day and to keep the town's books for the ensuing year, so the inhabitants wrote the name of a likely candidate on a slip of paper and handed it in to the moderator or his teller. Occasionally, if the incumbent or another man were an especially obvious choice, the town might dispense with the written ballots and elect him by show of hands, or by a simple resolution that he be elected to, or continued in, the office. Next came the election of the selectmen, the town's chief executive authorities, and once again the voters would write their choices on slips of paper, either singly or all at once, and hand the papers in to the moderator for tabulation. In Connecticut, Massachusetts, and New Hampshire the law provided that towns might choose three, five, seven, or nine selectmen according to local preference, and some towns adjusted the number frequently, although most chose the same number year after year. In Rhode Island the law provided for six town councilmen.

With the balloting for selectmen behind them, the voters had two other important elections to manage, one of them for a treasurer and the other for constables. Of the two, the choice of a treasurer was by far the easier. In New Hampshire it was no problem at all: the towns customarily entrusted their money to the selectmen. Elsewhere a special treasurer was chosen, very much as the town clerk was chosen, either by ballot or nomination. The election of constables, on the other hand, was often a difficult and time-consuming business. The office of constable was not a position of leadership and high status like the others with which it was grouped for electoral purposes, but the vital nature of its duties—the collection of taxes, the warning of town meetings, and the maintenance of order—made the election a crucial one. Moreover, because the duties were so arduous the first men elected often declined to serve, even at the risk of paying a stiff fine, and it was handy to have a tabulation of written votes to turn to for second and third choices.[3] So the voters turned in their slips of paper and prepared to vote on the resulting pleas of hardship, offers of substitutes, and outright refusals.

The election of the constables ended a distinct phase of the meeting. Many offices remained to be filled: highway surveyor, tithingman, hog reeve, fence viewer, sealer of leather, and a variety of others; but for these a more informal electoral procedure would suffice. Some towns emphasized the break in the electoral sequence by taking an hour's recess after the constables' election to sort out their preferences for the remaining positions, but many more plunged straight ahead, resolving to choose the rest by "nomination and vote," or as most phrased it, "by hand votes."[4] These elections were usually clear sailing, with nominees or volunteers quickly voted into office, and with relatively few contests for office or refusals to serve. When the election of minor officers was finished, the meeting turned to other local business, and finally adjourned.

To call the election meeting described here a typical one would be a mistake. First of all, there were too many variations in the order of election from place to place, and even from time to time within the same town. Sometimes a town would elect the constables before the selectmen, sometimes it would elect the town clerk after the selectmen, and occasionally it would elect one of the major officers near the bottom of the list, along with the hog reeves and pound keeper. But allowing for these variations in local custom, the broad pattern was clear enough. The offices of leadership and prestige—selectman, town clerk, and town treasurer—and the constableship were grouped for election and filled first; then the meeting turned to the lesser offices, and finally, to the remainder of the town's business.[5]

Procedures for voting and for the general conduct of meetings varied as well. Here, however, the most significant pattern of variation was not the adaptation of the general system to local convenience, but a strong trend over the course of the century toward more explicit and formalized rules of conduct. An early manifestation of that trend was the institutionalization of the office of moderator. At the beginning of the eighteenth century, the laws governing town affairs in all four colonies were silent as to who was to preside over town meetings, leaving the whole problem of maintaining order in the meetings to local choice. Practice understandably varied. In the largest seaport towns like Boston, Salem, and Portsmouth, procedures for the conduct of public business were consistently more formal and sophisticated than in the countryside as a whole. These towns followed what would become the general practice of electing a moderator at the beginning of each meeting, and indeed had done so since the middle of the seventeenth century.

In the small and medium-sized towns, however, no standard procedure existed. Three Essex County towns, Andover, Boxford, and Manchester, elected regular moderators by 1700, perhaps because of Salem's example. On the other hand, Topsfield and Lynn in the same county elected moderators only occasionally, and managed their affairs without one the rest of the time. New Haven customarily elected a man to serve as moderator "until Such time as the towne Se cause to make any other order," which was usually a matter of some years.[6] Springfield solved the problem of order by electing "the worshipful Colonell Pynchon" moderator for all the meetings in a year, although when he was unable to attend they elected no substitute and conducted their meetings informally.[7] Enfield followed Springfield's example and chose a moderator most of the time, but moderators were not a universal Connecticut Valley institution as Hartford, Connecticut's capital, never chose one until after 1717. Finally, the voters of Barnstable explored a whole range of possibilities in one year, 1715, when they did without a moderator in one meeting, elected one the next, and then decided on a troika of three simultaneous moderators for a third meeting.[8]

Exactly how the towns conducted their meetings when they did not choose moderators is not entirely clear, because in most cases the records do not specify the alternative. The experience of several towns, however, suggests some possibilities. In Watertown the alternative was a moderator appointed by the selectmen as part of the process of warning the meeting. The Medfield records reveal that there the "Constables were wont to assist" in managing "the affairs of the day," and since several towns elected their constables before any of the other officers, it is likely that they followed a similar practice.[9] Most likely of all, however, is the possibility that the selectmen, who had called the meeting and established the agenda in the first place, simply presided over it as well. This was certainly the case in Dedham's early meetings, and it remained a universal practice throughout the century in meetings for the election of representatives in Massachusetts, and for the drawing of jurors everywhere.[10] The management of town meetings at the beginning of the century was a matter of local custom and individualized practice.

Within a few decades, however, the varied procedures of 1700 disappeared as town after town began to elect moderators on a regular basis. Braintree, for example, which apparently had conducted its affairs informally in the seventeenth century, elected moderators regularly after 1695, and Medfield replaced its system of presiding constables with a regularly elected moderator in 1708. Other towns adopted the innovation gradually, electing moderators at scattered meetings for a few years, and then regularly at every meeting. In 1715 the General Court of Massachusetts, citing "the disorderly carriage of some persons in said meetings," ordered every town meeting to elect a moderator.[11] This action was more a confirmation of the general trend toward standardizing procedure than a response to a particular crisis; the provincial records reveal no surge in disorderly meetings in the years leading up to 1715.[12] By 1720 even outlying Massachusetts towns like Swansea, Hadley, and Hatfield fell into line, and began each meeting with the election of a moderator.[13]

The standardization of procedures in Massachusetts was paralleled by a similar trend in the other colonies. Confirming the traditional practice in old towns like Portsmouth and Hampton and new towns like Londonderry, the New Hampshire Assembly enacted a verbatim copy of the Massachusetts law less than five years later.[14] Rhode Island and Connecticut never enacted laws explicitly requiring the election of a moderator, but the practice gradually became universal. In New Haven the traditional manner of electing moderators gave way in 1718 to annual elections, and in 1739 to separate elections for each meeting.[15] Some new towns, like Ashford (incorporated 1718) and South Kingstown (1723), elected moderators from the beginning; Bolton (1720), on the other hand, adopted the practice a few years later, in 1728. The assemblies of both colonies tacitly admitted the universality of the practice in 1729, when they enacted laws governing the conduct of moderators, without specifically creating the position.[16]

Once the towns had created a standard focus of authority in their meetings, they turned to another major area of local variation, voting procedures. At the colony level, sophisticated methods for casting and counting votes had long been in effect. As early as the 1640s Massachusetts had articulated a system for the nomination and election of assistants by paper ballot and proxy voting, and specified by law that deputies be elected "by Papers."[17] Similar procedures became universal during the seventeenth century, so that by 1700 standard procedures for the election of representatives existed in all of the New England towns. The "freeholders" or "freemen" elected representatives at special meetings called by the selectmen in response to a "precept" from the sheriff or on their own authority under terms of the election laws. The "major part" of the selectmen presided over these meetings, received the written and unfolded votes of the freeholders, proclaimed the winner, and returned the completed precept to the General Court. This procedure remained virtually unchanged throughout the eighteenth century.[18]

For strictly local elections, however, procedures in the early years of the century were left to local discretion. As was the case with the governance of town meetings, local practices varied. Procedure in the seaports was most clearly established. In Boston ballots for the leading offices were "brought in" from an early date, and in Portsmouth the existence of numerical election results suggests that the clerk had something more tangible to work with than the result of a show of hands.[19] During the 1680s, Salem elected its selectmen by nominating ten or more candidates, and then balloting for the seven seats on the board. Whether or not that procedure continued was concealed in later years by the laconic notation that selectmen "were chosen," but the town was unlikely to have resumed a more primitive method.[20]

Procedure in the country towns was much less clearly explained. Hatfield chose its selectmen by written ballot from 1690 to 1700 at least, as the town clerk revealed by recording his tallies on the covers of the record book, although the scattering of votes reveals that, unlike Salem's practice, the town made no prior nominations. Dedham, on the other hand, did have a procedure for nominations, as a 1726 vote to choose the selectmen "out of the Eight that have been highest in Nomination" revealed, but in Dedham elections had not traditionally been by written ballots.[21] For most of the other towns, the early records merely relate the names of those "chosen" to office. The very brevity and simplicity of these records, however, suggests that procedures were not very elaborate. Most towns were small and intimate, and had never evolved a rigorous system of formal nominations and paper ballots to fill their offices. People knew almost instinctively which of their fellows were qualified to lead them, and which of those would prefer to have a year off. So they managed candidates and elections without ceremony, simply naming the obvious candidates and confirming the choice by a show of hands.

The proof of how informal this electoral system was came when the town meetings, ruled by their newly instituted moderators, began to question their electoral practices as they had their procedures for managing the meetings. On the one hand, they had the traditional town meeting system of hand voting, fast and convenient in time of unanimity but unsatisfactory for deciding controversial elections; on the other hand, they had the traditional system of representative elections, which provided far more adequate methods of screening voters and a concrete tabulation of the results. In town after town during the early decades of the century, the question of voting methods became an issue.

The first town to confront the issue directly was Manchester, which voted in March 1701 "to chuse town officers for the year insuing by holding up the hand." That vote settled the issue temporarily, but the town found it necessary to reiterate its position six times over the next twenty years, until finally in March 1721 it gave in and resolved "to chues selectmen, town Clark and tow tresuer by prox."[22] The issue apparently arose next in Dorchester, where the town clerk suddenly began to report exact voting totals in 1706, although written balloting was not explicitly mentioned until 1717, when the town voted to "bring in" its votes for selectmen separately instead of all at once.[23] In a number of towns the change to written ballots came between about 1715 and 1725. Braintree voted in 1717 "that a Town Clerk & Town Treasurer should be chosen for the time to come by written votes," while on the same day a constable was chosen "by their usual sign of lifting up the hand."[24] Medfield freeholders first "brought in their votes" in 1723; Dedham switched to "paper Voates" amidst an acrimonious sectional dispute during the late 1720s; and by 1730 at least four other towns had explicitly adopted the new policy.[25] By 1730 paper ballots were the accepted mode of election, and the occasional use of "handy votes" required specific authorization.[26]

Adoption of the written ballot did not complete the evolution of town meeting voting procedures; rather, that evolution continued throughout the century. Two major areas of change in the later years were the refinement of the use of the paper ballot in major office elections, and the establishment of more summary methods of election for the lesser officers. Concerning the major officers, two major kinds of decisions had to be made: whether or not to require a separate ballot for each individual position at issue, and whether the election could be decided by a plurality of votes if the leading candidates failed to gain an absolute majority. On the question of separate ballots the towns reached no final decision during the colonial period, and the issue was settled in each case on the grounds of expediency. By far the most common system was to fill multiple offices like selectmen all at once, because of the time consumed by collecting and sorting several sets of ballots. At times, however, special circumstances called for individual balloting, such as elections in which each selectman had to come from a distinct part of town, or contested elections in which control rather than speed was crucial to the success of the meeting.[27]

Decisions on the question of plurality versus majority showed a distinct trend during the century toward enforcement of more stringent standards of election. The issue arose with the change to written ballot, because while election by hand or verbal voting usually involved a "yes" or "no" vote on a nominated candidate, the usual method of written balloting eliminated the nomination process, allowed each man to vote for a slate of his own choice, and often resulted in a fragmented set of returns. When first confronting the question, a town usually decided in favor of a plurality. Boston, for example, voted in 1708 that the choice of a moderator be decided "by the greatest number of Votes and not confined to the majority of Voters," and Lynn resolved in 1736 that "the highes six in vot shall be the selectmen."[28] As time passed, however, men began to question the validity of such decisions. The problem seems to have surfaced first in Dorchester, where the clerk began to record the number of voters beside the election totals in 1733, and in 1736, when a man first failed to achieve election at the first "stroke," recorded that a second vote had taken place. In Boston, "A Doubt" arose at the 1743 annual meeting, and after debating the law for some time the inhabitants "determined by a Vote that the Town Apprehends the true Sense & meaning of said Law to be, that every Person Voted for to any Office must have a Major part of the Votes brought in & that otherwise he is not legally Chosen."[29] Other towns sought to maintain the practice of plurality elections but were forced to give in by disappointed candidates. In 1757 ten Braintree voters challenged the moderator's decision to proclaim two selectmen "chosen according to the usual custom of said town as having more votes than any other," and forced the town to pass a special resolution to legitimize the election.[30] That challenge was settled with a minimum of difficulty, but a similar one in Londonderry caused more trouble. There the supporters of a defeated candidate challenged the customary election of a representative by plurality, convinced the moderator to conduct the election again, and since the supporters of the original winner had left the meeting, carried the day. Eventually the election was set aside by the Assembly, but only after the town submitted a lengthy petition to that end citing their "Unacquaintedness with Law."[31] By the time of the Revolution a majority vote was necessary virtually everywhere to assure a legal election.

As the towns adopted more and more formal methods of electing their major officeholders, they began to seek ways of shortening their meetings by using more abbreviated procedures for filling the lesser offices. The requirements of the minor offices were, of course, very different from those of the major ones: on the one hand, the major offices were positions of substantial responsibility, so that the competition among community leaders to fill them might require sophisticated electoral methods; on the other hand, the minor offices were little sought after, and were more successfully filled by a system of nomination that searched for willing candidates to stand for a more or less perfunctory election. When the towns switched from hand votes to written ballots, however, many voters seem to have assumed that consistency would require the whole slate to be filled by the written method. Whether the towns ever attempted to ballot for hog reeves, field drivers, and the like is unclear, but in any case they soon realized that if they were going to be able to resist the efforts of purists like the Braintree voters who questioned the validity of elections by hand vote "Since they had urged written votes, etc," they would have to make more explicit the procedures for the election of minor officers.[32]

In town after town, therefore, the elections came to be divided into phases. First, the voters filled the major offices by written ballot, then they resolved to "Choose the Rest of the Town Offices by hand vote" and proceeded to fill the minor offices by "nomination and vote."[33] Some towns mentioned the procedural resolution only for a year or two, then silently followed it, but others, like Manchester, repeated it every year, which not only served to stress the legality of the custom, but also emphasized again and again the distinction between major and minor offices. To further simplify the selection of the lesser officers, other towns introduced another refinement, an hour's break in the meeting, during which the leaders could work up an acceptable list of nominees for the minor offices and thus speed the elections. Most towns did not explain the nominating process, but Bolton made it clear in 1778 when they voted that "the Selectmen for the future Shall Nominate the Town officers that they think proper to serve the next year."[34]

By the end of the colonial period, the conduct of town meetings and elections was a much more elaborate, formal, and standard process than it had been in 1700. In part this change was a manifestation of the transfer of power from the selectmen to the town meeting in the years around 1700 described by Kenneth Lockridge and Alan Kreider for Dedham and Watertown alone, but which was, in fact, a broad trend throughout New England.[35] As the meeting became the dominant decision-making body in a town, its business became simultaneously more lengthy and more a matter of originating policy rather than ratifying decisions made elsewhere. Under these circumstances questions of order and procedure became more important, and regular moderators and formalized voting methods came into wide use during the first quarter of the eighteenth century. But population growth and the increase in local contention, the factors behind the evolution in government, did not end in 1725, and neither did the evolution itself. As large towns became larger and more diverse and new towns were founded by men from many old towns, the pressure for increasingly formal governmental agencies and procedures became stronger, and the need for increasingly standard governmental methods grew as well. To men of the revolutionary generation the town meeting and the officers it elected were more a part of a formal structure of government and less an expression of community involvement than had been the case seventy-five years before.

If diversity and contention led to standardized institutions for maintaining order in meetings and formalized procedures for settling electoral

contests, it is important to emphasize that they did not cause, during the
colonial period at least, two other developments widely attributed to them:
the rise of the secret ballot and the transformation of local officeholders
from socially respected community leaders into partisan political operatives.
Instead, elections remained open in the interest of control; and the political
leadership of the towns remained in the hands of groups of clearly identified
social leaders, men whose broad authority in the community prevented
factional conflicts, even those in which they constituted one of the parties,
from developing into challenges to their hold on the major offices.

Both the purpose for which the towns adopted the written ballot and the
size of the communities worked to prevent the written ballot from becoming
a secret ballot. The appeal of the paper ballots in the colonial towns was not
secrecy, but control. First of all, it contributed to the speedy and orderly
conduct of elections because it obviated the establishment of elaborate
nomination procedures to assure, not only that all potential candidates had
their names put forward, but also that the voter would not be confused into
voting for candidates he did not prefer merely because their names came up
early in the voting.[36] Even more important, written votes produced a
concrete, visible record of the results of the voting. The outcome depended
not on the moderator's ability to judge whose supporters had shouted the
loudest, nor on his ability to see the hands raised or half raised at the rear of
the room, but on the counting of a stack of papers that could be piled on the
table for all to see. The coincidence of "paper votes" and explicit voting
tabulations in the records suggests the superiority of the ballot in providing
figures for deciding close elections, as does the insistence of the colonial
legislatures (as early as 1636 in Massachusetts) that deputies, whose elections
were subject to review by the House, be chosen by paper ballots.[37]

The procedures for insuring control militated against secrecy. Voters cast
their paper ballots by submitting them one by one to an official, who
received the ballot unfolded, checked the voter's eligibility against the local
tax list, and when the procedure was strictly enforced sent the voter to a part
of the room away from those who were waiting to vote. Thus, in 1721 the
proprietors of Swansea ruled that "there should Come but one Person at a
time: and deliver their vote into ye Clarks hand & ye Clark Should Inspect
Every vote of ye Authority of ye Voters."[38] Undoubtedly when the election
was uncontested, or the vote noncontroversial, these requirements were
relaxed, and they might also be relaxed in contested elections through the
connivance of an interested vote counter, but the ultimate result of such
lapses of control was to provoke even more draconian measures.[39] Faced with
widespread accusations of corruption and multiple voting during the
spirited Hopkins-Ward competition for the governorship in the 1760s, the
Rhode Island General Assembly responded by requiring each voter to sign
his name on the reverse of his ballot; a procedure that not only eliminated
secrecy at the time, but enabled several industrious town clerks to produce
permanent lists of voters showing the candidates they supported.[40] And even

when through one problem or another written ballots failed to decide an issue, the response of election officials was revealing. The ultimate recourse was to call for a formal division of the assembled electorate by sending the adherents of one candidate into the balcony and those of the other candidate into the body of the meeting house, a procedure that could not fail to reveal to the entire meeting where each man stood.[41]

That these control procedures ignored the requirements of a secret ballot should be no surprise, because in communities as small as most of the New England towns an attempt to insure secrecy would have failed anyway. On any issue worth contesting, a little effort served to reveal everyone's position. Thus, when Derryfield was split by a feud between Congregationalist and Presbyterian parties, the leader of one, Colonel John Goffe, was able to inform the governor that his opponent, John Hall, "obtained eighteen voters be side him self and there was eighteen voters on the opposite side of the most substantial men in town so that when they had don all they could that could not git hall any office without voting for himself," which in the course of revealing the taboo against voting for oneself makes clear that Goffe knew how each of the thirty-seven voters would vote. Similarly, an inhabitant of East Greenwich, Rhode Island, deposed that he knew how two questionable voters had voted in the election for deputies in 1763, because he had looked at their ballots as they walked up to hand them in.[42] A written ballot was secret only if the voter's neighbors neglected to keep track of his vote.

Equally revealing of the limits of change in the colonial period was the absence of attempts by contending factions to exploit horizontal social cleavages to oust the clearly defined town social elites from the major offices or to turn the offices into prizes in a politicized spoils system. Instead, disputes found expression in electoral contests only when they represented vertical divisions in society that pitted members of the recognized leadership as well as lesser inhabitants against one another. Three main kinds of evidence—overlapping personnel in the major offices, the makeup of the few surviving lists of candidates for major offices, and the behavior of towns when leaders refused election—confirm the existence of an identifiable leader pool, and reveal the consistency with which the voters filled the leading offices with members of that pool.[43]

An initial indication of the existence of a clearly defined pool of town leadership can be found in the increasing clarity with which voting procedures separated the major offices of moderator, town clerk, town treasurer, selectman, and representative from the rest of the town offices. Of the minor offices only the constable was included in the select group chosen by written ballot, and the broad spectrum of candidates, the frequent refusals, and the willingness of towns to accept hired substitutes and minor sons emphasize that office's difference from the major ones.[44] Clearly, the town electors considered the five major offices to be positions of special importance and set them apart to be filled with special care.

Just as the voters grouped the offices, they grouped the men who held them by electing the same men, at various times, to all of the major offices. In the seventy-three towns tabulated for this study, a total of 6,068 men served in the five major offices at one time or another during the years from 1700 to 1784. Of these men 5,167, or 85.2 percent, served at least one term as a selectman (see Table 1). This large proportion was due in part to the number of selectmen elected, as towns chose five, seven, or even nine at a time. But a more important factor was the overlapping personnel of the five offices. Nearly three-quarters (72.3 percent) of the men who served as representatives, clerks, treasurers, or moderators also served as selectmen.

At first glance such composite figures may not seem very meaningful, because they are drawn from towns as different in size as Boston, with 15,000 inhabitants near the end of the period, and Cornish with less than 200, but they do represent the behavior of the towns accurately. The predominate pattern was for all but a few of the other major officers to be chosen from the past, present, or future selectmen. Eighty percent or more of the leaders served as selectmen in all but thirteen of the towns studied, and two-thirds or more were selectmen in all but five.[45] Patterns for the other offices were a little more varied, but still exhibited the tendency of the towns to elect leaders to more than one office. Naturally, some leaders served in every possible combination of the five offices. Because as few as half a dozen men served in the offices of representative, town clerk, and town treasurer in some towns, however, individual actions would bias a tabulation of the combination of those offices severely. Selectmen, on the other hand, were numerous enough that the combinations of that office with the others produced more meaningful statistics; and therefore the concentration of offices has been studied in terms of the service of selectmen in each of the other offices.

Overall, the smallest percentage of representatives, 66.9 percent, served as selectmen (see Table 2). Two significant groups of towns demonstrated a distinct tendency to elect different men to the offices of selectman and representative. In the seaport towns of Boston, Portsmouth, Newport, and New Haven the offices were arduous enough, and candidates numerous enough, that some officeholders specialized, and only 42.8 percent of the representatives ever served as selectmen in these towns. A similar tendency existed in four of the other five Rhode Island towns studied, where only 52.4 percent of the deputies ever served as town councilmen, possibly because legislative elections in Rhode Island involved partisan competition that was not fully operative in the strictly local elections.[46] When Rhode Island and the seaports were excluded from the calculations, however, the proportion of representatives with experience as selectmen rises to about 80 percent. Except for the instances already cited, there were no significant differences between large and small towns, or between towns in different regional groupings. Altogether 43 percent of the representatives served their first term as a leader in that office, and for those who served as selectmen as well it seems to have made little difference which office came first. Throughout most of rural New

TABLE ONE

Leaders and their first Major Office

Town	Years	# of Leaders	# of Select-men	% of Leaders who were Selectmen	% of Selectmen serving first as Selectmen	% of Reps serving first as Reps	% of TC serving first as TC	% of TT serving first as TT	% of Mods serving first as Mods
MASSACHUSETTS									
Amherst	1759-84	45	44	97.8	93.2	20.0	66.7	33.3	8.3
Andover	1700-84	102	91	89.2	86.8	20.0	37.5	52.6	13.2
Barnstable	1714-83	59	36	61.0	80.6	37.5	72.7	0.0	42.5
Barrington	1718-44	18	15	83.3	86.7	0.0	33.3	12.5	20.0
Billerica	1700-84	82	80	97.6	98.8	18.8	0.0	n/d	n/d
Boston	1700-84	180	122	68.9	90.9	45.3	66.7	50.0	33.3
Boxford	1700-84	141	139	98.6	96.4	18.8	36.3	n/d	n/d
Braintree	1700-84	107	93	86.9	91.2	22.2	83.3	25.0	18.9
Brookline	1700-84	63	60	95.2	83.3	16.7	58.3	23.1	4.8
Cambridge	1700-84	108	92	85.2	92.4	37.0	66.7	28.6	22.6
Dedham	1700-75	94	90	95.7	98.9	5.9	0.0	16.7	12.5
Dorchester	1700-84	74	66	89.2	92.4	33.3	33.3	25.0	11.1
Duxbury	1700-84	53	41	77.4	82.9	53.3	100.0	n/d	59.0
Fitchburg	1764-84	29	27	93.1	85.2	0.0	16.7	20.0	25.0
Grafton	1728-84	92	91	98.9	93.4	0.0	22.2	37.5	16.7
Hadley	1700-84	127	127	100.0	97.6	0.0	75.0	0.0	64.7
Hanover	1727-84	65	44	66.7	68.2	0.0	75.0	60.0	10.0
Hardwick	1737-84	50	45	90.0	93.3	12.5	40.0	28.6	0.0
Hatfield	1700-84	66	64	97.0	92.2	18.8	75.0	0.0	0.0
Leicester	1722-84	72	68	94.4	85.3	44.4	15.4	30.0	16.0
Lunenburg	1728-84	79	69	87.3	91.3	9.1	37.5	38.9	14.3
Manchester	1700-84	59	49	83.1	79.6	16.7	33.3	31.3	30.0
Medfield	1700-84	140	135	96.4	90.4	18.2	30.0	31.3	11.4
Middleboro	1700-84	95	68	71.6	88.2	57.2	72.7	58.3	30.8
Norton	1711-84	68	55	80.9	65.5	39.1	70.0	68.2	5.6
Oakham	1759-84	39	34	87.2	82.4	----	62.5	33.3	23.1
Pelham	1743-84	78	77	98.7	92.2	0.0	75.0	44.4	0.0
Shirley	1753-84	31	29	93.5	89.7	0.0	14.3	57.1	n/d

TABLE ONE: continued

Town	Years	# of Leaders	# of Select-men	% of Leaders who were Selectmen	% of Selectmen serving first as Selectmen	% of Reps serving first as Reps	% of TC serving first as TC	% of TT serving first as TT	% of Mods serving first as Mods
MASSACHUSETTS Continued									
Springfield	1700-84	105	92	87.6	81.5	38.2	50.0	20.0	25.0
Sudbury	1700-84	143	137	95.8	90.5	19.2	25.0	20.8	14.3
Swansea	1700-84	109	70	64.2	88.6	66.7	22.2	63.2	37.0
Topsfield	1700-76	100	96	96.0	96.9	25.0	0	9.1	3.4
Waltham	1738-84	50	49	98.0	98.0	14.3	50.0	n/d	n/d
Watertown	1700-84	117	107	91.4	88.7	26.1	50.0	33.3	19.4
Westminster	1759-84	41	39	95.1	94.9	0	33.3	0	16.7
Worcester	1722-84	87	81	93.1	82.7	26.7	30.8	21.4	31.0
MAINE									
Biddeford	1717-84	43	39	90.7	97.4	41.7	0	n/d	n/d
Brunswick	1739-84	38	37	97.4	94.6	16.7	28.6	n/d	n/d
Falmouth	1719-86	105	93	88.6	n/d	n/d	n/d	n/d	n/d
Gorham	1764-84	24	21	87.5	76.2	42.9	60.0	50.0	n/d
Newcastle	1754-84	35	29	82.9	86.2	0	75.0	66.7	42.9
Scarborough	1720-84	50	47	94.0	95.7	18.2	50.0	n/d	n/d
NEW HAMPSHIRE									
Bedford	1750-84	51	45	88.2	97.8	16.7	42.9	0	20.0
Canterbury	1750-84	41	39	95.1	89.7	0	50.0	---	30.0
Chester	1724-84	79	71	89.9	100.0	10.0	20.0	---	35.4
Concord	1732-49 1765-84	39	32	82.1		50.0	57.1	25.0	28.6
Cornish	1767-84	34	32	94.1	96.9	25.0	33.0	---	0
Derryfield	1751-84	42	36	85.7	88.9	0	20.0	---	45.0
Dover	1700-84	91	82	90.1	86.5	27.3	28.6	---	20.0
Dublin	1771-84	18	16	88.9	87.5	33.3	50.0	0	40.0

TABLE ONE: continued II

Town	Years	# of Leaders	# of Select-men	% of Leaders who were Selectmen	% of Selectmen serving first as Selectmen	% of Reps serving first as Reps	% of TC serving first as TC	% of TT serving first as TT	% of Mods serving first as Mods
NEW HAMPSHIRE Continued									
Hampstead	1749-84	52	49	94.2	95.9	33.3	75.0	---	5.9
Hampton	1700-84	155	147	94.8	97.3	30.3	0	---	10.5
Hanover	1767-84	27	25	92.6	88.0	0	50.0	0	23.5
Londonderry	1719-84	121	111	91.7	94.6	28.6	27.2	---	36.8
New Ipswich	1762-84	33	28	84.8	92.8	18.2	0	---	62.5
Portsmouth	1700-84	120	92	76.7	93.5	57.9	60.0	---	25.0
Weare	1764-84	37	28	75.7	100.0	42.9	0	---	60.0
RHODE ISLAND									
Exeter	1742-84	75	62	82.7	74.2	42.2	100.0	20.0	34.8
Middletown	1743-84	60	42	70.0	71.4	62.2	100.0	33.3	n/d
Newport	1700-83	158	53	33.5	50.9	86.0	85.7	40.0	37.8
Providence	1700-84	214	112	52.4	69.6	66.9	66.7	37.5	29.7
Smithfield	1731-84	85	57	67.1	80.7	52.0	50.0	85.7	18.8
So. Kingstown	1723-84	112	70	62.5	75.7	58.2	71.4	55.6	37.0
CONNECTICUT									
Ashford	1716-84	73	61	83.6	70.5	48.3	83.3	28.6	24.3
Bolton	1721-84	53	48	90.6	87.5	33.3	16.7	42.9	5.6
Derby	1700-84	97	91	93.8	94.4	31.7	n/d	n/d	n/d
Enfield	1700-84	75	65	86.7	75.4	33.3	42.9	37.5	11.5
Kent	1739-84	61	50	82.0	80.0	47.6	100.0	50.0	7.4
Hartford	1700-84	236	221	93.6	n/d	n/d	n/d	n/d	n/d
New Haven	1700-84	205	188	91.7	87.8	51.1	66.7	46.2	12.5
Newtown	1712-84	126	124	98.4	96.8	14.3	0	n/d	n/d
Stonington	1700-84	125	112	89.6	79.5	47.7	100.0	n/d	n/d
Woodbury	1731-84	110	90	81.8	92.2	38.5	75.0	83.3	80.0

TABLE TWO

Overlapping Personnel in Major Town Office

Town	Years	# of Reps	% of Reps who were Selectmen	# of TC	% of TC who were Selectmen	# of TT	% of TT who were Selectmen	# of Mod	% of Mod who were Selectmen
MASSACHUSETTS									
Amherst	1759-84	6	100.0	3	66.7	3	100.0	12	100.0
Andover	1700-84	25	72.0	8	75.0	19	73.7	38	86.8
Barnstable	1714-83	16	75.0	11	45.5	6	83.3	40	62.5
Barrington	1718-44	2	100.0	6	66.7	8	87.5	10	80.0
Billerica	1700-84	16	87.5	8	100.0	n/d	n/d	n/d	n/d
Boston	1700-84	86	53.5	6	16.7	4	75.0	78	50.0
Boxford	1700-84	16	93.7	11	90.9	n/d	n/d	n/d	n/d
Braintree	1700-84	18	88.9	6	33.3	12	50.0	53	85.0
Brookline	1700-84	12	100.0	12	91.6	13	84.6	21	95.2
Cambridge	1700-84	27	66.7	6	66.7	7	85.7	31	74.2
Dedham	1700-75	17	88.2	12	100.0	12	83.3	16	93.8
Dorchester	1700-84	18	72.2	6	83.3	4	100.0	27	92.6
Duxbury	1700-84	15	60.0	4	50.0	n/d	n/d	14	71.4
Fitchburg	1764-84	2	100.0	6	83.3	5	80.0	16	93.8
Grafton	1728-84	4	100.0	9	100.0	8	87.5	12	100.0
Hadley	1700-84	11	100.0	4	100.0	6	100.0	37	100.0
Hanover	1727-84	9	77.8	4	50.0	10	70.0	43	60.5
Hardwick	1737-84	8	87.5	10	60.0	7	100.0	10	100.0
Hatfield	1700-84	16	87.5	4	100.0	3	100.0	16	100.0
Leicester	1722-84	9	88.9	13	100.0	10	80.0	25	96.0
Lunenburg	1728-84	11	90.9	8	75.0	18	77.8	35	85.7
Manchester	1700-84	6	100.0	15	93.3	16	81.2	30	80.0
Medfield	1700-84	33	100.0	10	100.0	16	93.8	35	97.1
Middleboro	1700-84	21	61.9	11	36.4	12	50.0	26	69.2
Norton	1711-84	23	82.6	10	80.0	22	63.2	18	94.4
Oakham	1759-84	0	-----	8	87.5	9	77.8	13	84.6
Pelham	1743-84	1	100.0	4	75.0	9	100.0	13	100.0
Shirley	1753-84	1	100.0	7	100.0	7	71.4	n/d	n/d

TABLE TWO: Continued

Town	Years	# of Reps	% of Reps who were Selectmen	# of TC	% of TC who were Selectmen	# of TT	% of TT who were Selectmen	# of Mod	% of Mod who were Selectmen
MASSACHUSETTS Continued									
Springfield	1700–84	34	73.5	10	70.0	10	90.0	40	85.0
Sudbury	1700–84	26	88.5	12	91.6	24	91.6	42	92.9
Swansea	1700–84	27	59.3	9	77.8	19	47.4	54	55.6
Topsfield	1700–76	20	90.0	6	100.0	11	90.9	29	93.1
Waltham	1738–84	7	85.7	2	100.0	n/d	n/d	n/d	n/d
Watertown	1700–84	23	82.6	10	80.0	12	75.0	36	88.9
Westminster	1759–84	5	100.0	6	83.3	3	100.0	6	83.3
Worcester	1722–84	15	93.3	13	77.0	14	92.9	29	93.1
MAINE									
Biddeford	1717–84	12	66.7	4	100.0	n/d	n/d	n/d	n/d
Brunswick	1739–84	6	83.3	7	100.0	n/d	n/d	n/d	n/d
Falmouth	1719–86	20	60.0	8	37.5	7	85.7	n/d	n/d
Gorham	1764–84	7	57.1	5	40.0	4	75.0	n/d	n/d
Newcastle	1754–84	1	0.0	4	75.0	6	50.0	7	57.1-
Scarborough	1720–84	11	81.8	6	83.3	n/d	n/d	n/d	n/d
NEW HAMPSHIRE									
Bedford	1750–84	6	50.0	7	85.7	9	100.0	15	80.0
Canterbury	1750–84	6	100.0	6	83.3	0	-----	10	90.0
Chester	1724–84	10	80.0	5	80.0	0	-----	17	58.9
Concord	{1732–49 / 1765–84}	6	50.0	6	66.7	4	100.0	8	75.0
Cornish	1767–84	4	75.0	6	83.3	0	-----	4	100.0
Derryfield	1751–84	1	100.0	5	40.0	0	-----	20	75.0
Dover	1700–84	33	82.8	7	71.4	0	-----	25	88.0
Dublin	1771–84	3	100.0	2	100.0	4	100.0	5	60.0

TABLE TWO: Continued II

Town	Years	# of Reps	% of Reps who were Selectmen	# of TC	% of TC who were Selectmen	# of TT	% of TT who were Selectmen	# of Mod	% of Mod who were Selectmen
NEW HAMPSHIRE Continued									
Hampstead	1749-84	3	66.7	4	75.0	0	-----	17	88.2
Hampton	1700-84	33	75.8	7	85.7	0	-----	19	89.5
Hanover	1767-84	1	100.0	2	100.0	2	100.0	17	88.2
Londonderry	1719-84	21	76.2	11	72.7	0	-----	19	89.5
New Ipswich	1762-84	11	81.8	9	100.0	0	-----	8	37.5
Portsmouth	1700-84	38	52.6	5	60.0	0	-----	36	61.1
Weare	1764-84	7	42.9	2	100.0	0	-----	10	40.0
RHODE ISLAND									
Exeter	1742-84	26	84.6	8	37.5	5	80.0	23	78.3
Middletown	1743-84	37	56.8	5	0	6	50.0	n/d	n/d
Newport	1700-83	121	28.1	7	42.9	10	30.0	45	37.8
Providence	1700-84	166	44.0	6	50.0	8	75.0	64	51.6
Smithfield	1731-84	50	50.0	8	50.0	7	57.1	16	68.8
S. Kingstown	1723-84	55	61.8	7	42.9	9	44.4	46	60.9
CONNECTICUT									
Ashford	1716-84	29	82.8	6	83.3	7	85.7	37	78.4
Bolton	1721-84	18	83.3	6	100.0	7	85.7	18	94.4
Derby	1700-84	41	85.4	n/d	n/d	n/d	n/d	n/d	n/d
Enfield	1700-84	21	66.7	7	85.7	8	75.0	26	84.6
Hartford	1700-84	36	63.9	3	66.7	3	66.7	29	79.3
Kent	1739-84	21	76.2	6	16.7	6	33.3	27	88.9
New Haven	1700-84	47	53.2	3	33.3	26	76.9	16	43.8
Newtown	1712-84	28	92.9	4	100.0	n/d	n/d	n/d	n/d
Stonington	1700-84	65	80.0	5	40.0	n/d	n/d	n/d	n/d
Woodbury	1731-84	26	57.7	4	50.0	12	25.0	20	50.0

England the selectmen and representatives came from a single group of leaders.

The offices of town clerk and town treasurer were even more closely associated with the selectmen than the one of representative. Some towns, like Billerica and Dorchester, systematically elected the town clerk to the Board of Selectmen, and a number of towns elected a man as both clerk and selectman much of the time simply because he seemed qualified for both offices. Some towns placed a premium on education in choosing a clerk, and would pick a young college graduate rather than an experienced leader with a more ordinary background.[47] But young men who began as clerk usually served in other leadership positions later in their careers, so it is clear that they were identified as leaders in the town's mind. Forty-five percent of the town clerks served in that office as their initial office, but 74 percent eventually served as selectman, and others undoubtedly served as representative, treasurer, or moderator. As with the representatives, differentiation of clerks from the other officers was more marked in Rhode Island and the seaports than elsewhere.

The identification of the selectmen and treasurer began in the seventeenth century, when most towns left the public money in the hands of the selectmen or a treasurer they appointed.[48] This practice continued in New Hampshire right down to the Revolution; only four of the fifteen towns surveyed in that colony elected treasurers on a regular basis in the eighteenth century. Even after towns began to elect treasurers regularly, the treasurers remained closely associated with the selectmen for a long time, in part because a town was unlikely to entrust its money to a man of unproven reliability. Topsfield, for example, did not venture to elect a treasurer without a previous term as selectman until 1759, and many other towns were nearly as careful. Seventy-six percent of the treasurers also saw service as selectmen, and only 37 percent began their service as leaders in that office.

The office of moderator was the most exclusive of the major offices. Because the duties of a moderator only lasted for the duration of the meeting, the position had appeal to men who were already busy with other offices, and that appeal was reinforced by the fact that the town's choice of a man to keep order through his personal prestige and authority was testimony to his status in the community. As a result, moderators were almost invariably established leaders. Seventy-seven percent of the moderators in all the towns were selectmen as well, and only 24 percent made their appearance as leaders in that office. Even in Rhode Island and the seaport cities the percentages of multiple service for moderators were higher than for the other offices generally, and in those towns men who became moderators without the benefit of service in other major town offices were likely to be high officials in the colonial government. The tendency of the towns to pick experienced holders of the other major town offices to the prestigious position of moderator is powerful evidence of the towns' identification of the holders of those offices with its circle of leaders.

Confirmation of the view that overlapping personnel in the major offices was due to the existence of a clearly identified pool of leaders can be found in the few lists of candidates for major office that have survived. Lists of nominees for office and tabulations of votes cast are very scarce for the eighteenth century, but enough exist to show what sort of man received support from his fellow townspeople at election time. The earliest lists to be considered, which are technically beyond the temporal limits of this study, are a set of lists of nominees for selectmen in Salem for 1683, 1684, and 1685.[49] At that time, and possibly in the early eighteenth century as well, Salem elected its selectmen by a procedure modeled on the system for electing assistants in Massachusetts under the first charter. First the town nominated a number of men to serve as selectmen, sometimes narrowing the field to ten men, and then balloted for the final seven positions. The most striking feature of the lists, however, is not the method of election, but the unfailing consistency with which the town nominated leaders, as defined in this study, for high office. In 1683 Salem nominated eighteen men as selectmen. Of these, sixteen had previously served as selectmen, one had not yet been a selectman but later became one, and one name was illegible.[50] The next year, 1684, the town nominated ten men, all experienced selectmen. For 1685 the town's actions are a bit unclear. Under the heading "Nominated for Selectmen at a towne meeting ye 9-1-84/5" are two partially repetitive lists, one containing ten names and the other thirteen. Whether both lists are for the same year, or whether one is from a later year and merely squeezed into a blank space to save paper, the lists are consistent with the town's nominating practices. The first list contains ten names in all, five previous selectmen, four future selectmen, and one man who never occupied a leadership position. The second list contains the names of ten previous and three future selectmen.

Taking the four lists together, it is clear that Salem was extremely careful to nominate men of established reputation for high office. All four lists included a majority of experienced town leaders, and one was composed entirely of such men. But even more significant was the town's ability to identify rising leaders among the men who had not yet served. All told, the voters named five men who were not proven leaders to nine places in the nomination lists. Four of these men, occupying eight places, fulfilled the town's expectations and became selectmen during the next decade, while only one man in all the lists failed to gain the confidence of a majority of the town, and he received a mere 10 votes out of the 1,005 cast in the four elections. The townspeople of Salem knew their leaders and wasted few votes on men outside the inner circle.

A set of voting tabulations for Hatfield from 1697 to 1700, which the town clerk obligingly entered on a flyleaf to the record book, tells a similar story, although in Hatfield the election was presumably managed without the benefit of nominations. In each of those elections the votes were divided among twenty to twenty-eight candidates, of whom no more than six were

ever men who did not become established town leaders at some time during
their lives.* Moreover, the nonleaders received far fewer votes than the more
prominent candidates. In 1700, their best year, five nonleaders polled 9.9
percent of the vote, and in 1697, their poorest year, two nonleaders polled a
scant 2.7 percent of the vote. Even without benefit of nominations, the voters
had a clear eye for men of leadership caliber, and did not waste votes on
lesser men.

At other times and in other places the results were the same. In 1739 New
Haven gave 499 votes to thirty-one leaders, 28 votes to nine nonleaders, and
11 votes to men whose names are no longer legible.[51] In Barnstable five men
were candidates for moderator at a meeting sometime about 1715, and all
were leaders.[52] Finally, nine candidates stood for election as representatives
in Portsmouth in 1744.[53] Of these, the seven who were leaders garnered 466
of the 507 votes cast, and even the two candidates who were not town leaders
were justices of the peace and prominent men.

The overall statistics of major office elections for most of a century, and
the detailed results of voting in several specific, but probably noncontroversial elections, indicate the general existence of established groups of leaders
in the eighteenth-century towns. But how did these leaders fare in contested
elections, and what happened to them in situations that pitted their interests
against those of a majority of the voters? One way of answering these
questions is to look at the behavior of the towns in elections at which, for
one reason or another, the established leaders refused to serve. The 1751 town
elections in Massachusetts provided a particularly good example of this
situation, because a law required town officers in that year to swear that they
would not accept or pass the inflated paper money of the neighboring
provinces, and leaders in many communities were unwilling to jeopardize
their personal economic interests by taking such an obligation.[54] The refusal
of leaders to serve placed the towns in a dilemma, because on the one hand
they had to have selectmen, and on the other they were unwilling to settle for
inferior men. In Hadley the town attempted to elect the customary seven
selectmen, but finally decided to make do with five after seven of the twelve
men elected to the office refused to serve. This decision averted the need to
elect men who were not recognized as leaders, because three of the five men
who agreed to serve were experienced selectmen and a fourth later saw
service as a selectman, while the fifth was an established leader of the eastern

*Support for Leaders and Other Candidates in Hatfield Elections

Year	Candidates	Leaders			Non-Leaders		
		Number	Votes	Percentage	Number	Votes	Percentage
1697	26	21	191	90.5	5	20	9.5
1698	20	18	146	97.3	2	4	2.7
1699	28	22	170	91.7	6	15	8.3
1700	23	18	136	90.1	5	15	9.9

precinct, which soon became the town of Amherst. Of the seven who refused three were experienced selectmen and three later served as selectmen.[55]

The refusal of the leaders to serve caused even more of a crisis in the town of Swansea. There the voters chose three slates of three selectmen and all refused.[56] Seven of these men were experienced leaders, while the other two later served for a number of years. After the third slate refused, the town adjourned the election for two months before electing three obviously inferior men: none of them had served as a leader before, and one was never elected again. These men did not refuse on the spot, but qualms about the legality and propriety of the election resulted in a petition to the General Court, and finally, at a meeting in August, the three men originally chosen by the town, who had among them twenty-one years of prior service, reconsidered their refusal and agreed to serve.

Both Hadley and Swansea changed the customary practice for electing selectmen rather than accept the election of inferior candidates, and that resolution was even more explicitly stated by the town of Norton. After the voters had elected twenty-one selectmen without success they became "Discouraged of proseding any farther [and] thinking it Imposabel to find Sutabel persons in sd town that can safely take the aforesd oath" they adjourned and petitioned the General Court to exempt them from the law that prescribed the oath.[57]

The need to choose selectmen from a group of appropriate leaders even governed a town's conduct when a controversy arose between those very leaders and the rest of the electorate. For four decades the leaders and voters of Brookline fought over whether to have three selectmen, as the voters insisted, or to share the duties among five, as the leaders wished. Most of the time the leaders accepted the inevitable vote to "chouse three Select Men" as final, but periodically they rebelled, and when they did they were able to bring the town to its knees simply by refusing to serve.[58] The first such battle came in 1725. The town began its meeting by voting to have three selectmen, and then proceeded to choose seven past or future leaders to the office, five of whom promptly refused. Obviously dumfounded, the town then adjourned for half an hour, after which they reconvened and elected three more candidates. When all these men refused, the town quickly capitulated, and agreeing to have five selectmen after all, filled out the board with two of the men who had refused earlier and one other. In all, they considered only eleven men eligible for election as selectmen, and ten of them were identifiable leaders.

Twice more the town fought over the issue, and each time the town confirmed that only its known leaders made satisfactory selectmen. In 1736, when the town compromised and elected four selectmen after a single slate of three had refused, all seven candidates were experienced leaders. Four decades later, in 1777, the town went through four meetings and fifteen elections before finding three selectmen who would serve, and of all the candidates only two, both of whom refused to serve, were not established leaders.[59] Whatever its leaders' motives for refusing office, a town had no alternative but to choose its candidates from among their ranks.

Even when towns were torn by open party or sectional controversy, the requirement that its major officers be "sutabel persons" remained in force. Throughout the century, factions sought to elect their adherents to the principal offices, but however the cleavages ran in the community, the candidates were invariably men recognized by the whole town as leaders in less heated times. When a faction representing the newly settled part of Dedham seized control of the town meeting in 1727 and 1728 and permitted unqualified men to vote, three of the six men it chose as selectmen had served as leaders before the crisis, two did so afterward, and all received the exemption from menial minor offices that Dedham granted its leaders.[60] When rival factions conducted simultaneous elections in Ashford in 1716, all claimants to the office of selectman served at least three other terms; and when factions in Swansea engaged in a similar dispute in 1721, nine of the ten men they put forward for major offices were established leaders.[61]

Whatever the system used for elections, and whether the election was routine or acrimonious, the New England towns unfailingly chose their leaders from universally recognized pools of leaders. Over the years the personnel of these pools gradually changed as new leaders emerged and old ones died or became disabled. Similarly, the composition of a town's leadership pool changed as the town changed, becoming more diverse if the town as a whole developed more varied interests and a less homogeneous population, or remaining more stable if the town itself changed little. Towns grew larger and more numerous as the century progressed, and the conduct of their affairs became more regular as practices of the powerful town meeting grew increasingly sophisticated and standardized. But political leadership remained a function of the most eminent members of the local community, men whose worth was recognized by all the inhabitants of the town.

·2·

THE TOWNSPEOPLE AND THEIR LEADERS

An analysis of how people at all levels of society participated in the affairs of the community must have a central place in the study of local leadership. Many systems of local government are possible, ranging from narrow oligarchies, in which only a few participate at all, to broadly egalitarian models, in which many, if not all, members of a community have a voice. In eighteenth-century New England, well-identified groups of leaders played a crucial role in managing the affairs of towns, but less prominent members of the communities also participated in the political process in significant ways. The nature of that participation and the relationship between the leaders and the community it reveals are important keys to an understanding of how the New England towns functioned.

Historians have often approached the question of participation from the standpoint of voting rights, and have exercised much ingenuity comparing legal franchise requirements with tax lists and probate records in an effort to determine how many people met the legal standards.[1] Such efforts, however, are plagued by great uncertainties about the assessment practices behind the tax lists, and about the typicality of recorded probate records.[2] Worse still is the fact that even when an accurate calculation is possible it tells only who could participate in theory and says nothing about whether the towns applied the legal franchise requirements strictly or whether those technically eligible to participate actually did so. Michael Zuckerman has demonstrated recently that towns frequently evaded the legal franchise tests when they conflicted with local realities, and historians have long puzzled over the tiny fraction of legally eligible voters who turned out for elections for which the results are known.[3] Voting rights have proven to be an inconclusive indicator of political participation in the colonial towns.

Another approach to the question of participation, however, avoids the pitfalls of studying unenforceable legal prescriptions and attributing eligibility to men who obviously never participated. Every New England town elected a large number of major officers and an even larger number of minor officers at annual elections. The men who filled these offices demonstrated an undeniable interest in community affairs by accepting office; the towns in

23

turn demonstrated conclusively that they considered those elected to be eligible for meaningful participation. Clearly, too, the men who filled the more important offices swung more weight in local affairs. Study of the numbers and kinds of men who filled minor and major offices, and comparison of both groups with the whole body of townspeople identified in a town's annual tax lists, then, suggests itself as a means of discovering who did and who did not participate in local affairs, and of estimating the relative influence of a town's inhabitants in the conduct of its affairs.

In terms of political participation, the towns might be envisioned as so many disks, each ruled off into bands by four distinct lines. Within the outer bounds of a disk, of course, would be the whole population of the town; within the second line would be all who participated actively in local affairs by filling one or more of the numerous town offices; within the third line would be the town leaders, the men who filled the five major offices; and finally, in the center would be the inner core of the leadership, those men who, by the experience and influence gained through long service, played a dominant role in the councils of the town. The size of each of the bands on the disk would naturally vary from town to town.

Although the outermost band, the members of the general population who never held town office, was invariably the largest, it can be dealt with quickly because most of its members were excluded from political activity by universally held cultural assumptions. Women made up about half of the population of any settled town in colonial New England, and although a few women were active in public affairs when, as widows, they acted as the head of an important family, they were excluded from office, and legally from voting as well.[4] Of the male population, the few colonial censuses indicated that about half was under sixteen years of age, while another eighth was between sixteen and twenty-one years. Members of the latter group were considered adults for tax purposes, for highway labor, and for military training, but for political purposes they were minors, and only participated in a few unusual cases.[5] To all intents and purposes, therefore, the actions of the "inhabitants" of a town could mean no more than the actions of the roughly one-fifth of the population who were adult males.[6] It is within this group that the breadth of participation in local affairs must be measured.

To find out which of the adult males participated in town affairs and which did not, it is necessary to focus on the lesser town offices and the men who held them. In addition to electing selectmen and other major office-holders the town meetings annually filled from about five to fifteen other offices. Because the duties of these offices involved performance of some of the town's basic public services, and because in the normal course of affairs between twenty and forty men were needed to fill them each year, the offices did not become the preserve of an elite group, and remained open to any man who was willing and able to take an active part in town affairs.[7]

Basically, the lesser offices fell into three main groups. The first group consisted of a large number of positions of a generally supervisory nature. Maintenance of the public highways was a town function, and all four colonies required their towns to elect highway surveyors or supervisors, each of whom was responsible for summoning the able-bodied male inhabitants of his neighborhood to repair the highways when necessary, and supervising them while they worked. Similarly, all four colonies provided for the election of fence viewers, who were charged with inspecting fences to make sure that they were sufficient to keep the owners' livestock from escaping and with ordering repairs when necessary.[8] Except in Rhode Island, laws required the towns to elect tithingmen annually to report violators of the laws licensing taverns and sabbath breakers to the county courts for punishment. Rhode Island left enforcement of the licensing laws to the town councilmen and required no specific official to enforce the laws governing the sabbath, although some towns elected "Sunday constables" on their own initiative.[9] All of these offices were unpaid except for the fence viewers, and perhaps the Sunday constables, in Rhode Island.[10]

A further group of supervisory officials consisted of the numerous "inspectors" and "sealers" who certified the quality or quantity of commodities involved in trade. Various laws in all four colonies required the widespread elections of clerks of the market, packers and gagers, or sealers of weights and measures to inspect the containers used in wholesale and retail trade; sealers of leather to certify that leather was properly tanned; sealers of timber or corders of wood to oversee firewood sales; viewers of lumber or measurers of boards to inspect construction timber; and sealers of flax and hemp to inspect those commodities. Other officials of a similar kind were especially common in coastal towns, among them cullers of fish, cullers of staves, and inspectors of grain.[11] Still other officials, like the ubiquitous pound keepers or the branders of horses peculiar to Connecticut, took care of the less menial aspects of livestock control. And finally there was a large and varied assortment of offices peculiar to one or two colonies, or even to a few towns. Among these were the deer reeves who sought out poachers in Massachusetts and New Hampshire, the vendue masters who auctioned the property of delinquent taxpayers and others in Rhode Island, the wardens who assisted in sabbath regulation for a few years in Massachusetts, and lotlayers and firewards in individual towns.[12] Of these officials, the various sealers and inspectors, the pound keeper, and the vendue masters could expect to receive fees for the performance of their duties, and often the same men would remain in one of those offices for a number of years.[13]

A second main group of officers consisted of those who performed menial tasks, most of which involved the catching and herding of stray livestock. The titles and exact duties of these officials varied. Towns in all four colonies at one time or another elected officers called "haywards" or "field drivers." In Massachusetts and New Hampshire these officials were responsible for neat cattle, sheep and horses; swine were entrusted to special hog reeves, who not only had to catch the strays, but also had to make sure that all hogs were ringed and yoked. Rhode Island and Connecticut laws did not differentiate the functions so extensively, and in those colonies single sets of officials were indiscriminately known as "field drivers," "haywards," or "hog reeves." Whatever their exact title, the haywards could expect to receive at least modest compensation for their trouble in the form of a share of the fee paid to reclaim an impounded animal.[14] Not all menial tasks, of course, involved livestock. Hartford, for example, elected chimney viewers for a number of years, and Boston elected scavengers and gravediggers.[15]

The third type of office was also menial in the sense that it involved running errands rather than supervising others or inspecting their conduct, but it also involved far more responsibility. Offices of this type, which included constables, tax collectors, and the town sergeants of Rhode Island, were also relatively arduous and time consuming. The towns had far more trouble filling these offices than any of the others. By law, ministers, colony officials, military officers, men who had served as constables within the past seven years, and certain other classes of people were exempted from serving as constables or collectors; while others were threatened with fines for refusing to serve.[16] But the office was demanding enough that men still refused to serve in substantial numbers, often requiring the towns to hold several elections.

Some towns solved the problem by making the office a paid position. This was the universal solution in Rhode Island, where a law of 1702 allowed the constables 5 percent of the taxes they collected and where the proliferation of fees for serving legal process soon made the offices of town sergeant and constable attractive enough that men would hold them for years at a time. Elsewhere the advent of paid constables was more gradual. Some towns tried valiantly to find unpaid constables, and some elected separate constables and collectors so that each office would be less time consuming.* Most towns, however, merely tried to avoid a direct drain on the town treasury by allowing paid substitutes to serve in the turn of the man elected so that he was assured of his seven years' exemption, or by electing wealthy men who were unlikely to accept until the fines collected would pay the wages of a willing candidate. During the 1760s and 1770s, Sudbury adopted the custom of electing one of the selectmen to the office of constable,

*Londonderry paid its constables a regular salary as early as 1732 (*Town Records*, March 6, 1731/2). Andover and Manchester presumably did not pay, however, and Andover had thirteen men refuse to serve during the 1740s, while Manchester had fifteen refuse (one constable a year was desired) from 1776 to 1785 (Andover Town Records, 1740–49; *Manchester Town Records*, 1776–85). Amherst, Lunenburg, Worcester, Londonderry, and most towns in Rhode Island and Connecticut eventually elected separate collectors. Barnstable and Brookline, among others, were openly paying their constables by the 1760s, and by 1780 Barnstable resorted to having the office "Bid off" to the lowest bidder (Barnstable Town Records, 8 March 1768, 22 March 1780; *Brookline Town Records*, vol. 1, 4 Mar. 1765, and following). See also the discussion of constable elections in Zuckerman, *Peaceable Kingdoms*, pp. 85–87.

apparently with the understanding that he would pay for the honor of serving as selectman by hiring a man to serve as constable.[17] Finally, many towns simply accepted the realities of the situation and hired a constable without even trying to find unpaid ones. By paying a man for his troubles, they could be assured that the enforcement of the laws and the collection of taxes did not have to be entrusted to men of limited abilities.

As this outline of the types of minor town offices demonstrates, the duties of town office were varied enough, and the offices themselves numerous enough, that a substantial portion of the male population had the opportunity to participate in the lower levels of the town government from time to time. Because the offices ranged from arduous but relatively menial ones that were suitable for young men with abundant energy but little experience, to responsible but not physically taxing ones suited to older men, townsmen of all ages were able to hold town offices. Similarly, men in a wide range of economic situations were able to hold office, either because the burden was so divided that no one suffered a hardship by serving, or because fees or other compensation made service at least modestly rewarding.

The most extensive evidence about the numbers and kinds of men who served in a town's minor offices is available for Dedham. Between the years 1705 and 1755, during a period in which the population of the town increased from somewhat less than 1,000 to somewhat less than 2,000, a total of 375 Dedham inhabitants served a total of 1,539 terms in ten minor town offices (see Table 3).[18] Exactly what these figures mean in terms of the percentage of population serving in town office would be obscured by the natural process of birth, death, and migration, except for the survival of numerous tax lists, which give a rough summary of the population at a point in time, and of abundant records, which permit the identification of the town officers with the names on the tax lists. A look at the results of collating the lists of taxpayers and officeholders confirms that participation was in fact broad.* Two-thirds or more of the taxpayers on all but the first

*Officeholders and Taxpayers in Dedham, 1705–1755

Date	Taxpayers	Officeholders Taxed	Ineligibles	% of Taxpayers who served
1710	218	128	10	58.7
1715	188	136	21	72.3
1720	221	163	28	73.8
1725	187	148	18	77.0
1730	231	164	29	70.9
1735	248	168	27	67.7
1740	310	208	34	67.2
1745	311	215	39	69.1
1750	321	207	44	64.5

Note: Ineligibles are women and nonresidents who could not become officers. The tax lists are in *Dedham Town Records*, 6: 55–59, 142–147, 200–205, 256–260, 310–316, 371–377; ibid., 7: 47–54, 121–128, 178–182.

TABLE THREE PART I

Age of Minor Officers in Dedham 1706-1755

Age	Constable	Surveyor	Tything-man	Fence Viewer	Field Driver	Hog Reeve	Deer Reeve	Horse Officer	Sealer	Total
21-24	0	9	1	0	1	4	0	0	0	15
25-29	7	26	6	10	22	29	2	8	1	111
30-34	20	52	10	24	51	32	4	10	1	204
35-39	30	64	24	27	20	27	6	3	5	206
40-44	43	48	20	35	20	15	7	5	16	209
45-49	16	28	29	29	18	9	5	1	19	154
50-54	16	48	22	20	6	5	3	3	13	136
55-59	4	38	19	21	1	2	1	1	13	100
60-64	0	15	8	12	3	2	0	0	5	45
65-69	0	17	10	6	0	0	0	1	0	34
70-74	1	5	3	1	0	0	0	0	1	11
75-79	0	0	1	0	0	0	0	0	0	1
Sub Total	137	350	153	185	142	125	28	32	73	1226
% Aged 25-39	41.6	40.5	26.1	33.0	65.5	70.4	42.9	65.6	9.6	
% Aged 40-54	54.7	35.4	46.4	45.4	31.0	23.4	53.6	28.1	65.6	
Unknown	22	62	19	32	37	31	1	8	11	313
Total	159	412	172	217	179	156	29	40	84	1539

TABLE THREE PART II

Age of Minor Officers in Dedham 1706-1755 : Leaders Only

Age	Constable	Surveyor	Tything-man	Fence Viewer	Field Driver	Hog Reeve	Deer Reeve	Horse Officer	Sealer	Total
21-24	0	2	0	0	1	0	0	0	0	3
25-29	4	6	3	2	4	2	2	0	1	24
30-34	10	7	3	5	14	2	0	1	0	42
35-39	10	22	9	10	1	2	0	1	3	58
40-44	19	12	8	12	2	3	0	1	10	67
45-49	4	7	11	7	1	1	0	0	14	45
50-54	2	10	4	4	1	0	0	1	12	33
55-59	0	5	7	8	0	1	0	0	7	28
60-64	0	6	3	2	0	0	0	0	0	11
65-69	0	9	3	3	0	0	0	0	0	15
70-74	0	2	2	1	0	0	0	0	1	6
75-79	0	0	1	0	0	0	0	0	0	1
Unknown	2	1	2	0	0	0	0	0	8	13
Total	51	89	56	54	24	11	2	4	66	346

and last lists served as minor officers at some time during the period, and even the terminal lists, which would have included many men who had served before 1705 or after 1755, approached that percentage. Moreover, because about a tenth of the taxpayers on any list were women or nonresident landowners, the true percentage of officeholding inhabitants must have exceeded three-quarters.

Another comparison of the tax lists and the list of officeholders, this time an examination of the amount of taxes paid by men who served within the decades centered on 1710 and 1735, further clarifies the picture of which Dedham inhabitants served in local office (see Table 4).* As might be expected, the wealthier inhabitants served the town more frequently than their poorer neighbors. In both decades well over three-quarters of the men in the top three deciles were town officers. The wealthier men would have had less need to devote all of their energy to supporting a family, and it does not seem too much to assume that a frequent correspondence existed between wealth and ability. Moreover, in colonial New England men normally reached the peak of their careers during the middle years of their lives, at the same time that men in Dedham were holding office. Men generally ranked lower on the tax list in their youth, when they were not yet established, and in their later years, when they were engaged in passing their estates along to grown sons, than they did in the prime of their lives.

But it would be a mistake to conclude that officeholding was an occupation for the wealthy, no matter how reasonable that possibility might seem. In Dedham, during both of the periods examined, men in moderate and even relatively poor circumstances held office. Between half and two-thirds of the men in the fourth, fifth, and sixth deciles, the middle ranks of the tax list, and between a sixth and a quarter of those in the next three deciles, the lowest-ranking property owners, were officers. Only men in the bottom decile, all of whom were dependent sons, servants, or hired hands who paid only a poll tax, failed totally to gain election to town offices. Moreover, a majority of these were relatively transient persons, who worked in the town for a few years and then moved on without establishing roots. Participation was nearly as broad in economic terms as it was in strictly numerical ones.

A look at the ages at which men served in minor office in Dedham also adds information on who participated in town affairs.[19] Not surprisingly, the vast majority of town officers, 82 percent, were mature men between the ages of thirty and sixty years. The pattern, however, varied significantly from the offices of one general type to those of the others. For offices of the menial type, the officeholders were predominantly young men. Sixty-five

---

*Of the taxpayers in the top three deciles of the 1710 tax list, 80.3 percent were town officers from 1706 to 1715, and 77.3 percent of those in the top deciles of the 1735 list were officers from 1730–1739. For the fourth through sixth deciles the percentages were 48.5 and 65.3 respectively, and for the seventh through ninth deciles they were 22.7 and 16.2 respectively. No man in the bottom deciles served in town office.

TABLE FOUR

Tax Standing of Minor Officers in Selected Towns

Town	Decade	Taxlist	# of Officers Taxed	Column 1 as % of all: Officers	Taxpayers	Percentage of Officers Taxed in Deciles 1-3	Deciles 4-6	Deciles 7-9	Decile 10
Amherst	1760s	1771	89	86.5	54.2	41.6	37.7	18.2	2.6
Andover	1710s	1720	116	83.5	44.4	46.6	34.5	18.1	.9
Andover	1740s	1740	189	84.8	52.9	43.9	34.4	20.6	1.1
Brookline	1765-74	1771	40	71.4	48.2	42.5	37.5	20.0	0.0
Dedham	1706-15	1710	99	94.3	45.4	53.5	32.3	14.1	0.0
Dedham	1730s	1735	119	89.5	48.0	48.7	41.2	10.1	0.0
Hadley	1706-15	1720	52	81.3	44.4	51.9	36.5	11.5	0.0
Hadley	1760s	1770	65	81.3	44.8	61.5	29.2	6.2	3.1
Oakham	1770s	1771	52	56.5	56.5	42.3	32.7	17.3	7.7
Sudbury	1710s	1722	47	46.1[1]	38.8	46.8	36.2	10.6	6.4
Sudbury	1760s	1771	134	89.9	30.6	57.5	36.6	5.9	0.0
Swansea	1760s	1771	92	63.4[2]	26.7	54.3	35.9	9.8	0.0
Watertown	1720s	1730	51	43.6[2]	35.2	43.1	41.9	15.7	0.0
Worcester	1760s	1771	99	75.6	29.9	48.5	30.9	17.5	3.1
Concord	1735-44	1737	43	70.5	89.5	39.5	37.2	16.3	7.0
Derryfield	1750s	1758	34	66.7	81.3	38.2	38.2	23.5	0.0
Derryfield	1770s	1775	36	73.5	57.1	47.2	38.9	13.9	0.0
Dublin	1770s	1771	29	53.7	53.7	58.6	34.5	6.9	0.0
Portsmouth	1710s	1715	100	84.0	27.5	56.0	31.0	11.0	2.0
Bolton	1720s	1732	29	87.9	41.4	48.3	37.9	13.8	0.0
Bolton	1750s	1753	64	88.9	39.5	45.3	35.9	14.1	4.7
New Haven	1710s	1702	124	68.5	33.0	33.9	37.9	26.6	1.6
Exeter	1766-75	1774	74	79.6	16.6	59.4	21.6	14.9	4.1
S. Kingstown	1726-35	1730	68	87.2	34.5	39.7	39.7	17.6	2.9
S. Kingstown	1766-75	1774	84	83.2	19.8	46.4	33.3	11.9	8.3

1) West Parish Only
2) East Parish Only

percent of the field drivers whose ages are known and 70 percent of the hog reeves were between the ages of twenty-five and forty years. For the most responsible office of constable, the men were slightly older. More than half of the constables were between the ages of thirty-five and forty-five years. Among the offices of a supervisory nature, the pattern was more varied, but the officeholders tended to be somewhat older men. The surveyors of highways were distributed widely among the age groups, presumably to share the burden of an office that required about ten men a year, but the tithingmen, fence viewers, and sealers were more often than not men over the age of forty. The division of minor offices into types that required varying amounts of physical exertion and mature judgment enabled the town to draw on men of all ages.

In Dedham, then, the town filled its offices with men of broadly differing ages and economic standing, so that nearly all of the permanent inhabitants held town office at some time during their adult lives. Exactly how that experience compared with the corresponding situation in other towns is harder to determine. Little systematic evidence is available on the ages of minor officers in other towns. During the second decade of the century the pattern in New Haven was similar to that in Dedham, with 89 percent of the officers between the ages of thirty and sixty.* Among the individual offices, some differences existed. New Haven, for example, chose its constables predominantly among men less than forty years old, and chose its field drivers among those over forty, exactly the opposite of the pattern of Dedham. These examples illustrate the variety of local practice. Throughout New England, towns chose mature and vigorous men, mostly between the ages of thirty and sixty, to their minor offices. The age at which a man commonly served in one office differed from that at which he served in another, according to the type of office in question. Towns elected younger men to the more menial offices and older men to the ones with supervisory functions. Legal prescriptions notwithstanding, however, towns differed in

*Minor Officers in New Haven, 1710–1719

Age	Constable	Surveyor	Fence Viewer	Field Driver	Sealers	Total
25–29	1		6	1		8
30–34	9	4	12	8		33
35–39	3	8	34	11	8	64
40–44	4	12	25	20	12	73
45–49	1	4	23	13	8	49
50–54		8	21	8	4	41
55–59		2	12	9		23
60–64			12	6	2	20
65 and up			7			7
Unknown	4	10	33	26	7	80
Total	22	48	185	102	41	398
Over 40	27.8%	68.4%	65.8%	73.7%	76.5%	67.0%

I am indebted to Bruce E. Steiner of Ohio University for supplying the ages of the New Haven officials. Professor Steiner is preparing a demographic study of early New Haven.

their assessments of the duties of the various offices, and might elect younger or older men to any particular office than was the general practice. With a generous allowance for local variation, the towns filled their offices with men from a broad but predictable range of age groups.

Evidence on the percentage of men who held office in the towns and on their place in the economic hierarchy, fortunately, is more accessible. Whereas study of the ages of the officers requires detailed vital statistics on all of the men in the town, study of the percentage participating merely requires a list of officeholders, and a tax list to establish approximate population. A comparison of twenty-five tax lists from eighteen different towns with lists of officers for ten-year periods around the date of the tax list reveals that the rate of participation in town affairs in Dedham was no aberration (see Table 4).[20] Because a tabulation of the officers serving in a single decade necessarily misses many men on a taxlist who served before and after, two ten-year samples drawn from the Dedham data show a rate of participation of between 45 and 50 percent, as opposed to 75 percent or more for the longer period. Eight of the other sample decades exhibited a participation rate of between 40 and 55 percent, roughly equal to the Dedham pattern, which presumably indicates a similar long-term rate of participation in the towns they represent.[21] These towns were mostly smaller or medium sized, not unlike the Dedham of the first half of the eighteenth century in size or in the predominantly agricultural activities of the inhabitants. Four other sample decades showed a sharply higher rate of participation than Dedham's, indicating that virtually all adult males were officeholders over the long run.[22] Three of these four samples came from frontier towns incorporated less than ten years, while the fourth, Derryfield in the 1770s, represented a town that had not yet grown out of frontier circumstances.

In another eleven sample decades, however, the rate of participation was sharply lower, ranging from 40.0 percent down to 16.6 percent for Exeter in the decade before the Revolution. These towns were larger than the towns that had higher rates of participation, and so had more men to compete for the local offices.[23] Several of them also included inhabitants with more varied economic activities. Portsmouth and New Haven were seaport commercial centers, and also provincial capitals; Swansea was a small-scale seaport; and Worcester and South Kingstown were county seats and local trading centers. Participation declined in these larger towns because men engaged in commercial or administrative work were less likely to be interested in the traditional local offices, most of which were agriculturally oriented, and also because the populations of the towns included more transients, servants, and artisans who never became established members of the community.

The relationship between size and complexity and a decreased rate of participation is also reflected in the tendency for participation in a town to decline as the century progressed. Of the seven towns for which two sample decades are included, four—Sudbury, Derryfield, South Kingstown, and Bolton—showed a decline in participation as population increased. Two others—Dedham and Hadley—yielded inconclusive results because the repeated creation of new towns within their borders eliminated those outlying inhabitants who were least likely to hold local office in the old town. Only Andover managed to increase the number of local offices in step with the growth of population and to maintain a similar rate of officeholding. Participation in local offices was broad nearly everywhere, approaching universality in some towns, and probably not declining much below 50 percent in those where it was narrowest. But the rate tended to decline as towns increased in population and became more complex.

Unlike the breadth of participation, the economic status of the minor officeholders did not vary significantly according to the size of the town. As was the case in Dedham, the inhabitants in the top three deciles of taxpayers filled a larger share of the offices in most towns than any other comparable segment of the population. In nineteen of the twenty-five sample decades they served between 35 and 55 percent of the terms. The taxpayers in the next three deciles, however, were not seriously underrepresented, filling between 30 and 40 percent of the offices in all but four of the samples. As might be expected from Dedham's example, the taxpayers in the bottom four-tenths of the list held substantially fewer offices than the wealthier townsmen, between 10 and 15 percent in most cases. Equally significant with the breadth of access to office this pattern reveals was the relatively random distribution of towns with high and low concentrations of officeholding among the wealthy. Towns with the highest concentrations included tiny Dublin and sizable Sudbury, as well as the provincial capital of Portsmouth. New Haven, the other capital city, by contrast, had the most even distribution of offices among the several ranks of taxpayers of any town, and both Derryfield and early South Kingstown divided the offices equally between the wealthy and those of moderate means. Most men in eighteenth-century New England were eligible for town office, whether they were rich or poor.

Having surveyed the patterns of minor officeholding in a number of towns, it is possible to describe the relative size of the outer two bands on the metaphorical disk with which this chapter began. The outside band, which was composed of those who did not hold office, was very large because it included all the women and children in the town, as well as any slaves who may have been present. Its proportion of the adult males, however, was quite small. According to the evidence provided by lists of officers in sample decades from a number of towns, and by more extensive data for the town of Dedham, upward of 75 percent of the adult males held office in towns with populations of about 1,200 or less, and according to the censuses taken shortly before the Revolution, 61 percent of all the towns fell in this category.[24] In the larger towns the proportion of nonparticipants was somewhat higher, but rarely reached half of the potential officeholders.

Nonparticipating male inhabitants of a town fell into several categories. Prominent among them were those men who as transient servants and hired hands or as mobile artisans and merchants failed to become established members of town society. These constituted about 10 percent of the population in agricultural Dedham, and must have been even more numerous in the commercial towns. Another noticeable group consisted of those too young and those too old for effective service in offices that required mature but vigorous men. The majority of this group appeared near the bottom of the tax list, either because they had not yet become established economically or because they had relinquished parts of their estate that they could no longer manage effectively, although a minority of both groups had substantial property. Finally, there was a small but predictable group of permanent inhabitants who failed to hold office because of persistent poverty, lack of ability, or unknown causes.

The second band on the disk, consisting of those men who held town office, was necessarily smaller than the outer one, but still of substantial size. In the smaller towns it included nearly all of the adult males, estimated at about one-fifth of the population, and in the larger towns at least half of the adult males. Most of these men were between the ages of thirty and sixty. The wealthier members of the community predominated, but all levels of income were substantially represented. This description of the band occupied by the minor officers is, however, still incomplete. Although it distinguishes the participants in town politics from the nonparticipants and thus locates the outer edge of the band, it is open sided toward the center of the disk because the relationship between the strictly minor officers and those who progressed from minor to major office remains to be described. Examination of this relationship must be the next subject of discussion.

Just as the term "leaders" implies, the men who emerged from the ranks of ordinary participants to hold the chief offices constituted a local elite. Exactly who belonged to this elite in terms of economic standing, family position, age, religious affiliation, and external political connections will be the subject of later chapters. For the present, attention will focus on the size of the elite pool of leaders, the process by which prospective leaders qualified themselves by service in minor office, the willingness of established leaders to serve in minor office, and finally on the structure of power within the pool of leaders itself.

At issue in a study of the size of the local elite is the question of the openness of the political system. The finding that from half to virtually all of the male inhabitants held minor office indicates that participation in the governmental process was relatively open in all towns, although progressively less so as the towns increased in size. But the duties of the lesser officers were very routine, and although matters like the maintenance of highways and the control of livestock affected the lives of most members in a predominantly agricultural society, execution of a minor office gave a man little opportunity to make important decisions. Apart from the town meeting, real power in the towns lay with the leaders, the holders of the major offices. Whether these offices were accessible to a few or to many is, therefore, crucial to an understanding of the openness of local government.

One way of establishing the size of the pool of town leaders is to compare the number of leaders and the number of minor offices serving in a town during a sample decade like those used to study the minor officers. Some of the leaders, of course, served simultaneously as minor officers and some did not, so that the groups are not mutually exclusive, but a comparison does help to measure their relative size. A glance at the data in Table 5 reveals that

TABLE FIVE

Leaders as a Percentage of Town Officers

Town	Dates	# of Leaders	Leaders as % of Officers	Dates	# of Leaders	Leaders as % of Officers
Amherst	1760-1769	21	23.6	1780-1789	33	26.2
Andover	1711-1720	24	17.3	1740-1749	23	10.3.
Barnstable	1721-1731[1]	20	17.2			
Barrington	1720-1729	13	28.3			
Brookline	1710-1719	14	29.8	1765-1774	12	21.4
Dedham	1706-1715	17	16.2	1730-1739	18	13.5
Fitchburg	1776-1785	21	18.4			
Hadley	1706-1715	20	31.3	1760-1769	24	30.0
Lunenburg	1730-1739	18	31.0	1750-1759	28	25.9
Manchester	1730-1739	11	20.4	1776-1785	12	15.6
Medfield	1700-1709	24	33.8			
Oakham	1770-1779	20	21.7			
Springfield	1720-1729	26	14.1			
Sudbury	1710-1719	27	26.5	1760-1769	18	12.1
Swansea	1700-1709	13	12.6	1761-1770	16	11.0
Topsfield	1710-1719	24	37.5	1750-1759	19	25.3
Watertown	1720-1729	22	18.8			
Worcester	1730-1739	16	15.5	1760-1769	23	17.6
Newcastle	1760-1769	14	22.6			
Concord	1735-1744	10	16.4			
Derryfield	1751-1760	15	29.4	1770-1779	24	49.0
Dublin	1771-1780	13	24.1			
Hampstead	1760-1769	19	22.1			
Hanover	1770-1779	16	24.2			
Londonderry	1754-1763	23	10.6			
Portsmouth	1711-1720	21	17.6			
Exeter	1742-1751	23	27.7	1766-1775	29	31.2
S.Kingstown	1726-1735	14	17.9	1766-1775	38	37.3
Ashford	1729-1738	11	20.8	1760-1769	16	12.0
Bolton	1721-1730	12	36.4	1751-1760	16	22.2
Enfield	1720-1729	17	16.2	1760-1769	10	12.5
New Haven	1710-1719	35	19.3			

1) Data for 1725 are missing.

the number of leaders varied widely from town to town.[25] In the most extreme cases, the group of active leaders might be only a tenth the size of the pool of minor officers, as was the case in Andover during the 1740s, and at the other end of the spectrum it might be half as large as the whole body of minor officers, as it was in Derryfield during the 1770s. As with the proportion of minor officers in the overall population, the variation depended mainly on the size of the town.[26] In twenty-seven small town samples the leader pool averaged about a quarter (26.5 percent) as large as the pool of minor officers.[27] The percentages for a few individual towns varied considerably, but the majority of cases fell reasonably close to the average. Since for most small towns the pool of minor officers approximated the available adult population, a quarter of that number meant that the leadership was quite a broad group.

In the twenty-two towns with a population larger than 1,200, however, the proportion of leaders to minor officers was substantially lower, only 17.6 percent. Except for three Rhode Island towns with percentages between 27 and 37 percent, moreover, the individual cases were mostly below the average.[28] Furthermore, because the minor officers constituted a smaller percentage of the adult population in the larger towns, a pool of leaders only 12 or 15 percent as large could be quite small indeed. The time in the century at which the samples were drawn seems to have had little direct influence on the general findings. In two-thirds of the cases where two samples were taken for the same town, the second one produced a lower percentage than the first, but then most towns increased in population as time went on. Significantly, when Rhode Island towns, which had unusually small groups of minor officers and normal-sized groups of leaders, are excluded the large town percentage fell from 17.2 before 1740 to 12.3 in the later period when there were more very large towns. The percentage of minor officers gaining entry into the leadership pool in a town of a given size apparently did not change during the century.

Comparison of the size of the leader pool and the total population confirms the findings described in the preceding paragraphs and produces a more comprehensive index of the position of each of the seventy towns in the overall pattern. The basic data for such a comparison are a tabulation of the leaders serving each town during three twenty-five year periods between 1700 and 1775, and a set of population estimates based on censuses and tax lists (see Table 6).[29] Of the three sets of figures resulting from the analysis of this data, the set for the last period, 1750–1774, is the most comprehensive, since reasonably exact censuses are available for virtually all the towns. This data confirms the impression, obtained by comparing the size of the leader pool with the size of the minor officer pool, that participation varied according to a town's population. Less than 1 percent of the population were leaders in the four cities of Boston, Newport, Portsmouth, and New Haven; between 1 and 3 percent were leaders in most towns with more than 1,000 inhabitants; between 3 and 6 percent served as leaders in most towns with 500 to 1,000

TABLE SIX

Leaders as a Percentage of Population by Periods

Town	Numbers of Leaders				Leaders as % of Population		
	1700-24	1725-49	1750-74	1775-84	1700-24	1725-49	1750-74
MASSACHUSETTS							
Amherst	xx	xx	25	31			3.9
Andover	36	39	41	26	3.1	2.4	1.7
Barnstable	20	31	22	20	2.5		1.0
Barrington	11	14	xx	xx			
Billerica	31	32	25	13		2.9	1.9
Boston	66	68	56	58	0.6	0.4	0.4
Boxford	63	48	46	28	11.4	8.6	5.5
Braintree	41	39	37	26			1.5
Brookline	19	25	23	18			6.8
Cambridge	28	39	32	37	2.7		2.0
Dedham	35	39	36		3.6	3.5	1.9
Dorchester	27	20	26	16		1.6	1.9
Duxbury	19	13	16	20			1.5
Fitchburg	xx	xx	16	21			6.2
Grafton	xx	44	41	37			5.4
Hadley	29	55	56	28	5.5	8.0	9.8
Hanover[1]	xx	34	24	21			2.2
Hardwick	xx	16	24	26			2.4
Hatfield	32	32	18	11		5.5	2.2
Leicester	13	34	36	23		4.2	4.7
Lunenburg	xx	31	49	27			6.0
Manchester	20	21	24	12	7.2		3.2
Medfield	36	50	51	34	6.5		7.8
Middleboro	21	25	39	31			1.1
Norton	22	25	31	14	7.3		1.6
Oakham	xx	xx	22	24			8.1
Pelham	xx	24	46	35			12.4
Shirley	xx	xx	23	16			5.3
Springfield	48	41	32	23		2.4	1.2
Sudbury	61	52	37	29	5.6		2.1
Swansea	33	37	34	30			1.9
Topsfield	38	46	33		10.7	6.4	4.6
Waltham	xx	21	23	18		3.2	3.5
Watertown	43	43	33	24	4.3	3.3	4.8
Westminster	xx	xx	17	25			3.6
Worcester	11	31	35	33			2.4
MAINE							
Biddeford	9	22	18	11			2.4
Brunswick	xx	17	21	11			4.2
Gorham[1]	xx	xx	15	15			1.8
Newcastle	xx	xx	26	16			5.7
Scarborough	5	22	24	18			1.9

1) Populations for Gorham and Hanover are conjectural.

TABLE SIX Continued

Town	Number of Leaders				Leaders as % of Population		
	1700-24	1725-49	1750-74	1775-84	1700-24	1725-49	1750-74
NEW HAMPSHIRE							
Bedford	xx	xx	40	25			11.0
Canterbury	xx	xx	29	19			5.8
Chester	xx	41	34	25		6.9	2.9
Concord	xx	16	20	15		5.8	2.7
Cornish	xx	xx	15	25			11.3
Derryfield	xx	xx	28	23			12.2
Dover	32	29	39	16		3.2	2.4
Dublin	xx	xx	9	13			
Hampstead	xx	xx	40	20			6.2
Hampton	70	66	48	20		5.7	5.5
Hanover	xx	xx	14	22			15.2
Londonderry	20	49	50	39		6.8	2.1
New Ipswich	xx	xx	24	22			5.6
Portsmouth	46	47	36	26	2.9	2.2	0.8
Weare	xx	xx	25	20			9.3
RHODE ISLAND							
Exeter	xx	22	45	35			2.8
Middletown	xx	18	48	25			5.8
Newport	62	50	54	24	2.8	1.1	0.7
Providence	65	74	77	53	4.5	1.9	2.1
Smithfield	xx	45	40	33			1.7
S. Kingstown	xx	46	65	41		3.0	2.7
CONNECTICUT							
Ashford	17	27	30	27			1.7
Bolton	6	18	26	19		5.7	2.9
Derby	27	27	43	22	10.2	9.7	3.0
Enfield	31	35	24	16			2.0
Kent	xx	19	36	36			2.4
New Haven	76	69	55	57	4.5	1.8	0.8
Newtown	34	46	67	38		7.2	3.8
Stonington	47	45	47	32	8.2		1.1
Woodbury	xx	48	59	36		5.4	1.4

inhabitants; and more than six percent served in towns with populations under 500. (Table 7, part III ranks the towns.)

For the period 1725 to 1749 specific population data has come to light for only twenty-seven of the fifty-five towns then existing, and for all but four towns that data consists of estimates based upon tax lists. Again, however, the percentage of leaders in the population decreased as the towns increased in size. Boston, the largest city, had less than 1 percent of its population in the leader pool; towns with populations of more than 1,000 had between 1 and 5 percent leaders; and towns with less than 1,000 people had more than 5

TABLE SEVEN

Leaders as a Percentage of Population

Part I 1700-1724			Part II 1725-1749		
Town	Percentage	Population	Town	Percentage	Population
GROUP I			GROUP I		
Boston	0.6	10,567	Boston	0.4	16,328
GROUP II			GROUP II		
Barnstable	2.5	806	Newport	1.1	4,640
Cambridge	2.7	1,040	Dorchester	1.6	1,104
Newport	2.8	2,203	New Haven	1.8	3,749
Portsmouth	2.9	1,638	Providence	1.9	3,916
Andover	3.1	1,175	Portsmouth	2.2	2,178
Dedham	3.6	941	Andover	2.3	1,606
Watertown	4.3	1,000	Springfield	2.4	1,692
Providence	4.5	1,446	Billerica	2.9	1,094
New Haven	4.5	1,692	S. Kingstown	3.0	1,523
Hadley	5.5	525	Waltham	3.2	666
Sudbury	5.6	1,089	Dover	3.2	1,233
			Watertown	3.3	1,296
GROUP III			Dedham	3.5	1,116
			Leicester	4.2	810
Medfield	6.5	558			
Manchester	7.2	279	GROUP III		
Norton	7.3	302			
Stonington	8.2	576	Woodbury	5.4	882
Derby	10.2	266	Hatfield	5.5	585
Topsfield	10.7	279	Bolton	5.7	315
Boxford	11.4	536	Hampton	5.7	1,157
			Concord	5.8	275
			Topsfield	6.4	720
			Londonderry	6.8	720
			Chester	6.9	592
			Newtown	7.2	639
			Hadley	8.0	684
			Boxford	8.6	558
			Derby	9.7	279

percent who served as leaders (Table 7, part II). An examination of the period 1700-1724, for which tax list estimates of population are available for nineteen of forty-one existing towns, yields very similar results. Boston had less than 1 percent leaders, towns over 1,000 in population had between 1 and 6 percent leaders, and smaller towns had more than 6 percent leaders (Table 7, part I).

Comparison of the three sets of percentages indicates that two interesting developments took place as the century progressed. First of all, it has been evident throughout this discussion of the size of the leader pool that access to the positions of power was less open in large towns than in small ones, but exactly what happened as an individual town grew has not been so clear. Now the data makes it clear that access did become progressively restricted:

TABLE SEVEN: Continued

Part III 1750-1774

Town	Percentage	Population	Town	Percentage	Population
GROUP I			GROUP III		
Boston	0.4	15,000	Derby	3.0	1,445
Newport	0.7	7,980	Manchester	3.2	739
New Haven	0.8	6,690	Waltham	3.5	663
Portsmouth	0.8	4,466	Westminster	3.6	468
			Newtown	3.8	1,741
GROUP II			Amherst	3.9	645
			Brunswick	4.2	504
Barnstable	1.0	2,146	Topsfield	4.6	719
Middleboro	1.1	3,438	Leicester	4.7	770
Stonington	1.1	4,465	Watertown	4.8	693
Springfield	1.2	2,755	Shirley	5.3	430
Woodbury	1.4	4,112	Grafton	5.4	760
Duxbury	1.5	1,061	Boxford	5.5	841
Braintree	1.5	2,445	Hampton	5.5	866
Norton	1.6	1,942	New Ipswich	5.6	c.400
Andover	1.7	2,462	Newcastle	5.7	454
Ashford	1.7	1,743	Middletown	5.8	830
Smithfield	1.7	2,405	Canterbury	5.8	503
Gorham	1.8	c.750	Lunenburg	6.0	821
Dorchester	1.9	1,360			
Billerica	1.9	1,334	GROUP IV		
Swansea	1.9	1,799			
Scarborough	1.9	1,272	Fitchburg	6.2	259
Dedham	1.9	1,929	Hampstead	6.2	644
Cambridge	2.0	1,582	Brookline	6.8	338
Enfield	2.0	1,205	Medfield	7.8	639
Providence	2.1	3,740	Oakham	8.1	270
Londonderry	2.1	2,389	Weare	9.3	268
Sudbury	2.1	1,773	Hadley	9.8	573
Hatfield	2.2	815	Bedford	11.0	362
Hanover, Mass.	2.2	c.1,000	Cornish	11.3	133
Worcester	2.4	1,478	Derryfield	12.2	230
Hardwick	2.4	1,010	Pelham	12.4	371
Biddeford	2.4	753	Hanover, N.H.	15.2	92
Dover	2.4	1,614			
Kent	2.4	1,498			
S. Kingstown	2.7	2,374			
Concord	2.7	752			
Exeter	2.8	1,634			
Chester	2.9	1,189			
Bolton	2.9	884			

the percentage of leaders in all but six of the towns for which comparative figures exist declined from period to period (Table 6). At first glance, this trend does not seem very significant. After all, a town's population usually increased as time passed, and since the number of offices available was small and relatively fixed, the elite was bound to become an increasingly smaller percentage of the population. Even the towns in which the percentage of leaders increased support this obvious conclusion, because five of them had lost major parts of their outlying areas, which were relatively underrepresented, before the apparent increases in the size of the leader pool took place. But a fixed number of offices did *not* necessitate a progressively smaller elite: frequent elections should have enabled a town to keep access to power open by increasing the turnover of men in office. That they did not do so suggests that growth brought qualitative changes in a town's political system that made fewer men eligible for office and made smaller elites more desirable.[30]

Even more suggestive is the outcome of an analysis of the changing percentage of leaders in towns of a given size. When the percentage of leaders in towns with populations of between 500 and 700, and between 1,000 and 1,300, are averaged for each of the three time periods, the result shows a progressive decline in the relative size of the leader pool at each population level. For towns with between 500 and 700 people the percentage of leaders declined from 7.9 in the first twenty-five-year period to 6.6 in the second period, then to 5.8 in the third period; and for towns between 1,000 and 1,300 the respective percentages were 3.9, 3.4, and 2.2. Not only did access to power become more restricted as towns grew in size, it also became restricted in smaller and smaller towns as the whole society grew in size and complexity.*

Conclusions about the size of the leader pool for towns with different populations and at different points in time provide answers to questions about the relative size of the groups of town leaders and secondary town officers, but they do not go very far toward explaining the overall relationship between the two groups. Heretofore it has been assumed that the leaders were a subgroup of those who participated in town affairs by holding minor office, just as those participants were necessarily a part of the whole population of the town. That this assumption was valid is confirmed by two customs of local politics, the habit of selecting men who had proven their ability in lesser offices to the top position, and the practice of continuing to elect established leaders to minor offices.

Understandably, when a town prepared to fill its major offices it looked for men of proven ability. The incumbents were, of course, strong candidates, as were those who had preceded the incumbents in major office, but new talent was also necessary. Fortunately, the New England towns provided many ways a man could demonstrate his fitness for major office. One could serve as a commissioned or noncommissioned officer in the militia, become a leader of the church, acquire a liberal education, gain a reputation

---

*The universal shrinkage in the relative size of elites suggests an important modification to the implication in Lockridge and Kreider's "Evolution of Massachusetts Town Government 1640 to 1740," pp. 549–74, that the turn of the century brought a one-time-only shift in power from the selectmen to the town meeting. That the length of service of town leaders declined from the early seventeenth century to about 1700 is well documented, but the declining size of the elite thereafter, which given the relatively fixed number of offices is the inverse of length of service, suggests that the trend soon reversed itself. In all likelihood the growing complexity of society and the institutionalization of more formal governing procedures, as discussed in Chapter 1, served to restore and then reinforce the power of the knowledgeable leaders. Figures in Table 20 confirm that after reaching a low point in the early 18th century, length of service increased in the years before the Revolution.

for financial acumen by building and maintaining a prosperous estate, or serve the town on ad hoc committees like those appointed to lay out highways or perambulate the town's boundaries. But by far the most common method of demonstrating ability was to serve in one or more of the minor town offices. Just how pervasive the minor offices were as testing and recruiting grounds for leaders is clear in a survey of the sample decades used to study the minor offices. Of 523 leaders who began their service in major town office during ten year periods beginning in the sixth year of each of the fifty-one samples of minor officers, 374, or 71.5 percent had served in minor office during that sample decade. Exactly how many others had served before, of course, is impossible to determine.[31]

A look at the backgrounds of new leaders in five scattered towns reveals that no particular office or group of offices was prerequisite for election to major offices. Of the leaders selected at random from the extensive Dedham data, two had been constables, three had been surveyors of the highways, three had been tithingmen, two had been fence viewers, two field drivers, and one a hog reeve. Many towns looked favorably on the claims of a man who had successfully completed a recent term as constable, not only because the office involved the responsibility of collecting substantial sums of money, but also because the numerous duties of a constable gave many people firsthand knowledge of his abilities. Four of seven new selectmen in Hampstead between 1765 and 1774 had served as constables within the five years previous to their election, and four of six new leaders in Ashford during the 1730s had been constables during the previous ten years. Other towns, however, paid more attention to other offices. In Andover between 1745 and 1754, six of eight new leaders were recent highway surveyors, and in Worcester half of the six new selectmen elected during the decade before the Revolution had recently been tithingmen.

More important to this apprenticeship system than individual offices was the willingness of a prospective leader to devote time and effort to the town's service. In a majority of the towns studied, the minor officers averaged two to three terms in office per man in a decade. (See Table 8, part I.) Even though their liability for election to the lesser offices was cut short by service as leaders during the course of the decade, however, the prospective leaders in Dedham, Andover, Worcester, Hampstead, and Ashford served about one term per man more than the town average.* This meant that a man was in

*Prior Service of New Leaders in Minor Office

Town	Average Terms, All Officers	Average Terms, New Leaders
Andover (1740s)	2.78	4.00
Dedham (1730s)	1.96	4.50
Worcester (1760s)	2.37	3.67
Hampstead (1760s)	2.66	3.28
Ashford (1730s)	3.91	4.50

office virtually every year. Josiah Pierce of Worcester, for example, served as deer reeve in 1760, 1761, and 1762; tithingman in 1761; constable in 1763; and highway surveyor in 1764, before becoming a selectman in 1765. Similarly, William Avery of Dedham served as constable in 1710 and 1711, fence viewer and tithingman in 1713, highway surveyor in 1714, tithingman again in 1715 and 1717, surveyor again in 1716 and 1717, and finally selectman in 1718. One of the many attributes of the leader pool was that it was made up of those town officers who were most willing and able to serve the town.

Promotion to the ranks of a town's leaders profoundly changed a man's status in the political life of the town, but it did not usually end his service in the lesser offices. When most of a town's adult population was needed to fill the local offices, as was the case in the smaller towns, the town scarcely would have exempted those leaders who were out of office from taking a turn. Even the larger towns, which theoretically had enough men to fill all their offices easily, were unwilling to exempt their ablest citizens from service. Leaders were therefore under substantial pressure to serve in minor offices during the intervals in their tenure of the major positions.

If leaders had considered the lesser offices beneath their dignity the situation might have generated considerable friction, but most leaders viewed continued service in minor offices as necessary and often as desirable. Eighteenth-century political values stressed the obligation of elite members to provide service to the community, as well as establishing their right to high office. In the opinion of those leaders who moved in intercolonial and trans-Atlantic circles, this obligation of service undoubtedly did not extend to viewing fences, but the vast majority of leaders were much more parochial men, who considered fence viewing and highway regulation fitting duties for one who aspired to a place of honor among his neighbors and fellow townspeople. For most town leaders, continued service in lesser offices, especially those of a supervisory nature, was entirely consistent with their sense of personal worth.

Even for those who did not particularly relish serving in minor office, judicious acceptance of selected offices could have its advantages. As further inquiry will reveal, a certain number of town leaders could claim their position on the basis of family status, superior education, wealth, or dazzling personal abilities; but others, probably a majority, were simply men of ordinary or slightly above average ability, who achieved the rank of leaders because they were more willing than most to devote time and energy to the public service. Such men were usually just as willing to serve in minor office after a term as selectman, as they had before. For others, service in minor office could be the lesser of two evils. All able-bodied men shared in the legal obligation to turn out for highway labor at the summons of the local highway surveyor, or to provide a substitute, on pain of a stiff fine for refusing. Unless a leader had a hired hand who was not busy, accepting election to the supervisory office of highway surveyor was a real alternative to reporting for work with pick and shovel.

Skillful administration of minor offices could also help a man build the "interest" a leader needed if he hoped to cut a figure in the politics of a large town, or especially of a colony. Historians—beginning with the inimitable Peter Oliver—have not been slow to draw large conclusions from the willingness of major figures like Elisha Cooke, Jr., and Samuel Adams to serve the town of Boston as tax collectors, and their assertions ring true, even though tax manipulation was something less than the main cause of the American Revolution.[32] Other offices held the possibility of equally useful favors, but mere willingness to provide cheerful service as well as frequent contacts with the townspeople while executing the duties of an office were enough to gain a man popular support. When shrewd old James Otis, Sr., found himself engaged in a struggle with Edward Bacon, a crypto-Tory, for political supremacy in Barnstable during the 1760s and 1770s, he agreed to serve as a regulator of the fish in Herring Brook in 1763, his first minor office in thirty years, and then as surveyor of highways in 1765, 1766, 1769, and 1770. Execution of these offices, as well as simultaneous service as selectman, representative, and moderator, moved the town to vote Otis its formal thanks for his service in 1772, the first time it had ever passed such a vote, and enabled Otis to pass his positions as selectman and moderator to his son, Joseph, when he retired from town politics.[33] Minor town office could be a useful tool in the hands of a resourceful leader.

The willingness of leaders to serve in minor offices does not mean, however, that the towns treated them as ordinary inhabitants. Leaders were expected to serve the town, but the towns agreed that they should serve only in the supervisory offices and virtually exempted them from election to the menial positions. Leaders served a total of 2,237 of 12,664 terms in the fifty-one sample decades used to study the minor offices, for an overall average of 17.7 percent of the offices (Table 8, part I). While this comprehensive statistic is not very meaningful, masking as it does a set of individual cases in which leaders served as few as 1.5 percent of the terms and as many as 35.4 percent, the figures for individual offices were much more consistent. Men who had previously held major office served more than 10 percent of the terms as hog reeve in only three samples, for an average of 4.2 percent of the terms, and more than 10 percent of the terms as field driver in only six samples, for an average of 7.0 percent. By contrast with the low percentages for these menial offices, the leaders served a substantial portion of the terms in the supervisory offices. More than 19 percent of the surveyors of highways, 17 percent of the fence viewers, 13 percent of the tithingmen, and 30 percent of the various sealers and inspectors were established leaders (Table 8, part II). Only 7.6 percent of the constables, a menial but responsible office, were leaders, and even this figure is misleading. Nearly half of the leaders who became constables served in the last two decades of the period, after the job had become a paying position. One such man was William Davis of Brookline, a one-term selectman, who volunteered to serve as constable each year from 1765 to 1769, each time setting his own salary.[34] A paid position,

TABLE EIGHT

Statistics of Minor Officeholding

Part I : All Minor Offices

Town	Years	Minor Terms Served by Leaders #	%	# Officers	# Terms	Average Terms	New Leaders with Minor Experience #	%	Leaders as Constable #	%
MASSACHUSETTS										
Amherst	1760-69	42	19.5	89	215	2.42	5	71.4	1	5.6
Amherst	1780-89	54	18.9	126	286	2.27	11	91.6	1	4.0
Andover	1711-20	53	15.1	139	352	2.51	10	90.9	0	0
Andover	1740-49	19	3.1	223	621	2.78	8	80.0	1	2.9
Barnstable	1721-31	13	5.7	116	230	1.98	2	40.0	2	8.7
Barrington	1720-29	14	21.9	46	64	1.42	3	60.0	3	25.0
Brookline	1710-19	2	2.4	47	83	1.77	6	66.7	0	0
Brookline	1765-74	23	16.2	56	142	2.54	5	71.4	6	60.0
Dedham	1706-15	35	13.7	105	255	2.43	15	100.0	0	0
Dedham	1730-39	27	10.3	133	261	1.96	10	83.3	0	0
Fitchburg	1776-85	36	16.4	114	219	1.92	N/A	N/A	4	22.2
Hadley	1706-15	49	32.9	64	149	2.33	4	100.0	2	11.8
Hadley	1760-69	69	26.8	80	257	3.21	10	90.9	2	11.8
Lunenburg	1730-39	52	35.4	58	147	2.53	6	75.0	5	33.3
Lunenburg	1750-59	36	11.3	108	320	2.96	7	63.6	0	0
Manchester	1730-39	57	30.3	54	188	3.48	4	80.0	1	10.0
Manchester	1776-85	123	29.1	77	423	5.49	1	33.3	2	20.0
Medfield	1700-09	7	5.6	71	124	1.75	10	66.7	2	10.0
Oakham	1770-79	50	20.0	92	250	2.76	13	76.5	4	36.4
Springfield	1720-29	74	18.2	185	406	2.19	6	75.0	0	0
Sudbury	1710-19	55	27.1	102	203	2.01	8	61.5	5	23.8
Sudbury	1760-69	47	13.7	149	343	2.30	8	80.0	4	10.5
Swansea	1700-09	13	6.1	103	213	2.07	2	50.0	0	0
Swansea	1761-70	31	7.0	145	444	3.31	9	75.0	0	0
Topsfield	1710-19	35	27.1	64	129	2.02	9	90.0	1	5.0
Topsfield	1750-59	20	12.9	75	155	2.07	11	91.6	1	5.0
Watertown	1720-29	3	1.5	117	200	1.71	11	78.6	0	0
Worcester	1730-39	31	14.0	103	221	2.13	3	60.0	0	0
Worcester	1760-69	79	25.4	131	311	2.37	6	75.0	6	28.6
Newcastle	1760-69	78	31.3	62	249	4.02	3	42.8	8	40.5

TABLE EIGHT: Continued

Town	Years	Minor Terms Served by Leaders #	Minor Terms Served by Leaders %	# Officers	# Terms	Average Terms	New Leaders with Minor Experience #	New Leaders with Minor Experience %	Leaders as Constable #	Leaders as Constable %
NEW HAMPSHIRE										
Concord	1735–44	67	25.7	61	263	4.32	1	33.3	5	50.0
Derryfield	1751–60	30	18.3	51	164	3.22	4	66.7	0	0
Derryfield	1770–79	51	27.9	49	183	3.73	7	63.6	3	33.3
Dublin	1771–80	30	20.0	54	150	2.78	6	66.7	4	19.0
Hampstead	1760–69	35	15.3	86	229	2.66	7	77.8	5	27.8
Hanover	1770–79	38	20.2	66	188	2.85	11	78.6	0	0
Londonderry	1754–63	61	15.6	218	390	1.79	11	91.7	0	0
Portsmouth	1711–20	52	15.6	119	333	2.71	8	53.3	1	2.7
RHODE ISLAND										
Exeter	1742–51	62	24.5	83	253	3.05	8	80.0	0	0
Exeter	1766–75	103	29.9	93	344	3.70	8	44.4	2	5.0
Middletown	1743–52	69	28.3	57	244	4.28	6	42.9	0	0
S. Kingstown	1726–35	20	7.8	78	258	3.31	8	61.5	0	0
S. Kingstown	1766–75	61	20.1	101	304	2.98	8	42.1	0	0
CONNECTICUT										
Ashford	1729–38	39	18.8	53	207	3.91	6	75.0	0	0
Ashford	1760–69	33	9.1	133	363	2.73	7	70.0	0	0
Bolton	1721–30	14	15.9	33	88	2.67	7	77.8	2	18.2
Bolton	1751–60	42	18.2	72	231	3.16	5	62.5	4	20.0
Enfield	1720–29	40	15.6	105	256	2.44	8	88.9	0	0
Enfield	1760–69	33	13.3	80	248	3.10	2	100.0	0	0
Hartford	1700–09	37	14.6	150	253	1.69	14	60.9	0	0
New Haven	1710–19	93	19.7	185	473	2.56	26	86.7	0	0

TABLE EIGHT: Continued

Part II : Leaders in Minor Office

Town	Surveyor #	%	Fence Viewer #	%	Tythingman #	%	Sealers #	%	Field Driver #	%	Hog Reeve #	%
MASSACHUSETTS												
Amherst 1	12	28.6	14	63.6	2	6.9	3	60.0	-	-	0	0
Amherst 2	12	20.7	6	21.5	9	15.0	13	65.0	0	0	1	2.4
Andover 1	32	27.1	3	15.0	3	6.1	8	26.7	2	2.9	1	2.9
Andover 2	16	6.2	-	-	2	2.5	0	0	1	-	1	20.8
Barnstable	7	18.4	0	0	0	0	2	7.1	1	20.0	0	0
Barrington	8	36.4	0	0	3	18.8	0	0	1	-	0	0
Brookline 1	2	6.9	0	0	-	-	0	0	1	10.0	0	0
Brookline 2	9	24.3	3	16.7	12	30.8	2	6.9	1	10.0	0	0
Dedham 1	9	12.3	6	10.9	7	23.3	8	88.9	0	0	1	33.3
Dedham 2	7	9.5	2	5.0	4	20.0	10	90.9	0	0	1	2.5
Fitchburg	19	22.6	3	33.3	8	40.0	-	-	1	16.7	0	0
Hadley 1	5	22.7	17	26.2	4	18.2	10	100.0	0	0	0	0
Hadley 2	16	55.1	8	22.2	10	45.4	0	0	2	28.6	0	0
Lunenburg 1	15	46.9	4	20.0	2	6.3	12	70.6	-	-	2	4.8
Lunenburg 2	16	15.1	2	7.4	1	3.9	9	22.0	1	2.9	12	30.7
Manchester 1	15	36.6	12	38.7	2	8.7	15	36.6	1	14.0	8	12.3
Manchester 2	27	49.0	16	43.2	1	3.2	60	39.2	7	-	-	-
Medfield	3	8.1	1	3.2	1	3.2	-	-	1	0	0	0
Oakham	23	31.9	0	0	2	7.1	11	29.0	x[2]	x	0	0
Springfield	6	7.3	15	13.0	7	14.0	16	72.7	x	10.0	0	0
Sudbury 1	9	19.6	12	32.4	14	35.0	14	66.7	1	4.0	-	-
Sudbury 2	11	15.7	11	36.7	4	9.2	9	18.8	2	4.0	0	0
Swansea 1	2	3.0	2	4.3	1	8.7	6	40.0	0	0	0	0
Swansea 2	17	10.1	9	30.0	0	0	3	3.9	1	10.0	1	10.0
Topsfield 1	7	19.4	10	45.4	12	42.9	4	40.0	-	-	2	10.0
Topsfield 2	4	8.7	6	20.7	4	13.8	2	25.0	-	-	-	-
Watertown	2	3.8	0	0	1	2.4	0	0	1	-	0	0
Worcester 1	15	17.2	0	0	0	0	13	56.5	0	0	3	8.3
Worcester 2	34	3.6	1	5.0	1	5.0	28	75.7	0	0	0	0
Newcastle	19	39.0	9	23.1	7	29.2	10	25.0	6	21.4	8	26.7

TABLE EIGHT: Continued

Town	Surveyor #	%	Fence Viewer #	%	Tythingman #	%	Sealers #	%	Field Driver #	%	Hog Reeve #	%
NEW HAMPSHIRE												
Concord	27	47.4	10	19.2	6	30.0	14	50.0	4	8.7	1	2.4
Derryfield 1	8	21.6	4[1]	36.4	1	7.1	9	33.3	0	0	1	5.3
Derryfield 2	19	32.8	x[1]	x	4	22.2	15	55.5	-	-	1	3.9
Dublin	16	25.0	5	25.0	4	20.0	0	0	1	6.3	0	0
Hampstead	14	15.4	8	21.1	4	15.4	0	0	0	0	1	3.9
Hanover	12	15.8	3	15.8	4	13.8	14	63.6	0	0	1	5.6
Londonderry	38	16.7	7	36.8	3	8.6	2	10.5	-	-	3	7.7
Portsmouth	27	33.0	1	2.2	2	5.4	8	21.6	-	-	0	0
RHODE ISLAND												
Exeter 1	29	24.2	-	-	-	-	13	20.6	-	-	-	-
Exeter 2	77	34.7	-	-	0	0	10	25.6	0	0	-	-
Middletown	13	32.5	0	0	-	-	26	37.7	0	0	-	-
S. Kingstown 1	3	4.2	-	-	-	-	17	22.7	0	0	-	-
S. Kingstown 2	43	37.1	-	-	2	6.1	3	7.9	3	13.6	-	-
CONNECTICUT												
Ashford 1	5	11.6	7	16.3	4	20.0	18	34.0	0	0	-	-
Ashford 2	17	12.5	4	20.0	0	0	3	10.3	-	-	-	-
Bolton 1	2	9.1	0	0	1	50.0	8	36.4	-	-	-	-
Bolton 2	5	12.8	2	10.0	1	7.7	23	44.2	-	-	2	11.1
Enfield 1	11	26.2	11	19.6	12	33.0	5	50.0	1	3.1	0	0
Enfield 2	7	7.4	1	3.3	3	15.0	21	28.4	-	-	-	-
Hartford	2	5.0	1	1.3	-	-	0	0	0	0	-	-
New Haven	6	12.5	36	19.5	-	-	26	89.7	17	16.7	-	-

1) Selectmen acted as Fence Viewers.

2) Fence Viewers were also Field Drivers.

for which a man could name his price, was a far cry from the unpaid menial position of earlier years.

The statistics of service in themselves are impressive evidence of the understanding in the towns that leaders should not serve in menial offices, but the records go even farther. Throughout most of the century towns were under great pressure to use any stratagem to secure the election of constables, as the Sudbury custom of making the selecmen hire substitutes and the Boston custom of forcing the wealthy to pay the fine testify.[35] Most towns, however, made no effort to thrust the position on their leaders, even though there was no legal obstacle to establishing a quid pro quo as Sudbury did. In addition to the eighty-seven leaders who served as constable during fifty-one sample decades, twenty-one refused to accept the towns' election. Dedham tried to elect only one leader to the office in fifty years, and gave up the effort when he refused indignantly.[36] For the really menial offices like field driver and hog reeve, the towns knew better than to try. Barnstable once chose Captain Joseph Lothrop, a veteran selectman and moderator of the election meeting itself, to the office of hog reeve only to be told in no uncertain terms that the Captain considered the office beneath his dignity.[37] Twenty years later the town found itself in a humorous mood and chose all the resident justices of the peace to be hog reeves. Fortunately, however, they had the presence of mind to elect four humbler men as well, and offered no objections when the justices declined to take the oath.[38] The disparity in status between respected leaders and those who served in the more menial offices was such that the election of most leaders to an office like hog reeve could be a joke, and nothing more.

As men who had begun their careers in the lesser offices worked their way to the top by demonstrating their ability in offices like constable and highway surveyor, and often continued to serve in minor offices throughout their lives, the leaders were an important part of the pool of minor officers. But they were, at the same time, a clearly defined group in their own right, holding a set of major offices that were beyond the reach of the ordinary town officers, and holding minor offices only on special terms. Whereas 75 to 100 percent of the able-bodied males held some minor office in small towns, and 50 percent or more in large towns, the group of officers who went on to become leaders was much smaller. In most small towns about a quarter of the officers became leaders, and in the larger towns the proportion ranged down to about 10 percent. Analysis of the size of the leader pool and of the minor officeholding activities of the leaders completes the task of ascertaining the size of the purely minor officeholding band in the disk model of town political activity. Subtracting the leaders from the total group that held minor office leaves between half and three-quarters of the population in the class of ordinary participants in town affairs.

With the relative sizes of the bodies of minor officers and town leaders determined, only the internal structure of the pool of town leaders remains to be described. The town leaders were all prominent and respected men, of course, but like any such group its members varied considerably in power and stature. Some leaders were towering figures whose influence dominated the community and extended well beyond its limits, while others were of more modest standing, men who were respected for experience, good judgment, and diligence, but only slightly above the ordinary run of townspeople in power and influence. These differences in power gave the leader pool of each town a structure that was revealing of the political order in the town, and since the structures varied from town to town, helped to determine the order in the whole region as well.

That differences in power existed is undeniable; the problem arises in trying to measure those differences. Social scientists have studied power relationships in twentieth-century communities extensively, and have developed three distinct methods of analysis: the reputational method, the decisional method, and the positional method.[39] Since the first two require exhaustive information available only in contemporary communities, however, historians have little choice but to use the third, or positional, method. This method involves counting the holders of key offices and inferring power relationships from the length of service and specific offices held by various individuals. Such strategy has been employed in this study, and requires several assumptions about power and officeholding that should be mentioned.

First of all, it is assumed that powerful individuals were, indeed, officeholders, and in particular that they were holders of the five major offices tabulated in this study. Hypothetically, a man could have held real power in a town without holding office, as some twentieth-century political managers do by nominating officials and then influencing their actions behind the scenes, and thus avoid appearing in the records. Such behavior would have been strange in a political system that selected candidates on the basis of personal prestige, and in which institutionalized political organizations did not exist, but it might have occurred. If so, however, the men involved have evaded all attempts to uncover them. Surviving diaries and literary sources give no hint of such men, and as will be seen in Chapter 5, virtually all men who can be identified as prominent from lists of provincial officials and college graduates held major town offices. All available evidence confirms the wisdom of assuming that officeholders were a town's real leaders.

A second major assumption is that length of service is a reasonable measure of a man's relative power. This assumption could be a problem if analysis focused on a single office, or on a small fraction of the influential positions, especially if the object of the study was to assess the role of some particular individual. A tabulation of Boston selectmen, for example, would not reveal that Samuel Adams was a power in town affairs, because he never held that particular office. But in fact this study includes all or most of the important positions. The case of Adams, therefore, would pose no real problem: tabulation of representatives and moderators would credit twenty-three terms of service and accord him his rightful place in Boston politics. Even if a few men did slip through, moreover, that would not seriously affect an investigation that seeks to discover the relative concentration of power among the leaders in a great many towns. The study of length of service may obscure the careers of the few who preferred not to hold office, but the preference of the voters for men with prestige and personal authority insured that the idiosyncratic few would have little effect on the overall structure.

The study of concentrations of power through analysis of length of service, like the study of the overall size of the leader pool aims at an understanding of the openness or closedness of the political order. Historians have frequently used measures of length of service in major town offices, especially average length of service as a selectman, to support generalizations about the distribution of power cast in terms of democracy and oligarchy, deference and consensus. But incredible as it may sound, they have accepted figures like four or five terms per man as a priori evidence of the contention they wished to advance, without making any effort to discover how such a rate compared with similar figures for other towns, especially those thought to have different power distributions. The same figure, therefore, has been advanced to support diametrically opposed conclusions: what one man interpreted as "broad popular participation" becomes "a kind of eighteenth-century Whig democracy which was controlled by those who had 'a stake in society' " to another, and simply "oligarchy" to a third.[40] Without a statistical frame of reference, attempts to subject the distribution of power in New England towns to quantitative analysis are inconclusive indeed.

Fortunately, the data assembled for this study permits a systematic survey of the length of service of town leaders all over New England (Table 9).[41] In terms of the average length of service of selectmen, figures for seventy-five towns suggest a small, but potentially significant, range of experience. The averages varied from 2.2 terms per man in infant Hanover, New Hampshire, to 6.9 terms per man in Newport. For towns with averages as low as two or three terms per man, the turnover of selectmen was very high; few men can have served long enough to achieve disproportionate power, and few restrictions on access to office can have existed. For towns with averages of four, five and even six terms per man, the situation must have been different. Because some men served only one or two terms in all of the towns, the higher averages for some towns meant that some men were serving very many more terms than the town's average number. Repeated reelections marked such men as special favorites of the voters, while long service in itself gave a man extensive resources in terms of experience and knowledge of town affairs, all of which tended to invest a man with unusual power. Access to power was likely to be more restricted in towns where the average length of service was higher.

Town averages, such as those presented here for length of service in the office of selectman, are valuable tools for the comparative analysis of behavior in many towns because they provide a single statistical summary for each town that incorporates all of the bits of data gathered on individual townsmen.[42] On the other hand, averaged lengths of service have two important disadvantages. First of all, the town average reveals comparatively little about the distribution of length of service within each town. If the average is very low (one or two), the service of each individual is likely to be short, because a great many single terms would be required to offset a single case of fifteen or twenty terms. If the average is somewhat higher, however, the distribution it summarizes is not so clear. An average of four or five terms might mean that a few men served ten to twenty terms, and a large number served one or two, or it might mean that all of the leaders served between three and six terms. This same ambiguity hampers the use of an average as a comparative figure. By concealing variations in the overall town distributions, averages can make very different patterns of behavior appear the same, and so suggest misleading categories, or alternatively suggest that no meaningful categories exist. Discussion of power distributions solely in terms of averaged figures is an uncertain business.

Confirmation of the hypothesized relationship between average length of service in the office of selectman and the concentration of power among a town's leaders can be found in an examination of the proportion of terms as selectmen filled by men who served one term, a few terms, and many terms. Of all the men who served as selectmen in seventy-three New England towns just under one-third (30.5 percent) served a single term and were not elected again (Table 10). Reasons for such short service understandably varied. In towns where the distribution of offices was egalitarian, some men might have come up for only one turn as a selectman. Other one-term selectmen were busy leaders who served mainly in other offices. Selectmen everywhere died, or moved, or underwent a change in health or fortune that disqualified them from further service. Finally, some one-term selectmen were marginal leaders who were never elected again because their execution of the office was unsatisfactory or undistinguished. Whatever the reason for their short service, however, one-term leaders served only a small percentage of all the terms as selectmen, and can have had little real power. Their total service ranged from 1.3 percent of the terms in Barrington to 21.5 percent in Weare. In one group of towns, most of which were small, one-term selectmen made up a third or more of the whole list of selectmen, and served 10 percent or more of all the terms. In most of the other towns the one-term men totaled less than a third of the selectmen, and served well under 10 percent of the terms.

What these contrasting patterns meant can best be understood by looking at the one-term selectmen in conjunction with those at the opposite end of

TABLE NINE

Average Service in Major Office

Town	Terms per Selectman	Terms per Rep.	Terms per T.C.	Terms per T.T.	Terms per Mod.	Terms per Leader
MASSACHUSETTS						
Amherst	2.8	2.7	8.3	8.3	2.1	4.8
Andover	4.6	3.4	10.6	4.4	4.9	7.4
Barnstable	6.5	4.5	6.4	11.5	4.9	10.7
Barrington	5.3	1.0	4.3	3.3	3.6	9.4
Billerica	5.3	4.5	10.6	n/d	n/d	7.3
Boston	5.1	4.4	14.2	21.3	3.2	7.8
Boxford	3.0	5.3	7.7	n/d	n/d	4.2
Braintree	4.4	4.9	14.2	7.1	3.8	8.2
Brookline	5.1	4.1	7.1	5.7	4.5	9.7
Cambridge	5.1	3.9	14.2	12.1	4.8	8.3
Dedham	4.3	4.5	6.4	6.4	6.1	7.6
Dorchester	6.5	4.5	12.7	14.3	4.5	10.6
Duxbury	4.5	4.3	21.0	n/d	4.7	7.6
Fitchburg	3.1	2.5	3.3	4.0	3.3	6.3
Grafton	3.1	3.3	5.4	6.1	4.1	4.8
Hadley	3.6	2.6	21.3	11.5	4.1	6.3
Hanover	3.8	3.1	14.5	3.0	3.7	6.8
Hardwick	4.2	3.8	4.6	6.9	4.8	7.2
Hatfield	6.6	4.0	21.3	18.7	8.6	11.3
Leicester	4.5	3.9	4.9	6.0	4.9	8.2
Lunenburg	4.1	3.2	7.2	3.2	3.1	6.8
Manchester	4.8	1.5	5.2	4.1	4.3	8.7
Medfield	3.1	1.9	8.5	3.3	4.2	5.6
Middleboro	5.2	3.0	7.9	7.0	3.5	7.1
Norton	4.5	2.8	7.4	3.0	3.7	7.5
Oakham	3.4	---	3.3	2.8	2.1	5.0
Pelham	2.7	1.0	10.5	4.6	3.2	4.3
Shirley	3.6	1.0	4.7	4.6	n/d	5.4
Springfield	4.9	3.3	8.5	8.1	4.0	8.4
Sudbury	4.2	3.2	7.1	3.5	4.7	7.2
Swansea	3.8	3.1	9.4	4.5	3.3	6.4
Topsfield	4.0	3.8	12.7	4.7	5.5	7.4
Waltham	4.8	6.6	18.5	18.5	n/d	7.1
Watertown	4.3	3.8	8.8	7.2	4.1	7.4
Westminster	4.1	1.8	4.8	7.7	3.5	5.8
Worcester	4.0	3.9	5.2	4.5	3.9	7.2
MAINE						
Biddeford	5.6	2.3	17.3	n/d	n/d	7.4
Brunswick	3.9	2.0	1.7	n/d	n/d	5.3
Falmouth	3.3	3.5	8.6	n/d	n/d	4.3
Gorham	2.9	2.0	2.8	5.3	n/d	4.7
Newcastle	3.0	1.0	7.8	4.7	4.3	5.0
Scarborough	4.1	2.3	10.7	n/d	n/d	5.6

TABLE NINE: Continued

Town	Terms per Selectman	Terms per Rep.	Terms per T.C.	Terms per T.T.	Terms per Mod.	Terms per Leader
NEW HAMPSHIRE						
Bedford	2.3	1.7	5.0	3.4	2.3	4.2
Canterbury	2.6	---	5.5	---	3.3	4.2
Chester	2.5	2.2	12.2	---	3.6	4.0
Concord	3.7	2.2	5.4	5.3	5.7	5.9
Cornish	2.5	1.8	3.2	---	4.5	3.8
Derryfield	3.0	1.0	7.0	---	3.6	5.1
Dover	4.3	3.1	12.6	---	5.2	7.4
Dublin	2.8	1.0	7.0	3.3	2.8	5.0
Hampstead	2.3	4.3	9.0	---	3.2	4.1
Hampton	2.8	3.2	12.1	---	4.5	4.5
Hanover	2.2	1.0	9.0	3.0	2.4	4.5
Londonderry	2.9	2.3	6.0	---	3.4	4.1
New Ipswich	2.6	1.4	2.4	---	1.5	3.7
Portsmouth	4.6	3.4	17.0	---	3.5	6.3
Weare	2.3	1.6	10.5	---	2.1	3.2
RHODE ISLAND						
Exeter	4.2	6.7	5.5	8.6	5.4	8.6
Middletown	5.7	4.1	8.6	7.0	n/d	7.8
Newport	6.9	4.7	8.7	6.6	3.1	7.6
Providence	4.6	4.5	14.2	8.0	10.8	7.5
Smithfield	5.6	2.2	6.8	7.1	3.4	6.8
S. Kingstown	5.4	2.3	8.9	6.9	3.8	7.2
Coventry	4.4	n/d	8.7	6.5	2.6	
CONNECTICUT						
Ashford	4.3	7.2	11.3	7.4	4.2	10.2
Bolton	4.0	7.3	10.8	7.6	5.1	10.1
Derby	3.7	2.9	n/d	n/d	n/d	4.7
Enfield	6.1	7.3	12.1	8.5	5.3	11.2
Hartford	2.3	9.3	26.3	24.3	5.9	5.0
Kent	4.2	5.0	7.5	6.3	3.5	8.1
New Haven	3.4	7.2	28.3	2.7	5.6	5.9
Newtown	3.1	6.4	16.8	n/d	n/d	5.0
Stonington	5.0	5.3	17.0	n/d	n/d	8.0
Windham	3.6	5.0	16.0	8.0	4.6	7.1
Woodbury	3.8	8.1	13.5	4.1	4.5	6.8

the spectrum, the men who served five years or more. Whereas single-term selectmen had little opportunity to consolidate and wield power, those who remained in office for five years or more had time to gain a substantial knowledge of the details of government, and the experience necessary to sense how favorable decisions could be obtained on certain crucial issues, and conflicts over others avoided. Knowledge of governmental procedures

TABLE TEN

Distribution of Service as Selectman

MASSACHUSETTS	Serving 1 Year			Serving 2-4 Years			Serving 5 Years or More		
	# Men	% of Men	% of Terms	# Men	% of Men	% of Terms	# Men	% of Men	% of Terms
Amherst	27	45.0	13.6	18	30.0	25.1	15	25.0	61.3
Andover	18	19.8	4.3	39	42.9	25.3	34	37.4	70.4
Barnstable	6	16.7	2.6	12	33.4	16.6	18	49.9	80.8
Barrington	1	6.7	1.3	5	33.3	18.7	9	60.0	80.0
Billerica	21	26.3	5.0	35	43.8	21.9	24	29.9	73.1
Boston	15	12.3	2.4	57	46.7	26.1	50	41.0	71.5
Boxford	45	32.4	10.9	66	47.5	42.5	28	20.1	46.6
Braintree	27	29.0	6.6	34	36.6	24.2	32	34.4	69.2
Brookline	15	25.0	5.0	21	35.0	18.2	24	40.0	76.8
Cambridge	24	26.1	5.1	32	34.8	18.8	36	39.1	76.1
Dedham	13	14.4	3.3	50	55.6	34.0	27	30.0	62.7
Dorchester	10	15.2	2.3	27	40.9	17.9	27	43.9	79.8
Duxbury	16	39.0	8.6	14	34.2	21.0	11	26.8	70.4
Fitchburg	13	48.1	15.5	9	33.3	31.0	5	18.6	53.5
Grafton	34	37.4	11.9	44	48.4	42.1	13	14.2	46.0
Hadley	47	37.0	10.2	41	32.3	23.9	39	30.7	65.9
Hanover	14	31.8	8.3	21	47.7	34.9	9	20.5	56.8
Hardwick	13	28.9	6.9	18	40.0	27.1	14	31.1	66.0
Hatfield	15	23.4	3.5	19	29.7	11.1	30	46.9	85.5
Leicester	21	30.9	6.8	19	28.0	15.6	28	41.1	77.6
Lunenburg	14	20.3	5.0	34	49.0	32.7	21	30.7	62.3
Manchester	15	30.6	6.4	15	30.6	15.7	19	38.8	77.9
Medfield	54	40.0	12.7	53	39.3	33.0	28	20.7	54.3
Middleboro	19	27.9	5.4	22	32.4	17.2	27	39.7	77.4
Norton	13	23.6	5.3	22	40.0	25.7	20	36.4	69.0
Oakham	9	26.5	7.8	15	44.1	31.0	10	29.4	61.2
Pelham	28	36.4	13.3	36	46.8	47.6	13	16.9	39.1
Shirley	6	21.4	6.0	16	57.2	42.0	6	21.4	52.0
Springfield	18	19.6	4.0	35	38.0	21.0	39	42.0	75.0
Sudbury	42	30.7	7.3	57	41.6	26.0	38	27.7	66.7

TABLE TEN: Continued

	Serving 1 Year			Serving 2-4 Years			Serving 5 Years or More		
	# Men	% of Men	% of Terms	# Men	% of Men	% of Terms	# Men	% of Men	% of Terms
MASSACHUSETTS Continued									
Swansea	26	37.1	9.8	25	35.7	25.2	19	27.2	65.0
Topsfield	25	26.0	6.6	41	42.7	27.3	30	31.3	66.1
Waltham	6	12.2	2.5	25	51.0	31.4	18	36.8	66.1
Watertown	24	22.4	5.3	47	43.9	26.8	36	33.6	67.9
Westminster	11	28.2	6.9	17	43.6	28.1	11	28.2	65.0
Worcester	33	40.7	10.3	30	37.0	26.4	18	22.3	63.3
MAINE									
Biddeford	12	30.8	5.5	9	23.1	11.0	18	46.1	83.5
Brunswick	12	32.4	8.3	16	43.3	29.9	9	24.3	61.2
Falmouth	35	37.6	11.2	37	39.8	33.2	21	22.6	55.6
Gorham	9	42.9	15.0	7	33.3	30.0	5	23.8	55.0
Newcastle	11	37.9	12.8	13	44.8	44.2	5	17.3	43.0
Scarborough	21	44.7	10.8	14	29.8	22.7	12	25.5	66.5
NEW HAMPSHIRE									
Bedford	20	44.4	19.0	22	48.9	56.2	3	6.7	24.8
Canterbury	20	51.3	19.4	12	30.8	28.2	7	17.9	52.4
Chester	33	46.5	18.4	28	39.4	43.6	10	14.1	38.0
Concord	9	28.1	7.6	16	50.0	33.6	7	21.9	58.8
Cornish	15	46.9	19.0	12	37.5	36.7	5	15.6	44.3
Derryfield	16	44.4	14.8	12	33.3	33.3	8	22.3	51.9
Dover	25	30.5	7.1	27	32.9	20.6	30	36.4	72.3
Dublin	8	50.0	17.8	4	25.0	22.2	4	25.0	60.0
Hampstead	23	46.9	20.5	20	40.8	45.5	6	12.3	34.0
Hampton	61	41.5	15.0	66	45.1	43.9	20	13.4	41.1
Hanover	10	40.0	17.9	13	52.0	62.5	2	8.0	19.6
Londonderry	43	38.7	13.4	48	43.3	41.3	20	18.0	45.3
New Ipswich	12	42.9	16.6	12	42.9	41.7	4	14.2	41.7
Portsmouth	20	21.7	4.8	39	42.4	24.6	33	35.9	70.6
Weare	14	50.0	21.5	9	32.1	33.8	5	17.9	44.7

TABLE TEN: Continued

	Serving 1 Year			Serving 2-4 Years			Serving 5 Years or More	
# Men	% of Men	% of Terms	# Men	% of Men	% of Terms	# Men	% of Men	% of Terms

RHODE ISLAND

	# Men	% of Men	% of Terms	# Men	% of Men	% of Terms	# Men	% of Men	% of Terms
Exeter	16	25.8	6.1	22	35.5	19.2	24	38.7	74.7
Middletown	5	11.9	2.1	19	45.2	21.9	18	42.9	78.2
Newport	9	17.0	2.5	14	26.4	11.5	30	56.6	86.0
Providence	22	19.6	4.3	47	42.0	25.0	43	38.4	70.7
Smithfield	12	21.1	3.8	23	40.4	18.9	22	38.5	77.3
S. Kingstown	16	22.9	4.2	22	31.4	15.8	32	45.7	80.0

CONNECTICUT

	# Men	% of Men	% of Terms	# Men	% of Men	% of Terms	# Men	% of Men	% of Terms
Ashford	18	29.5	6.9	18	29.5	19.2	25	41.0	73.9
Bolton	15	31.3	7.7	20	41.7	29.0	13	27.0	63.3
Derby	22	24.2	6.6	37	40.7	30.7	32	35.1	62.7
Enfield	17	26.2	4.3	21	31.3	14.7	27	42.5	81.0
Hartford	101	45.7	19.7	95	43.0	50.4	25	11.3	29.7
Kent	12	24.0	5.7	25	50.0	32.4	13	26.0	61.9
New Haven	67	35.6	10.5	73	38.8	30.4	48	25.6	59.1
Newtown	38	30.6	9.8	63	50.8	44.3	23	18.6	45.9
Stonington	24	21.4	4.3	49	43.8	24.9	39	26.6	70.1
Woodbury	15	16.7	4.3	48	53.3	39.6	27	30.0	56.1

and the ability to influence others toward desired goals are the very warp and woof of political power, and these were preeminently at the command of the experienced leaders.

One indication of the power of the experienced leaders was that although men with five years' service as selectmen were invariably a minority of the total number, they served a large proportion of all the terms. The exact proportion varied from town to town, but unlike the variations noted earlier for the size of the pool of minor officers and for the size of the leadership group, the groupings of towns according to this index of the concentration of local power did not depend strictly upon population size. Longtime selectmen served less than half of the terms in one group of towns, many of which were small, but a few of which had well over a thousand inhabitants. All were established towns, incorporated before 1750.[43] These were also towns in which one-term selectmen served 10 percent or more of the terms. The basic pattern was to have many leaders fill the office of selectmen, each serving a few terms. In Boxford, for example, one-term selectmen filled 11 percent of the seats on the board, two- to four-year men filled 43 percent of the seats, and no selectman served for more than ten years. In Hampton 4 men served more than ten terms each, but the 127 men who served four years or less filled 59 percent of the seats, a substantial majority; and similar patterns can be traced for towns like Londonderry, Newtown, and Pelham. The distribution of power among the leaders in these towns was relatively equal because few men served long enough to establish a dominant position in town affairs.

In a larger and more diverse group of towns, those selectmen serving more than five years filled a clear majority of the seats. Most of the towns in this group exceeded 1,000 in population, and all of the seaport cities, as well as all of the county seats, were in this category.[44] Several towns were smaller, however, and some of them had well under 1,000 inhabitants. Why these small towns had officeholding concentrations as great as the larger towns will be made clear in later chapters; attention now much focus on describing their characteristics. Whereas many men shared the office of selectman in the more egalitarian towns, service was more restricted in towns of this second group. One-year selectmen were numerically fewer and served a smaller percentage of the terms in most of these towns. The real difference, however, lay in the balance between those who saw moderate service, two to four terms, and those who saw long service. In the egalitarian towns these two groups were evenly balanced, each with about 40 percent of the terms; but in the second class of towns the long-serving group was clearly predominant and the group with moderate tenure filled only a quarter to a third of the positions. The leadership of these towns was stratified, with real power concentrated in the hands of the minority of leaders who served more than five years.

While established towns divided into groups with egalitarian and restricted power distributions, the pattern for newly settled towns was not so clear.[45] Historians have long argued that frontier towns were "democratic," which in this context would mean egalitarian, but the evidence does not entirely bear out this contention. Some towns, like Bedford, filled a substantial portion of their terms with new men and continued very few men in office for more than four years. On the other hand, towns like Oakham followed the restricted pattern, with few terms served by one-year men and a majority served by longterm selectmen. Still other towns combined elements of both the egalitarian pattern and the restricted pattern. Fitchburg elected one-year men to 15 percent of its terms at one end of the spectrum, and longterm selectmen to 53 percent at the other end. Newly settled towns had too few political leaders and too unstable a population to follow either model of power distribution consistently.

The analysis of the relative concentration of service and power within a town's leadership helps to make up for the shortcomings of an analysis of average length of service alone. In the context of the individual town, it makes clear that power could be so concentrated that men serving five years or more filled 80 percent of the terms, and that power could be so equally shared that the same kind of leader occupied no more than 20 percent of the places. In the context of comparative study, this analysis clarified the meaning of averaged figures. A high average length of service as selectmen, it would seem, invariably meant that power was concentrated in the hands of a few individuals. No town with an average of more than four terms belonged to the egalitarian group suggested by the study of concentration of offices. Low average length of service, however, was a less reliable index of overall leadership patterns. Established towns with averages of less than three were always in the egalitarian group, but as the average rose from three to four the likelihood increased that the town would belong to the restricted group. Most newly incorporated towns also had low average lengths of service, but the relationship between this figure and the degree of concentration in officeholding patterns was inconsistent. Dublin and Canterbury both had averages of less than three terms, and both elected longterm selectmen to more than half of all the terms. Average length of service as selectman, supplemented by a more detailed study of the distribution behind the averages, provides as complete information on the concentration of power among town leaders as can be obtained from data on a single office.

A more complete picture of the meaning of differing lengths of service emerges from an analysis of the average length of service of leaders in all five major offices, which is a more inclusive and hence a more reliable indicator. These overall averages ranged from a low of 3.2 terms in Weare to a high of 11.3 for Hatfield (Table 9). The figures are higher than those for selectmen alone, not only because town clerks, town treasurers, and moderators served more terms on the average than selectmen, but also because leaders so often served in more than one office. Like the selectman averages, however, the averages for all leaders provide groupings of towns according to the concentration of power within the pool of town leaders.

For one group of established towns, average service ranged from three terms per man up to about five terms. Selectmen in these towns usually served only a few terms, and the average service in each of the other major offices was also low.[46] Comparison of the data in Table 9 with that in Table 2 reveals that the overlap in personnel between selectman and each of the other offices was relatively high for most of the towns under discussion, so even though leaders commonly served in more than one office they did not serve long enough in any one of them to consolidate power. This interpretation is confirmed by the fact that these were also the towns in which short-term selectmen filled most of the seats on the board. In these towns power was fairly equally distributed among the town leaders.

In another group of established towns the averages were higher, ranging from about six terms up to eleven terms. These were usually towns in which the selectmen served a high average of terms, and often towns in which the average service in each of the other major offices was high. On the other hand, the rates of overlap between selectman and the other offices were mixed. In towns like Norton and Worcester, men compiled a record of long service by serving a few years in each of the several offices, while in other towns, such as Boston, Portsmouth, and South Kingstown, a high rate of average service depended more on long service in individual offices. In either case, however, high average service in all offices combined with consistent election of longterm leaders as selectmen to indicate that real power was concentrated in the hands of the leaders with the most extensive service.

Just as average service for established towns varied according to the groupings suggested by the data on the distribution of terms as selectman, average service in newly established towns followed the inconsistent pattern suggested by that data. Most towns incorporated after 1750 had low averages, but Fitchburg and Westminster had averages that suggest substantial concentration of power. Moreover, since some of the new towns had existed less than fifteen years in 1784, it would be perilous to conclude that their low averages were meaningful.

The data on average length of service by town leaders, and on the distribution of power among the leaders, casts new light on the perennial debate about the openness of the colonial political structure. If who served was any indication of who could serve, both proponents of an open or egalitarian interpretation and proponents of a closed, elitist view can find comfort in the figures. Interpretation of town politics in these terms is not a question of validating one hypothesis and rejecting the other, but rather of deciding which one, with suitable refinements, best fits the town or group of towns under discussion.

Moreover, the notion that the eighteenth-century towns represented a whole spectrum of political behavior gains further credence when the actions of the leaders are related to the role of other members of the community in the political process. Political structure as measured in the length of service by town leaders did not vary strictly according to population size, but the tendency for small towns to be egalitarian and towns of increasing size to be more and more uniformly restrictive in access to power was pronounced enough for parallels to be drawn to variations that seem closely related to population. First of all, towns varied in officeholding participation in local government from nearly full adult male involvement in the smallest towns to participation by about half of the male inhabitants in the largest towns. The pool of leaders varied in size in a similar fashion. Leaders constituted as many as half of all town officers, or 15 percent of a town's whole population in some small towns and less than 10 percent of all officers or 1 percent of the population in the largest towns. The leader pool also decreased as a percentage of the population as towns grew larger. The political structure of colonial New England cannot be represented by a single model or described in a single catchword.

·3·

THE ECONOMICS OF LEADERSHIP

A man's wealth has much to do with his status in society, and so the examination of the position town leaders held in the economic structure of the community is a fitting way to begin the study of those attributes which made some men leaders in the eyes of their fellow townspeople. In the theory of social stratification the primary determinants of status are the roles a person fills, and one of the principal high status roles is that of political leader or high public official. Wealth is also a determinant of status, but it is a secondary factor that operates indirectly by enabling the possessor of riches to purchase the educational and material trappings of a high status role, or by permitting him to use economic power as a compensatory mechanism in other ways. Equality in wealth does not always mean momentary equality in status, but in the long run wealth can be expected to have a profound effect on status.[1]

The problem of tracing the influence of wealth on leadership status in the New England towns is a complex one. One direct approach involves determining the relative wealth of a town's leaders by plotting their position on the town's tax list. This method has been followed, and in aggregate terms it reveals that nearly three-quarters of all town leaders were wealthy enough to rank in the richest quarter of their town's population. Such a general figure, however, is of limited value because it reveals nothing about the quarter of the leaders who were not rich or about the wealthy men who did not become leaders. Furthermore, towns varied widely in total wealth, in degree of economic stratification, and in the kinds of economic opportunities available to their inhabitants. Consideration of the impact of wealth on town leadership involves a discussion of the economic standing of the leaders in their town, of how wealth functioned as a criterion for election, and of the overall relationship among wealth, town leadership, and high social status. First, however, the basic patterns of economic stratification and of commercial activity in the towns must be traced in order to provide a basic understanding of the economic conditions under which the social and political system operated.

One of the central difficulties in studying the economic status of the town leaders was the existence of major differences in total wealth and in kinds of

63

economic activity from town to town, and the consequent fact that men in the top or middle deciles in one town might be much richer than men in the corresponding deciles in another town. The merchant princes of Boston or Newport and prominent gentry families like the Leonards of Norton, the Chandlers of Worcester, and the Hazards and Gardners of South Kingstown are extreme examples of men who enjoyed a vastly higher standard of living than the farmer-selectmen of the smaller towns, but more subtle differences in the social and economic structure also existed.[2] Property in some towns was concentrated into a few hands, so that men in the top decile were much richer than those in the second or third, and vastly richer than those in the levels of society that produced leaders less frequently. In other towns gradations of wealth were more gradual, so that the leaders were all at about the same income level, and in some towns the property was so evenly distributed that men in the top deciles were not appreciably richer than those at the middle of the list. Some of the towns with little stratification were poor, so that all of the inhabitants were ordinary husbandmen, but other towns contained homogeneous populations of well-do-to yeomen and gentlemen because the size of the landholdings effectively excluded poor people.

The problem of analyzing the economic structures of the towns and the relative wealth of their leaders would be quickly solved if all tax lists showed the total value of a man's estate, or at least specified the rate of taxation so that historians could compute the total valuation. But most tax lists simply record the amount of money assessed on each inhabitant and provide no further information. Worse still, lists that purport to value all property in a town really show a conventionalized "tax value" that ranged from 100 percent of the actual cash value of the property down to 5 or 10 percent, while laws in the several colonies changed the rules for assessing some classes of property at different times, and required the assessors to provide a subjective estimate of the income potential of men whose income came from a craft or skill, or from intangible property.[3] Because of these omissions and uncertainties, the tax lists can not support a comparison of the absolute wealth of men in many communities over any time span.[4]

One way of overcoming these difficulties is to evaluate the relative positions of the leaders on the tax lists by computing the amount of property owned by men in different segments of the population. An analysis of the percentage of a town's taxable property owned by the men in each decile of the population provides an index of the amount of economic stratification in a community and permits comparison of the wealth of the leaders in the top deciles with that of leaders lower in the list. To a lesser degree, such an analysis also allows a comparison of the relative wealth of leaders in different towns by means of a comparison of the overall distributions of wealth. It does not reveal directly whether men in equivalent positions in equally stratified communities had the same amount of property, but once the economic position of men in a given stratum has been established with respect to other members of their own communities, records that show each town's share of colony-wide taxes provide some basis for comparing the wealth of similarly placed men in similarly stratified towns.

Data on the distribution of property is available in 106 tax lists from 58 towns, and it reveals not only that the concentration of property holdings differed from town to town, but also that that concentration increased as the period progressed.* During the last years of the seventeenth century and the first quarter of the eighteenth century, property was fairly equally distributed in most towns.[5] Because some tax lists included the value of the poll tax in the total and others did not, and because the addition of the uniform poll tax to the estates of both rich and poor tended to exaggerate the amount of property owned by the poorer inhabitants, lists with and without polls must

*See Table 11. Surviving tax lists take a bewildering variety of forms, and the notations in the column headed "Type" represent an attempt to point out the major kinds of lists. Lists marked "P" are valuations of all real and personal property, excluding the poll, and taxes based on such valuations; those marked "T" are valuations or taxes based on all property including polls; those marked "R" are strictly real estate taxes or valuations; those marked "M" are rates to pay a minister or complete a meeting house; and those marked "C" are commons division lists based on rateable estates. The biases that result from comparing different kinds of lists are hard to measure, but some generalizations are possible. Commoners' lists and minister's rate lists were likely to exclude nonproprietors of the commons and men who attended church elsewhere respectively, but if such exclusions existed in the lists used here, they did not have any clear effect on the distribution of property. Somewhat surprisingly, the distribution of property differed little whether a list included real and personal property or just real estate. Of twenty-three lists for which both distributions can be calculated, the amount of property held by the top decile of taxpayers varied by more than about 3 percent in only four, and two of those four were Cambridge and the North Parish of Braintree, which contained unusual groups of personal property-rich West Indian planters and absentee landowners who lived in Boston respectively:

Town	Real—(Real+Personal) (% difference)	Town	Real—(Real+Personal) (% difference)
Billerica 1771	.93	Norton 1711	3.11
Boxford 1745	.72	Shirley 1771	1.73
Boxford 1761	.25	Sudbury 1771	1.79
Boxford 1774	1.08	Sudbury 1722	1.61
Braintree 1774	-6.88	Topsfield 1725	2.42
Brookline 1693	-.48	Topsfield 1744	-.07
Cambridge 1770	-6.62	Topsfield 1765	-.43
Dedham 1710	6.06	Waltham 1740	.26
Dedham 1735	1.79	Waltham 1770	1.90
Leicester 1732	-.42	Gorham 1771	1.12
Lunenberg 1770	-.23	Bedford 1750	8.38
		Concord 1737	2.20

The presence or absence of the poll tax, on the other hand, made a substantial difference in the apparent distribution of property, depending upon the total percentages of the tax paid by the polls, and upon the number of men who paid only the poll tax or, alternatively, had their poll tax paid by someone else. Table 11, therefore, included a number of lists for which the distribution has been calculated both with and without the poll, and also a number of lists (marked with an *) for which a hypothetical distribution without the poll tax has been calculated by deducting the value of one poll from the tax of each taxpayer who paid the value of a poll or more.

TABLE ELEVEN

Cumulative Property Holdings

Name	Date	Type	1st	2nd	Deciles 3rd	4th	5th
Part I - Lists Before 1725 That Do Not Include Polls							
Boston	1687	P	46.9	66.8	78.6	85.8	92.2
Boxford	1687	P	25.7	41.1	54.1	64.8	74.1
Brookline	1693	P	21.1	37.0	51.7	63.6	72.3
Cambridge	1688	P	27.3	45.4	59.0	70.2	79.4
Dedham	1710	P	27.4	45.1	59.7	71.3	80.4
Manchester	1696	M	28.1	41.8	53.9	64.0	71.7
Manchester	1717	P	30.6	55.7	69.3	80.4	88.2
Norton	1711	P	33.3	52.0	66.6	77.6	86.2
Sudbury	1722	P	25.6	42.2	56.7	68.7	77.8
Topsfield	1687	P	30.4	47.8	59.6	70.1	78.6
Kingstown	1687	P	39.3	61.1	75.6	85.7	92.3
Andover*	1720	T	28.5	47.7	62.7	74.0	82.2
Barnstable*	1702	C	25.4	41.8	56.2	69.0	80.4
Salem*	1683	T	53.4	70.3	79.9	88.0	91.3
Springfield*	1685	T	39.7	59.6	74.0	83.4	90.6
Providence*	1705	T	32.2	50.4	63.8	75.0	84.3
Derby*	1718	T	31.9	49.7	64.1	74.3	82.9
New Haven*	1702	C	32.0	50.5	64.3	75.4	84.2
Part II - Lists Before 1725 That Include Polls							
Andover	1720	T	21.7	37.4	50.6	61.5	70.5
Barnstable	1702	C	20.1	34.5	47.5	59.4	70.5
Boxford	1687	T	25.8	40.6	53.1	63.1	71.6
Cambridge	1688	T	23.9	40.0	52.2	62.9	82.2
Dedham	1710	T	23.5	39.1	52.1	63.0	72.2
Hadley	1720	C	28.1	46.7	61.2	72.2	80.8
Medfield	1697	C	19.0	34.0	47.4	58.9	69.4
Norton	1711	T	25.8	40.8	53.8	65.4	76.0
Salem	1683	T	31.2	45.0	55.3	64.7	71.8
Springfield	1685	T	34.5	52.8	66.5	76.0	83.8
Topsfield	1687	T	26.2	43.3	55.7	66.1	74.8
Portsmouth	1715	T	31.5	46.9	58.8	68.3	76.6
Providence	1705	T	25.3	41.1	53.6	64.6	74.3
Derby	1718	T	26.0	41.9	55.2	65.6	74.8
New Haven	1702	C	24.9	40.9	53.6	64.7	74.1
Part III - Lists 1725-1749 That Do Not Include Polls							
Boxford	1745/6	P	28.8	49.2	64.7	76.9	85.5
Dedham	1735	P	29.1	48.4	63.8	76.4	86.4
Leicester	1732	M	27.4	45.4	58.9	70.2	79.8
Topsfield	1725	P	26.7	46.1	62.4	75.5	85.9
Topsfield	1744	P	30.5	52.5	70.0	83.0	91.4
Waltham	1740	P	29.6	48.6	63.7	76.9	87.2
Watertown	1730	P	31.0	50.5	64.7	76.0	85.1

TABLE ELEVEN: Continued

Name	Date	Type	1st	2nd	Deciles 3rd	4th	5th
Concord	1737	P	36.2	51.4	64.1	75.4	85.0
Bolton	1732	R	32.4	51.3	68.1	81.7	91.3
Andover*	1740	T	29.5	49.4	65.0	77.1	86.0
Billerica*	1733	M	33.2	56.1	71.6	81.5	89.0
Hadley*	1731	C	37.7	61.7	78.9	88.9	94.9
Leicester*	1743	T	33.7	55.6	69.7	79.4	86.8
Derby*	1728	C	33.7	53.5	66.9	76.9	85.2
Kent*	1744	T	32.4	53.9	70.2	80.7	87.5
New Haven 1st*	1745	T	32.9	53.7	68.7	79.3	87.0
New Haven 4th*	1745	T	26.6	45.0	59.1	70.9	80.6
Newtown*	1739	T	28.2	48.2	62.5	73.5	82.2
Woodbury*	1736	T	25.8	43.0	57.1	68.6	78.3

Part IV - Lists 1725-1749 That Include Polls

Name	Date	Type	1st	2nd	3rd	4th	5th
Andover	1740	T	22.6	39.1	52.9	64.4	73.9
Billerica	1733	M	22.4	39.6	53.1	63.5	72.6
Boxford	1745	T	23.9	41.5	55.9	67.6	76.4
Hadley	1731	C	34.4	56.8	73.1	83.1	89.6
Hatfield	1738	T	25.0	44.0	58.0	69.7	79.1
Leicester	1732	M	21.3	35.0	46.6	56.6	65.9
Leicester	1743	T	22.2	38.5	50.7	60.7	69.6
Topsfield	1725	T	24.3	42.5	56.4	67.4	76.9
Waltham	1740	T	24.3	42.5	57.6	70.0	80.3
Watertown	1730	T	24.9	42.2	55.2	66.4	76.2
Concord	1737	T	23.9	38.4	49.0	58.4	67.0
Dover	1741	T	25.2	40.9	53.2	63.7	72.4
S. Kingstown	1730	T	46.0	64.9	76.9	85.1	90.0
Derby	1728	C	29.3	47.3	60.0	70.1	78.7
Kent	1744	T	23.6	40.8	55.0	65.8	75.1
Woodbury	1736	T	21.6	37.1	50.2	61.4	71.3
Newtown	1739	T	23.6	41.3	54.5	65.3	74.5
New Haven	1745	T	24.8	41.8	55.3	66.5	75.8
New Haven 1st	1745	T	26.7	44.8	58.8	69.6	78.4
New Haven 2nd	1745	T	27.1	44.6	59.0	70.0	79.3
New Haven 3rd	1745	T	25.7	42.3	56.0	67.8	77.3
New Haven 4th	1745	T	22.0	38.1	51.2	62.7	72.7
New Haven 5th	1745	T	21.9	38.4	52.0	62.6	71.8

Part V - Lists After 1750 That Do Not Include Polls

Name	Date	Type	1st	2nd	3rd	4th	5th
Amherst	1759	P	24.6	44.3	60.7	72.9	82.7
Billerica	1771	P	32.0	52.0	67.5	79.8	89.1
Boston	1771	P	60.4	77.3	84.5	90.0	93.5
Boxford	1761	P	30.4	50.2	65.5	77.6	87.4
Boxford	1774	P	33.9	54.8	69.9	81.3	90.2
Braintree	1774	P	59.1	76.1	85.0	91.0	95.2

TABLE ELEVEN: Continued II

Name	Date	Type	1st	2nd	3rd	4th	5th
Brookline	1771	R	33.3	53.3	69.1	80.7	88.4
Cambridge	1770	P	50.1	68.9	80.0	87.3	92.3
Dedham	1771	R	35.8	58.0	72.5	83.1	90.5
Dorchester	1771	P	51.1	69.7	81.2	89.0	93.4
Fitchburg	1771	R	26.8	44.6	57.8	68.7	78.5
Hadley	1771	P	35.1	57.4	74.0	84.3	91.5
Lunenburg	1770	P	28.8	47.2	62.0	74.5	85.0
Manchester	1769	P	53.7	72.1	83.0	89.6	93.8
Medfield	1771	R	28.5	50.0	67.2	79.9	89.7
Norton	1771	R	40.8	62.0	76.5	86.6	93.7
Oakham	1771	R	34.3	56.5	70.0	80.4	88.9
Pelham	1771	R	28.5	47.9	64.3	78.6	89.2
Salem	1764	P	52.2	69.3	80.1	87.1	92.3
Shirley	1771	P	32.0	53.3	69.4	81.5	90.9
Springfield	1771	R	38.2	59.6	74.8	85.2	92.1
Sudbury	1771	P	35.0	54.8	68.9	79.8	88.7
Swansea	1771	R	51.5	70.5	82.3	90.0	94.6
Topsfield	1765	P	36.4	57.5	73.9	86.4	93.6
Waltham	1771	P	34.7	56.0	70.7	81.7	86.7
Westminster	1759	P	37.0	53.7	66.9	77.9	86.3
Worcester	1771	R	36.1	56.7	72.0	85.0	93.3
Brunswick	1771	R	34.2	57.0	74.5	86.7	94.4
Falmouth	1761	R	42.2	63.7	78.3	88.6	95.2
Gorham	1770	P	37.5	59.4	75.4	88.0	96.2
Scarborough	1771	R	43.6	64.1	77.3	86.7	93.5
Bedford	1750	P	27.9	47.4	64.4	78.5	89.7
Concord	1757	P	25.2	46.5	63.5	75.6	85.1
Exeter	1774	P	47.0	65.7	77.4	85.9	91.9
Middletown	1783	P	47.4	67.5	81.0	90.4	96.0
Andover*	1760	T	30.7	52.1	68.5	79.6	88.1
Billerica*	1755	M	33.0	54.4	70.3	81.4	89.3
Concord*	1776	T	30.6	50.9	66.4	78.6	87.6
Derryfield*	1775	T	32.7	53.4	71.0	82.5	90.7
Dover*	1753	T	34.3	55.6	70.2	80.6	88.7
Dublin*	1771	T	39.4	59.0	73.9	85.5	92.2
New Ipswich*	1763	M	31.6	52.5	69.9	81.4	89.3
New Ipswich*	1774	T	38.7	59.7	74.9	85.5	91.8
Exeter*	1763	T	44.4	64.7	76.6	84.6	90.2
Newport*	1760	T	61.4	80.9	90.4	95.4	98.1
Providence*	1751	T	40.8	58.6	71.2	80.0	87.1
Providence*	1773	T	58.9	77.5	88.1	94.1	97.3
Smithfield*	1760	T	42.7	62.3	75.1	84.5	91.3
Bolton*	1753	T	33.7	53.2	65.9	75.8	83.7
Bolton*	1774	T	33.5	53.4	68.8	80.3	87.9
Kent*	1771	T	32.1	51.9	66.5	77.8	85.4
New Haven*(city)	1766	T	40.9	62.3	77.1	87.4	94.6
Newtown*	1767	T	31.4	49.5	63.2	74.5	83.7
Woodbury*	1765	T	33.5	51.5	65.1	76.0	84.6

TABLE ELEVEN: Continued III

Name	Date	Type	1st	2nd	3rd	4th	5th
Part VI - Lists After 1750 That Include Polls							
Amherst	1771	T	24.6	40.9	53.0	63.2	71.9
Andover	1760	T	25.5	44.1	59.0	70.1	79.2
Billerica	1755	M	25.0	42.8	57.2	68.6	78.1
Boxford	1761	T	24.6	40.9	53.3	64.1	74.0
Boxford	1774	T	27.6	46.4	60.8	72.1	81.6
Braintree	1774	T	48.5	64.4	73.8	80.5	85.7
Cambridge	1770	T	42.1	59.8	71.7	80.0	86.3
Dorchester	1771	T	43.5	61.1	72.9	81.4	87.3
Hadley	1771	T	29.5	50.0	65.3	76.4	84.5
Hardwick	1776	T	25.5	42.7	55.4	67.0	76.3
Lunenburg	1770	T	22.3	38.6	51.4	62.2	71.8
Salem	1764	T	38.3	54.5	65.9	74.4	81.4
Shirley	1771	T	23.6	39.0	52.2	63.3	73.1
Sudbury	1770	T	28.5	46.3	59.6	70.6	80.0
Bedford	1770	T	41.8	54.4	64.8	73.6	80.6
Canterbury	1782	T	30.4	48.6	62.1	72.7	81.0
Concord	1757	T	24.8	45.7	62.4	74.6	84.0
Concord	1775	T	24.1	40.7	54.6	66.3	75.8
Derryfield	1758	M	25.4	41.5	53.7	62.7	71.2
Derryfield	1775	T	24.4	41.6	56.9	67.8	76.9
Dover	1753	T	24.1	40.9	53.8	64.4	73.6
Dublin	1771	T	26.1	42.7	57.1	69.5	77.7
Londonderry	1750	M	24.6	43.3	56.6	68.7	78.0
New Ipswich	1763	M	23.1	39.9	54.6	65.9	75.0
New Ipswich	1774	T	27.4	44.2	57.8	68.7	77.0
Portsmouth	1758	T	47.4	62.3	71.9	79.4	85.2
Weare	1764	T	23.2	39.3	52.2	61.3	69.8
Exeter	1763	T	41.4	60.9	72.6	80.8	86.7
Middletown	1783	T	38.5	56.3	69.3	78.7	84.8
Newport	1760	T	55.2	73.5	83.1	88.7	92.1
Providence	1751	T	34.8	51.0	63.2	72.3	79.9
Providence	1773	T	43.7	59.7	70.2	77.5	82.8
Smithfield	1760	T	37.0	55.0	67.4	76.9	84.3
S. Kingstown	1774	T	56.4	77.4	86.7	91.9	94.7
Bolton	1753	T	26.3	43.0	54.9	65.0	73.7
Bolton	1774	T	27.1	44.7	59.2	70.8	79.6
Kent	1771	T	25.3	42.3	55.7	66.8	75.5
New Haven	1766	T	27.7	44.9	58.6	69.8	78.7
New Haven (city)	1766	T	29.5	47.0	60.3	70.9	79.5
Newtown	1767	T	25.8	41.9	54.8	66.0	75.6
Woodbury	1765	T	27.1	43.2	56.0	68.0	77.3

be considered separately. During the early period, however, the differences between the two types of lists were seemingly at a minimum. The top decile of taxpayers owned between 20 and 30 percent of the property in most lists, the top half of the taxpayers owned between 70 and 80 percent, and of course the taxpayers in the bottom half of a list owned the remaining 20 to 30 percent. This distribution of property rates as egalitarian both in comparison to the patterns that developed for some towns later in the century, and in comparison with the patterns described by other historians.[6] Notable exceptions to the usual distribution of property were Boston, where 10 percent of the taxpayers already held nearly half of the property; Kingstown, where the top decile of the taxpayers owned 40 percent of the property; and Portsmouth, Salem, and Springfield, where apparent concentrations of about a third of the property in the hands of the top decile would certainly be more pronounced if the dampening effect of the poll figures could be eliminated. Boston was, of course, the metropolis of the whole region, Kingstown was the corporate name for the rich Narragansett Country, and Portsmouth, Salem, and Springfield were commercial and government centers for northern New England, Essex County, and the upper Connecticut Valley region respectively. Norton, the only other town to differ appreciably from the general pattern, was incorporated in the same year the tax list was made, and newly settled towns were notably erratic in social structure throughout the eighteenth century.

Lists from the second quarter of the eighteenth century reveal that the predominantly egalitarian social structure of the early years was gradually changing. The share of property owned by the top decile of taxpayers remained in the 20 to 30 percent range, but in the lower part of the list the concentration of property tended to tighten. Some towns maintained the old egalitarian pattern, but in many the amount of property owned by the top half of the taxpayers rose from the 70 to 80 percent range to about 85 percent. This trend was clear among the towns that excluded polls from their tax totals; and several of the towns that included polls would probably have matched the trend if the polls had been eliminated. Even better evidence of the decline in the percentage of property owned by the poor exists for the few towns providing two separate lists. Two Manchester lists, both in the early period, show a substantial increase in the property owned by men in the second and third deciles over a twenty-year period from 1696 to 1717, and a corresponding decline of 16 percent in the property owned by men in the bottom half of the list. In nearby Topsfield and Boxford, taxpayers in the bottom half of the list lost substantial ground, and in Derby the poorer taxpayers lost 5 percent of the property in ten years.

As in the first period, several towns had greater concentrations of property in the hands of the richer inhabitants than was general in the country towns. South Kingstown, shiretown of newly established King's County and economic heart of the Narragansett country, had nearly half of its property in the hands of its top decile, and Hadley, a secondary center in the Connecticut Valley and a rapidly growing town in the mid-eighteenth century, developed greater concentrations of wealth both at the top and in the middle of the list. Concord, a frontier town but a highly atypical one because of its role as the test case in Massachusetts' attempt to make good its claim to the Merrimac Valley, also showed a significant concentration of property at the top of the list.[7]

During the third quarter of the eighteenth century, the trend toward concentration of the property at the top of the tax list continued in many established towns, and the results of that trend, as well as the availability of a much larger number of tax lists, provide evidence of a varied pattern of town types. In many frontier towns and in most small country towns, the social structure remained fairly egalitarian. The share of wealth held by the top decile of taxpayers increased slightly to a range of 25 to 35 percent in the towns that did not include polls in the tax lists, and remained about the same in the towns that did include their polls. Most of the established towns now had 80 to 90 percent of their property in the hands of men in the top half of the list, although the increase was not as pronounced in the lists that included polls. A relatively egalitarian distribution of property, however, was no longer the only normal pattern for the country towns. A few major towns like Boston and Portsmouth had always had more stratification than the majority of the country towns, and now their stratification increased until the top decile held 60 percent of the property in Boston, and more than 45 percent in Portsmouth. Other towns acquired an urban character during the period. Providence developed as a commercial center after mid-century, and the top decile increased its holding from 35 percent in 1751 to 44 percent in 1773.

In the third quarter of the century, marked stratification spread into the countryside as well. Tax lists from towns in eastern Massachusetts like Waltham, Dorchester, and Braintree show that men in the top decile owned 35 percent or more of the property in what might be viewed as Boston's suburbs, and the same was true for Manchester, a satellite of Salem, and Middletown, which was adjacent to Newport. Many major towns in the strictly rural parts of the colonies also had substantially stratified social structures. Worcester, Springfield, and South Kingstown, all county seats, had concentrations of more than 35 percent of the property at the top of the list, and similar concentrations existed in some other country towns, like Norton, Swansea, Scarborough, and Smithfield, that were not administrative centers.

The existence of a wide variety of stratification patterns reveals much about the conditions of life in the towns, but the information would be more useful for such purposes as comparing the wealth of leaders in several towns if it could be related to an absolute measure of town wealth. Unfortunately, no such measure exists, largely because the only convenient forms of data, tax records and population statistics, have survived in such fragmentary fashion, but statistics that partially serve the purpose can be constructed. The most promising method is to compute the per capita share of a colony's tax assessment in each town for the year in which that colony took a census, and then to compare the wealth of leaders in corresponding deciles of tax lists in towns with similar stratification. Presumably, if the distribution of property among the deciles of the population in two towns is similar and the per capita colony tax in one town is greater, the men in a given decile would be richer in the town that pays more in taxes. The absence of censuses before 1750 and the difficulty of producing accurate enough population estimates for a single year to support delicate calculations make this method unprofitable for the first half of the century, but the data for the third quarter of the century will support the analysis.

The sample towns in Massachusetts fall into four different groups according to the percentage of property concentration: six had concentrations of 50 to 60 percent of the taxable property in the hands of the top decile of taxpayers, nine had concentrations between 35 and 45 percent, seven had concentrations between 30 and 35 percent, and six had less than 30 percent.[8] In the first group, Boston's per capita tax assessment was the highest, and naturally the capital had the wealthiest leaders.* Next came Cambridge and Dorchester, one a county seat and college center, and both suburban towns in the first ring around the metropolis. Third in wealth was Salem, a county seat and the colony's second largest seaport. Then came Braintree and Swansea. Braintree, like the third-place towns, was in a suburban location, but its larger area stretched farther back into the country. Swansea was a secondary port town on Narragansett Bay. The final town, Manchester, was a satellite fishing port to Salem and Marblehead, and to all appearances a comparatively poor town.

Each of the other three groups of towns divided into similar categories. The secondary group included three suburbs (Dedham, Topsfield, and Sudbury), two western county seats (Worcester and Springfield), a substantial country town (Hadley), and two Maine coastal towns (Scarborough and Falmouth), all with similar social structures and all with similar amouns of per capita wealth, as well as an interior town (Norton), and two newly

*Property Concentration and Per Capita Taxes: First Group

Town	Top 10%	Per Capita Tax ($\pounds$)
Boston	60.4%	.364
Braintree	59.08%	.183
Cambridge	50.12%	.280
Dorchester	51.08%	.279
Manchester	53.72%	.143
Salem	52.23%	.220
Swansea	51.51%	.186

settled towns that were much poorer.* Towns in the third group were all relatively egalitarian and all were essentially farming communities, but their leaders and other inhabitants were not uniformly middle-class farmers.† Brookline was a wealthy Boston suburb with the highest per capita tax assessment of any community in the sample and a population of exceptionally wealthy landowners. The other towns included four small established towns of average wealth and two infant settlements. The fourth group contained a similar mix, including the large and important town of Andover, which retained a uniquely egalitarian economic structure for a town of its size and wealth.[9]††

Stratification patterns combined with per capita tax assessments provide similar comparisons of the wealth of the taxpayers in two of the remaining colonies, although the small number of tax lists in each colony does not create as rich a picture as the Massachusetts data. No New Hampshire town, for example, compared with Portsmouth in social structure. The other

*Property Concentration and Per Capita Taxes: Second Group

Town	Top 10%	Per Capita Tax (£)
Dedham	35.8%	.224
Falmouth	42.16%	.183
Hadley	35.05%	.225
Norton	40.82%	.158
Springfield	38.17%	.203
Sudbury	35.04%	.209
Topsfield	36.39%	.235
Westminster	37.06%	.162
Worcester	36.11%	.205
Gorham	37.45%	.100 (est.)
Scarborough	43.55%	.207

†Property Concentration and Per Capita Taxes: Third Group

Town	Top 10%	Per Capita Tax (£)
Billerica	31.96%	.183
Boxford	30.42%	.238
Brookline	33.25%	.500
Oakham	34.32%	.107
Shirley	32.03%	.139
Waltham	34.67%	.239
Brunswick	34.23%	.216

††Property Concentration and Per Capita Taxes: Fourth Group

Town	Top 10%	Per Capita Tax (£)
Amherst	24.57%	.143
Andover	25.59%	.255
Fitchburg	26.81%	.129
Hardwick	25.52%	.131
Lunenburg	28.76%	.194
Medfield	28.47%	.307
Pelham	28.50%	.251

towns were all relatively egalitarian, ranking tightly in wealth from Dover, a county seat, through a group of established towns, most of which happened to be in the Merrimac Valley, to two newly settled towns, Weare and Dublin, which were significantly poorer than the others.* In contrast to New Hampshire, all of the towns in Rhode Island were comparatively stratified. Middletown, a Newport suburb, and South Kingstown, a county seat, both ranked with the most stratified group of Massachusetts towns, and both were wealthy.† Newport was equally stratified but appeared slightly less wealthy, presumably because the assessment formula missed much commercial property. Providence and Smithfield, both primarily agricultural towns at mid-century were less stratified and less wealthy; while Exeter, an inland town on the fringe of the Narragansett region, had a few families, comparable in status to the leading families of South Kingstown, who stood out above a generally poor population. The Connecticut tax lists yield no significant information.[10]

To generalize for the whole region, the data suggests that the richest men lived in towns where the centralizing influence of commercial and political activities was strongest, and that leading men from towns where political and economic activities were more localized were of more modest means. Known commercial centers like the seaport towns, and political centers like

*Property Concentration and Per Capita Taxes: New Hampshire

Town	Top 10%	Per Capita Tax (£)
Portsmouth	47.39%	7.24
Bedford	41.82%	8.17
Canterbury	30.37%	7.95
Concord	24.12%	8.64
Derryfield	27.40%	8.70
Dover	24.12%	9.11
Dublin	26.07%	6.25
Londonderry	24.62%	7.21
New Ipswich	27.36%	8.33
Weare	23.24%	5.59

Note: The tax data is from the list of rateable estates for 1767, published in *Provincial Papers of New Hampshire*, 8: 166–67. The source is a valuation rather than a tax, which explains why the per capita figures are higher than those for Massachusetts.

†Property Concentration and Per Capita Taxes: Rhode Island

Town	Top 10%	Per Capita Tax (£)
Exeter	41.36%	1.06
Middletown	47.35%	2.76
Newport	55.19%	2.07
Providence	34.77%	1.55
Smithfield	37.04%	1.95
So. Kingstown	56.40%	2.72

The tax of 1755 is recorded in *Rhode Island Colonial Records*, 5: 465.

the county seats (which were also likely to be local trading centers), ranked high both in stratification and in per capita taxation, so that the men at the top of town society were often persons of considerable property. Suburban towns ranked slightly below the centers in both stratification and per capita taxation, but as part of the centralized political and economic network they contained some men of substantial means. Farther inland and away from the county centers were towns whose inhabitants were engaged almost exclusively in agricultural and local trading activities. These towns were relatively unstratified, and most ranked low in per capita taxation, which suggests that their inhabitants were overwhelmingly yeoman farmers of modest and roughly equal means.

The apparent connections between wealth and economic structure on the one hand and apparent economic activities in a town on the other hand indicate that the economic roles of the various towns need further attention. Many observers and historians have attempted to describe the economies of the New England towns, but owing in part to the lack of systematic information on internal trade, and in part to the willingness of many writers to accept the delusive existence of self-sufficient farming, little is yet known about economic affairs in most of the towns.[11] A substantial body of information exists on the seaport towns, including studies that attempt to rank them in wealth and commercial importance; occasional biographers have attempted to describe the careers of country merchants as well as their more spectacular maritime counterparts, and a few impressionistic studies attempt to describe the economies of limited regions.[12] None of these, however, provides the detailed information on the economies of individual towns needed in the present study.

Logically, economic development in New England could have followed one of three patterns. First, regions in a similar state of development might have appeared as bands on the map, with a distinctly commercial coastal region succeeded by an established inland agricultural area and finally by a primitive frontier zone. Second, development might have taken place along major communications routes like highways and river valleys so that the overall pattern would consist of corridors of rich and commercially developed towns, bordered by poorer and more self-contained areas. And third, the pattern for development might be described by something like the central place models created by geographers to explain the relationships between large cities and their satellite towns and hinterland areas.

The first model has served most often as the basis for historians' generalizations, and forms the framework for the most sophisticated and impressive existing study of the economic structure, Jackson Turner Main's *Social Structure of Revolutionary America*. Working from voluminous research in tax and probate records, Main has described four types of society.[13] Along the coast were a number of cities, large and small, containing numerous merchants, artisans, and professional people, as well as many propertyless laborers. Reaching some twenty miles inland from the cities, and stretching along the coast and along navigable rivers, was a band of commercial farming towns that contained some merchants, some artisans and professional men, and most notably, a number of very large farmers. The next and most common type of town society, the subsistence farm area, filled most of the rest of the settled part of the colonies and was characteristically a "frontier in arrested development," with few artisans or professional men, no merchants, and a host of small farmers. Finally, on the western and northern fringes of the area were frontier regions, with no appreciable social development and few men not readily identifiable as farmers. These town types were easily identifiable on the basis of the wealth of the richest inhabitants; the top 10 percent of the taxpayers owned a quarter or so of the property on the frontier, no more than 40 percent in the subsistence regions, up to half of the property in the commercial farming regions, and half or more in the cities.

Like all good generalizations, Main's summarize the available data well, but not without some problems. First, the system of homogeneous bands relegates a large proportion of New England's population to a subsistence way of life, although colonists in the back country were certainly not attempting to live without manufactured and imported commodities like iron, cloth, books, tea, and, of course, rum, as both the continual agitation for paper money as a medium of trade and the pre-revolutionary rage over nonimportation testify. Even more to the point for this study, the descriptions of the economic areas do not mesh well with figures on concentration of wealth that should correspond. As the preceding pages have shown, highly stratified and egalitarian towns were not arranged in bands, but were scattered throughout the countryside. Some stratified towns showed an understandable tendency to congregate around the principal cities, but that tendency was not strong enough to dispel suspicions that the model of homogeneous bands is an inadequate representation of the New England economy.

A second possible pattern would have been for development along the river and highway routes of communication. Navigable rivers, however, were few in New England, and except for the Merrimack and the Connecticut, none served as a line of communication for more than a few miles.[14] Roads, on the other hand, were of major importance in the settled parts of the colonies. During the first quarter of the eighteenth century, highways were few and rarely mentioned in almanacs, which are the best source of information. The Post Road, running through the coastal towns from Portsmouth to Boston, by way of Dedham and Attleboro to Providence, down the west side of Narragansett Bay, and then along the coast to New Haven and New York, was by far the most important highway. Lesser roads of note ran from Boston to Cape Cod through the coastal towns, from the Post Road to Newport, and from Boston to Springfield through Worcester and Brookfield, and then down the Connecticut River to Hartford and New Haven.[15]

During the second quarter, the road network increased greatly in extent and in the frequency with which almanac makers described it.[16] The Post Road now extended northeastward to Brunswick, Maine; a "Middle Road" from Boston to Hartford through eastern Connecticut now joined the established routes west and south; and a number of very secondary routes led from Boston toward the upper Merrimac Valley, and toward north-central Massachusetts. This network was even more significantly extended in the third quarter of the century. Almanacs now described routes from Providence and Worcester to Hartford and New London; from Boston to Northampton and to Deerfield, running to the north of the established Springfield road; from Deerfield, Northampton, and Springfield to Albany; and from both central Massachusetts and eastern New Hampshire into the southwestern part of the latter colony.[17]

A relationship might be hypothesized between location on a through highway and a town's ability to establish the communications necessary for commercial development, but both the available data on social structure and data on relative commercial development, which will be discussed presently, indicate that the connection between communications and commercialization was not so direct. By 1775 a through road of at least secondary importance entered almost every established town, but the towns along the road did not exhibit similar concentrations of property. All of the major towns, or at least all of the towns that had wealthy inhabitants at the top of a highly stratified social order, lay along well-traveled highways, and many of the main towns, such as Boston, Providence, Hartford, and New Haven, were located at road junctions. Many intervening main road towns, however, had the egalitarian social structures of farming communities. Medfield and Bolton, for example, both of which were on the "Middle Road" from Boston to Hartford, were small, poor, and egalitarian towns, and many of the towns on the secondary roads were of the same general type. A model of development along communication routes, like a model of development in homogeneous regions, is helpful in understanding the relative economic development of the towns, but it falls short of providing an adequate explanation of the observable variations.

A third model for regional development is central place theory, a theory developed by economic geographers to explain the relationships among the various centers of population in an area. The key concept in this theory is "centrality." By centrality is meant simply that many types of goods and services can be most efficiently and profitably offered in a place that serves as a population center for a region, and that the "central place" will consequently grow in size and importance, while the population of its "complementary region" will remain relatively dispersed and tributary. Moreover, because some central goods and services, for example the merchandise in a retail shop, are necessary to large numbers of people on a daily basis, and other goods or services, such as the distribution services provided by a large wholesaler, are necessary only to specialized groups of people on an intermittent basis, central places are organized on a hierarchical basis, with the more widely needed goods and services available at lower-order central places and the more specialized ones available only at higher-order central places. Under ideal conditions, towns of the same order would be equally spaced and surrounded by hexagonal hinterlands of a size determined by the number of subordinate lower order towns, but under real conditions the size and shape of complementary regions of the central places may vary considerably.[18]

In terms of the degree of stratification in a town, a measure by which the first models for development seemed wanting, central place theory fits the data nicely. Around Boston, where extensive data is available, the most stratified town was the metropolis itself, and the percentages declined regularly as one followed the road from Boston to Dorchester, Dedham, and Medfield, or alternatively from Boston to Cambridge, Watertown, and Waltham. Boston, of course, was something of a special case, because it was the largest city in New England and presumably a central place of a higher order than any of the other towns.* The expected pattern, however, exists even more clearly in the countryside. County seats like Worcester, Springfield, and South Kingstown, and colonial capitals like Portsmouth and New Haven, provide evidence of the wide distribution of higher-order central places, while egalitarian villages like Boxford, Fitchburg, Pelham, and Newtown illustrate the existence of lower-order dispersed places in all parts of the region. Towns like Scarborough, Norton, Sudbury, and Hadley would seem to be places of a higher order, but secondary to the leading local centers. On the basis of the pattern of social stratification alone, central place theory provides the best model for economic relationships in eighteenth-century New England.

Before a survey of regional economic models can lead to a real understanding of the pattern of commercial development in the towns, however, a measure of commercialization that is more directly related to economic function than stratification must be found. In the absence of systematically collected economic data, and in spite of theoretical warnings to the contrary, a student instinctively turns to town population as a measure of town size and importance, but in New England, where the town was a territorial unit

---

*According to the theory, the places immediately adjacent to a high-order central place should be very low-order dispersed places, and the satellite central places of an intermediate order should be some distance away. The theory, however, presupposes that the immediate environs of a city would be incorporated into it, as is true of most twentieth-century cities, but not of colonial Boston. An immediate parallel to the Boston situation was the tendency, described by James T. Lemon, for colonial Philadelphia to overpower all nearby central places, and arrogate all central functions to itself. Lemon, "Urbanization in Southeastern Pennsylvania," pp. 504–10.

rather than a distinctly urban area, population figures are an especially inaccurate measure.[19] A much more useful set of figures can be obtained by dividing each town's share of the colony's taxes by the total area of the town, and thereby computing an index of the hypothetical average value of the property in the town.[20] Such a measure depends directly on the value of property in a community, corrected for variations in the geographical area, and since property values would be highest in an urban area, and roughly proportional to the potential for the marketing of goods in rural areas, the index is related to commercialization in a clear way.

The distribution of towns with similar values in this commercialization index shows why more than one model of commercial development has been applied to colonial New England.[21] A band of towns with fairly high values stretched along the coast from Plymouth to York, and a similar groups of towns lined the shores of Narragansett Bay. Behind these towns lay a second band with moderate values that stretched from eastern New Hampshire into southeastern Massachusetts. Connecticut deviated somewhat from this pattern in that the towns with the highest ratings were scattered across the middle of the colony, but values throughout the southern half of the colony were all at least moderately high. A third large group of towns, most of which had very low ratings in the index, stretched north from Hartford and west of Worcester and the Merrimac River. Presented this way, the data lends support to a theory of homogeneous bands.

A further look at the data, however, reveals that a regional interpretation glosses over the existence of a few towns in each region with unusually high ratings. Many of these towns had a high degree of social stratification, and many were also key road junctions and points for land-to-water transshipment in the communications network. Although all of eastern Massachusetts and New Hampshire ranked high in the commercialization index, Boston, its immediate neighbors, and Salem, Marblehead, Newburyport, and Portsmouth-Newcastle were spectacularly higher than the other towns. Newport and Providence stood out as notable centers in Rhode Island, as did Norwich, Hartford, Middletown, and New Haven in the more ambiguous Connecticut data. Even the low ranking western and northern region had clear centers at Springfield, Northampton-Hadley, Brookfield, and Worcester in Massachusetts, and at towns like Keene, Charlestown, and New Ipswich in New Hampshire. Two-thirds of the county seats ranked distinctly higher than most of the surrounding towns.

The commercial development of the towns, then, followed a central place model modified by important regional considerations. Overall commercial activity was greater in the long-settled eastern and southern parts of the region than in the more remote and more freshly settled interior sections. But towns varied considerably within each area, and each area had its commercial centers. In terms of social stratification and of the ability of men in leading towns to build substantial fortunes, a town's function within its county or local area was more decisive in shaping the local society than the general level of commercial involvement in the area as a whole.

Information on how the towns varied in the overall distribution of wealth and on the types of economic activities in which their inhabitants are likely to have participated is necessary for studying relationships among wealth, town leadership, and high status, because of the complexity of the question. Just as examination of the wealth of the towns showed that men in corresponding strata of the town populations did not belong to a common economic class, study of the data on the wealth of individual leaders reveals that town leaders did not share a common economic position. Wealth was an important factor in establishing a man's eligibility for town leadership, but it was not the direct determinant of elections, because factors like family position, religion, age, education, and demonstrated ability were equally important.

Exactly how the wealth of the town leaders compared with that of their fellow townspeople becomes clear when the position of each man who served as a leader within the decade surrounding the date of a tax list is plotted for each of the ninety-five tax lists from fifty-five towns available for study. Overall, about 40 percent of the leaders ranked in the wealthiest ten percent of the population and about 73 percent were in the top quarter. Another 20 percent of the leaders ranked in the second quarter of their tax list, leaving only about 7 percent who were below the middle of the list (see Table 12).[22] Furthermore, these gross averages provide a reasonable summary of the data for individual towns. Three-quarters of the leaders ranked in the top quarter of the population in forty-three lists, and more than half of the leaders were in the top quarter in all but six isolated cases. Only one town chose more than a quarter of its leaders from men who ranked below the middle of the list, and twenty-six towns chose no leaders at all from that segment of the population.

Such general figures give little information about how the towns came to choose most leaders from among the wealthiest inhabitants, but it is clear that wealth did not determine leadership in the most direct way. No town ever entrusted all of its major offices to the top five or seven men on the tax list. Since an intelligent observer would not demand such extreme behavior to prove the influence of wealth, however, it is equally important that no town came remotely close to electing only its richest inhabitants. Most towns were large enough that all of the fifteen to twenty-five leaders who ordinarily served during a decade could have come from the top decile of the tax list, with enough men left over to ensure that a town could avoid electing an unwilling or unpopular man. A majority of the men in the top decile, however, served as leaders in only twenty-five of the ninety-five cases, and most of these towns were so small that the top decile leaders were still a minority of the whole leadership.[23] None of the towns chose more than about two-thirds of their leaders from the top decile, and most chose well under half from that group. These figures meant that many rich men never became leaders, and that wealth alone did not insure a man's place in a town's political elite.

That towns did not view political leadership as an activity for the richest few alone is confirmed by the absence of a progressive contraction in the range of property owned by leaders in towns of increasing size. Figures on the size of the pools of town leaders presented in Chapter 2 revealed that the elites remained about stationary in number as towns grew larger, so that the leaders constituted an increasingly smaller percentage of the population in towns of greater size. As elites became proportionately smaller, however, they were not chosen from a smaller and smaller group at the top of society. The percentage of leaders in the top decile of the population was not consistently larger in cities like Boston and Portsmouth or in large towns like Cambridge, Worcester, and South Kingstown than it was in tiny settlements like Bedford, Pelham, and Bolton. Single towns tended to draw more leaders from the top quarter of the population as they became larger, but few towns excluded men from the lower half of society as would be predictable if leadership had become restricted to a fixed group of gentry at the top of society. Clearly, the towns took some leaders from the top decile of the tax list and some from farther down the list as convenience and individual fitness for office dictated. Town leaders did not constitute a narrow economic class at the top of society.

Most leaders stood somewhere in the top quarter of their town's tax list, but even such relative wealth was not an essential criterion for election. No town restricted its selections entirely to the top quarter, although that group invariably would have been large enough to provide a range of choice.[24] Willingness to choose men from the second or third quarter of the list was an important matter, because few men that far down the list paid even half as much in taxes as the men in the top decile, and most would appear to be ordinary inhabitants if wealth were the main source of information. The relatively random pattern of towns that chose their leaders substantially from the top decile or two of the population in comparison with the data on the stratification and relative wealth of the towns makes clear that the majority of town leaders were not an economic class on a colony-wide basis; and the same information reveals that leaders within a single town ordinarily did not maintain a common standard of living. All of the leaders in a frontier town like Dublin, which took its leaders from the top half of a tax list that showed only 26 percent of the property in the hands of the top decile of taxpayers, or all of the leaders in a small town like Boxford, which took its leaders from the top half of a similarly stratified tax list, might have been on a level of rough equality. In many other towns, however, the leaders at the top of the tax list were so much richer than their fellows in the third or fourth decile of the list that the conclusion that they maintained different standards of living and experienced different styles of life seems justified.

TABLE TWELVE

Tax Standing of Leaders

Town	Years	Tax List	# of Leaders	# of Leaders Taxed	Top 10%	Top 1/4	2nd 1/4	3rd 1/4	Bottom 1/4
Amherst	1759-65	1759	20	11	27.3	72.7	27.3	0	0
Amherst	1766-75	1771	22	20	40.0	65.0	25.0	10.0	0
Andover	1715-24	1720	25	25	36.0	76.0	16.0	4.0	4.0
Andover	1735-44	1740	24	24	41.6	83.3	16.7	0	0
Andover	1755-64	1760	25	24	45.8	62.5	25.0	8.3	4.2
Billerica	1728-37	1733	16	13	30.7	61.6	30.7	7.7	0
Billerica	1750-59	1755	15	14	21.4	92.9	7.1	0	0
Billerica	1766-75	1771	10	9	33.3	66.7	11.1	22.2	0
Boston	1766-75	1771	27	18	66.7	77.8	5.6	11.1	5.6
Boxford	1687-96	1687	24	21	23.8	42.9	42.9	14.2	0
Boxford[1]	1741-50	1745/6	25	16	31.3	68.8	12.5	18.7	0
Boxford	1756-65	1761	22	20	40.0	80.0	20.0	0	0
Boxford	1770-79	1774	25	24	41.7	62.5	37.5	0	0
Braintree[1]	1770-79	1774	23	8	62.5	75.0	25.0	0	0
Brookline	1766-75	1771	14	10	30.0	70.0	20.0	10.0	0
Cambridge[1]	1766-75	1771	22	13	30.7	61.5	21.4	7.7	7.7
Dedham	1706-15	1710	18	18	27.8	77.8	16.7	5.6	0
Dedham	1730-39	1735	19	18	50.0	83.3	16.7	0	0
Dedham	1766-75	1771	20	19	47.4	84.2	10.5	5.3	0
Dorchester	1766-75	1771	15	15	26.7	86.7	13.3	0	0
Fitchburg	1766-75	1771	16	14	35.7	78.6	21.4	0	0
Hadley	1716-25	1720	20	19	40.5	78.9	15.8	5.3	0
Hadley	1726-35	1731	25	24	50.0	83.3	12.5	4.2	0
Hadley	1766-75	1771	25	25	44.0	84.0	16.0	0	0
Hardwick	1771-80	1776	21	21	47.6	81.0	9.5	9.5	0
Hatfield	1733-42	1738	22	20	30.0	65.0	30.0	5.0	0
Leicester	1727-36	1732	17	17	23.5	47.1	41.2	11.8	0
Leicester	1738-47	1743	26	24	37.5	75.0	20.8	4.2	0
Lunenburg	1757-66	1762	26	25	32.0	64.0	36.0	0	0
Lunenburg	1766-75	1770	25	24	37.5	62.5	37.5	0	0
Manchester	1695-1703	1696	14	11	36.4	54.6	27.3	9.1	9.1
Manchester	1714-25	1717	13	12	16.7	41.7	50.0	8.3	0
Manchester	1765-74	1769	13	13	69.2	100.0	0	0	0
Medfield	1766-75	1771	30	28	32.1	75.0	21.4	0	3.6
Norton	1711-20	1711	14	11	45.5	90.9	0	9.1	0
Norton	1766-75	1771	15	15	53.3	86.7	13.3	0	0
Oakham	1766-75	1771	13	13	46.2	92.3	0	0	7.7
Pelham	1766-75	1771	23	23	30.4	56.5	30.4	13.0	0
Shirley	1766-75	1771	10	10	40.0	80.0	10.0	10.0	0
Springfield	1680-89	1685	20	15	46.7	73.3	20.0	6.7	0
Springfield	1766-75	1771	23	22	54.6	68.2	18.2	13.6	0
Sudbury[1]	1717-26	1722	35	17	23.5	76.5	11.8	11.8	0
Sudbury	1766-75	1771	22	22	59.1	86.4	13.6	0	0
Swansea	1766-75	1771	21	14	21.4	71.4	21.4	7.1	0
Topsfield	1719-28	1723	34	24	29.2	54.2	29.2	4.2	12.5
Topsfield	1740-49	1744	21	16	31.3	81.3	12.5	6.3	0
Topsfield	1760-69	1765	19	18	50.0	72.2	27.8	0	0
Waltham	1738-47	1740	17	17	41.2	58.8	35.3	5.9	0

TABLE TWELVE: Continued

Town	Years	Tax List	# of Leaders	# of Leaders Taxed	Top 10%	Top 1/4	2nd 1/4	3rd 1/4	Bottom 1/4
Waltham	1766-75	1771	13	13	69.2	84.6	15.4	0	0
Watertown[1]	1726-35	1730	31	15	40.0	86.7	6.7	6.7	0
Westminster	1759-68	1759	14	12	25.0	66.7	33.3	0	0
Worcester	1766-75	1771	16	15	33.3	80.0	6.7	6.7	6.7
Brunswick	1766-75	1771	11	10	40.0	70.0	20.0	10.0	0
Gorham	1766-75	1771	15	11	36.4	54.6	45.5	0	0
Scarborough	1766-75	1771	14	11	36.4	54.6	27.3	0	18.2
Bedford	1750-59	1750	21	17	23.5	58.8	29.4	5.9	5.9
Bedford	1766-75	1770	21	18	33.3	72.2	22.2	0	5.7
Canterbury	1776-85	1782	18	15	66.7	93.3	6.7	0	0
Concord	1733-42	1737	13	13	30.8	61.5	23.1	0	15.4
Concord	1770-79	1775	15	13	53.8	69.2	23.1	0	7.7
Derryfield	1753-62	1758	17	14	21.4	50.0	21.4	21.4	7.1
Derryfield	1770-79	1775	24	20	30.0	55.0	40.0	5.0	0
Dover	1736-45	1741	15	11	36.7	81.8	0	9.1	9.1
Dover	1748-57	1753	18	16	62.5	81.3	12.5	6.3	0
Dublin	1771-80	1771	16	15	33.3	73.3	26.7	0	0
Londonderry[1]	1746-55	1750	27	10	10.0	20.0	60.0	10.0	10.0
New Ipswich	1762-71	1763	21	17	47.1	76.5	11.8	11.8	0
New Ipswich	1770-79	1774	18	17	47.1	100.0	0	0	0
Portsmouth	1710-19	1715	21	20	65.0	90.0	10.0	0	0
Portsmouth	1754-63	1759	14	12	33.3	58.3	41.7	0	0
Weare	1764-73	1764	23	13	15.4	38.5	46.2	7.7	7.7
Exeter	1758-67	1763	23	23	39.1	78.3	17.4	4.4	0
Exeter	1770-79	1774	35	33	33.3	75.8	21.2	3.0	0
Middletown	1779-85	1783	21	19	26.3	52.6	36.8	5.3	5.3
Newport	1756-65	1760	32	30	50.0	83.3	13.3	3.3	0
Providence	1700-09	1705	36	33	45.5	87.9	3.0	6.1	3.0
Providence	1746-55	1751	41	38	34.2	71.1	15.8	13.2	0
Providence	1769-78	1773	54	52	63.5	88.5	5.8	3.8	1.9
Smithfield	1756-65	1760	22	21	61.9	81.0	9.5	9.5	0
S. Kingstown	1726-35	1730	13	13	46.2	69.2	30.8	0	0
S. Kingstown	1770-79	1774	41	38	39.5	73.7	21.1	5.3	0
Bolton	1727-36	1732	14	13	15.4	46.2	46.2	0	7.7
Bolton	1748-57	1753	15	15	66.7	73.3	20.0	6.7	0
Bolton	1770-79	1774	16	15	53.3	86.7	13.3	0	0
Derby	1713-22	1718	15	13	38.5	61.5	23.1	7.7	7.7
Derby	1723-32	1728	24	19	31.6	52.6	5.3	31.6	10.5
Kent	1739-48	1744	19	14	35.7	64.3	21.4	0	14.3
Kent	1766-75	1771	23	20	55.0	85.0	0	10.0	5.0
New Haven	1700-09	1702	35	34	32.4	61.8	20.6	14.7	2.9
New Haven	1740-49	1745	32	31	48.4	74.2	6.5	16.1	3.2
New Haven	1761-70	1766	30	27	63.0	85.2	7.4	3.7	3.7
Newtown	1735-44	1739	30	27	28.9	63.0	28.9	3.7	3.7
Newtown	1762-71	1767	41	38	52.6	78.9	15.7	5.3	0
Woodbury	1731-40	1736	25	24	45.8	66.7	25.0	8.3	0
Woodbury	1760-69	1765	28	26	50.0	69.2	23.1	3.9	3.9

1) These tax lists cover one precinct of a multi-precinct town, and the number of leaders taxed is underrecorded accordingly.

Leaders who ranked in the second or third quarter of a tax list in towns with any significant degree of stratification stand as clear confirmation of the sociological observation that men can attain positions of authority and respect without great wealth, although wealth and high status tend to converge in the long run.[25] Such men clearly owed their elevation to qualities other than wealth, and this was even more true of those who ranked near the bottom of the tax lists. The forty-odd town leaders who ranked in the bottom quarter of their town's list became leaders, not because they were rich men, or even because they were prosperous men with additional qualities, but because their relative poverty did not diminish the town's confidence in their ability to provide good service.

An examination of the number of terms served by the poorer leaders adds certainty to the view that wealth was not a prerequisite for effective leadership. The election of men of ordinary means to major office in significant numbers indicates that towns were willing to entrust them with major responsibilities, but it does not prove that poor leaders could compete on equal terms with the wealthy for power and influence. Data on the number of terms served by the leaders, however, reveals no significant correlation between the length of time a man remained in office and his position on the tax list. Some of the poorer officeholders served only one or two terms, suggesting that they were marginal leaders, but others served for fifteen or twenty years, which indicates that they were respected and powerful men. Of ten towns chosen from the larger sample, eight showed a higher average length of service for leaders who appeared in the bottom three-quarters of the tax list. Even more impressive are the figures for the longest service, which show that some poorer leaders served as long as anybody.* Nine of the towns had leaders of ordinary means who served more than twenty terms in major office, while the tenth, Gorham, was incorporated so late in the period that few leaders had time to compile more than half a dozen years of service.

Some of the long-serving leaders may have ranked higher on the tax lists in earlier or later stages of their careers than when they were caught by the

*Leaders Below the First Quarter in Taxes

Town	No. of Men	No. of Terms	Ave. Terms	Longest Service	Town Ave.
Amherst	10	97	9.7	27	4.8
Andover	16	150	9.4	28	7.4
Cambridge	5	45	9.0	24	8.3
Pelham	10	97	9.7	27	4.3
Gorham	5	19	3.8	7	4.7
Bedford	12	75	6.3	35	4.2
Portsmouth	7	113	16.1	31	6.3
Providence	21	210	10.0	27	7.5
Bolton	13	111	8.5	56	10.1
New Haven	19	191	10.1	48	5.9

tax lists used here, but others never rose above the middle of the spectrum. The Bishops of New Haven are a good example of prominent men who were never wealthy. Three generations of Bishops served the town as selectmen, town clerks, and representatives for twenty to fifty years each without ever climbing out of the middle deciles of the tax lists. The high averages for the poorer men thus do not mean that they served longer than their rich neighbors, because a tax list a decade earlier or later might have shown that an older leader had declined in fortune or that a young one was on his way to greater wealth, but they do indicate that modest means was no obstacle to long service and power.

Since the towns did not select their leaders from an economic class, and did not make wealth a necessary precondition for election to high office, an explanation of why so many town leaders were relatively wealthy men must be sought elsewhere. One important clue is in the nature of the service demanded of the leaders. In the first place, offices like selectman, town clerk, and town treasurer were time consuming. Town meetings usually convened three or four times a year, and in addition to attendance on those days and at ensuing adjournments, the selectmen and town clerk had to meet before the meeting to draw up and record the warrant that established the agenda for the town. The number of routine executive meetings of the selectmen varied considerably, but such meetings must have averaged at least one a month over the whole period when such varied duties as regulating taverns and retail establishments, caring for the poor, supervising the inferior town officers, conducting church, parish, and school business, maintaining town property, preparing estimates of town expenses to guide the town meeting in its appropriations, and responding to petitions of individual inhabitants for alterations in roadways and fence lines are considered. In addition, most towns elected some or all of the selectmen to assess the taxes, many town proprieties made the selectmen their executive committee, and the boards were continually delegating individual members to repair bridges, perambulate town boundaries, view suggested changes in roadways, go to Cambridge or New Haven in quest of a schoolmaster, and to handle many other similar tasks. Town clerks and town treasurers were burdened with like chores.

All these duties took up a great deal of time, and since with minor exceptions the major offices were unpaid positions, town leadership could be a financial drain on a man. Representatives received an allowance for each day of service, when the towns did not force them to agree to serve gratis as a condition of election, but in any case they had to live on their money until accounts were approved and taxes collected, and there was no assurance that the per diem wages would pay for all expenses. Similarly, some town clerks received small fees for recording vital statistics and other business involving private individuals, and selectmen could submit accounts for time and money spent in town service although such accounts often remained unapproved, and unpaid, for years.[26] No major town office paid enough to support a man and his family, and even if office is considered as part-time employment, the terms were not always favorable. The office-holder had to advance money to cover his expenses in hopes of later reimbursement; and he had to provide services at the town's convenience, not at his own. This meant that even fair per diem compensation could not repay, for example, a farmer who was forced to delay planting or harvesting his crops while he attended to the public business. Since leadership on these terms could be an expensive proposition, the towns turned most frequently to their richer inhabitants, who were likely to be able to withstand the strain.

Town voters cast their ballots with a sense of the economic implications of their actions clearly in mind. Calculating that candidates for representative would be willing to serve without pay in return for the honor of sitting in the General Court, a few towns required the representative to promise to turn his wages over the town treasurer, although they were careful not to suggest such a bargain if it eliminated the most acceptable candidate.[27] At most times, however, towns were more concerned with preventing public office from becoming too much of a burden. As early in 1674 Northampton voted to elect a single man selectman no more than every other year, "it being too great a burthen for the same men to be so often employ'd," and in the neighboring town of Hadley that policy was scrupulously followed throughout the eighteenth century.[28] Other towns were less explicit about their policies, but all were willing to discharge an officer if he could show that service would seriously interfere with his personal business. Not only were the wealthy most likely to have time to devote to political activity, and hence a willingness to serve in public office, but they were also likely to be able to fill the offices effectively because they were not under continual pressure to attend to urgent day-to-day affairs.[29]

The tendency of the voters to arrive at this practical evaluation of the advantages of electing well-to-do leaders was further strengthened by the dominant system of political thought in eighteenth-century New England, the "country" ideology. This ideology stressed the necessity for electing "independent" men to office, because men who were not dependent on the provincial or imperial governments for favors or on other inhabitants for their livelihood were least likely to succumb to corruption or influence and most likely to conduct public business with the common good firmly in mind. Most statements of country ideas stressed the component of "independence" that required vigilance against corruption by the central government; but independence also meant independence from economic influences, and the wealthier townsmen were most calculated to fulfill that condition.[30]

The desire to have independent leaders influenced the towns to pick their wealthier men, but it did not lead to the election of a homogeneous group of gentry, or squirearchy, to local office. Eighteenth-century probate records and deed books, which frequently list occupations, contain many references to "gentlemen," but the meaning of such labels is uncertain. Old men writing wills often called themselves "gentlemen" and their middle-aged sons "yeomen" or "husbandmen," which suggests that they had turned much of the heavy labor over to the sons and so had become gentlemen by virtue of retirement. In the cases of administrators of estates and men registering deeds, the records suggest that the term "gentlemen" was losing its meaning. Officials often used precise occupational designations at the beginning of legal proceedings, but then shifted to blanket references to the same men as "gentlemen" in subsequent documents. A few leaders appear to have been gentry in the strict sense of being men of honorable birth who lived on landed or invested income without performing manual labor, but the majority were yeomen, artisans, tradesmen, or professional men who ordinarily worked for a living.[31]

Two kinds of sources provide detailed information on the occupations of town leaders, although both have serious weaknesses. First, the occupational labels mentioned in probate records confirm that the leadership was open to prosperous artisans as well as to landowners. Probate records for the sample towns in the largely agricultural province of New Hampshire during the 1760s reveal that although a majority of the men declaring specific occupations were yeomen farmers, a substantial minority followed trades such as blacksmith, joiner, and housewright.* Maine wills for the sample towns between 1730 and 1760 indicate a similar pattern, although the minority of trades corresponds to the maritime nature of the region's economy.[32] The leadership, therefore, included men with a variety of occupations, but the overall pattern of involvement remains unclear because the probate records included few individuals from any one town, because an occupational label provides only a crude indication of an individual's economic and social status, and because the labels of "esquire" and "gentleman" adopted by the most prominent leaders provide no real evidence of occupation at all.

The second source of information on occupations, tax lists that categorize property or estimate earning potential, provides clearer information about the recruitment of occupational groups into the leadership of specific towns and about the economic status of leaders with distinctive occupations. These lists either indicate the proportion of taxes assessed on "faculty"—that is, the income potential of a skill or craft—or itemize ownership of shops, mills,

---

*Provincial Papers of New Hampshire, 37–39 (1939–41): Probate Records, 1760–1771, contain the following occupational information for leaders in the fifteen sample towns:

Occupation	Decedents	Administrators	Occupation	Decedents	Administrators
Esquire	10		Blacksmith	1	2
Gentlemen	11	11	Bookbinder		1
Merchant	1	3	Cooper	1	
Yeoman	10	6	Housewright	1	
Husbandman	2	2	Joiner	1	1
Innholder	1	1	Mariner		1

and other commercial property, although they do not list a taxpayer's exact occupation. Examination of ten such tax lists, all but one of them from Maine and Massachusetts, reveals that as many as half of the men with nonagricultural holdings were town leaders, while the proportion of leaders to adult males was considerably smaller.* Furthermore, the nonagricultural holdings of leaders tended to be larger than those of less prominent men. These facts harmonize with the finding that leaders tended to rank in the top quarter of a tax list, especially in view of the likelihood that only the more successful tradesmen or professionals would own the kinds of tangible, nonagricultural property that would attract the attention of the assessors.

The prominence of many men with nonagricultural incomes, however, did not reflect a sharp distinction between agricultural and nonagricultural careers. For most of the men involved, in fact, a trade or profession merely supplemented an essentially agricultural income. In four inland towns where the assessors listed taxes on each man's income from "faculty" separately from taxes on the usual agricultural properties, the nonagricultural tax represented less than 15 percent of the overall assessment for nineteen of thirty-four leaders, and more than 33 percent of the assessment for only four. Prominent men presumably derived a larger proportion of their incomes from commercial or professional activities in the coastal towns, but even in a seaport like Falmouth investments tended to be limited to

*Leaders' Holdings in Nonagricultural Property

I: Lists Taxing "Faculty"

Town	No. of Leaders	% of Holders	Leaders' % of Holdings	All Ldrs as % of Adult Males	No. of Ldrs Paying less than 15% for Faculty	No. of Ldrs Paying more than 33% for Faculty
Concord 1757	4	57	60	14	1	0
Lunenburg 1770	7	33	56	30	5	1
Sudbury 1770	20	21	44	11	10	3
Waltham 1740	3	33	35	16	3	0

II: Lists Itemizing Commercial Property

Town	No. of Leaders	% of Holders	All Ldrs as % of Adult Males	Percentage Owned By Leaders					
				Shops	Mills	Ware-houses	Wharves	Ship-ping	Trading Stock
Falmouth 1760	17	27	–	–	19	60	86	43	40
Fitchburg 1771	1	50	31	50	–	–	–	–	–
Oakham 1771	3	43	41	50	50	–	–	–	–
Scarborough 1771	9	26	10	–	36	100	–	29	0
Springfield 1771	6	14	6	10	11	–	–	–	–
Swansea 1771	7	21	10	21	43	0	0	30	37

Note: Only those shops which were structurally distinct from the owner's dwelling were included in the valuation list. The valuations provided no basis for establishing the monetary value of the types of property listed.

fractional shares in mills or ships and to be balanced with substantial farming operations. The frequency with which men combined several sources of income explains why occupational labeling tended to be confused and suggests that distinctions based on occupation were less likely than other variables to influence a man's status as a leader.

From all appearances, a division between two occupational types of town leaders was much more important than the differences between specific trades. The first type consisted of substantial but rather ordinary country men who might be either farmers or rural artisans and shopkeepers, but who in all probability were both. Such men could call themselves "yeomen" or "blacksmiths" interchangeably. As leaders they tended to serve relatively few terms, and rarely achieved prominence beyond the borders of their native town. The second type of leader, those who achieved the distinction of "esquire" and many of the men who called themselves "gentlemen," enjoyed more prestige. These men were particular favorites of the local voters, serving considerably more than the average number of terms in town office, and they also might aspire to become justices of the peace, judges, or councillors.[33] The precise occupational status of such individuals, however, was no more clear than that of their less prominent fellow citizens. Nearly all were merchants, lawyers, physicians, or landed gentlemen, but most were several of those at once. The two types of leaders had one major quality in common. They were men who earned a large enough income that they could neglect their business from time to time or who managed a large enough establishment that they could rely upon sons, apprentices, or hired hands to perform critical tasks in their absence. Men of limited means could serve only when small families or the willingness to live at an unusually modest scale counteracted their need to devote full time to earning a living.[34] Both the financial and the ideological aspects of the political system worked to establish a modest, but very real economic threshold for town leadership.

Beyond these rational and ideological calculations of economic fitness, of course, the role of wealth as a broad influence on individual status played a part in the choice of town leaders. The general influence of wealth on status is almost impossible to analyze and measure precisely in a historical context, however, because status is a matter of perception rather than of objective placement in a tax list or list of officials. For this reason, social scientists prefer to study status and power in contemporary communities by means of questionnaires and opinion samples rather than solely by studying assessors' records and organizational tables of municipal government.[35] But the subjective evaluations of bystanders are largely unavailable to the twentieth-century student of eighteenth-century society, and even the status meaning associated with recorded activities and practices must be studied with caution.

The status associations of several kinds of physical labor in eighteenth-century New England, for example, require especially careful attention because the distinctions were extremely fine and not always in line with twentieth-century suppositions. Accumulations of wealth allowed some men to live in relative luxury with servants, expensive household furnishings, and socially gratifying associations with other men of wealth and prominence, but they were not great enough to allow oligarchical elite groups with a contempt for physical labor to develop. A few clergymen, such as James MacSparren of South Kingstown and Ebenezer Parkman of Westborough, considered manual labor a source of "great Trouble and affliction" for professional reasons, but most New Englanders, even those who could justifiably be called gentlemen, did not mind mowing hay or mending a fence.[36] As Chapter 2 has shown, the line between honorable town office and menial town office did not separate the major offices from the minor offices so much as it separated the offices that combined discretionary power and responsibility from offices that involved strictly prescribed messenger-boy functions. Established and acknowledged leaders willingly served as fence viewers and highway surveyors despite the labor involved, but they avoided offices like hog reeve and field driver, which were entirely routine as well as laborious.

The honorable nature of labor allowed town leaders to perform apparently menial chores without stigma for the sake of convenience. Tasks like sweeping the meeting house often went to men who lived nearby or who had frequent business in the area rather than to poor laborers. The north parish of Braintree employed Joseph Parmenter, a respected leader who was repeatedly elected town clerk and treasurer by acclamation, to chase dogs out of the meeting house without lowering his standing in the eyes of the town, and towns like Lunenburg, Barrington, and Amherst hired veteran selectmen to sweep the meetinghouse and ring the bell. Similarly, selectmen were frequently willing to replace planks in bridges, rebuild pounds, and repair the meetinghouse themselves, if that seemed easier than finding someone else to do the job.[37]

Some would-be aristocrats disdained physical labor and scorned those substantial citizens who lived by their own labors. In a famous incident in 1705, Governor Joseph Dudley and his son William attempted to force two carters out of the highway in Brookline, calling them "rogue," "rascal," and "dogs," and subsequently had the two arrested. A principal cause of the Anglicized Dudley's irritation was that John Winchester maintained that he was "as good flesh and blood as you," and refused to remove his hat throughout the encounter. Winchester's stand was not an expression of pure egalitarianism as has sometimes been supposed, because the young man was the son of a principal town leader of Brookline, a respected neighbor of Judge Samuel Sewall's, and a man who became a town leader in his own right and left a substantial estate of some £1,100 on his death. No less a person than Judge Sewall viewed the roadway, agreed with the carters' contention that the road was wide enough for both parties, and ordered the prisoners released. The exaggerated views of aristocratic dignity expressed by

Dudley appeared among gentlemen occasionally, but they were not the prevailing opinion of how leading men should act.[38]

The willingness of prominent men to perform many kinds of labor does not indicate that social distinctions did not exist. Aside from data on the wealth of elected officials, records of how townsmen were seated in the meetinghouses provide the most direct evidence of how wealth affected status. Where a man sat at meeting was a symbolic indication of where he stood in the eyes of the community, and towns struggled hard to articulate rules that would define each man's place correctly. Ordinarily, seating a meetinghouse involved two separate decisions. First, the town had to decide how much of the floor space to devote to private pews, and distribute them among the leading men of the town. Then the town meeting "dignified" the public seats by declaring which were to carry the most prestige, and charged a committee to assign the inhabitants to seats according to a set of rules.[39] Seating rules involved three major components: age, the valuation of real and personal estate, and a category called "usefulness" or "honor," which involved service in public office and occasional special consideration for the first settlers of a town. The value of estates was an invariable component of rules for the assignment of both pews and seats, age was generally a criterion for seating, and usefulness was involved in a majority of cases. But no matter how these components were combined to form a rule, they seldom produced an undisputed assignment of places. Most towns found it necessary to appoint several committees and change the system for seating several times before a satisfactory arrangement could be achieved.

A good example of the problems encountered in seating was provided by the town of Bolton. In 1730, ten years after the town was incorporated, the voters decided to seat the meeting house properly, appointed a committee, and enacted one of the most complicated seating rules on record. Basically, the system depended on a series of calculations in pounds and shillings, with ages and places of honor assigned values in money. The first criterion was to be age, with men to be seated at age thirty and "Every year after to be called one Pound." Secondly, the town established public usefulness as a criterion by voting that "every Commission from the Governor Shal be Reckned Att five Pound"; and third, it voted to consider property according to the latest list, crediting only one poll to each man's account. When the committee reported a month later, however, the results were far from satisfactory. After some debate the town rejected the report and returned the committee to its deliberations, this time with instructions to order the seats according to their own discretion. This rule was more efficacious, and the committee's new report proved more to the town's liking.[40] Regardless of how precisely the rules for seating were explained, they were merely to serve as an expression of the voters' instinctive evaluations of each man's status.

Complicated rules for seating were often abandoned in favor of discretion, and even when they were ostensibly in force they were honored most often in the breach. Exactly how rules requiring "Due and Strict Regard" for the list of estates contributed to seating arrangements can be seen in the experiences of Watertown and Murrayfield, Massachusetts. When the east parish of Watertown set out to build pews in its meetinghouse in 1727, the town initially had difficulty establishing ground rules. The town voted to "have Regard to what Persons have disbursted and have Bin Rated as to Reall and Personall Estate for the Building of sd meetinghouse; and to have Regard to Persons of Honnour and Usefallness in Sd Precinct," but the report of the committee was rejected. A year later the town voted to reconsider; and after still another year and three more committees, a plan of the pews was entered in the records, based in theory on what each man had paid toward building the meeting house, but more likely on the prejudices of the voters. The nineteen pewholders ranged from first to seventy-fifth on that year's tax list.[41]

Three years later, in 1732, the town finally confronted the problem of seating the body of the meetinghouse, and, surprisingly, completed the project within two months. The rules were age and estates, and estate was clearly a secondary criterion, serving mainly to separate the members of an age group. All of the men born in the 1650s and 1660s sat in the front seat, and their estates ranged between twenty-first and one hundred-first.[42] Men born in the 1670s were seated in the second and third seats, along with a number of wealthier men born in the 1680s. Other men born between 1680 and 1700, most of whom were relatively poor, sat in the remaining four seats on the meetinghouse floor. Most of the younger and wealthier men in the precinct (born between 1680 and 1703, and including two members of the seating committee) sat in the front seats in the front and side galleries, which were officially equal to the third and fourth pews in dignity. Those in the front gallery ranked between the seventh and thirty-fourth places in the tax list, and those in the side gallery ranked between thirty-second and seventy-second. Younger and poorer men (all born after 1700) sat in the rear seats in the galleries. All of the older, retired leaders were accommodated in the pews, and all of the active leaders sat either in pews or in the first three seats. With one exception, all of the younger men who later became leaders sat in the front seats in the galleries. Despite the fact that "usefulness" was not listed as a seating rule in Watertown, public service and age were decisive in the seating arrangements, with wealth an important but less consistently applied factor.

Wealth played a similarly limited role in seating the meetinghouse in the new town of Murrayfield in 1773, despite the town's decision to make position on the valuation list the sole criterion.[43] Since the town was less than ten years old, it contained few really old people, and to all appearances few men of real prominence. Under these circumstances wealth might be expected to play a decisive role in status arrangements, but that clearly was not the case. Three deacons, all of whom ranked in the second quarter of the tax list, sat in the highest pew, followed by a group of moderately wealthy men. The highest taxpayer stood tenth on the list of seatings, the third taxpayer stood eighth, and three of the five men in the bottom two pews paid more in taxes than two of the deacons who headed the list. The seating system may have followed an evaluation of each man's usefulness in the town, but that is not clear because the town had been divided recently and the leadership was in flux.

Seating lists from two towns may seem a rather slim basis for describing the influence of wealth upon the most formal institutionalization of status in the New England colonies, but the votes and debates of other towns provide no reason for questioning their reliability. Wealth was but one of three often-articulated criteria for estimating status, and when a town voted flatly to seat the house according to the rate list, a wise seating committee took the instructions with a grain of salt. Towns did not vote to reseat at every redrawing of the tax list, but only when changes in the town or the building of a new meetinghouse made old arrangements unsatisfactory.[44] Reseating committees sought to approximate the town's intuitive evaluation of each man's status, and both age and public service figured prominently in the formal calculations. Towns that voted to raise money for the new meetinghouse by selling pews usually intended to make sure that the buyers were suitable persons, just as they retained the right to proper representation when they voted to elect a representative who would serve without pay.[45] Injunctions to seating committees to search the tax list did not mean that status was in such flux that high status went automatically to the richest men.[46] Most men in prestigious seats were wealthy, but towns like Watertown had acknowledged leaders who ranked high even when they were relatively poor. Wealth was a contributing factor to the status of the leading men, although position on the tax list was most crucial when the towns sought to distinguish among middle- and lower-class individuals whose relative status was not so clearly defined.

Wealth, then, influenced the selection of town leaders and the social stratification of the towns in two significant ways. First of all, wealth was a factor in establishing a man's overall status in the community. Towns differed widely in the degree to which property was concentrated in a few hands, and in the overall amount of wealth at the disposal of their inhabitants. These factors did not directly affect the proportion of the population that contributed leaders, but as later correlations between the data on the leader pools and the economic structure will show, they did influence the patterns of town politics. Wealth enabled some men to devote time to acquiring the personal contacts and educational polish that were associated with social and political eminence, while relative poverty limited the ability of other men to gain high status, and especially their ability to establish and maintain prestige on a family basis.

Few town leaders were aristocrats, however, even in a comparative sense, and personal wealth also had the more limited function of defining a sort of threshold standard of living above which men were eligible for major public office. Men of substantial property were most able to spare the time necessary for unpaid public service, and they were preeminently qualified in ideological terms to be the independent freeholders upon whom the political culture of the period placed such a heavy value. Most town leaders ranked above a point about a quarter of the way down the tax list, and a much smaller number ranked below that point because town leadership was a financial strain as well as a source of prestige and personal satisfaction.

·4·

THE INFLUENCE OF FAMILY

In a famous passage in his *Defense of the Constitutions*, John Adams attempted to explain the differences in political influence among the inhabitants of his native province, linking the influence of wealth as a source of distinctions with that of family prestige. Great wealth, he said, inspired a degree of admiration and respect that engendered disproportionate influence, while "children of illustrious families" enjoyed advantages in education and acquaintance with public affairs as well as in the "habitual national veneration for their names." As a result, he asserted, the principal offices in every New England town had "generally descended from generation to generation, in three or four families at most."[1] Adams's comments on the influence of wealth, of course, greatly simplified a complex subject, and his comments on family have not met with universal acceptance. Some historians have supported Adams's deferential thesis, but others have advanced arguments about "middle-class democracy" and "consensual communalism" to deny the existence of stable and acknowledged elite groups.[2]

Firm conclusions about the role of family relationships in qualifying men to be local leaders require substantive investigation of the demographic and genealogical characteristics of the town elites, as well as consideration of the scattered records and documents that revealed how the townsmen regarded the leading families. Analysis of the proportion of the surnames in a town represented among its leaders provides an indication of the influence of family, in a comparatively broad sense, on elections, while tabulation of the frequency with which sons succeeded their fathers in the pool of town leaders provides evidence of the influence of family in a narrower sense. Examination of the age structure of the leader pool clarifies the extent to which sons could succeed their fathers in office directly and the extent to which leaders in each generation were chosen from among eligible men in a restricted age bracket. And finally, evaluation of the early age at which men of eventual eminence first became town leaders supports a discussion of the extent to which deference to "illustrious families" influenced the political decisions of the New England towns.

95

An initial step in establishing the influence of family on the selection of town leaders is to measure the amount of family continuity in each town from generation to generation, but such measurements are far easier to propose than to carry out. Assertions such as John Adams's that three or four families dominated each town are basically untestable because "family" is so hard to define. A family might mean the nuclear family of husband, wife, and children; it might include the members of an "extended family" of several generations living under one roof; or it could encompass all the members of a community with a common surname and even those with other names who were related by marriage. In terms of actual experience, moreover, family is even harder to define, because to any man his family includes those with whom he perceives some tie of kinship and excludes those with whom he shares no such feeling, regardless of the actual genealogical details.

After a lapse of two hundred years, historians are hard pressed to reconstruct the genealogical relationships in any community, and the perceptual complications are almost wholly beyond reach. One method of coping with these difficulties is to use more than one measure of family continuity. A measure that considers all persons with a common surname as one family provides a fairly broad degree of inclusiveness, although it risks sweeping unrelated persons with the same surname (for example, Smith) into a single family, and might prove absolutely meaningless in a small community in which everyone is at least vaguely related to everyone else. By contrast a measurement of strict father-son continuity makes allowance for the possibility that the effective family unit may have been small, while risking a certain amount of leakage in the cases of men who made brothers, nephews, or other relatives their political heirs when they lacked sons, or at least sons of suitable ability.

An index of the first sort is one that tabulates the number of surnames among a town's leaders over the first eighty-five years of the eighteenth century, and then relates that total to the number of surnames in the whole population of town taxpayers. Among the thirty towns for which the necessary data is available, two distinct patterns emerge (Table 13).[3] One group of towns, most of which had populations of more than a thousand by the end of the period, had 40 percent or less of the towns' families represented among the leaders. About a third of the families produced leaders in most substantial towns, and the proportion fell as low as 17 to 20 percent in large and economically stratified towns like Portsmouth and Springfield. A few unusual small towns, like Hadley and its recently separated daughter-town Amherst, or Manchester, with its stratified society of well-to-do farmer-merchants and poor fishermen, also had low percentages of leader-producing families.

Most small towns, on the other hand, included members of 40 percent or more of the resident families among their leaders. In one group of small but

TABLE THIRTEEN

Participation by Patrimonial Groupings

Town	1 Names in Taxlist	2 Names in List of Leaders	3 Column 2 as % of Column 1
Amherst	71	28	39.4
Andover	131	29	22.1
Billerica	122	41	33.6
Boxford	87	46	52.9
Brookline	57	27	47.4
Cambridge	168	57	33.9
Dedham	133	40	30.1
Fitchburg	50	24	48.0
Hadley	77	29	37.7
Manchester	91	32	35.2
Medfield	79	45	56.9
Norton	110	43	39.1
Oakham	62	28	45.2
Springfield	214	38	17.3
Sudbury	162	59	36.4
Topsfield	75	35	46.7
Bedford	74	32	43.2
Concord	92	24	26.1
Derryfield	58	32	55.2
Dover	138	56	40.6
New Ipswich	137	26	18.9
Portsmouth	400	84	21.0
Exeter	139	45	32.4
Providence	264	88	33.3
South Kingstown	161	38	23.6
Bolton	103	30	29.1
Kent	182	37	20.3
New Haven	321	90	28.0
Newtown	103	56	54.4
Woodbury	272	52	19.1

long-established towns typified by Boxford and Medfield, well over half of the local families shared the major offices, and even in frontier towns with more mobile populations nearly half of the families produced leaders. Only one town with over a thousand souls revealed a proportion of leadership families much over 40 percent, and that town, Newtown, was the sort of exception that proves the rule because it behaved in every respect but population like the towns of the Boxford-Medfield group.[4]

In light of figures that show participation by members of 20 to 70 percent of each town's families in the local leadership, the definition of family as a group with a common surname clearly does not support the assertion that three or four families monopolized the offices in each town. But as suggested before, other factors indicate that that definition of "family" by itself is not entirely satisfactory. Close examination of the tax lists reveals that most of the common-surname families that were substantially established in a town produced at least one leader during the century and that most of the surnames that went unrepresented in the list of leaders belonged to transient taxpayers, often servants, or to members of very small and marginal families. Concentrations of leaders and service, then, are the essence of family power rather than mere token representation, but even if the percentage of all offices held by men with a given surname was tabulated, the results would be inconclusive as long as members of common-surname families were separated by five to seven generations by the time of the Revolution, intermarried with each other freely, and showed no awareness of special kinship relations. Figures on broad family groups must be supplemented by figures narrowly derived from the study of father-son relationships to yield more conclusive results.

While the figures on broad family groupings indicated that no town conferred all its offices on a small number of families, data on father-to-son continuity in officeholding reveals that the political benefit to be derived from having a prominent father was considerable, especially in certain towns. Because of the complexities involved in relating the number of leaders' sons who held office, their length of service, and the corresponding information on the general leader pools in towns of differing size, variations in father-to-son continuity cannot be expressed in an index, and it can be summarized only partially in a table. Furthermore, such generational continuity cannot be studied effectively in towns less than two generations old at the end of the period under consideration, and many additional towns have left insufficient genealogical information. When all of the data on family is considered for a group of fifteen towns that seems generally representative of the larger sample, however, four distinct patterns of town behavior emerge (Table 14).[5]

First of all, in urban towns like Boston and Portsmouth, family continuity was a minor factor in leadership selection. Only 7 percent of the leaders in Boston and only 21 percent of the leaders in Portsmouth were sons of other leaders, and a large majority of the leaders in each town were the only representatives of their family name to hold major office. Family political dynasties, like that of the Cushing family in Boston, did exist, and sons of leaders served more terms on the average than the other leaders, but the total service of the established political families represented only a small percentage of the total number of terms.* Major offices in the cities went overwhelmingly to the current merchant princes and to the leaders of popular political factions, many of whom were recent immigrants or newly risen to prominence.

*Thomas Cushing (1663-1740) and his son and grandson of the same name (1694-1746 and 1724-88) served twenty-one terms as selectman, thirty-seven terms as representative, and eighteen terms as moderator between 1707 and 1778. Each was Speaker of the House of Representatives in turn. Shipton, *Sibley's Harvard Graduates* (Boston, 1933-72), 5: 568-74; Ibid., 11: 377-95.

TABLE FOURTEEN

Comparative Service by Sons of Leaders

Town	# of Leaders	# of Leaders' Surnames	Average Terms	# of Sons	Sons' Average Terms	Sons as % of all Leaders
Andover	102	29	7.4	40	8.5	39.2
Boston	180	148	7.8	12	10.6	6.6
Cambridge	108	57	8.3	22	11.3	20.4
Dedham	94	40	7.6	24	7.2	27.7
Grafton	92	51	4.5	29	4.5	31.5
Hadley	127	29	6.3	59	6.2	46.5
Medfield	140	45	5.6	50	4.9	35.7
Springfield	105	38	8.4	31	12.7	29.5
South Kingstown	112	38	7.2	42	7.8	37.5
Bolton	53	30	10.1	12	4.8	22.6
Emfield	75	31	11.2	22	15.2	29.3
Stonington	125	48	8.0	39	11.6	31.2
Chester	79	58	4.0	14	4.4	17.7
Hampton	155	61	4.5	49	6.5	31.6
Portsmouth	120	84	6.3	25	6.8	20.8

Family continuity was of equally limited significance in towns at the other end of the social spectrum, the small, egalitarian farming communities. Sons of leaders often became leaders in towns like Medfield, Grafton, or Bolton; but so did virtually every other reasonably prosperous and capable individual. Grafton, Bolton, and Chester, a similar town, had high percentages of different surnames among the town leaders, while in the older village of Medfield the offices were widely divided among the numerous branches of the local families. Sons of leaders showed no tendency toward long service in these towns. In Medfield, for example, 50 of 140 leaders were sons of leaders, but no son served more than nine years as a selectman and only 4 served more than 10 terms in all major offices combined. As a group they served an average of 4.9 terms, somewhat less than the average of 5.6 terms for all of the leaders. A similar situation existed in Grafton, where only one of 29 leaders who were leaders' sons served 20 terms, making him a prominent personage. Overall, the 29 averaged 4.5 terms apiece, a figure virtually indistinguishable from the general average of 4.46. This pattern of limited family continuity in office existed in newly settled towns as well as in the more established towns discussed here, although on the frontier the willingness to elect newcomers to office was an aspect of the town's recent settlement and not a significant feature of a developed political structure.

In contrast to the patterns in the largest and the smallest towns, family continuity was an important element in the politics of most moderate- and large-sized towns. Generally these towns divided into two groups. In towns of the first type, leaders' sons were relatively numerous in the overall group of leaders, but did not necessarily serve more terms on an average than the other leaders. Instead, the crucial distinction was not between leaders' sons and nonleaders' sons, but between the members of six to eight prominent families, or branches of families, and the men of other, less favored lineage. In Dedham, for example, the town conferred high office on the three successive eldest sons in the Avery family, the Daniel Fisher branch of the Fisher family, the Joseph Ellis family, and the Nathaniel Gay family, and on the senior members of the Metcalf family, whose genealogy was complicated by the presence of two lifelong bachelors in the officeholding branch.[6] Other families, like the Richards and the Fales, were as numerous as any of the leading ones, and often as wealthy, but no Fales ever became a leader, and the only Richards to achieve that distinction was a college graduate and ultimately a provincial figure by virtue of his marriage to Governor Dudley's granddaughter.[7]

Similar groups of hereditary elite families existed in towns like Andover and South Kingstown. The Andover records reveal no fewer than sixteen cases in which father, son, and grandson were all town leaders in the Farnum, Frye, Osgood, Stevens, and two Abbott families during the first eighty-five years of the eighteenth century. These families were among eleven family groups in the town that produced ten or more taxpayers consistently throughout the century, and together accounted for 76 percent of the towns' leaders.[8] Even among the most prominent families, however, leaders were not evenly distributed; the Abbotts, with twenty-five to thirty-five taxpayers each year, provided twenty-six leaders over the century, while the second largest family, the Holts, with fifteen to twenty-five taxpayers, provided only one.*

All of the leading families in towns like Dedham and Andover were yeomen, or apparent yeomen who styled themselves gentlemen, but the same sort of multifamilied elite could be made up of more aristocratic individuals. South Kingstown's government was largely managed by interrelated gentlemen of the Gardner, Hazard, Helme, Niles, Potter, Robinson, and Watson families, who accounted for 70 percent of all the town's terms in major office and among them produced thirty-one leaders who were leaders' sons.[9] As evidence of their higher status, these families also produced three deputy governors and twelve assistants of Rhode Island, as well as numerous judges, militia colonels, and justices of the peace.

Unlike South Kingstown, however, the town elites of most country towns that produced especially prominent leaders were dominated by a single officeholding family. In Cambridge, for example, three successive Andrew Boardmans served as town clerk and town treasurer almost continuously from 1700 to 1779, and served a total of 93 terms as selectman, representative, and moderator into the bargain. Similarly, John Chandler of Worcester and his two sons served 149 terms in major offices between 1733 and 1775, and nine members of the Pynchon family served 24.5 percent of all the leadership terms in Springfield.[10] All of these towns were county seats, but the same pattern existed in other important country towns. The Leonards of Norton filled 22 percent of the offices in that town and the Partridges filled 29 percent of the offices in Hatfield.

Leaders' sons in such towns did not compose an especially large proportion of the pool of leaders, and except for the members of the great family did not provide especially long service. In Springfield, for example, the leaders' sons averaged 12.7 terms each, 4 terms above the general average when all families are considered, but only 7.8 terms when the eight descendents of Colonel John Pynchon are omitted. Similarly, the inclusion of the sons of the Boardman family raises the average service of the sons of Cambridge town leaders from 5.8 terms to 11.3 terms, in comparison with an average of 8.3 terms for all leaders. The predominant influence of a single family in the affairs of towns like Cambridge, Worcester, and Springfield was all the more remarkable because Cambridge as a college town, and the other towns as

---

*By comparison, family concentrations among officeholders were much less extensive in egalitarian Medfield. In that much smaller town the Adams, Allen, Ellis, Morse, Plimpton, Smith, Turner, and Wight families averaged five or more taxpayers on the 1697 and 1771 tax lists and accounted for 44 percent of the town's population and for 53 percent of the town leaders.

county seats, attracted large numbers of lawyers, merchants, and other educated and able men. Cambridge drew men like Councillor Samuel Danforth and Attorney-General Edmund Trowbridge into town politics, and Springfield elected Judge Josiah Dwight and Councillor John Worthington to an impressive number of local offices, but such men were never able to challenge the special position of the leading family in the confidence of the voters either by establishing parallel dynasties or by transforming town politics into a genuinely open arena.

Both in terms of the service of leaders' sons and in terms of the broader family measure of common surnames, the role of family relationships in the selection of town leaders varied from town to town. In some towns a large percentage of the families with common surnames produced leaders, and the likelihood that sons of prominent leaders would became leaders in due course was limited. In other towns the leaders accounted for only a small percentage of the surnames in the town, and sons in one or more prominent families routinely succeeded their fathers as town leaders. And finally, in the largest towns the leaders came from only a small percentage of the towns' families, but recruitment was open and sons rarely succeeded their fathers in town office. Life in a town dominated by three or four of John Adams's "illustrious families" was the experience of some New Englanders, but it was not a universal situation.

Closely related to the study of family continuity in town office is an examination of the age at which the towns usually recognized men as leaders. Modern students from Sir Lewis Namier to the recent historians of the New England towns have found in the officeholding patterns for many local and even parliamentary offices in England one model for the relationship between family influence and access to high office: an oligarchial model in which access was severely limited and sons entered office as soon after attaining their majorities as the electoral details permitted, considerations of ability and efficiency notwithstanding.[11] Where such a pattern of behavior existed family influence was indeed extreme, and if examples of that sort of influence existed in eighteenth-century New England, they would be revealing. For a contrary opinion of the necessity for age and experience as qualifications for high office, however, one need look no further than the United States Constitution, which, drawing on the experience and beliefs of Americans, prescribed age qualifications that increased with the responsibility of the office. Age qualifications indicated a desire to ensure that political officials possessed a degree of experience and mature judgment, and marked, whether they were prescribed by custom or enacted by law, a political system in which social status played a less distinct role in influencing electoral decisions. The degree to which age qualifications applied to the holders of local office in New England, therefore, is one measure of how powerfully ascriptive family status influenced the political structure.

Four kinds of statistics contribute to an understanding of the age qualifications expected of town officials, figures on the age at which the average selectman entered the town leadership, detailed distributions of age at first service for all selectmen in sample towns, comprehensive listings of all selectmen who began to serve at the age of thirty-five and under, and finally data on the average age of last service and on the unusual cases in which a generation of leaders precipitated conflict in their town by refusing to step aside when the leaders of the next generation sought to replace them. In the fifty-one towns for which the age data on selectmen is reasonably complete, the average age at first service was 42.7 years, and since a large majority of the town leaders served first as selectmen, that figure provides an effective minimum for the average of the leadership as a whole (Table 15).[12] Averages for the individual towns ranged from a low of 37 recorded in Weare to a high of 51 in Gorham, and except for the fact that six of the eight towns with averages below 40 were small, the respective averages do not suggest a meaningful pattern of variation.[13] The mythical average selectman in virtually every town was middle-aged when he began his service.

The usefulness of averaged figures, of course, varies with the spread of the data they summarize, but in the case of the selectmen's ages a series of sample distributions suggests that the concentration in the middle years was sufficient to give the mean real validity.[14] Detailed accounting of the ages at which selectmen first served in a dozen towns with exceptionally complete data shows that clear majorities of the selectmen in ten towns began serving between the ages of thirty-five and forty-nine, which is to say in a fifteen-year period bracketing the overall average of forty-two (Table 16).[15] New leaders in that age group composed 53 percent of the total recruitment in Hardwick, where five of the nine very young men had served in the town's first two years, and up to 82 percent in Billerica where the pattern of middle-aged leadership was most undeviating. Most towns had substantial minorities at the ends of the age spectrum, but the group that began its service when aged over fifty was generally larger than the group at the opposite extreme, and in terms of age qualifications constituted a much less significant deviation from the dominant pattern.[16]

The substantial clustering of ages around the mean value indicates that selection of middle-aged leaders was the generally accepted practice, although as presented it does not establish the existence of a normative age qualification for town leadership. Clearly, however, the emergence of town leaders in their middle years relates to the practice, discussed in Chapter 2, of subjecting potential leaders to an apprenticeship in lesser offices and to the requirement, described in Chapter 3, that unpaid leaders be able to bear the financial strains of public service. These aspects of the system for selecting leaders served essentially the same purpose as an age qualification, to assure election of men of mature judgment and financial probity; and together they provide justification for interpreting the frequent selection of middle-aged

TABLE FIFTEEN

Average Age at First and Last Service

Town	% of Men for whom data are complete	Average Age at First Service					Average Age at Last Service
		1710-24	1725-49	1750-74	1775-84	1710-74	
Amherst	91	-	-	41	41	41	49
Andover	94	48	48	43	44	45	54
Barnstable	78	-	39	42	45	42	53
Barrington	100	54	44	-	-	49	56
Billerica	95	45	44	43	44	44	53
Boston	64	42	46	43	61	44	51
Boxford	85	40	37	40	42	38	49
Brookline	81	47	43	46	40	45	53
Cambridge	88	48	43	49	45	45	53
Dedham	96	47	49	42	48	45	52
Dorchester	94	46	45	45	42	45	54
Duxbury	73	46	48	48	44	47	55
Grafton	76	-	44	43	40	43	50
Hadley	95	44	47	42	41	44	53
Hanover	92	-	47	44	43	45	49
Hardwick	90	-	40	45	44	42	51
Hatfield	80	44	39	40	53	40	56
Leicester	68	-	41	44	38	43	51
Lunenburg	86	-	37	45	36	40	49
Manchester	80	36	37	39	41	37	47
Medfield	96	45	46	41	42	43	51
Oakham	71	-	-	43	37	42	43
Shirley	84	-	-	40	40	40	44
Sudbury	75	43	49	46	44	46	53
Swansea	80	45	44	46	49	45	51
Springfield	87	45	48	49	50	46	56
Topsfield	90	42	41	43	44	42	49
Waltham	95	-	49	48	40	48	51
Watertown	89	44	45	47	40	45	53
Westminster	98	-	-	39	43	39	47
Worcester	87	45	44	41	45	42	49
Gorham	82	-	-	51	42	51	51
Cornish	83	-	-	38	41	38	43
Dover	68	48	41	40	35	41	49
Dublin	85	-	-	43	35	42	42
Hampstead	85	-	-	44	39	43	47
Hampton	95	43	44	42	41	43	52
Londonderry	49	39	38	40	39	39	45
New Ipswich	82	-	-	38	46	39	45
Portsmouth	72	39	37	43	37	38	47
Weare	79	-	-	37	38	37	41
Newport	62	45	45	45	65	45	58
Providence	81	49	42	43	43	43	50
Smithfield	80	-	42	43	45	42	49
S. Kingstown	85	49	37	42	41	41	49

men as evidence of such a qualification. Only the demonstration that young men became leaders in substantial numbers and under normal circumstances would tend to undermine that interpretation.

Since the size and composition of the group of very young leaders provide the clearest evidence for evaluating the normative significance of the

TABLE FIFTEEN: Continued

Average Age at First and Last Service

Town	% of Men for whom data are complete	Average Age at First Service					Average Age at Last Service
		1710-24	1725-49	1750-74	1775-84	1710-74	
Bolton	90	50	41	49	47	46	54
Derby	70	39	38	45	41	41	49
Enfield	73	40	41	39	43	40	52
New Haven	94	43	44	43	46	43	50
Stonington	87	41	43	45	45	43	52
Woodbury	76	-	44	43	38	43	47

apparent pattern of middle-aged officeholding and for determining whether family influence, social status, or other meaningful factors provided the basis for deviation from the probable norm, the young town leaders deserve close attention. Men who served their first term at the age of thirty-five or less comprised 570 of the 3,845 selectmen in fifty-one towns with good age data, or about 14 percent (Tables 17, 18).[17] This was a comparatively small group, and its significance is further diminished by the unequal distribution of young town leaders from decade to decade and from town to town, in patterns that suggest that youthful leaders were exceptional in most towns at most times.

When the list of youthful selectmen is broken down by decade, it shows that men thirty-five years old and younger entered the leader pool rapidly during the first decades of the century and during the early 1780s, and much more slowly during the intervening years. An average of more than 3 young men became selectmen for each town in existence from 1700 to 1709, and about 2.5 young men became selectmen for each town studied during the 1780s, while in the intervening years the rate of entry never exceeded 1.7 men per town per decade. The first decade of the century was a period of rapid change in town government, as town after town adopted new and more elaborate procedures for handling broad-based political participation, and according to Kenneth Lockridge and Alan Kreider, as the towns replaced their seventeenth-century patriarchs with new, untried, and, apparently in some instances, very young men.[18] The young men entering town office during this period were not only numerous, but were also slightly more ordinary individuals than would be true in succeeding decades. Only 23 percent qualified as "prominent men," that is, members of famous families, college graduates, or men who made their way into offices above town level.

After 1710 the number of young town leaders diminished, and the percentage who were prominent climbed steadily until, at mid-century, it reached a third of the total number. Overall rates of entry hovered around 1.5 men per decade per town, which meant that most towns in most years had no one under thirty-five on the board of selectmen, especially in view of the fact

TABLE SIXTEEN

Age of First Leadership Service

Town	% under 35	% 35-39	% 40-44	% 45-49	% 50-54	% 55 and over	% 35-49	# of leaders
Amherst	20.0	12.5	32.5	12.5	20.0	2.5	57.5	40
Andover	9.0	15.4	19.2	28.2	15.4	12.8	62.8	78
Billerica	1.6	25.8	25.8	30.6	11.3	4.8	82.0	62
Dorchester	7.0	25.0	22.9	14.6	14.6	12.5	62.5	43
Hadley	13.3	19.4	24.5	20.4	9.2	13.3	73.9	98
Hardwick	20.9	20.9	9.3	23.3	18.6	7.0	53.3	43
Medfield	13.0	13.9	19.4	26.9	9.3	8.3	61.2	98
Dublin	40.0	20.0	6.7	6.7	6.7	20.0	33.4	16
Hampton	16.5	24.7	19.6	12.4	15.5	11.3	56.7	97
S. Kingstown	42.5	22.5	13.8	13.8	3.8	3.8	50.1	80
New Haven	7.9	18.5	29.2	22.5	13.5	8.4	70.2	178
Stonington	19.5	18.4	16.1	27.6	11.5	8.0	62.1	94

TABLE SEVENTEEN

Temporal Distribution of Entry of Selectmen Aged 35 Years and Under

Decade	Men	Prominent Men	% Prominent	# of Existing Towns	Men per Year	Men per Town per Decade
1700-09	86	20	23.3	28	8.6	3.07
1710-19	37	9	24.3	30	3.7	1.23
1720-29	57	14	24.6	38	5.7	1.50
1730-39	67	18	28.4	41	6.7	1.63
1740-49	52	18	34.6	42	5.2	1.24
1750-59	71	22	31.0	43	7.1	1.65
1760-69	59	13	22.0	49	5.9	1.20
1770-79	82	15	18.3	50	8.2	1.64
1780-84	59	6	10.2	48	11.8	2.46
1700-84	570	135	23.7	51	6.7	1.31

that the majority of those who did begin young clustered near the upper age limit (see Table 18). Recruitment of young men revived only in the 1780s, presumably because of the increased demands on public servants and possibly because of increased opportunity for young men to gain experience in responsible positions in the military. Then the rate of entry increased sharply to 2.5 men per town per decade, and the number of prominent men among the new young leaders declined, although the exact figures are suspect because colonial civil lists and biographical dictionaries of college graduates do not continue uniformly into the revolutionary era as a source of comparable data.

TABLE EIGHTEEN

Distribution of Ages of Entry for Selectmen Aged 35 and Under

Age	Mass.	N.H.	Conn.	R.I.	Total	%	Cumulative %
35	59	20	11	6	96	16.8	16.8
34	56	22	10	6	94	16.5	33.3
33	39	10	13	6	68	11.9	45.2
32	35	18	13	9	75	13.2	58.4
31	34	15	12	6	67	11.8	70.2
30	33	13	8	2	56	9.8	80.0
29	13	8	3	3	27	4.7	84.7
28	17	11	3	3	34	6.0	90.7
27	6	8	1	1	16	2.8	93.5
26	9	3	1	1	14	2.5	96.0
25	6	1	0	1	8	1.4	97.4
24	5	1	1	0	7	1.2	98.6
23	2	3	0	1	6	1.0	99.6
22	0	1	0	0	1	0.2	99.8
21	1	0	0	0	1	0.2	100.0

Just as young men were not uniformly important in the recruitment of town leaders from decade to decade, their numbers varied significantly from town to town. Hypothetically, towns could elect young men to office for three sorts of reasons: first, because they placed little or no reliance on age qualifications; second, because they were so short of manpower that whatever age qualifications existed became inoperative; or third, because the particular young men in question were exempted from a general age qualification because of family influence, educational qualification, or exceptional ability. In fact, all three explanations were valid in one group of towns or another, although the third one was clearly the most important.

The first explanation, relative absence of age qualifications, deserves careful attention for a group of eight to ten towns of the sample fifty-one. Many of these towns, like Boxford, Grafton, and Medfield, have appeared in one context or another as representative of an egalitarian pattern of behavior, and all seem to share that characteristic.[19] Usually small, usually unstratified in wealth, often with little family continuity and rapid rotation in office, these towns seemingly regarded their offices as burdens to be shared as widely as possible. All were basically agricultural towns, and since none had very large populations or especially complex economic or political functions, the responsibilities of major town office were not extensive. Such towns seemingly had little need to enforce qualifications designed to ensure the election of the most mature and experienced men to high office, but the evidence fails to show that they did much more than relax slightly the common practice of electing middle-aged men. Together the towns chose 16.3 percent of their town leaders from men who were thirty-five or younger, only slightly above the overall average, while only 11.8 percent of these, far below the general average, rose above their fellow townsmen in prominence. The small number of young leaders indicates that the egalitarian towns preferred older men, although the voters' willingness to consider young men, and ordinary ones at that, suggests that the informal age qualification was only weakly enforced.

A second group of nine towns clearly elected young men to the board of selectmen because they lacked a large enough population to demand leaders of mature years and still fill their offices.[20] These were essentially frontier towns, newly settled and sparsely populated. About a quarter (25.3 percent) of their selectmen began their service as young men, and only a small minority of these (7.2 percent) ever became prominent. In some cases family groups of a father and several grown sons settled a town and father and son served simultaneously on the first board of selectmen. In Cornish, for example, four of five members of the first board were Chases: Samuel, aged sixty; his younger brother Moses, aged forty; and Samuel's sons Dudley, thirty-seven, and Jonathan, thirty-five. Eight of the nine frontier towns studied, all incorporated after 1750, were in this stage of development, while the ninth, Hardwick, illustrates that the leadership did not necessarily remain open to young men once the town had passed the frontier stage. In Hardwick's first two years, 1737 and 1738, five men under thirty-five dominated the board of selectmen. The five remained in office year after year until they compiled an average of twenty-six years of service in major town office, and in the ensuing forty years Hardwick chose only two young men to the board, both relatives of the original five, and both men of prominence. On the frontier young men served as a matter of necessity, and their service reveals little about how the town would behave later when more men were present to broaden the range of choice.

For the largest group of sample towns, young leaders were clearly men who were exempted from the age qualifications required of others because of their status or abilities. In contrast to the figures for the distinctly egalitarian towns and for the frontier towns, men of known prominence made up nearly 35 percent of the youthful selectmen in this third group of towns. Another 22 percent of the young men were prominent within the confines of their town, serving more than ten terms in major office, and a further 9 percent were not prominent in their own right, but apparently owed their early election to their father's leadership status. All told, two-thirds of the young leaders elected in this third group of towns are attributable to demonstrated ability, family status, or a combination of the two.

The special claim of the youthful candidates, rather than the low percentage of young selectmen, was the distinguishing feature of this group of towns. The combined percentage of selectmen in the lower age bracket remained at 12.4 percent, only moderately below the average for the whole sample because the percentages for individual towns varied widely. At one end of the spectrum were towns like Billerica, which elected only four young men, all in their mid-thirties and two of them future justices, and Barnstable, which chose only three thirty-four-year-olds, including a college graduate and a future judge and councillor. Such towns held strictly to the practice of selecting middle-aged leaders, and made exceptions only for men with unusual credentials. At the other end were communities like Portsmouth, with its twenty-three youthful leaders, including thirteen who became high provincial officials and six who were sons of very prominent men, and South Kingstown, where eighteen members of the local gentry became selectmen at early ages, often as a stepping stone into the colony's elite. These towns frequently overlooked age as an indication of suitable experience for young men with the right connections, but required more ordinary townsmen to meet the normal standards for election.

As study of the minority of leaders who became selectmen in their early years confirms, the normal practice in eighteenth-century New England was to elect middle-aged town leaders, and for most men that practice was so strict as to constitute an unwritten age qualification. Given this requirement, careers in town politics had a predictable rhythm. Until his middle thirties, an aspiring town leader served his town in the minor offices, if at all, while devoting most of his time to a growing family and, he hoped, a growing estate. Then, as he approached middle age, a man became eligible for the responsible town offices that served as a practice ground for potential leaders, and finally, if his service proved satisfactory, he could expect to become a leader sometime before his fiftieth year.

Implicit in the kind of typical career in town office sketched above, however, is the expectation that as each generation reached middle age the preceding one would step aside and make a respectable quota of major offices available to aspiring leaders of suitable experience and wealth. By and large, such transitions did occur and took place smoothly. On the average, leaders last served at the age of 50.2, and town averages varied from 41 in new and highly mobile Weare to 58 in more stable Newport (see Table 15). More important than such figures were the average ages of the men in office each year from decade to decade. In Dorchester, for example, five-year averages ranged erratically from 44 to 54 years, in Hatfield the range was from 44 to 55, in South Kingstown it was from 39 to 55, and in Stonington it was from 44 to 52. As these examples suggest, average ages on the board rose and fell as younger men succeeded older ones in a natural, haphazard pattern.[21]

Exactly how most leaders felt about giving way after relatively short careers cannot be known, although some must have been glad to retire to the status of elder statesmen and others must have left office unwillingly. One town leader, James Blake of Dorchester, complained bitterly of his replacement as town clerk at the age of sixty-one, charging that the measure had been carried "by a discontented Factious party," although he was bedridden and unable to attend meetings.[22]

More important to the political system, however, was the discontent among younger men that arose when veteran leaders refused to give way. Dedham, for example, was particularly slow in developing a system of gradual replacement of leaders, and twice in forty years Dedham exploded into contention as one generation of leaders fought to displace its predecessor. First, in 1689 that town replaced all its experienced selectmen, most of whom were born between 1620 and 1630, with men born between 1645 and 1655, and never elected the older men to office again.[23] Then the generation of the 1640s and 1650s remained in office overlong, excluding the men born in the 1660s from their turn in the major offices, and finally gave way to a group born in the 1670s. It was consequently no accident that, when the contentious movement to incorporate the outlying parts of Dedham as separate precincts began in the 1720s, resentful men born during the 1660s and their sons born after 1680 who anticipated sharing their fathers' fate were in the forefront of the agitation.[24]

The smooth and steady cycle of movement into office in early middle age and departure from office as old age approached that characterized the careers of the majority of ordinary, locally influential town leaders reveals much about the day-to-day social assumptions underlying New England town politics. When choosing leaders from among themselves, the voters preferred to elect men of mature years, substantial experience in public service, and visible success in private business. This preference extended not only to the sons of ordinary townsmen, but also to the sons of most leaders, so that when family dynasties appeared among ordinary yeoman town leaders, they were rooted in the repeated ability of family members to demonstrate their fitness to serve. For most town leaders election to major office depended on personal achievement rather than inherited status.

Most aspiring town leaders could expect to make their own way in town politics, but that expectation was not shared by the minority hitherto labeled "prominent." Men with distinguished ancestors, or with personal reputations reaching beyond the towns' borders, contributed a sizable proportion of the leaders who began to serve in their twenties and early thirties; and in view of both the relatively small numbers of prominent individuals in most towns and the concentration of the prominent young leaders in the larger, more established towns, the number of prominent men who began their careers as leaders at an early age provides grounds for supposing that different social assumptions governed the political participation of the prominent. Before concluding that election on the basis of personal achievement and open access to office were universally dominant aspects of the political system, therefore, examination of the recruitment of prominent individuals into local politics is necessary.

An effective way of identifying prominent individuals in each town is to count the resident judges, justices of the peace, councillors, and those college graduates who held major town office. The list of province- and county-level officials comprises those who held high political office in a society that used official position as a measure of social status, including those who achieved their position by their own efforts as well as those who inherited their status. A list of college graduates, on the other hand, includes those whose placement in society was aided by acquisition of a liberal education, together with the attendant advantage of contacts throughout the New England elite.[25] By comparing the career patterns of men whose prominence is measured in ultimate success with those of men whose prominence resulted from educational achievement, and by isolating the subgroups in both areas whose status was materially aided by familial prominence, it becomes possible to estimate the relative advantages in elite selection of ability and educational qualifications on the one hand, and of birth and elite social connections on the other.

An initial examination of the data on the age of entry of prominent men to town service in sixty-nine sample towns confirms that the electoral pattern for prominent men differed from the general pattern for town leaders. Whereas the overall group of leaders entered their first major office at an average age of 42.7 years, a group that might be termed the provincial elite began to serve at an average age of 35.2 years, a significantly lower figure (Table 19).[26] This low average age at entry into service, combined with the high percentage of prominent men among the very young leaders, illustrates the way in which elite members clustered at the bottom end of the distribution of ages. The largest numbers of elite members entered the pool of leaders during their early thirties, while the curve for ordinary leaders peaked in the early forties.

This pattern of early selection indicated that town electors were able to identify future elite members at a very early stage in their careers, even though elite status (as defined here) depended most often on performance in offices held later in a man's life. Such an ability to predict success was all the more remarkable because prospective elite figures assumed leadership in town politics with little or no apprenticeship background in minor offices. Few men in colonial New England were settled enough to hold any office until after their middle twenties, so that when potentially prominent men like the Otises of Barnstable, the Pynchons of Springfield, or the Hazards of South Kingstown became selectmen or representatives at the age of twenty-eight or thirty, the office was usually their first town position. Consequently, provincial offices were not filled by the most experienced and successful town officials in open competition; instead, those destined for higher office became town leaders at a tender age as a result of the same process of pre-selection that fated them for the higher positions.

Exactly what the distinctive electoral treatment of leading men meant in social terms depends, of course, on an understanding of the voters' reasons for discriminating. If the voters chose some men early in life because of raw ability, or because of educational qualifications, access to office might still be open in a meaningful way; while if the prevailing basis for early selection was family background or social status, equality of access would be clearly circumscribed.

Problems of measurement and definition about ability as a criterion for selection make firm conclusions impossible. After two hundred years, and in the absence of a standard other than performance for measuring ability, successful officeholding provides the only comprehensive means of judging leadership ability. Because such success is the principal basis for considering men part of the provincial elite, the conclusion that ability was a distinguishing characteristic of elite members would be virtually tautological. Furthermore, ability, or education for that matter, is not entirely independent of social status because personal contacts and a man's whole climate of experience play a role in fitting him for political office.

In spite of these qualifications, some indications of the relationship between status and ability exist. First of all, provincial offices always remained open to a substantial number of self-made men, as the data make clear. The average age of first town service for justices of the peace, a figure that involves men counted solely on the basis of success, was 36.3 years,

TABLE NINETEEN

Average Age of Entry into Town Office of Prominent Men

	Massachusetts	Massachusetts without Boston	New Hampshire	New Hampshire without Portsmouth	Rhode Island	Connecticut	Totals
Number of Prominent Men	321	x	70	x	117	50	558
Average Age	37.1	x	35.9	x	38.2	35.7	37.1
Number of Prominent Men omitting men who moved after age 40	x	209	x	28	108	48	393
Average Age	x	34.2	x	33.0	37.5	35.4	35.2
Number of Justices of the Peace	x	164	x	18	43	15	242
Average Age	x	36.4	x	33.8	38.5	32.9	36.3
Number of Judges and Councilors	x	48	x	3	79	3	133
Average Age	x	32.4	x	28.0	37.6	35.3	35.5
Number of College Graduates	x	110	x	11	11	35	167
Average Age	x	32.4	x	34.1	37.1	36.6	33.7
Civil Officers of Prominent Families	111	89	20	x	44	5[1]	180
Average Age	32.7	32.1	31.2	x	35.5	31.4	33.1
College Graduates of Prominent Families	83	56	14	x	5	8[1]	110
Average Age	32.0	30.7	30.2	x	34.2	31.6	31.8
Civil Officers and College Graduates of Prominent Families	63	46	11	x	4	2[1]	80
Average Age	31.8	30.7	29.7	x	37.0	31.0	32.3

1) Data for Connecticut, although limited, appears to be representative. Of 25 Connecticut Assistants from non-sample towns for whom biographical sources specified age at first service in major town office, all began serving by age 35. The average age at first service was 29.5. Twelve of the men were college graduates.

while the general average, which includes other factors, was only 35.2. Furthermore, all of these statistics exclude two of the principal cities in the sample, Boston and Portsmouth, where family continuity in politics was markedly lower than in the other towns that produced members of the provincial elites, and where new men were especially welcome to serve (see Table 14 and the discussion on p. 98).[27] The seventy-six justices who held town office in the cities began to serve at an average age of 40.3 years, a figure that accounts for nearly half of the difference between the gross average age at entry and the adjusted average used in this discussion. These higher averages reveal the inclusion of men who had proven their fitness for provincial offices by long years of service in lesser offices. On the other hand, the average for justices remained much lower than the average for ordinary town leaders, and the average for judges and councillors, 35.5, was lower still, which suggests that many of these very eminent men began their public service too early to have proven themselves by prior service.

Education provided some men access to high office, but as with sheer ability, the evidence is mixed. The average age at which college graduates entered town office, 33.7 years, was as much below the general average as the average for justices of the peace was above it, although neither variation is terribly impressive. Skills like fluency in public speaking and the ability to write coherently were at a premium in many country towns, and their command explains the early rise to prominence of a number of college graduates. Another part of the college experience, however, was the set of contacts and friendships with other educated men it provided, but such ties, although crucial to seekers of provincial office, were not equally open to all. P. M. G. Harris has shown that, beneath a pattern of short-term cyclical variation, a clear majority of the college graduates attaining upper class positions in colonial New England came from upper-class families in the first place.[28] This finding is confirmed explicitly for the towns in the present sample: of the 167 college graduates judged to have become prominent men, 66 percent were sons or near relatives of prominent men in previous generations. When a man like Henry Sherburne, Jr., became selectman of Portsmouth at the age of twenty-two, his father's status as a member of the council and a leader of the popular faction in New Hampshire was certainly a more important consideration than his Harvard diploma.[29]

In the end the social status of the candidates provides a more satisfactory explanation for the early town elections of most members of the provincial elites than factors like education and ability. Nearly a third of the civil officers elected or appointed in sample towns and fully two-thirds of the college graduates who achieved prominence in civil pursuits were members of families that had produced individuals of similar status in the past.[30] Of these 210 sons of illustrious families, more than 90 percent entered town service before the age of forty, for an average age at entry of thirty-two, which was low even in comparison with the rest of the provincial elites. No town or colony was so foolish as to keep an incompetent man in public office merely because of his birth, and a liberal education was always advantageous, but at election time high social status often proved to be an indispensible element in the election of a young and untried man. The status of a prominent man's family, as well as educational polish and politically useful contacts, largely exempted sons of distinguished parentage from the qualifications of age and experience that bound ordinary men.

The information presented here on the role of family status in shaping political opportunities, and the supporting information on the ages at which men became leaders, reaches to the core of the longstanding historical debate over whether or not eighteenth-century America was a deferential society.[31] New England voters demanded that most candidates for high office meet generally accepted standards of maturity, economic independence, and experience in lesser offices. At the same time, however, the electorate stood ready to vote young, unestablished men of high social status into office without requiring the slightest evidence of official experience. Clearly, candidates of the latter type were beneficiaries of political deference and candidates of the former type were not. In political terms, deference refers to the degree to which the majority of citizens willingly accepts the peculiar capacity of elite members to fill the highest public offices and to speak with authority on the basic public issues because of their social status, personal prestige, or some other criterion at least partially distinct from the rational calculation of abilities and interests. As Michael Zuckerman, one participant in the debate, has aptly observed, such deference "occurs in some degree in all complex social systems."[32] But most historians, Zuckerman not excepted, have ignored the idea that variations in deference are essentially variations in degree, and have reduced the issue to crudely dichotomized choices between "consensualism" or "democracy" on the one hand and "deferential politics" or "oligarchy" on the other.

Theoretically, political communities might be arranged in a spectrum with those in which deference is most pervasive at one end and those in which it is minimal at the other. In one community, political power might be exercised exclusively by the heads of certain families regardless of age or personal ability; in another, elections might take place and voters might practice some discrimination among elite members on the basis of ability; in a third, rival elite members might gain election to office only when the measures they advocated harmonized with the perceived interests of lower class voters; and so the sequence of political types would proceed until it reached a community in which previous elite status or great fame would provide absolutely no political advantage or authority.

On the level of internal town politics such a spectrum of deferential behavior clearly existed in colonial New England. At one extreme were towns like Springfield where, in the early eighteenth century, the predominant voice of the Pynchon family in town affairs was unchallenged and unquestioned. From 1664 until his death in 1703 Springfield's only moderator was the "Worshipful Colonel John Pynchon Esq.," and so undisputed was his family's position in the town that when the Longmeadow section organized itself as a separate precinct in 1714, it promptly voted "Hon[ere]d Col. Punchon," the old man's son and successor, moderator "for said meeting, and for all sutch meetings when present among us."[33] In family-dominated towns like Springfield the leading family held town office continually, and repeated elections grew out of the awe with which the townspeople regarded family members.

A second pattern of deferential behavior existed in towns where elites were larger and more frequently divided. In Portsmouth, for example, gentlemen of both the Wentworth-Atkinson connection and Waldron-Sherburne alliance began their public service at the tender ages that were characteristic of recognized elites, but year to year electoral decisions followed the shifting issues of New Hampshire politics.[34] The shifting political fortunes of elite candidates did not alter their standing in the social order, and defeated candidates felt no compulsion to minimize their social distance and become champions of characteristically lower-class measures. During the Hopkins-Ward era, for example, elitist Rhode Island politicians maintained an intensive and expensive contest for the votes of the freemen over a period of more than ten years without ever proclaiming their candidates as partisans of the ordinary man and without denouncing their opponents as proponents of narrow upper-class interests.[35]

A third pattern of political behavior occurred in towns where some social and political stratification existed, but where the leading families were socially less distant from the mass of the population, and where their access to provincial office was less consistent. Such towns generally recognized the claim of leading families to political leadership, but that recognition did not stem from the kind of awe that led a town to elect a young man to high office without prior experience. Towns like Dedham, Andover, or Dorchester were predisposed to elevate members of certain families to town leadership, but only after the men in question had served a suitable and conventional apprenticeship in the lesser offices.

In the political behavior of a fourth group of towns, deference played a minimal role. These were mainly egalitarian towns, where really prominent men were few, the social distance among local families slight, and traditions of family continuity in office rare. In addition, these towns were usually small and likely to place few demands on town government, so that the responsibilities of a town leader were not substantial. Egalitarian towns placed little premium on age, experience, or parentage in selecting leaders, because no candidate worth deferring to sought offices that were of so little consequence.*

---

*Young leaders of ordinary means were sometimes very numerous in small egalitarian towns. While Dedham, Andover, and Dorchester elected eleven, nine, and five men to office before their thirty-sixth birthday, Boxford elected twenty-nine, Hampton elected twenty-seven, and Derby seventeen.

While a hierarchy of town types governed the political variations in internal town behavior, a different sort of distinction separated the forms of political behavior that were characteristic of the careers of strictly town leaders and of members of the provincial elites. Fundamentally, variation in deference patterns depended not on differences in the composition of town elites as a whole, but on the presence or absence of prominent individuals or families capable of commanding deference. In every town the majority of leaders were relatively ordinary men, for whom the dominant political criteria were maturity, experience in public service, and visible success in private life. Such men expected to enter the town leadership in middle age after serving a substantial apprenticeship in the lower offices, to serve their towns as first among equals without any real opportunities to rise above the purely local offices, and to find access to town office relatively open, with family influence playing little part in elections.

In contrast with their more parochial associates, town leaders with entry into the provincial elites maintained a different relationship with their constituents, and expected treatment according to a different set of rules. Where ordinary men expected to prove their fitness for the town's highest offices, gentlemen of high status assumed that their social position and family background fitted them for leadership beyond the necessity for further proof. Where lesser men sought the opportunity to make their own way, provincial leaders demanded recognition as town leaders as a matter of course. And finally, where ordinary leaders expected to hold high town office as the capstone of a successful career, members of the provincial elite viewed town office as a youth's stepping stone to greater prominence and as a service to society performed in return for suitable recognition of elevated social status. In short, the social and political elite expected due deference to their standing in society.

Grounds for reconciling these apparently conflicting views of politics and society can be found in the conception of high and low cultures familiar to anthropological students of complex societies. According to this notion, societies contain both a "high culture" or "great tradition" associated with the thought and values of the elite, and a "low culture" or "little tradition" expressed in the daily lives of ordinary people, but incomplete without an understanding of its dominant elite counterpart.[36]

In this context, the conflicting political cultures of eighteenth-century New England become more understandable. At the level of ordinary affairs, New England town life contained profoundly egalitarian forces and operated, as Michael Zuckerman has argued, on a model that maintained social cohesion by seeking the consensual participation of every established inhabitant.[37] This set of consensual social assumptions provided a theoretical justification for most political decisions at the strictly local level, but once removed from the intimate context of the town, it conflicted with the traditional hierarchical view of society and with the theoretical underpinning it provided for Anglo-colonial constitutional arrangements.[38] At the provincial level, therefore, the hierarchical social model was dominant, and with it a set of assumptions that stressed political deference to social superiors. As the political expression of the society-wide "great tradition," the set of deferential assumptions applied not only in the provincial capitals, but also in every town whenever the townspeople considered their relationship with an individual or family whose social identity stemmed from its place in the overall social hierarchy. Thus John Adams could at once be mistaken in claiming that town political power descended "in three or four families at most," and correct in asserting that wealthy and prominent families could expect "a degree of admiration, abstracted from all dependence, obligation, expectation, or even acquaintance" and "an habitual veneration for their names . . . [which] secures them in some degree the favor, the affection, and the respect of the public."[39]

·5·

TOWN AND CHURCH

In popular history the most prominent attribute of the early New England leader is not his wealth or family status, but his Puritan sainthood. The Congregational deacon has become a virtual archetype of the town leader, and lists of founding church members frequently serve local historians as handy registers of prominent men. Professional historians have reinforced the impression created by their amateur brethren by conducting exhaustive studies of the early Massachusetts freemanship and devoting little attention to the relationship between church membership and political activity in the other colonies or in Massachusetts after 1684.[1] Most historical readers are aware that church membership was the prime qualification for political participation in seventeenth-century Massachusetts, and in the absence of suitable information from other times and places have accepted the church-member franchise as a symbol of the religious context for political involvement throughout colonial New England.

Despite long neglect, information for the broad-based study of the participation of church members and church leaders in local and colony-wide political affairs exists in the records preserved by hundreds of Congregational churches and in the archives of the minority sects. Private record-keeping and casual record storage have adversely affected the completeness, survival, and accessibility of the church records, so that complete runs for all of a town's churches are rare, especially in large towns with several churches, but enough records have survived to support research conducted on a sampling basis. Of the seventy-four towns examined intensively in the present study, thirteen have virtually complete records for all churches and for political affairs during the entire period, while seven have complete records for shorter periods of time. A further thirty-two towns lack records for some churches for extended periods, but have complete enough records for the remaining churches that many generalizations are possible.[2]

Research based on the extensive body of town and church data eliminates the necessity, implicit in the use of freemanship rosters, of understanding religious affiliation as a formal qualification for public participation. Instead, it places religion in a broader context of individual status and community structure that reveals much more about the workings of the New

England towns. Like wealth or family prestige, religious status was an attribute of individual townsmen and an influence on their position in the community. Whether or not a man was a full member of a local church was a consideration when many towns selected leaders, as the literature on the Massachusetts franchise suggests. By the eighteenth century a number of towns contained Anglicans, Baptists, Quakers, or other dissenters, so that sectarian issues complicated the religious aspect of leadership selection beyond a choice between members and nonmembers in the Standing Order churches.

Study of church affiliations also provides information unlike that based on tabulations of individual attributes, because churches were quasi-corporate entities and formed community units distinguishable from the towns in which they existed. Each New England church selected a minister to lead its religious observances and elected lay leaders to manage its prudential affairs. Each church of the Standing Order also served as the focus of a subordinate unit of government, the parish, in Connecticut, Massachusetts, and New Hampshire towns containing more than one church. Data on church membership and church leadership thus provides an opportunity for considering the relationship between town activities and the operation of coordinate community institutions.

Appropriately, discussion of the religious aspect of local leadership begins with a consideration of the influence of Congregational church membership on the selection of town leaders. As is well known, most inhabitants of seventeenth- and eighteenth-century New England attended and supported the Congregational churches that existed in virtually every town. In 1700 85 percent of the approximately 150 churches in New England belonged to the majority Congregational order, and on the eve of the Revolution 70 percent of the 800 churches were of the same persuasion.[3] Laws in Connecticut and Massachusetts required each town to support the "publick worship of God" by appropriating tax money to settle and pay an "able, learned and orthodox [Congregational] minister or ministers" chosen by the members of the local church and accepted by the taxpayers in town meeting. The churches so supported by public policy constituted the New England establishment or "standing order." As the eighteenth century wore on a series of laws exempted Anglicans, Baptists, and Quakers from ecclesiastical taxes, provided that they filed acceptable certificates from their own clergymen testifying that they attended services regularly; but the certificate system remained a limited and controversial procedure. In New Hampshire the law required each town to settle and pay a minister, but in that colony the denominational identification of the official minister depended on the wishes of the local majority, so that Presbyterian towns such as Londonderry, Bedford, and Chester were able to settle ministers of their own sect, even though the majority of settled ministers in the colony were Congregationalists. Only in Rhode Island was the exercise of religion a strictly private affair, in conformity with the Charter injunction "to hold forth a lively experiment" in religious liberty.[4]

A peculiarity of the Congregational establishment was the membership system that distinguished among church members, "halfway" members, and the congregation or general body of adherents. Most established churches, including the Churches of England (Anglican) and of Scotland (Presbyterian) which had adherents in New England, operated inclusive territorial parishes, and automatically considered all well-behaved inhabitants of a parish to be communicants of the Church. The puritan New Englanders, however, stressed the necessity of making the earthly church approximate the heavenly church of true believers, and reserved full membership and the privilege of taking communion to those who appeared to be members of the elect. All others were expected to support the churches and to attend services, but they were excluded from active participation in church affairs. Halfway membership was an innovation adopted gradually after 1662 that permitted the noncommunicating sons and daughters of church members (and eventually others as well) to obtain baptism for their children by "owning" or reaffirming the commitment to live Christian lives and accept church discipline made for them at the time of their own baptism.[5] The rosters of church members in the Congregational church records, and the records of the Baptists and Quakers who made roughly similar divisions, enable historians to draw distinctions between the more committed adherents and the general population that are impossible with Anglican and Presbyterian records.

To assess the impact of full church membership on town leadership, information about the identities of full members and about the age at which they joined the church has been added to the rosters of selectmen from fifty-two towns with reasonably full church records for all or part of the eighteenth century. A computer calculated the service records of selectmen belonging to each church in a town, including dissenting sects, as well as the records of selectmen not listed as members by any church, and compared the ages of church admission with the ages of officeholding. Data on halfway membership, unfortunately, was too scanty to justify analysis. Separate tabulations for thirty-six towns over the whole period from 1700 to 1784, and for smaller numbers of towns with good records in each of the three periods 1650 to 1699, 1700 to 1749, and 1750 to 1784, make possible both an overall discussion of the eighteenth-century situation and an investigation of changing patterns over most of the colonial period.

Several factors indicate that a brief discussion of change in the religious attributes of political leaders in New England over the entire colonial period is a useful preliminary to a fuller discussion of the role of church members in eighteenth-century town affairs. In the first place, if leadership patterns changed little from a seventeenth-century situation in which virtually all leaders were church members, little would be gained by an elaborate analysis of differing patterns among the towns: it would be enough to observe that leaders were normally drawn from the church membership. By contrast, if patterns changed rapidly during the eighteenth century, study of data compiled for the entire century might yield misleading results. The presentation of data will begin, therefore, with a discussion of change in three periods between 1650 and 1784.

The association between orthodox church membership and political leadership was most striking in the seventeenth century, when the region's puritan mission seemed most urgent. At least 70 percent of the 366 selectmen elected in eight Massachusetts and Connecticut towns from 1650 to 1699 were members of the local church, and the proportion undoubtedly would appear higher if the church records of several towns were more complete (see Table 20).[6] To some extent the prominence of church members reflected the Massachusetts law of 1647 that required a majority of each town's selectmen

TABLE TWENTY

Comparative Service of Church Members and Non-Members

Town	Members #	Ave. Terms	Non-Members #	Ave. Terms	Town	Members #	Ave. Terms	Non-Members #	Ave. Terms
PERIOD 1650-1699					**PERIOD 1750-1784**				
Andover	8	3.5	22	4.7	Andover	30	3.4	16	4.1
Boston	67	5.5	3	4.3	Barnstable	8	4.1	11	6.1
Cambridge	27	9.2	15	2.4	Boston	30	6.2	16	4.3
Dedham	45	7.7	14	3.5	Boxford	31	3.2	29	2.8
Dorchester	40	5.5	2	5.5	Braintree	25	4.2	15	4.1
Medfield	10	7.9	31	5.3	Cambridge	21	7.4	22	2.6
New Haven	39	6.3	12	5.6	Fitchburg	10	3.7	15	2.6
Stonington	18	7.5	13	4.7	Grafton	22	4.4	37	2.0
					Norton	10	4.4	20	3.5
PERIOD 1700-1749					Topsfield	14	4.1	17	4.3
					Brunswick	14	4.5	12	3.5
Andover	31	4.6	25	4.2	Gorham	7	3.7	14	2.5
Barnstable	7	6.1	13	7.2	Cornish	8	3.9	23	2.0
Barrington	7	5.7	8	5.0	Dublin	9	3.2	7	2.4
Boston	45	4.2	38	4.5	Hampstead	26	2.4	22	2.1
Boxford	45	2.8	46	2.6	Hampton	38	3.6	17	1.7
Braintree	38	4.7	22	3.0	Hanover, N.H.	17	2.3	8	2.1
Brookline	10	6.8	23	4.4	New Ipswich	5	2.8	22	2.4
Cambridge	31	4.9	23	4.6	Portsmouth	15	6.3	14	5.6
Dorchester	9	11.9	31	4.8	Weare	9	2.1	19	2.4
Hardwick	8	4.4	6	2.8	Enfield	13	7.3	11	5.0
Norton	19	4.8	11	3.7	New Haven	42	3.1	44	3.7
Topsfield	45	3.6	27	2.9	Newtown	19	3.0	62	2.3
Hampton	60	2.3	50	2.1	Stonington	10	6.3	35	3.9
Portsmouth	27	4.1	42	3.1	Newport	13	7.8	10	7.1
New Haven	51	3.7	60	2.7					
Stonington	41	4.7	20	4.7					
Newport	17	6.1	15	6.1					

to be colony freemen, but the law was not a sufficient explanation of the towns' selection of leaders. The Massachusetts towns chose church members to fill 78 percent of all terms as selectmen, much more than was required by law, and the Connecticut towns, which had no religious qualification, elected saints a similar percentage of the time. The first generation of settlers in New England has long been famous for its high proportion of church members, and the town leaders of that generation are also known for their long service.[7] Virtually all of the first-generation leaders in towns with good early church records were members, while the few nonmember selectmen in towns such as Boston, Cambridge, or Dedham were second-generation men serving a few terms at the end of the century. Individual church members served longer than nonmembers, averaging 6.6 terms as selectmen in the eight sample towns to 4.3 selectmen terms for nonmembers.

The deaths of the first-generation leaders and the growing ascendancy of the relatively unchurched second generation presaged a reduction in number of church members among the town leaders as the seventeenth century gave way to the eighteenth. Known church members comprised only half of the selectmen elected between 1700 and 1749 in seventeen towns drawn from all four New England colonies. Such a proportion suggests that religious status had become less important in the election of leaders once the formal link between the churches and political participation was broken, but the exact dimensions of the change remain unclear. On the one hand, voters no longer allowed a few men, most of whom were church members, to dominate the boards of selectmen but instead shared the offices among many men. The average service of selectmen in six towns appearing in both the late seventeenth- and early eighteenth-century sample decreased from 5.8 terms to 4.3 terms.[8] On the other hand, the number of church members in the population was presumably small, so that the towns were still giving disproportionate influence to the churches when they elected half of the leaders from their membership. Also, church members continued to serve more terms than did nonmembers, with average service in the sample towns of 4.2 terms and 3.5 terms respectively.

Data drawn from twenty-five sample towns for the period from 1750 to 1784 indicate that the changes in the selection of leaders from the seventeenth century to the early eighteenth century marked a discrete shift in town behavior rather than a continuing trend. In many ways patterns in the two eighteenth-century samples were strikingly similar.* The proportion of

---

*See Table 21. Orthodox church members include Rhode Island members of all sects. Figures in the "Joined After Election" and "Other Members" columns omit Amherst, Leicester, Falmouth, Providence, Smithfield, and South Kingstown because of inadequate data. "Other Members" includes a few men whose dates of membership are uncertain, but probably earlier than first election to office. The town categories "A," "B," and "C" in the table represent cities, large country towns, and small country towns respectively. Individual towns are grouped as in Table 22.

orthodox church members among the town leaders in the later period, 43 percent, was slightly lower, but church records in which leaders were identified were slightly less complete. Members of dissenting churches, who had appeared among the leaders for the first time in the early eighteenth century, increased slightly from 1.5 percent of the selectmen to 3.1 percent. Orthodox church members continued to outserve nonmembers as selectmen, with average service figures of 4.3 terms and 3.2 terms respectively. Taken together, the statistics drawn from the three samples indicate that a substantial change in the political influence of Congregational church members occurred at the end of the seventeenth century, but that the religious correlates of political leadership remained stable through most of the eighteenth century. The continuity in eighteenth-century leadership patterns observed in the examination of town samples over several limited time periods confirms the validity of treating the century as a unit for more thorough analysis of the role of Congregational church members in the selection of local leaders.

In summary terms, detailed data from thirty-six towns over most of the eighteenth century provide results similar to those obtained from the smaller samples. Forty-two percent of the 3,032 selectmen elected between 1700 and 1784 appeared in the membership rolls of the local church, another 3 percent belonged to a variety of dissenting sects, and the remaining officeholders were not identified as church members in the extant and accessible records (see Table 22 and the summary statistics in Table 21). The average service of members as selectmen also exceeded the average service of nonmembers by a similar margin of almost one term per man.

More revealing about the relationship between church membership and leadership than summary measures is the detailed analysis of town behavior.[9] First, an examination of the statistics on each town reveals a division into town types similar to that encountered in the study of other measures of political behavior. The differences between the average service records of members and nonmembers remained about the same for all kinds of towns, but communities varied in other respects. Towns in a first category, including the major cities of Boston, New Haven, Newport, and Portsmouth, had relatively long-serving town officers and a distinctively high percentage of orthodox church members among the selectmen. About half of the urban selectmen were full church members, a status which was valuable for signaling a candidate's orthodoxy to the voters in cities that contained several dissenting congregations.[10]

A second category included large country towns such as Cambridge, Andover, Dover, and South Kingstown. These towns also had long-serving town leaders but the proportion of full church members, 42 percent, was somewhat lower than in the cities. Dissenting churches were common in the larger country towns, but their members were few and well known, so that voters had less reason to be concerned about the loyalties of candidates who

TABLE TWENTY-ONE

Aggregate Service Records of Church Members

Sample	All Selectmen		Orthodox Members		Dissenters		Non-Members		Joined After Election		Other Members	
	#	Ave. Terms	#	Ave. Terms	#	Ave. Terms	#	Ave. Terms	#	Ave. Terms	#	Ave. Terms
1650–1699	366	5.9	254	6.6	–	–	112	4.3				
1700–1749	951	3.9	477	4.2	14	3.1	460	3.5				
1750–1784	964	3.6	416	4.3	30	3.3	518	3.2				
1700–1784 A	453	4.5	224	4.9	16	3.4	213	4.1	84	5.0	156	4.7
1700–1784 B	1864	4.6	785	5.1	56	4.7	1023	4.2	195	5.7	550	4.7
1700–1784 C	715	3.3	276	3.7	26	3.2	413	3.0	101	4.4	186	3.3
1700–1784 All	3032	4.3	1285	4.8	98	4.0	1649	3.9	380	5.2	892	4.4

TABLE TWENTY-TWO

Service Records of Church Members as Selectmen

Town	Number of Churches Cong. Other Providing Data			Orthodox Members		Dissenters		Non-Members	
	Cong.	Other	Providing Data	#	Ave. Terms	#	Ave. Terms	#	Ave. Terms
CITIES									
Boston	11	7	12	74	5.4	3	2.3	45	4.6
Portsmouth	3	1	4	32	5.4	8	4.6	50	4.0
New Haven	8	4	11	87	3.6	5	2.2	96	3.2
Newport	2	5	7	31	6.7	-	-	22	7.3
LARGE TOWNS									
Andover	2	-	2	53	4.1	-	-	38	4.5
Barnstable	2	1	2	14	5.4	-	-	22	7.3
Braintree	3	1	4	60	4.8	2	4.5	31	3.7
Cambridge	2	1	2	48	6.5	-	-	44	3.5
Dedham	4	1	4	49	5.5	-	-	41	2.8
Hanover	1	2	3	16	4.8	2	2.5	21	3.8
Leicester	1	3	3	7	5.9	9	6.4	52	4.0
Lunenburg	1	-	1	40	3.8	-	-	24	4.7
Middleboro	3	3	3	22	5.1	4	6.0	41	5.1
Norton	2	1	3	28	5.1	-	-	27	3.8
Springfield	6	1	2	29	5.8	-	-	31	5.1
Sudbury	2	-	1	57	4.9	-	-	80	3.7
Swansea	-	3	2	-	-	23	4.8	47	3.3
Watertown	3	1	2	30	6.1	2	7.0	74	3.5
Biddeford	2	-	1	22	7.2	-	-	17	3.6
Falmouth	4	2	5	29	4.7	8	3.0	56	4.3
Scarborough	1	-	1	20	4.8	-	-	27	3.7
Dover	4	1	5	15	3.5	4	2.3	63	4.6
Ashford	1	2	2	27	5.0	2	3.0	32	3.7
Bolton	2	-	2	35	4.3	-	-	12	3.6
Stonington	3	1	3	49	5.7	-	-	49	4.3
Woodbury	6	1	6	56	3.7	-	-	34	4.1
Providence	2	4	4	37	5.3	-	-	75	4.3
Smithfield	-	2	1	15	5.5	-	-	42	5.6
S. Kingstown	1	4	5	27	7.3	-	-	43	4.3
SMALL TOWNS									
Amherst	2	-	2	13	4.1	-	-	47	3.1
Boxford	2	-	2	73	3.2	-	-	67	2.7
Medfield	1	1	2	14	5.7	8	2.8	113	2.9
Topsfield	1	-	1	55	4.1	-	-	39	3.8
Hampton	3	1	4	80	3.4	5	2.4	62	2.0
Derby	2	2	3	9	3.9	13	3.7	69	3.7
Kent	3	-	3	32	3.8	-	-	16	4.7

were not orthodox members. In a third and final category were many of the smaller country towns, including Boxford, Derby, and Hampton. Leaders in such towns served few terms in office as part of an egalitarian political order that shared office widely. Under these conditions church membership was less important for election, and the small towns elected fewer members, 39

TABLE TWENTY-THREE

Leadership and Age of Church Membership

| Town | Men Who Were Members First | | | | Men Who Were Leaders First | | | |
	#	Ave. Terms	#	Ave. Age Joined	#	Ave. Terms	#	Ave. Age Joined
Ashford	22	4.1	17	37	7	7.3	7	62
Bolton	24	3.5	23	31	11	5.8	11	43
Derby	16	3.2	11	30	6	5.2	6	56
Kent	23	3.0	12	36	9	6.0	9	44
New Haven	61	3.8	56	31	31	3.1	31	57
Stonington	29	5.5	26	31	20	6.0	20	54
Woodbury	47	3.7	42	30	4	4.0	4	44
Andover	37	4.8	34	31	16	4.1	16	52
Barnstable	8	4.3	6	32	6	7.0	6	53
Boston	62	5.5	41	31	13	4.7	13	52
Boxford	49	2.9	45	31	24	3.9	24	51
Braintree	48	4.7	29	32	14	5.1	14	54
Cambridge	42	6.0	40	30	6	10.2	6	45
Dedham	21	4.7	21	34	13	6.2	13	54
Hanover, Mass.	12	4.0	11	33	4	7.0	4	43
Lunenburg	31	3.5	29	35	9	4.9	9	42
Medfield	8	1.4	4	34	11	6.6	11	55
Middleboro	20	5.0	15	28	6	6.2	6	58
Norton	16	4.0	12	36	12	6.6	12	55
Springfield	18	6.4	15	32	8	4.9	8	60
Sudbury	31	5.2	27	34	26	4.6	26	48
Swansea	8	4.0	6	32	4	2.8	4	46
Topsfield	34	3.7	32	32	21	4.6	21	47
Watertown	22	5.3	20	30	8	8.9	8	52
Biddeford	13	6.9	5	30	9	7.7	9	49
Scarborough	14	5.6	8	31	6	2.7	6	52
Dover	9	2.7	8	35	6	4.8	6	46
Hampton	55	3.5	54	32	30	3.1	30	51
Portsmouth	13	6.3	10	30	20	4.8	20	52
Newport	11	3.6	8	35	20	8.4	20	56

percent, than any other class of towns, although church members still served longer on average than other townsmen.

A key to understanding the towns' preference for church members as leaders appears in the relative ages at which leaders joined the churches and reached high offices. So far this analysis has relied on figures showing how many leaders were church members at some time in their lives and how long each leader served. A useful distinction exists, nevertheless, between those selectmen who became church members before election to major office and those who were already leaders when they experienced religious conversion. As a full examination of the behavioral pattern for each group shows, church affiliation served less as a prior qualification for election and more as an indication of the multiple community ties characteristic of a town leader.

That church membership was not a general qualification for leadership is abundantly clear in further comparisons of the service records of selectmen who were already church members when first elected, of those who became members after serving several terms, and of nonmember selectmen. Evidence cited earlier has shown that about half of the eighteenth-century selectmen were not church members, but that the towns manifested their preference for members by electing them to longer terms. Division of the half of all selectmen who were members shows that about 70 percent had experienced religious conversion before serving their first term in office and that the remaining 30 percent had served for some time before joining the church. Church members were thus a distinct minority among beginning selectmen, and membership could scarcely have been a qualification for election. Moreover, in the long run the towns showed their highest favor to the minority of selectmen who joined a church after holding office. In the thirty towns with the best records, such men served an average of 5.2 terms, while those who began their careers as members averaged 4.4 terms and nonmembers averaged 3.8 terms (see detailed data in Table 23 and summaries in Table 21).[11] The influence of church membership on the selection of leaders was a subtle one, and not a simple matter of formal or tacit religious qualifications.

The precise role of church membership in the electoral process becomes clearer when the ages at which leaders experienced religious conversion are compared with one another and with normal membership patterns in New England churches. Comprehensive studies of the age at which men became church members are few in number and focus heavily on the Great Awakening period. Studies of four individual towns show mean ages of between thirty and thirty-five years for the first half of the eighteenth century, with means of thirty to thirty-nine years in the early decades of the century and a decline to means in the twenty- to thirty-year range during the Awakening.[12],* In these towns the church member population ranged in size from Andover and Woodbury, where the number of male members admitted from 1711 to 1759 and 1702 to 1742 respectively almost equaled the number of taxpayers in each town at the close of the period; to Norton, where approximately 120 male admissions from 1711 to 1743 contrasted with an estimated 250 adult males in 1740; and to Norwich, Connecticut, where only about 25 percent of the men seated in the First Society meeting house in 1734

*Mean Ages of Full Church Membership

Town	Period	Age	Period	Age	Mean Age
Andover	1711–29	36.5	1730–49	26.2	33.3
Norton	1711–39	39.7	1740–44?	29.9	?
Norwich	1717–44	30.3	—	—	30.3
Woodbury	1702–38	29.8	1739–42	22.6	26.8

Similar data compiled by Robert Pope (*The Half-Way Covenant*, pp. 280–85) for the seventeenth century showed the following *median* ages for males joining churches in full communion: Roxbury, 29.2 (1680s); Charlestown, 30.9, 30.2, 32.7 (1660s, 1670s, 1680s); Boston Third Church, 32.6 (1680s); and Dorchester, 25.6, 27.8, 20.8 (1660s, 1670s, 1680s).

were members. Regardless of the size of the membership, communicants came from established local families: in Woodbury more than two-thirds of the Great Awakening converts belonged to families with lengthy associations with the Woodbury church, while in Norwich at least half of the converts belonged to families descended from the original town proprietors. Sons and daughters of substantial local families tended to join the church as they matured and either married or prepared to marry, with the bulk of the admissions concentrated in the years of early adulthood. The authors of all four studies treat membership as a life-cycle phenomenon, while emphasizing factors that help to explain the relatively small shifts in age of conversion at the time of the Great Awakening.

Age data for the majority of church member leaders throughout New England who joined a church before election to major office conforms well to the overall membership history of the four towns. In the thirty towns for which information is available, the average age at which leaders in this group joined ranged from twenty-eight in Middleborough to thirty-seven in Ashford, with nineteen towns clustering in the thirty- to thirty-two-year-old bracket (see Table 23). In Andover future leaders joined at an average age of thirty-one, close to the overall average of thirty-three years, and leaders in Woodbury and Norton conformed just as closely to the town averages. The similarity of the membership patterns for future leaders and for other townsmen suggests that all were responding to the same maturation process and that potential leaders were indistinguishable from others in religious terms. The lack of differentiation accords with the evidence presented in Chapters 2 and 4 that most leaders were only beginning to serve as minor officers at the age when many joined the church, and that few emerged as leaders before their fortieth birthday. Unlike advanced education or high family status, early church membership did not identify a young man as a potential leader.

Since membership was not a qualification for office, and since early conversion did not mark a man as a leader, the electoral advantage enjoyed by church members must be sought elsewhere. In this search, the life histories of the minority of selectmen who became church members after emerging as leaders is particularly revealing. Predictably, the experiences of members of this group were more varied than those of the majority who joined the church at a conventional age. Length of service varied from the single terms served by some men to the fifty or more terms served by others. Age of admission also varied widely, because the group included prominent men who became leaders and members at an early age, as well as men who joined in old age. Also included were a large number of men who migrated from one town to another, becoming leaders and then members in their adopted homes.

Because the diversity of the late-joining minority limits the value of statistical generalizations, a discussion of the common patterns of behavior can best be presented through individual histories drawn from selected towns. Representative of the most significant pattern were the four late-joining selectmen of Cambridge, all of whom were prominent leaders.[13] Collectively the men served more than 60 terms as selectmen, and more than 109 terms in other major offices, with an individual minimum of twelve years of service. Individually, two men were scions of leading families who entered office in their early forties and became church members one year and three years later respectively. A third man was a leader's son who began serving at the age of thirty-six and joined the church a year later, while the fourth man was a longterm selectman who joined the church in his late forties, some seven years after first election. To say that such men became church members as a further mark of their involvement in the community and its affairs seems crude, but essentially accurate. Given puritan assumptions about the spiritual qualifications for church membership, the decision to join must not have been direct or calculating. But it does seem reasonable to suppose that leaders would find active church participation attractive, and that the visible evidence of public respect inherent in community leadership might make a proud man without a dramatic conversion experience more willing to risk presenting a conventional conversion experience in a public relation.

Individuals conforming to a second pattern also became church members as they identified themselves with their community, but their behavior can be explained more directly. When the new town of Bolton formed a church in 1725, four years after its incorporation, three early leaders were among the original members, while two others joined soon after and a sixth man transferred membership from his native town some years later. Subsequent church membership was common among a new town's founding fathers, and occurred under circumstances that necessitated violations of the usual age pattern for membership. Two other Bolton leaders became church members at a conventional age, but as members of the illustrious Pitkin and Talcott families they were already town leaders by their early thirties. The remaining three Bolton late joiners followed the pattern set by the Cambridge leaders and joined in middle age after several years of service.

Men of a final type, those who became members as old men and without apparent reference to leadership status, were especially numerous in Middleboro. In that town two leaders joined the church in middle age shortly after beginning office holding careers of at least sixteen terms, but the remaining four men followed a different pattern. Each man served one or two terms as a selectman without becoming especially prominent, and then joined the church from three to thirty years later, in three cases after the new member's sixtieth birthday. Such men existed in many towns, but as the high average number of terms served by late joiners indicates, they constituted only a minority of the entire group.

Placing the individual histories of late-joining selectmen in the context of earlier findings about political service makes clear the usefulness of the concept of community identification and involvement as an explanation of the link between church membership and town office. Evidence presented in earlier chapters has shown that most towns preferred leaders who had served an apprenticeship in lesser town offices, who had the economic resources to devote time freely to public affairs, and who had family traditions of public service.[14] Discussions in this chapter have shown that most towns refused to make church membership a mechanical qualification for high office, choosing some 65 percent of new selectmen from men who were not yet members, and that most towns failed to give future leaders who shared in the common pattern of religious conversion in early adulthood special treatment by electing them to office earlier than was the rule for other men. Instead, the towns showed preference for church members by keeping them in office longer once they were identified as leaders. Men who were founding fathers or who demonstrated concern for the community in other ways gained particular favor, even though their church membership followed initial election, while leaders in general who were linked to the community by religious bonds enjoyed greater favor than those who lacked the distinction. Church membership was one of several factors identifying a man with the community and as a leader in it.

A fuller understanding of how church membership performed the function just discussed depends on a consideration of the role of the churches and of their increasingly numerous civil coordinates, the parishes, as subcommunities within the towns. The churches themselves formed corporate groups, holding meetings, electing deacons and elders as leaders, and intensifying acquaintanceships among the members. Until the blossoming of voluntary societies in the post-revolutionary period, the churches formed the primary nongovernmental institution providing frequent social intercourse in the country towns.[15] When members of the churches and their congregations sought candidates for election to town office, they turned frequently to the men who served their churches as deacons. More than 60 percent of the 791 deacons who served in 106 churches in sample towns during the eighteenth century were leaders as well (see Table 24 and footnote on p. 132). Deacons were especially prominent as leaders in country towns, but they held office less frequently in the coastal cities where local society had more numerous focal points. Also significant was the high proportion of deacons from the first church in each town among the leaders. First churches usually served the central village or the most prosperous area within a town, and their deacons were town leaders in more than three-quarters of the cases.

As with church members in general, the question of why deacons were often leaders is a complex one. Although 60 percent of the deacons were leaders, four of ten were not, so it would be erroneous to conclude that election to town office was automatic. Even in the seventeenth century, when towns chose large majorities of their leaders from among church members,

TABLE TWENTY-FOUR

Leadership Service of Congregational Deacons

Sample	All Churches			First Churches		
	# Deacons	% Leaders	% Deacons First	# Deacons	% Leaders	% Deacons First
1650-1699 All	87	65.5	8.0	75	76.0	9.3
1700-1749 A	108	33.3	13.9	26	53.9	15.4
1700-1749 B	278	73.0	13.7	192	81.3	13.5
1700-1749 C	51	72.6	11.8	45	80.0	13.3
1700-1749 All	437	63.2	13.5	263	78.3	13.7
1750-1784 A	102	41.2	20.6	24	62.5	16.7
1750-1784 B	316	63.9	17.1	208	74.0	17.3
1750-1784 C	105	70.5	11.5	85	78.8	12.9
1750-1784 All	523	60.8	16.6	317	74.5	16.1
1700-1784 A	177	36.7	16.4	41	58.5	17.1
1700-1784 B	475	65.7	14.7	315	77.5	14.9
1700-1784 C	139	71.9	10.8	116	77.6	12.1
1700-1784 All	791	60.3	14.4	472	75.8	14.4

more than a third of the deacons failed to impress the voters as suitable candidates for office. Further qualifications follow from a consideration of the ages at which deacons were selected. Chapter 4 has shown that leaders first served at an average age of about forty-three years, with large numbers of men beginning to serve in their late thirties and forties. Deacons followed a similar pattern, but with an average of forty-six years and a clustering in the forties and early fifties.[16] Such an age pattern suggests that few men came to the initial attention of the town voters through service as deacons, and, indeed, less than 15 percent of the deacons held that position when first selected as town leaders. Deacons stood out among the officeholders for long service rather than for the circumstances of original selection. Overall, they averaged 10.3 terms as leaders (11.5 terms for first church deacons) compared with 6.8 terms for all leaders in the fifty-four towns contributing records on the diaconate.* The qualities demanded of leaders and deacons differed sufficiently that no church limited the search for deacons to prominent officeholders, and no town automatically elevated deacons to high office. Given the centrality of religious matters in town life and the status of the church as a primary institution of social intercourse, however, voters were

*Deacons' Length of Service

Town Group	Average Terms All Deacons	Average Terms 1st Ch. Deacons	Average Terms All Leaders, Same Towns
1700-84 A	8.9	12.9	6.9
1700-84 B	10.7	11.8	7.6
1700-84 C	9.8	10.3	5.1
1700-84 All	10.3	11.5	6.8

predisposed to respect their chosen deacons and to regard those endowed with political and administrative abilities as especially suitable candidates for election to public office.

The prospects of deacons for repeated election to townwide office were further enhanced by the practice, increasingly common as the eighteenth century wore on, of regarding churches and their secular counterparts, the parishes, as constituent elements of the towns. During the seventeenth century New Englanders assumed that communities should be unitary in all respects, so that creation of a new church within a town implied the prompt division of the town into two communities, each maintaining the unified focus of one town, one church, one land proprietorship, and, usually, one central residential village. In 1700 a bare 12 of the 119 New England towns contained more than one orthodox church; and with the exception of Boston, which had outgrown the unitary community concept within a few years of its settlement, and of towns such as Hartford and Salem, which had histories of nasty religious divisions, the multiparish towns were products of the 1690s.[17] As the new century progressed the unitary community ideal became increasingly unworkable and even undesirable for residents of towns with populations too large for one church but too small for convenient division. By 1750, 106 of the approximately 260 towns contained parish divisions, including more than two-thirds (81) of the towns that had existed at the turn of the century. Increasing numbers of New Englanders lived in towns too populous and too diverse for unitary town politics, and felt a need to apportion town offices among groups of townsmen in ways that would ensure the proper representation of all legitimate interests.[18]

The usual expression of the need for apportionment was a town vote to divide seats on the board of selectmen and other town offices among the parishes or neighborhoods within a town. As early as 1697 Hartford was electing two selectmen from the "North Side" of town, two from the "South Side," and one from the "East Side of Great River," areas that approximated the three parishes in the town. Such votes became increasingly frequent as more towns underwent subdivision, and similar apportionment plans appeared in other towns without formal votes.[19] The common expression of such plans in terms of parishes, however, should not suggest that parishes themselves were the dynamic institutional embodiments of local solidarities. Most parishes were merely the secular arm of a local church and met in formal session little more than once a year, except when a new minister was being settled or a new meeting house was under consideration.[20] Parish voters met most frequently as the congregation at weekly church services, occasions at which deacons were the most prominent laymen and at which, presumably, church members were more consistently present than non-members. Because few parishes nominated formal slates of candidates for town office, informal contacts, especially those associated with church attendance, were crucial to the identification of candidates and help explain why church members and their leaders, the deacons, were prominent among town officials.[21]

A further indication of the importance of churches to town politics occurs in a final area of discussion, the role of religious dissenters in town affairs. As statistics presented earlier in this chapter indicate, an overwhelming majority of New Englanders adhered to the dominant Congregational order, but a persistent and growing minority espoused other beliefs. Historians have documented minority claims of religious intolerance and have studied those claims in local contexts, but few have succeeded in explaining why some towns ostracized their dissenters while others accommodated them. Systematic evidence on the electoral history of dissenters, combined with other indications of how towns responded to the political aspirations of dissenters, helps to illuminate town behavior.

During the eighteenth century, Anglicans, Baptists, Quakers, and Presbyterians constituted the major religious groups outside the Congregational Standing Order. Earliest to appear were Baptist and Quaker groups, which emerged in the mid-seventeenth century and rapidly achieved majority status in Rhode Island. Quakers enjoyed their greatest growth during the later seventeenth century, establishing meetings in the old Plymouth colony, in areas of Connecticut and Massachusetts bordering on Rhode Island, in Essex County, Massachusetts, and in adjacent southeastern New Hampshire and Maine. After 1700 growth slowed, and involved mainly the migration of small parties of Maine and New Hampshire Quakers into the frontier areas of those colonies.[22]

Baptist history was more complicated, because the sect contained so many internal divisions. Early Baptists divided over theological points into Five Principle and Six Principle groups, plus a flourishing Seventh-Day Baptist congregation in Newport and Westerly, Rhode Island. Six Principle Baptists were most numerous in rural Rhode Island, while the Five Principle Baptists had sizable churches in Newport and Providence and in such scattered Massachusetts towns as Boston, Swansea, and Leicester. Together these "old Baptists," as well as the Quakers, had stabilized into recognized communities by 1740, and had achieved a variety of accommodations with the standing order. These included limited tax exemption under the certificate system, cooperation of college-educated Baptist ministers with Congregational ministers at ordinations, acceptance of the Swansea First Baptist Church as an official town church, recognition of the Leicester church's elder as a tax-exempt minister, joint attendance of Baptists and Congregationalists at Congregational services in that town, and other local compromises.

Further fragmentation of the Baptist ranks occurred after 1740, when large numbers of New Light separatists found Baptist teachings more convincing than Congregational doctrines and changed sects, bringing a new spirit of militancy as well as rapid growth to New England Baptists. Small Separate Baptist churches appeared in towns throughout the colonies during the second half of the century, and renewed controversies with the Standing Order by refusing to present certificates when seeking tax exemption and by rejecting local compromises even when offered on easy terms. Many of the persecutions recorded by Baptist historians resulted as much from the stubborn insistence by Baptist minorities that all differences be settled entirely on their terms as from the unreasonable intolerance of the orthodox majority.[23]

The Anglicans, like the Baptists, began with small numbers before 1700 and gradually gained converts as the century progressed. From two small churches in Boston and Newport in 1700, the Church of England gradually expanded its foothold in Massachusetts and Rhode Island until by 1775 churches existed in most of the larger coastal and suburban towns. In Connecticut growth was even more rapid, especially in the western half of the colony. From beginnings in the 1720s, converts multiplied until on the eve of the Revolution they comprised an estimated 9 percent of the colony's population, with shares as large as 55 percent in the population of individual towns.[24] Anglicans experienced some hostility throughout the colonial period, because of puritan antipathy toward episcopal church organization and because of the aggressiveness of many of the missionary clergymen supported by the Society for the Propagation of the Gospel in Foreign Parts, but they also were well disposed to arrange local compromises because they supported the principle of local ecclesiastical taxation as long as a share of the receipts went to Anglican clergymen.

Throughout the eighteenth century Presbyterians enjoyed a status that differed markedly from that of other dissenters. Presbyterians agreed with the Congregational majority on most points of doctrine, differing mainly over methods of church government and matters of practice that both groups considered to be of a secondary nature though sufficient to justify maintaining separate sects. In addition, most New England Presbyterians were Scotch-Irish immigrants who preferred to retain their ethnic and cultural identity by settling in separate townships from their Congregational neighbors and by maintaining distinctive churches served by Irish-born clergymen.[25] The Standing Order recognized Presbyterian bodies as acceptable churches, and the Presbyterian churches in towns such as Pelham and Londonderry became the official town churches, while Chester, which had an existing Congregational church when the Irish arrived, soon split into two parishes, one Congregational and one Presbyterian. A few churches, such as that at Brunswick, succeeded in combining Congregational and Presbyterian members by adopting elements of each form of polity, but the two groups more often proved incompatible. Newcastle and Derryfield failed to form stable churches because the mixed populations could not agree on ministers or procedures, and the migration of Congregationalists into Oakham resulted in the transformation of the Presbyterian church there into a Congregational one and in the departure of most of the Irish settlers.[26]

Because Presbyterian churches normally achieved official status as town churches, the situation of their members with respect to the town leadership was more similar to the situation of Congregational church members than to the situation of other dissenters. Unfortunately for comparative purposes, Presbyterians kept no formal lists of communicants, and the best available evidence consists of lists of elders for Londonderry and of parish officials for Chester, both elected on an annual or frequent basis. These data suggest that Presbyterian laymen enjoyed a status like that of their Congregational counterparts. Eleven of sixteen elders chosen during Londonderry's first two decades were leaders, and the elders served an average of 3 terms as selectmen, slightly above the town average. In Chester twenty-four of the fifty-one Presbyterian wardens chosen during the period were leaders, and they served an average of 2.6 terms, also slightly above the town mean. These figures also indicate that Chester's Presbyterian leaders enjoyed electoral success equal to that of the Congregationalists in the town's other parish.

Churches of the other three dissenting sects normally held minority positions in largely Congregational towns, isolating their members from the meetinghouse contacts so useful to potential leaders. Twenty-six of the thirty-six towns listed in Table 22 contained Anglican, Baptist, or Quaker churches, and nineteen had identifiable leaders who served as selectmen between 1700 and 1784.[27] Of these, the four Rhode Island towns and Swansea were special cases because they enjoyed effective religious liberty.[28] In the aggregate, dissenting leaders in the remaining towns experienced surprisingly little discrimination because of their minority position: the seventy-five dissenting selectmen averaged 3.8 terms in comparison with a general average of 3.9 terms in the same towns (see Table 25).[29]* As a group the Baptists, whose historians have been most conscious of discrimination, fared best, with an average above the mean for all selectmen in the towns they served.[30] Anglican selectmen enjoyed close to average periods of service, and only Quaker leaders, whose religious values often discouraged active involvement in public affairs, served conspicuously less than their fellow townsmen. Such averages meant that dissenters were less successful office seekers than orthodox church members, but distinctly more successful than nonmembers.

*Service Averages for Towns with Each Dissenting Sect

Sect	Towns	Dissenters' Av. Terms	General Av. Terms
Anglicans	8	3.7	4.1
Baptists	4	5.0	4.0
Quakers	5	2.3	3.6

TABLE TWENTY-FIVE

Service of Dissenters as Selectmen

Town	Anglicans		Baptists		Quakers		All Selectmen	
	#	Ave. Terms	#	Ave. Terms	#	Ave. Terms	#	Ave. Terms
STANDING ORDER TOWNS								
Ashford			2	3.0			61	4.3
Derby	13	3.7					91	3.7
New Haven	5	2.2					188	3.4
Boston	3	2.3					122	5.1
Braintree	2	4.5					93	4.4
Hanover	1	4.0			1	1.0	45	3.8
Leicester			7	7.7	2	2.0	68	4.5
Medfield			8	2.8			135	3.1
Middleboro			4	6.0			68	5.2
Watertown	2	7.0					107	4.3
Falmouth	5	3.0			3	3.0	93	3.3
Dover					4	2.3	82	4.3
Hampton					5	2.4	147	2.8
Portsmouth	8	4.6					92	4.6
TOWNS EXERCISING RELIGIOUS FREEDOM								
Newport	8	5.6	15	6.3	4	5.8	53	6.9
Providence	4	8.8	18	5.3	1	7.0	112	4.6
Smithfield					15	5.5	57	5.6
S. Kingstown	1	6.0	2	6.5	20	8.0	70	5.4
Swansea			18	4.2	5	7.0	70	3.8

More revealing than overall statistics were the experiences of potential leaders in individual towns. Dissenters found office hardest to obtain when their numbers were very small, when their ties to out-of-town churches interfered with local loyalties, and especially when their expression of dissent was new or calculated to place them in conflict with the majority in the town. Members of the Braintree Anglican church, which consisted of about fifteen families in the first half of the century, had to wait nearly forty years before electing their first selectman; Ashford Baptists produced no leaders until they stopped presenting certificates from churches in other towns and founded their own church in the 1760s; and the Middleboro Baptist leaders belonged to a branch of the conciliatory Swansea church rather than to Isaac Backus's militant Separate Baptist church. Leaders who suddenly joined a new dissenting group often did so after an acrimonious departure from the orthodox church, and were likely to find themselves left out at the next election. Cases in point were Henry Sherburne of Portsmouth, dropped as a selectman when he turned Anglican in 1734 but promptly returned to office when he reconverted to New Light Congregationalism in the 1740s, and Captain Thomas Cheney of Dudley, Massachu-

setts, who disappeared from town office when he presented a certificate from
the Sturbridge Baptist Church and a demand that he be reimbursed for the
ministers' taxes collected from him by distraint, and returned to office two
years later when he offered to make the money in question a present to the
town.[31] Dissenters also met with hostility in newly settled towns where the
limited resources available to pay for a meetinghouse and a minister set their
refusal to contribute in stark relief.

Once a dissenting church became established and the sharpest conflicts
were resolved, community dynamics pressed hard for conciliation and
accommodation of conflicting interests. Public affairs ran most smoothly
when the whole community consented to their conduct, so once a dissenting
group contained sufficient numbers or distinguished enough members to
influence town politics, the safest course was to recognize their voice. Towns
could achieve electoral accommodations in one of three ways: by placing
religion formally outside political channels, by dividing available offices
among religious groups on a regular basis, or by simply electing individual
minority members to enough offices to keep them satisfied.

The method of excluding religious considerations from electoral politics
operated most frequently in towns where the dominance of the Standing
Order was in doubt or where dissenters held a clear majority. Among the
sample towns Swansea used this method most self-consciously, and Leicester
used it equally successfully if less formally. Throughout the eighteenth
century Swansea maintained its agreement to forego tax support for its
quasi-established Baptist church, and repeatedly reaffirmed its public commitment to keep church and state separate. A religious minority group, the
Quakers from the Shawomet area, produced the most prominent leaders, and
when the town decided in 1774 to apportion its selectmen, it did so not by
church or parish but by the districts within which militia companies were
raised. Leicester never formally voted to exclude religion from its public
processes, but the town worked to avoid contention. The first settlers in the
1720s included Baptists and Quakers as well as Congregationalists, and by
1732 the town clerk was routinely recording the dissenters' certificates. In
1741 the town recognized Elder Thomas Green as a tax-exempt clergyman,
and two years later opposed the creation of a new parish on the ground that
it would disrupt the religious balance, including an arrangement under
which one group of Baptists attended the Congregational meeting. The
town elected dissenters to major office freely and several Baptists ranked
among the most prominent town leaders. Characteristically, the sharpest
political dispute over religion occurred not between the orthodox and the
dissenters, but between a second Baptist church organized in 1764 and the
rest of the town. The new church served members from several towns beside
Leicester, so the town felt little responsibility toward it; and when the
church demanded tax exemption for its elder, ordained under allegedly
irregular circumstances, and other concessions, the town refused and pro-

voked a long court battle.[32] Towns such as Swansea and Leicester had little difficulty in achieving religious harmony among all legitimate members of the community.

A second method of handling the political aspirations of dissenters was characteristic of towns where dissenters were numerically insignificant although individual men were of leadership stature, or where dissenting groups were unorganized or fragmented. This method is exemplified in the history of Medfield. Originally a homogeneously Congregational town, Medfield began to experience religious divisions in 1746, when several members separated from the church in protest against the antirevival views of the minister. Some of the "aggrieved brethren" eventually returned to the church, but seven men declared themselves to be Baptists, organized a Baptist mission, and formed the nucleus for a Baptist church gathered in 1776. As Separates the Medfield Baptists developed an irreconcilable opposition to the Standing Order and its certificate system that led to newspaper polemics about the tax system in 1771 and to the selection of Medfield as the site for Isaac Backus's anti-establishment strategy convention in 1773. Throughout this period of Baptist agitation, the town of Medfield maintained its commitment to the Standing Order, voting in 1750 to dismiss the Separates' "Awfull Petition" for exemption from the ministerial tax and refusing in 1771 and 1772 to place the support of the ministry on a voluntary footing that would have ended the seizure of the property of dissenters unwilling to present certificates.[33] Because neither side was prepared to compromise, Medfield and her dissenters remained in frequent conflict in the later eighteenth century, but that conflict did not prevent dissenting leaders from participating actively in town affairs and holding office. Medfield's Baptists belonged to well-established local families, and despite their small numbers and slowness in forming a church, comprised a significant segment of town society. The town traditionally drew upon many inhabitants for official service and dissenters were no exception, especially in years when religion was not an overt public issue. Of fifteen men identifiable as Baptists before the gathering of a church in 1776, seven were town leaders and three first served in high office after declaring their dissent. The irregular pattern in which Baptists filled several offices in some years and none in others indicates that they served as individuals and not as regular representatives of their group.[34]

The third method of accommodating dissenters in town affairs involved including the dissenting church in the increasingly common system of apportioning offices among parishes or neighborhoods. Adoption of this method presupposed that the dissenting group was organized tightly enough to constitute a plausible representative unit, and that it was large enough to warrant its designation as one of three to five constituent units. In addition, the group had to make manifest that its principal loyalties were local rather than to some distant religious community of which it was a mission or subordinate part. During the early part of the eighteenth century, these requirements made apportionment plans more attractive to towns with Baptist societies, which were even more committed to local congregational autonomy than the Standing Order, or with Quaker minorities than to towns with Anglican missions tied to England and the Society for the Propagation of the Gospel. Dover had begun to elect Quaker selectmen regularly by 1700, and Sutton, Massachusetts, a town near Worcester, included the Baptist society in an apportionment plan instituted when the town divided into parishes in 1744.[35] Anglican churches were slower to attain political recognition because most remained small and because their status as missions raised the suspicions of neighboring Congregationalists. Anglicans, however, did obtain representation in a number of towns after mid-century as their numbers increased and as the missions stabilized into locally dominated parishes.[36]

A clear example of the process by which dissenting societies achieved political representation is the history of Braintree's Anglican church. The mission in Braintree began about 1700 with visits by George Keith and other clergymen to a body of up to thirty listeners. By 1704 ten adult males were adherents, in 1713 there were twelve communicants, and in 1727 the mission finally obtained a permanently resident Anglican minister. During these early years, the mission faced unrelenting opposition from the town's majority, as repeated petitions to the Society for the Propagation of the Gospel testify. By 1740 hostility had subsided sufficiently for Colonel Joseph Gooch, the most prominent parishioner, to obtain an occasional office, but he soon left town, frustrated by the town's refusal to satisfy his desire for frequent election. The church gradually grew to a membership of fifty families, and in 1763 obtained a minister who forswore further proselytizing to care for his flock.[37]

Numbers, longstanding, and particularly the new willingness to live and let live had its prompt reward in the regular election of Ebenezer Miller, Jr., son of the late Anglican minister, as a selectman after 1762. Exactly how the accommodation worked is revealed in a remarkable passage in John Adams's *Diary* describing his temporary defeat of Miller in 1766 and 1767. During the 1760s, Braintree consisted of three parishes, with two selectmen chosen from each of the northern and middle parishes and one selectman from the newer southern parish. At the same time local politics were organized into loose factions led on the one hand by the eminent Quincys of the North Parish, Adams, and an assortment of Congregational deacons, and on the other hand by justice Ebenezer Thayer of the Middle Parish. Thayer had apparently formed an alliance with the Anglicans, most of whom lived in the northern parish, to gain support in that area, and in return had helped Ebenezer Miller to sit as a North Parish selectman along with a Quincy candidate. In 1766 Adams unexpectedly unseated the Toryish Miller, frightening Thayer's partisans and provoking the Anglicans, some of whom threatened to boycott town meetings while their leader was excluded. Adams declined reelection in 1768, and Miller promptly returned to his seat.[38]

The process by which Braintree Anglicans established a claim to political representation is illustrative at once of the political integration of dissenters into town politics and more broadly of the role of churches as units of local political organization. Dissenters could take their place in town affairs once they stopped threatening the community and symbolically became loyal members of it, and local peace then demanded that the town accommodate their personal ambitions and policy preferences immediately. Town politics worked by balancing the interests of all groups with legitimate standing in the community, and the dynamics of rural life assured that churches would provide an organizing focus for most groups. The integration of dissenting religious groups into town society and the elevation of their members to the status of town leaders thus depended less on the operation of general Congregational intolerance for religious minorities and more on the ability of the dissenters to develop the numerical weight and cooperative attitude of a community subgroup. In the broader sphere as well, the key to understanding the religious dimension of town life involved the centrality of churches to the organization of local society rather than either formal religious qualifications for public participation or formal votes of exclusion against dissenting groups. Because churches were a primary meeting place for townsmen in their day-to-day lives, church members were better situated to be active citizens and influential leaders than those outside the churches, and the most visible church leaders, the deacons, enjoyed a favored position among the church members.

·6·

THE PROVINCIAL HIERARCHIES

An analysis of the social composition of the New England town leadership concerns itself primarily with the internal structure of town government and the relationships among individuals within each town; but towns were part of larger entities, and eventually attention must also be given to the relationship of town government to the county and provincial administrations and to the interaction of leaders at all three levels. As an examination of the age structure of the town elites has shown, a man's status in provincial politics influenced his status in town politics and the political order of the larger society had a direct relationship to the order in a town. One way of studying this relationship is to look at the local origins of colonial officials and then to try to assess the relative importance of various towns in the overall political structure and the consequent influence of provincial affairs on local arrangements. Whether or not a town produced leaders of sufficient consequence to hold provincial office, and how high those leaders progressed, are, like the internal structures of the towns, important indicators of local patterns in the political order.

On the surface, all four New England colonies had similar governmental structures. The principal unit of local government was, of course, the town, with its corporate organization and locally elected officials. Next in the hierarchy came the county, which was primarily a judicial subdivision with very limited administrative functions. The principal officials at the county level were justices of the peace, who had both individual jurisdiction over minor disputes and collective jurisdiction over more important ones when assembled as a court of general sessions of the peace, which had criminal jurisdiction, and a county court or inferior court of pleas, which had jurisdiction over civil cases. Above the county courts in the judicial ladder were the superior courts, and at the top of society in each province were the councils, which combined legislative and judicial functions, and shared executive power with the governors.

Similar governing bodies existed in each colony, but they varied widely in exact constitutional provisions and in the social position and geographical distribution of their members. Some officials were elected by the voters of a colony at large, others were elected by the legislatures, and still others were appointed by the governors. Each of these procedures favored the selection of different sorts of candidates in terms of their personal connections, position in provincial politics, and status in the community. Other differences between offices at a similar level of government in separate colonies stemmed from variations in the nature of their functions owing to disparities in size between the colonies and to divergences in local usage. These and other factors had a profound influence on the social status and geographical distribution of the provincial officeholders, and that in turn has a bearing upon one's conclusions about the relationship between the political order in the towns and the functioning of elites in the larger society. A survey of the mode of selection, social and political function, and social and geographical composition of the groups of provincial officeholders is therefore of primary importance to a study of local leadership.

Of the four colonies under consideration, town life in New Hampshire was related least clearly to the functioning of the province's political elite. New Hampshire was a royal colony, operating without benefit of a charter, and all provincial officials from the councillors down to the justices of the peace were appointees of the governor, or on occasion, of his superiors in London. Officeholders were selected on the basis of friendship with the governor or for their usefulness to the imperial administration, and appointments reflected the structure of local society only in terms of the governor's calculation of the appointee's influence on local political affairs. The political hierarchy paralleled the colony's social structure as long as settlement remained confined to a small area along the coast, and the dozen odd towns remained tightly integrated into the political system through legislative representation and other means; but as settlement sprawled rapidly to the west and north, especially after mid-century, the integration of the political and social systems became subject to increasing qualification.[1]

The trend in the social context of political power is graphically illustrated in the history of the New Hampshire Council. During the twenty years after the institution of provincial government in 1679, appointments to the Council were distributed among the leading families of five of New Hampshire's six towns. Weares of Hampton and Waldrons of Dover joined inhabitants of the provincial capital at the board so that no one town provided more than 26 percent of the councillors.[2] As the eighteenth century progressed and the old councillors retired, however, representation became restricted increasingly to Portsmouth natives. Only twelve men from other towns entered the Council after the turn of the century, and a mere three came from the 150-odd towns incorporated between that date and the Revolution. The contraction of the sphere of recruitment was progressive even within the capital city. During the first four decades of the century, when New Hampshire politics were open, twenty of twenty-three new councillors were also Portsmouth town leaders, and the Council represented a cross-section of the town's leading families; but after the Wentworth family won overwhelming political supremacy, the colonial appointments went to an interrelated, Anglicanized group, of whom only about one-third ever held town office. Wentworth family government, embodied in the Council, stood testimony at once to the economic, social, and political predominance of the capital city in New Hampshire, and to the limited integration of the town and country elites into the provincial political structure.[3]

Appointments to the New Hampshire judiciary, although few in number, were somewhat more representative of the country elite than appointments to the Council. Since the division of the province into counties did not take place until 1769, little can be learned from the membership of the county courts, but the Superior Court of Judicature was in continuous existence after 1693 and provides a usable body of membership data.[4] As with the Council, the Superior Court appointments in the late seventeenth century included prominent men from most towns in the province. Portsmouth provided six of the sixteen judges appointed before 1700, but Dover, Hampton, and Exeter, the other major towns, provided two to four each. During the first quarter of the eighteenth century, most judges came from Portsmouth, but after 1725 men from other eastern towns predominated. The geographical range was, however, modest: only one judge, Joseph Blanchard of Dunstable, lived more than twenty miles from Portsmouth.

In social terms the Superior Court judges provided a representative sample of the established leading families of eastern New Hampshire. Judgeships went regularly to families like the Weares of Hampton and Hampton-Falls, the Gilmans of Exeter, and the Wiggins of Stratham, whose forebears had been founders of the colony but whose members were excluded from the increasingly cliquish Council.[5] In addition, the judiciary provided for the mobility of new men like Thomas Millet and Thomas Wallingford of Dover. Almost without exception, and unlike the councillors, the judges were active in the leadership of their native towns, and owed their appointments to their standing as respected local notables rather than to family or mercantile connections with the Portsmouth oligarchy.

The significance of the lowest office in the provincial hierarchy, that of justice of the peace, apparently changed with the growth of the province and the development of a stable pattern in New Hampshire politics. In New Hampshire alone of the New England colonies, no comprehensive list of justices' commissions has survived, so generalizations depend on a single list of the justices commissioned in 1717, and a group of similar lists in the decade preceding the Revolution.[6] According to the 1717 list, however, the appointed justices represented the leading families of the country towns even more fully than the Superior Court judges of the period. Portsmouth, as usual, contributed the largest number of justices, but five other towns were also represented, and the country towns provided a substantial majority (twelve of twenty-one) of the officials.* Clearly the list was constructed with an eye both to confirming the status of the established, Portsmouth-based provincial leaders and to providing judicial services in the country towns. On the one hand, eleven sitting councillors and two future councillors headed the commission, and twelve of the thirteen belonged to the fourteen-man quorum. On the other hand, while eight of the quorum councillors lived in Portsmouth, the governor was careful to see that the three main outlying towns received representation, not just at the bench, but in the quorum as well. The two quorum positions conferred upon noncouncillors went to James Davis of Dover and John Gilman of Exeter, whose towns would otherwise have lacked quorum seats. The justices, like their counterparts in the Superior Court, were overwhelmingly active town leaders.

Although early justices' commissions encapsulated the colony's active political elite, by the 1760s the status of the justices of the peace was in considerable doubt. According to the authoritative study of New Hampshire politics, Governor Benning Wentworth's principal methods of managing the poorly integrated western portions of the province were to issue justices' commissions to his supporters, and to enfranchise well-disposed western towns in assembly elections regardless of their smallness or of the competing claims of larger, though less docile, eastern communities.[7] Whereas in earlier days commissions were reserved for gentlemen and councillors, by the 1760s many small western towns believed that they were entitled to have one of their inhabitants in commission as a matter of routine and petitioned accordingly. By 1765 the list of justices had grown so long as to make justices seem, to one observer, to "run down the streets in streams."[8]

A look at the 1768 list of justices indicates that the derisive attitude toward justices was partly justified and partly mistaken. Justices were both more numerous and more widely dispersed through the province. Seventy-five men from thirty-eight towns held commissions, and the towns represented ranged as far west as the Connecticut River and as far north as Lake Winnipesaukee. As might be expected, many of the western justices were relatively ordinary town leaders. From the point of view of eastern gentry and merchants, the inclusion of yeoman farmers like Jeremiah Clough of

*Distribution of Justices—1717

Town	Justices	Quorum
Portsmouth	9	8
Exeter	3	1
Dover	3	2
Hampton	2	1
Newcastle	3	2
Stratham	1	—

The only full-fledged towns not represented were Greenland and Kingston.

Canterbury and Matthew Patten of Bedford indicated a definite cheapening of the once exclusive commission of the peace.[9]

The larger commissions of the pre-revolutionary years contained a smaller proportion of high-status individuals, but the commonness of the justices and the growth in their numbers can be easily overemphasized. New Hampshire's population in 1768 was approximately five times as great as it had been half a century before, while justices of the peace were less than four times as numerous. Moreover, justices were not randomly distributed throughout the colony. Eighteen, or about one-fourth, lived in Portsmouth, while thirteen hailed from Dover, Durham, and Exeter, and another twenty lived within twenty-five miles of the capital. Ten of the Portsmouth justices, two in Exeter, and one in Dover were present or future councillors, so the claims of the leading families of the old towns to a place in the commission of the peace did not go unrecognized. Even Governor Wentworth's favorite tactic of packing the assembly with obscure clients from insignificant western towns was not reflected in his appointment of justices. Thirteen of the twenty justices who lived in towns that were more than twenty-five miles from Portsmouth belonged to towns that ranked well above their neighbors in the economic index described in Chapter 3.[10]

In social and political terms the changes in the body of justices of the peace mirrored the changing structure of the New Hampshire elite. Whereas in the early decades of the eighteenth century the Council, judiciary, and justices all represented a unified elite of eastern town leaders of distinguished lineage, by the 1760s the Council represented one elite constituency, the higher judiciary represented another, and justices of the peace included elements of three distinct elite groups. First in influence was the Anglicanized Portsmouth merchant-aristocracy, which rarely engaged in town officeholding and owed its political position to family alliances, wealth, and social connections. Next came a group of eastern gentry families, which derived some political benefit from the tradition of family participation in provincial government, but which still based its position on a solid record of leadership in the day-to-day affairs of established and politically active towns. And finally, in the newly developing western part of the province were groups of emergent local and county leaders, often with ordinary or immigrant backgrounds, who were as yet poorly integrated into the colony's political and social elites and owed their position almost entirely to their role as leaders of their communities.

Despite the unique institutional arrangement in Massachusetts by which the legislature elected the Council annually and the governor appointed the rest of the major province and county officials to serve during his pleasure, that province enjoyed a stable political structure with deep and clearly visible roots at the local level. Massachusetts was too large and populous for a small clique around the appointed governor to gain effective control of the governmental machinery, as happened in New Hampshire, and whatever tendencies existed in that direction dissolved in the face of the tradition of local autonomy that was a legacy of the electoral politics of the seventeenth century and of the charter that brought Maine and Plymouth under the government at the Bay. Political elites at every level were open to new men, but a hierarchy of towns and a traditional set of officeholding families combined to give political organizations at the county level a pattern of stability and to make the ability to speak for local interests a primary criterion for successful participation in provincial affairs.

How local interests weighed in provincial politics is clear in the composition of the Massachusetts Council, which was elected by the House of Representatives and the previous year's councillors and was therefore partially subject to the manipulations of legislative careerists and to shifts in the political winds. According to the charter, the Council consisted of twenty-eight members, of whom eighteen were to be inhabitants or proprietors of lands in the old Bay Colony, four were to be inhabitants or proprietors from the old Plymouth Colony, three were to be inhabitants or proprietors of the part of Maine that had previously belonged to Massachusetts, one was to be an inhabitant or proprietor of Sagadahock, the newly annexed eastern part of Maine, and two were to be chosen at large.[11] The provision that councillors could be proprietors rather than inhabitants of the area they were supposed to represent was a potentially significant loophole in the apportionment scheme, because many Boston merchants were proprietors of lands in remote parts of the province.

Historians have made much of the potential for abuse inherent in the proprietor clause, but in reality the General Court was quite scrupulous to maintain reasonable representation from the outlying areas.[12] In the eighty-two years after the election of the first Council in 1693, the old Plymouth Colony was entitled to 328 councillor terms and bona fide Old Colony residents filled 347 places, with one man each year coming from each of the three counties and the extra terms served in rotation.[13] Maine was supposed to provide councillors for 246 terms and actually filled 188, which was reasonable in view of the fact that most of the underrepresentation occurred in the first third of the period when all but three Maine towns were abandoned to the Indians. Only the Council seat assigned to Sagadahock territory was filled systematically by an absentee, and that region remained virtually uninhabited until after 1760. Regional apportionment was also a custom in Massachusetts proper, where it was not legally required. Essex County consistently elected four or five councillors, Middlesex regularly sent three, and the western counties of Hampshire and Worcester furnished one councillor between them in the early years and two or more after settlement accelerated in the 1740s and 1750s.

The representation of the outlying counties never reached a level commensurate with their share of the population, but the disproportionate number of residents of Boston on the Council served the interests of men in all parts of the province. A primary factor in filling the Council with Bostonians was the necessity that a quorum be readily available at all times to consult with the governor on executive matters and to take action in case of emergency. Councillors from the more remote counties expected to be in Boston during the regular sessions of the General Court and occasionally at other times, but for the most part they preferred to be spared the inconvenience of remaining in the capital on a longterm basis. Essex was the only outlying county to provide councillors in proportion to its population, and most of Essex lay within a few hours' boat trip of Boston. A second and related factor was that a seat on the Council was not always an especially prestigious position in the local status order. During most of the period, for example, Hampshire County was separated from the rest of Massachusetts by an unsettled wilderness and remained in constant danger of Indian attack, so that the command of the county militia and commissions to attend intercolonial defense conferences were far more important to the local leaders than a seat on a council sitting in remote Boston.[14] Leading men in the outlying counties acquiesced in their underrepresentation in part because they could not conveniently fulfill the duties of the office and in part because the office didn't necessarily mean as much to them as it did to men nearer Boston.

In addition to the geographical distribution of the membership, the relative influence of political alignments on elections was a factor in determining whether Council service reflected status in the county and local elites. Legislative elections made membership in the Massachusetts Council more susceptible to the influence of the political factions that flourished in the General Court than would have been the case if councillors had been appointed by the crown or elected by the freeholders, but in practice the gentlemen of the board were rarely the creatures of any organized political group.

One indication of the social status of the councillors was the stability of the membership and the ability of many incumbents to enforce their position as political neutrals who remained in office year after year in spite of shifts in factional power.[15] During the seventy-three years between the proclamation of the charter and the beginning of the purge of prerogative supporters in 1766, the twenty-eight-man Council averaged fewer than three new members a year, a rate that, in theory, could be explained by death and voluntary retirement, and the Council members averaged nearly ten years of service.[16] While elections often were managed by popular majorities in the House of Representatives, the governors found it necessary only twice to veto more than two nominations. On seventeen other occasions the governors "negatived" one to two individuals apparently as a result of personal vendettas, because they simultaneously allowed the supporters of the men they vetoed to take their seats.[17] The councillors were also firmly rooted in the local political level. Forty-nine of the fifty-one councillors who lived in country towns for which data has been assembled were town leaders, while even in Boston only seventeen of the fifty-nine men reached the Council without serving the town in one of its major offices.

Appointments to the provincial judiciary reveal the structure of the county elites, and confirm the political necessity of respecting their claims to high office. The highest court in the province, the Superior Court of Judicature, was too small to reflect the balance of local interests accurately, and, in addition, the unwritten requirements that a prospective judge have extensive experience in the law and preferably a liberal education eliminated many social and political leaders from consideration.[18] In a general way, however, the composition of the court indicated that members of leading country families were unwilling to have Bostonians dominate a court that heard cases in their local county seats and that they had the political influence to prevent it. Only five of the twenty-seven judges appointed after 1700 were natives of Boston, and, significantly, when Bostonian Thomas Hutchinson claimed the chief justiceship in 1760 and brushed aside the claims of several country candidates, the appointment became a cause célèbre in Massachusetts politics.[19]

Although appointments to the Superior Court were few in number and required professional qualifications, appointments to the Inferior Court of Pleas depended on personal authority and prestige, and the members of the court in each county epitomized the county's social and political elite. Judgeships were systematically awarded to the most prominent men in each of several large towns, so that the county bench would represent the interests of inhabitants of the whole region.[20] In Essex, Ipswich and Salem regularly provided a judge, while the remaining positions rotated among several towns; in Middlesex three judgeships alternated between Cambridge and Charlestown, and the fourth went to men from western towns such as Groton and Dunstable. Town politics did not determine appointments entirely, however, because there were also family interests to be considered. County judgeships were filled by Bradfords and Winslows, Pynchons and Williamses, Cushings and Saltonstalls, so that town-based appointment patterns often had to be changed to accommodate members of notable families who did not fit neatly into the rotation. Four members of the Cushing family served for fifty-eight years on the Plymouth Court, six Pynchons served forty-nine years in Hampshire, and five Leonards from three towns served ninety-four years in Bristol. At one time in the 1760s three of the four judges on the Bristol Court were Leonards.

Judges of the Inferior Courts were not only members of prominent local families, but also their towns' most important and influential leaders. Excluding Boston, fifty-two of the fifty-nine judges who lived in towns for which data is available served their town in major offices like selectman and moderator, which involved strictly local duties, and another four served their town only as representative, an office that enabled them to gain attention in Boston as well as to serve their constituents. Most judges were among the minority of town leaders who were especially influential and long serving. The thirteen Hampshire judges in sample towns averaged thirty-six years of town service, the four Plymouth judges averaged twenty-one years, and the five Worcester judges averaged thirty-one years. In Boston ten of the twenty judges were clearly town leaders and another judge had served as a representative, while the others included governors' relatives like Eliakim and Foster Hutchinson and prerogative-oriented merchants like Edward Lyde and Joseph Green.*

The lists of justices of the peace present an even clearer picture of the county elites than the lists of Inferior Court judges, because the greater numbers of justices provide the basis for quantitative estimates of the contributions of the respective towns to the elite. Actually, the justices of the peace included two distinct groups. In the larger group were the ordinary country justices, whose primary duties involved the adjudication of small causes, the swearing-in of local officials, the solemnization of marriages, and the like. These justices also had a nominal role in the decisions of the Court of General Sessions of the Peace, which had jurisdiction over criminal cases equivalent to that of the Inferior Court of Pleas over civil cases, and which served as a county's governing body. Members of the smaller group of justices, those who were designated as "of the Quorum" had to be present for the General Sessions to be lawfully convened, and the justices of the quorum, who were more distinguished or more experienced men, dominated the decisions of the county court.[21] The justices of the quorum constituted an elite group similar to the judges of the Inferior Court, although a slightly larger group because the quorum was not limited to a fixed number of justices.[22] Indeed, the personnel of the two groups largely overlapped because when fresh commissions of the peace were issued, as in 1761, the sitting judges of the Inferior Court usually led the list of justices of the peace and quorum. Ninety-one percent of all Inferior Court judges were also justices of the peace, and the vast majority belonged to the quorum.[23]

A look at the numerical distribution of the whole body of justices gives an indication of the distribution of local political power. During the first third of the provincial period, from 1693 to 1724, seven or more justices lived in a

*Judges as Town Leaders

County	Sample Town Judges	Representative Only	Other Major Office
Barnstable	11	0	11
Bristol	5	0	4
Essex	13	2	10
Hampshire	13	0	13
Middlesex	7	1	5
Plymouth	4	0	4
Suffolk (without Boston)	1	1	0
Boston	19	1	10
Worcester	5	0	5
	78	5	62

group of thirteen towns, which included the county seats of the seven mainland counties, and the then important towns of Scituate, Eastham, Charlestown, Ipswich, Marblehead, and Newbury. In the next twenty-five years the number of towns receiving seven or more commissions rose to thirty-two, with at least three such towns in each of the old counties, and two in newly formed Worcester County. And finally, thirty-seven towns produced seven or more justices in the quarter century before the Revolution, with the largest increases occurring in Essex and Suffolk, where justices became numerous in secondary towns like Lynn and Amesbury and in the Boston suburbs respectively.[24]

Because justices of the peace were appointed rather than elected officials, selection depended on an evaluation by the governor and his advisers of a man's social and political status and of his ability to use his status and prestige to maintain the authority of the central government among his neighbors. Most governors were sensitive to local political situations, and the majority of the justices were recognized local leaders. Sixty-four percent of the justices who lived in the forty-two sample towns in Massachusetts were town leaders, and with Boston, Cambridge, and Salem excluded, the figure was 89 percent.* Exactly how candidates came to the attention of the authorities in Boston, however, remains uncertain. Among the more prominent families, traditional involvement in politics, wealth, and usually connections gained while attending college are enough to explain particular appointments, but more is necessary to account for the appointment of many of the ordinary local leaders who became country justices. Frequently commissions went to men who had served in the House of Representatives and so had established a reputation in Boston, and the recommendations of the judges, sitting justices, and other local political leaders presumably carried great weight.[25]

*Justices as Town Leaders in Sample Towns (by County)

	Justices	Leaders	
Barnstable	26	23	
Bristol	14	14	
Essex (Salem omitted)	13	12	
Salem	58	42	
Hampshire	29	26	
Middlesex (Cambridge omitted)	21	20	
Cambridge	31	17	
Plymouth	17	14	
Suffolk (Boston omitted)	43	35	
Boston	214	84	
Worcester	25	22	
Maine (3 counties)	20	18	
Total	509	327	(64.2%)
Boston, Cambridge, Salem only	303	143	(47.2%)
All other sample towns	206	184	(89.3%)

Most justices were active local leaders, but there were important exceptions dictated by the custom of granting governmental authority to men of economic and social distinction and by purely political considerations. During most of the eighteenth century, justices who were not town leaders came most frequently from Boston, where they comprised 60 percent of the number commissioned, and to a lesser extent from other major eastern towns like Cambridge and Salem. Some of these men, like Dean Winthrop, Lieutenant Governor William Dummer, and several of the Hutchinsons were members of old New England families who had grown too proud to accept election to town office, while some, like Andrew Belcher and Francis Bernard, Jr., were relatives of high officials and often men of very limited ability whose appointments clearly resulted from nepotism. Others were wealthy and often self-made merchants who were too busy to attend to town politics, but who welcomed the social recognition of a commission of the peace, and may even have found the office an advantage in business. Finally, many were Anglicans, custom officials, or other persons too closely associated with the court interest in politics to be popular in electoral politics.

With the tightening of the Hutchinson-Oliver clique on the executive machinery after 1760 and the subsequent imperial crisis, the appointments of prerogative-oriented men with limited local followings became more numerous and began to spread to other towns. The engrossment of offices by the Hutchinsonian leaders, as well as their policy decisions, aroused increasing hostility among the active political leaders in Boston and in the counties, and in response the Hutchinson-Oliver clique compounded the problem by abandoning the traditional policy of neutralizing opposition with popular and well-chosen appointments. Instead, Bernard, Hutchinson, and their associates tried to ensure reliable local support by commissioning men whose political views were congenial, but who previously had not been active in politics. In Cambridge, where fifteen of twenty justices had been town leaders, commissions now went to a group of relative outsiders which included Anglican merchants such as John Apthorp and Richard Lechmere, and Antigua planters such as Thomas Oliver and John Vassall, and which had traditionally maintained a self-contained and exclusive society in their great houses along what came to be called "Tory Row."[26] The same phenomenon occurred in other towns and counties; and in addition the governors began to issue commissions to obscure men in the smaller country towns whose chief qualifications seem to have been ignorance of the dominant issues and lack of entry into the traditional local elites.

The novel policy of appointing justices of the peace without regard for the social and political realities in the countryside combined with the popular purge of the Council to reverse temporarily the traditional orientations of the elite offices. Between 1766 and 1770 the Council, which had always embodied a compromise between local interests and the requirements of central government, became increasingly representative of the county elites as prerogative men and family oligarchs were replaced with men risen from the ranks of the county judges and the justices of the peace.[27] At the same time, however, the county offices were increasingly filled with administration supporters, especially in counties like Suffolk, where several offices fell vacant in a short space of time; and the commission of the peace reached a nadir of local authority that was exemplified by the appointment in 1768 of James Murray, a Scottish-born North Carolina merchant who had recently arrived in Boston, not only to a justiceship but to the quorum.[28] By 1775 the elected Council was serving the interests of the country better than it had in decades, while the appointive judicial system, traditionally the bastion of local authority, was in universal ill repute.

In contrast to the situation in the more northerly provinces, a distinction between local concerns and the political decisions of imperial officials did not blur the meaning of elite recruitment in Rhode Island and Connecticut, because all offices were elective and all officials depended upon influence with the voters for their places. In both colonies the governor, deputy governor, and assistants were elected annually by the freemen of the governmental corporation, and both Superior Court judges and county court judges, who sat for both civil and criminal cases, were elected annually by the legislature. The legislatures also elected justices of the peace, but their significance in the study of elite structure is minimal because every town, no matter how small, was entitled to have one or more inhabitants placed in commission. The constitutional similarities between the two colonies, however, were not paralleled by similarities in political practice, so that the colonies displayed strikingly different patterns of behavior.

Eighteenth-century Connecticut has earned the reputation of a land of "steady habits," and the composition of that colony's Council justifies the nickname. Like Massachusetts under the Old Charter, Connecticut elected its assistants by soliciting nominations from the freemen in the fall, and then balloting in the spring to choose a governor, deputy governor, and twelve assistants from the top twenty nominees. No one prearranged slates of nominees, and the names of sitting magistrates were read in order of seniority, so that the voters usually reelected the incumbents in order until they died or became infirm. Men in the nineteenth and twentieth places in the list of nominees gradually rose in the standings until they became assistants, and of the nine governors between 1700 and 1785, seven began as assistants, worked their way up the list to deputy governor, and then took the governor's chair in course.[29] Connecticut's magistrates averaged nearly twelve years of service.

Unlike the Councils in Massachusetts and New Hampshire, residents of the capital did not predominate in the Upper House. Neither Hartford nor New Haven dominated Connecticut economically the way Boston and Portsmouth dominated the northern colonies, and the corporate integrity of

Connecticut tended to make the political society more tightly integrated than it was in the colonies already discussed. The secretary and treasurer always lived in the immediate vicinity of Hartford, but the Council drew together the most distinguished men in Connecticut's six counties. Hartford County, which included most of the Connecticut River Valley, consistently provided between one-third and one-half of the assistants, and the other counties sent two or three men each, a formula that agreed well with the distribution of population.[30] The assistants headed an elite of traditionally prominent families that were interrelated on a colony-wide basis. High office was not hereditary, but there were five magistrates named Huntington, four each named Pitkin and Stanly, and two with each of fourteen other surnames. Many political leaders lived in large towns like Hartford, Fairfield, or New London, where they were active town leaders; but family connections were so pervasive, and the colony so tightly integrated, that a large town power base was not essential.[31]

The judiciary, which was elected annually by the General Assembly, was composed of members of the same prominent families. The Superior Court, which had only thirty-two members from the time it assumed the judicial function of the Court of Assistants in 1711 to the Revolution, was a comparatively professional body. At least fourteen judges were college graduates, and virtually all had judicial experience at the county level. In addition, all but two judges were assistants at the time of their appointment, or became assistants shortly afterward, so that the intention in constituting the court was clearly to limit the traditional judicial function of the assistants to the most highly qualified members of the Upper House rather than to create a distinct body. The social and geographical composition of the Superior Court was a virtual microcosm of the Council.[32]

At the county level the Connecticut judiciary included three distinct elements. First the Assembly elected a judge of the county court, who was in effect the chief justice for the county. Second, the legislators chose between three and five justices of the peace and quorum to sit as associate judges on the county court.[33] This court served both as a court of general sessions of the peace for criminal cases and as a court of pleas for civil cases. Finally, the Assembly elected as many as fifty or sixty justices of the peace for each county at the nomination of the freemen of each town to handle small cases.[34]

The judge and justices of the peace and quorum formed the only court with county-wide jurisdiction, and their numbers included the leading political figures in the most important towns. About 90 percent of the county court justices in the sample towns were active town leaders in the eighteenth century, and the exceptions were old men who presumably had been leaders before 1700. Nearly two-thirds of the assistants served on the county court at some time in their careers, but the justices were more than twice as numerous as the assistants, and most of the additional men came from the larger towns.[35] Justices from major towns such as Hartford,

Windsor, New Haven, Fairfield, and New London served more than one hundred terms on the court between its creation in 1698 and 1785, while men from lesser towns like Stonington, Derby, or Middletown served about half as long. Minor towns such as Ashford, Bolton, and Newtown provided very few justices, and in most cases none at all. Like most Connecticut officials, the county court justices remained in office for long periods of time: the average term of service was eleven and one-half years.

Despite Rhode Island's general reputation for unorthodoxy and turmoil, the colony's government did not differ drastically from that of its neighbors at the beginning of the eighteenth century. The last of the turbulent first-generation leaders had retired after the overthrow of the Dominion of New England, and in 1700 Samuel Cranston was serving the fourth of thirty placid terms as governor.[36] At that time the colony consisted of only nine towns and about five thousand inhabitants, and the government was correspondingly simple.[37] According to the provisions of the Charter of 1663, the colony freemen elected a governor, deputy governor, and ten assistants annually to form the upper house of the General Assembly, and the towns elected deputies to the lower house semiannually. The assistants composed the Court of Trials, the only formal court, and between one and three justices of the peace in each town rounded out the judiciary.[38] The Assembly divided the colony into two counties, one in the islands and one on the mainland in 1703.[39]

During the first quarter of the century, the membership of the upper house reflected the general stability of politics. The magistrates served an average of 6 terms per man during the quarter century, and those entering the Council during the period served an average of 8.5 terms during their careers.* Social distance was not very great in the tiny colony, especially outside of Newport, but the assistants were primarily descendents of the founding fathers of Rhode Island. Roger Williams's son Joseph served several terms, as did the Greenes and Holdens of Warwick, the Coddingtons and Eastons of Newport, and the Coggeshalls of Portsmouth. In geographical terms, the pattern differed only slightly from the seventeenth-century distribution of five Council seats to Newport, three to Providence, and two each to Portsmouth and Warwick. Implementation of the provision in the act incorporating Kingstown that granted the town two seats reduced the representation of Newport and Providence by one seat in most years, but the upper house remained the exclusive preserve of leaders from the colony's five largest towns.[40]

*Statistics of Service by Rhode Island Magistrates

Period	Total Men	Total Terms	Average	First Serving	Terms	Average
1700–1724	58	349	6.0	47	400	8.5
1725–1749	76	352	4.6	55	300	5.5
1750–1774	84	350	4.2	67	298	4.4

Political stability foundered in 1731 on the issue of paper money, when Governor Joseph Jenckes, Cranston's successor, attempted to veto a land-bank bill; and Rhode Island began its celebrated and precocious practice of openly partisan politics. With the parade of Wanton and Greene, Hopkins and Ward in and out of the governorship, the degree of continuity in the upper house plummetted. Between 1700 and 1731 the voters elected forty-four new men to the upper house, but after 1732 they took only seventeen years to introduce another forty-four. Rhode Island had no fall primary election, and each party distributed printed ballots listing their nominees for the use of the freemen.[41] The lists were not mutually exclusive, which indicated that the normal eighteenth-century practice of electing distinguished men who stood above party was not entirely inoperative, but control of the upper house was essential to party supremacy, and the factions acted accordingly. In 1745 the Wantons swept into office, replacing eight of the twelve magistrates, and the next year the Greenes returned, replacing eleven. The average service of magistrates first elected in the second quarter of the century was only 5.5 years, and in the next twenty-five years the average fell still further, to 4.4 years.

The growth of political rivalry had only limited effect on the social status of the assistants, and caused even less change in their geographical distribution. The contending parties were organized as alliances of politically active families, and as such maintained the traditional elite character of colonial politics. The Wantons and Wards of Newport, the Greenes of Warwick, and the Browns of Providence all had founding fathers of the colony as ancestors. These leaders continued to reside in the older and richer coastal towns, and the distribution of seats changed only gradually. During the third quarter of the century, Warwick and Portsmouth each lost a seat. One went to Little Compton, which had just been annexed from Massachusetts, and the other went most often to growing Providence or neighboring Cranston, while the small towns averaged less than one assistant a year.* Because all of the leading towns except Newport and Providence were primarily agricultural, the majority of the assistants were not spectacularly wealthy, and their eminence was more an outgrowth of

*Distribution of Assistants in Selected Years

Town	1700	1720	1740	1760	1770
Newport	5	4	4	4	3
Providence	2	2	2	3	4
Portsmouth	1	2	1	0	1
Warwick	2	2	2	1	1
N. Kingstown	†{ 2	†{ 1	1	1	1
S. Kingstown		1	1	1	1
Little Compton				1	1
Cranston				1	
Smithfield			1		

†North and South Kingstown, separated 1723.

traditional family leadership in town and county politics than of extreme social distance. Eighty-three percent of the assistants in the sample towns were town leaders, and most were sons or near relatives of other leaders. A few magistrates, like Darius Sessions of Providence and Abraham Redwood of Newport, were self-made merchants and newcomers, but the majority were of native birth.[42]

Rhode Island erected its county court system and Superior Court in 1729 and 1747 respectively, just in time for them to become political footballs. The superior courts in other colonies quickly became professional bodies, but although the assumption of the judicial function of the Rhode Island assistants by five special judges marked a step in the same direction, the court proved to be a highly political body. Both Samuel Ward and Stephen Hopkins, the principal political leaders, served as chief justice when they were out of the governor's seat, and the court was as famous for deciding cases according to the political loyalties of the litigants as the General Assembly was for reversing the judgments at the next change of political fortunes.[43] Granting that the judges at any one time represented only one party, however, the membership of the court reflected the distribution of the colony's elite accurately.[44] Newport, Providence, Bristol, and South Kingstown, all county seats, contributed between three and six judges each, and Portsmouth, Warwick, and Little Compton, which were important towns for the recruitment of assistants, provided two apiece. But Superior Court elections were not governed by a traditional distribution of seats, and the office provided an outlet for political talents in the smaller towns. Seven towns that did not usually produce assistants contributed judges to the Superior Court in the decades before the Revolution. In terms of social status, more than half of the judges were assistants, and twelve of sixteen judges in sample towns were respected town leaders.

Below the Superior Court in the judicial hierarchy were the county courts and the justices of the peace. Technically, the laws that divided Rhode Island into three counties in 1729 erected separate Courts of Common Pleas and General Sessions of the Peace, and for a few years the Assembly elected the judges, usually the same men, of each court separately.[45] By about 1735, however, the two courts were effectively combined, and the men elected to be justices of common pleas were simply commissioned to sit in the Court of General Sessions. The Assembly also elected justices of the peace, who apparently had no part in the sessions of the county courts. These increased in numbers from between 1 and 3 in each town in 1700 to as many as 167 in the colony in 1764, with the number in each town adjusted to reflect the town's support of the prevailing party.[46]

The Inferior Court seats were at once political prizes and indications of high social and political status. Like the assistants and the Superior Court judges, the justices moved in and out of office as the parties moved in and out of power. Ten of the fifteen justices left office when the Wantons replaced the Greenes in power in 1747, and similar shifts occurred during the Hopkins-Ward era.[47] Some justices, however, were nonpolitical local dignitaries who remained in office regardless of which party was dominant, while many of the party-oriented men managed to regain their old offices again and again. The average tenure on the Inferior Court was 6.1 years, substantially higher than that for the assistants and the Superior Court. As might be expected, the justices were leading figures in the principal county towns. Fifty of the fifty-seven who lived in sample towns were town leaders. Newport and South Kingstown dominated the courts in their respective counties, while elsewhere Providence and Smithfield, Warwick and East Greenwich, and Bristol and Warren were paired in relative strength on the courts.[48]

As the foregoing analysis indicates, most members of the colony-wide elites of all four New England colonies were social and political leaders at the local level as well. Where the higher offices were elective, a man needed to earn the support of the freeholders in his section of the colony as well as to make the acquaintance of leaders from other areas, because both informal lists of candidates and formal political tickets incorporated customary balances of regional representation designed to give voice to local interests. Where the higher offices were appointive, the sanction enforcing broad geographical balance was less direct, but equally forceful. Imperial administrators needed to ensure that civil peace and political tranquillity existed in the countryside so that they could govern effectively, and the most practical method of gaining local political support was to appoint officials who were acceptable to politically active members of local society, and who had sufficient authority and influence to safeguard imperial interests in their localities. The colonial elites therefore included men from many country towns as well as from the capital cities.

The inhabitants of all towns, of course, were not equally able to gain entry into the higher elite. County seats were obvious centers for regional political leadership, and certain other towns were centers of political activity because of their place in the traditional distribution of offices (Warwick and Portsmouth, Rhode Island, are examples), or because of their relative size or the relative wealth of their leading inhabitants. As Chapter 4 has shown, moreover, members of the colonial elites often belonged to traditionally prominent families or qualified for their status by obtaining an unusually extensive education so that they did not participate in local politics on an equal footing with men of more ordinary backgrounds. The presence or absence of such individuals and the internal political structures of the towns were therefore mutually related, and the position of a town in the larger political structure was a partial explanation of its communal behavior.

A general survey of the distribution of the more important and more numerous provincial officials suggests how the principal officeholders were

TABLE TWENTY-SIX

Index of Prominence

	JPs	Quorum	Pleas	Council	College	Total	Index[1]
MASSACHUSETTS 1692-1774							
Amherst	2	0	0	0	2	4	6.20
Andover	7	1	0	1	6	15	6.92
Barnstable	26	18	11	6	10	71	33.09
Barrington	2	0	0	0	0	2	---[2]
Billerica	4	0	0	0	0	4	3.00
Boston	214	48	23	71	51	407	26.22
Boxford	3	0	0	0	1	4	4.70
Braintree	13	3	0	2	11	29	11.86
Brookline	8	4	0	0	7	19	56.21
Cambridge	31	7	6	13	18	75	47.41
Dedham	8	2	0	1	4	15	7.78
Dorchester	14	1	1	1	4	21	15.44
Duxbury	6	1	2	0	1	10	9.43
Fitchburg	0	0	0	0	1	1	3.86
Grafton	2	0	0	0	0	2	2.60
Hadley	8	2	1	1	5	17	13.95[3]
Hanover	4	5	1	0	1	12	12.00[2]
Hardwick	2	1	1	1	3	8	7.92
Hatfield	6	1	2	2	4	15	18.40
Leicester	2	1	1	0	2	6	7.79
Lunenburg	5	2	1	0	2	10	12.18
Manchester	3	0	1	0	2	6	8.09
Medfield	1	1	0	0	1	3	4.70
Middleboro	7	1	1	0	2	11	3.20
Norton	6	5	3	2	2	18	9.27
Oakham	0	0	0	0	0	0	0.00
Pelahm	0	0	0	0	0	0	0.00
Salem	55	15	16	19	26	131	30.80
Shirley	0	0	0	0	0	0	0.00
Springfield	13	10	6	4	7	40	14.58
Sudbury	7	0	0	0	2	9	5.08
Swansea	9	3	1	0	2	15	8.34
Topsfield	0	0	0	0	0	0	0.00
Waltham	3	2	0	0	1	6	9.05
Watertown	7	1	0	0	3	11	15.87
Westminster	1	0	0	0	0	1	2.13
Worcester	10	7	2	3	3	25	16.92
MAINE 1692-1774							
Biddeford	7	1	0	0	2	10	8.33[3]
Brunswick	5	2	2	0	1	10	19.84
Falmouth	24	7	7	3	10	51	13.48
Gorham	2	1	0	0	3	6	12.00[2]
Newcastle	0	0	0	0	1	1	2.20
Scarborough	4	1	1	0	0	6	4.70

TABLE TWENTY-SIX: CONTINUED

	JPs 1717	JPs 1768	Supreme Court	Council	College	Total	Index
NEW HAMPSHIRE 1700-1775							
Bedford	-	1	0	0	0	1	2.76
Canterbury	-	1	0	0	1	2	3.98
Chester	-	2	0	0	0	2	1.68
Concord	1	1	0	0	3	5	6.65
Cornish	-	0	0	0	0	0	0.00
Derryfield	-	1	0	0	0	1	4.35
Dover	3	5	1	1	2	12	7.43
Dublin	-	0	0	0	0	0	0.00
Hampstead	-	1	0	0	1	2	3.11
Hampton	2	2	1	1	3	9	6.21[3]
Hanover	-	0	0	0	1	1	10.87
Londonderry	-	3	0	0	1	4	1.26
New Ipswich	-	1	0	0	2	3	5.00[2]
Portsmouth	9	18	11	41	17	96	21.50
Weare	-	0	0	0	0	0	0.00

	County Court	Supreme Court	Council	College	Total	Index
RHODE ISLAND 1700-1775						
Exeter	3	1	0	0	4	2.38
Middletown	5	0	1	0	6	7.23
Newport	18	4	51	6	79	9.90
Providence	10	6	33	4	53	14.17
Smithfield	5	0	6	0	11	4.58
S. Kingstown	13	5	15	3	36	15.16
CONNECTICUT 1700-1775						
Ashford	0	0	0	0	0	0.00
Bolton	0	0	0	0	0	0.00[4]
Derby	2	0	0	0	2	4.26[4]
Enfield	1	0	0	2	3	7.50[4]
Hartford	16	6	18	15	55	40.95[4]
Kent	0	0	0	2	2	4.01[4]
New Haven	15	2	5	21	43	19.28[4]
Newtown	0	0	0	2	2	3.45[4]
Stonington	5	0	1	4	10	7.59[4]
Woodbury	7	0	1	2	10	9.73[4]

1) The Index represents the total number of positions of prominence (column six) divided by the town's population in 1765 (Appendix I), and the result multiplied by 1,000 to yield an index of prominence per 1,000 inhabitants.
2) Populations for Hanover, Gorham, and New Ipswich are estimates. No population figures for Barrington exist.
3) Hadley, Biddeford, and Hampton all were divided late in the period. The populations of Amherst, Pepperrellborough, and North Hampton, respectively, have been added to the census population to minimize distortion in the Index.
4) The Index for all Connecticut towns has been tripled to compensate for the limited turnover in offices in that colony.

distributed, but for purposes of constructing a system for classifying the towns, a more precise and systematic index is desirable. Fortunately, the councillors, judges, and justices in the several provinces were numerous enough to give meaning to statistical measures, and most of the individuals concerned were prominent enough that their place of residence could be identified. For New Hampshire the justices of the peace, judges of the Superior Court, and councillors provide the most satisfactory information, while for Rhode Island and Connecticut the county court judges take the place of the justices of the peace, because justices were appointed for every town regardless of its size and importance. In Massachusetts figures on justices of the peace, justices of the peace and quorum, judges of the Inferior Court of Pleas, and councillors are all helpful, while the number of Superior Court judges was too small in comparison with the size of the province's elite to be meaningful. In addition, the number of college graduates among the leading town officers has been tabulated, because a college education provided a man with powerful contacts in elite circles and because the towns recognized college graduates as prominent individuals by choosing so many of them to high office at early ages.[49]

The number of justices of the peace, judges, and councillors resident in a town, and of college graduates among the town leaders, forms an "index of prominence," which, when it is divided by the population of the town in 1765, can be expressed as the number of prominent men in the town between 1700 and 1775 in relation to a thousand inhabitants in the census year (see Table 26). Reliance on a single population figure risks some distortion for towns that became more or less important during the century and for towns that were incorporated late, but potential distortion must be balanced against the substantial gain in accuracy achieved by using longterm figures on officeholding instead of short-term figures that often reflected the behavior of a single man rather than of a town as a whole. Remarkably, in view of the use of different groups of officials for each colony, towns in Massachusetts, New Hampshire, and Rhode Island that seemed intuitively to be similar in prominence had similar numerical ratings, and figures for Connecticut fell into line when the ratings were tripled to compensate for the slow turnover in that colony's offices.

Overall, the towns fell into three categories. First was a class of small or moderate-sized towns with an index of 5 or less. Some of these, like Topsfield, Pelham, and Ashford contained no prominent men at all, although many had a few exceptional leaders in the course of the century. Most of these leaders were at best college graduates of local importance or justices of the peace; the lesser towns rarely sent men to the Council or into the higher judiciary. This class of towns contained many frontier communities, as well as a number of egalitarian towns like Boxford, Medfield, and Newtown.

In the second category was a class of towns, usually of moderate or large size, in which the index ranged between 5 and 10. These towns produced a substantial number of justices and college graduates, and quite often one or two men who achieved the rank of judge or councillor. Towns of this class were common in the suburbs of the provincial capitals, and were interspersed with towns of less prominence in the countryside. The group contained only one county seat (Dover, which became a county seat in 1773), and few of the large county towns that supported a prominent baronial family.

Towns of the third class, which had an index of 10 or more, were the leading towns in their colony and contained substantial numbers of judges and councillors. Boston and Portsmouth, both provincial capitals, and Hartford and New Haven, both half capitals, belonged to this class because they had literally dozens of prominent men among their large populations. Newport achieved a remarkably low rating of 9.9, apparently because the traditional apportionment formulas in Rhode Island restricted representation, but the colony's leading city demonstrated its preeminence through the unusual prominence of those who did serve. Newporters served forty-nine years as governor and forty-three years as deputy governor during the eighty-five-year period. County seats like Barnstable, Worcester, and South Kingstown were also in this third group, as were unique towns such as Cambridge, which was at once a suburb, a county seat, and a center of learning, and Salem, which was both a major seaport and a county seat. Not all major towns, however, were government centers. Brookline, Dorchester, and Braintree were wealthy suburbs, while Hatfield and Lunenburg were inland towns of secondary prominence, and Brunswick and Biddeford were minor commercial towns on the Maine coast.

The distribution of political leaders among the towns, and the related distribution of politically important towns, moderately important towns, and politically insignificant communities throughout the New England countryside indicates that a sort of political central place theory paralleled the economic structure revealed by an analysis of wealth distribution and of commercialization. Every county-sized region contained a hierarchy of towns, ranging from communities in which the most prominent leaders operated on a purely local level to towns in which the leaders engaged in county-wide decision-making and influenced the county leaders, and finally to towns that produced leaders who were knowledgeable and influential in colony-wide and even extracolonial affairs. The existence of such a political hierarchy is perfectly compatible with the existence of a central place-oriented economic structure, and with a hierarchy of town types in such internal matters as the size of the town elite, the distribution of power among the local leaders, and the influence of family prestige on local politics. The crucial question, which will be taken up in the next chapter, is to determine whether all of these factors combined to create a structurally consistent typology of towns.

·7·

THE TYPOLOGY OF TOWNS

An examination of the size and tenure of town elites, the distribution of property in the towns, the role of family and church in political recruitment, and the classification of towns by prominence and economic function provides five comprehensive indices of town behavior, as well as several other indicators that must be used on a sample basis because of the enormous amount of information they require. No one aspect of town behavior fully illustrates the variety of town types, but analyzed together the five indices delineate a five-part typology of towns in colonial New England. An understanding of the components of this typology, moreover, gains in strength and clarity when the town types are fully described by adding information gained from the more fragmentary indicators to the basic outline.

As the preceding chapters have shown, none of the five indices suggested more than four groupings of towns, and while some measures arranged themselves according to population, others followed no clearly explained pattern. The first comprehensive measure of the internal political behavior of the towns, the percentage of the population serving in the town leadership, suggested four apparent categories of towns.[1] These categories seemed closely related to population, with the smallest percentage of the townsmen serving as leaders in the largest cities and with the percentages increasing steadily for groups of towns with populations over 1,000, between 500 and 1,000, and under 500 respectively. Towns like Hatfield and Concord, which had much smaller elites than other towns of their size, and Newtown, which had a much larger elite, however, remained unaccountable exceptions.

The second measure of internal political behavior, the average number of terms served by each leader,[2] and the third measure, the percentage of all terms served by those influential leaders who served five times or more,[3] seemed less closely tied to population. Both indices showed a three-way division in town behavior, with one group of towns combining a high average length of service and a concentration of power in the hands of the longest serving leaders. A second group combined a low average length of service and a relatively equal distribution of power among the leaders, and

165

the third group, which consisted of newly settled towns incorporated after 1750, followed a pattern of inconsistency. Most towns in the first group were comparatively large, and most towns in the second group were comparatively small, indicating a tendency toward variation according to population size. But there were significant exceptions in each group. The whole third group, of course, was distinguished by age rather than by size.

The fourth and fifth indices, the percentage of taxes paid by the wealthiest tenth of the taxpayers and the proportion of prominent individuals in the town, measured the general economic and social composition of town society rather than local political practices, and proved to be even less clearly tied to population.[4] Towns fell into three groups when ranked on each of these indices. In terms of property concentration, the groups consisted of egalitarian towns, which were small more often than they were large; stratified towns, which were often large; and frontier towns, which were small but unpredictable in their degree of stratification. In the index of prominence, the politically obscure towns were usually of small or moderate size, the modestly prominent towns were commonly moderate or large sized, and the really prominent towns varied widely in size. Population size was of limited use in explaining the economic structure or prominence of individual towns. Pairs of towns like Billerica and Dorchester, Cambridge and Dover, or Middletown and Bolton, which were very similar in size, revealed wide disparities in structure and prominence.

Since the natural groupings in the five indices do not create an obvious typology, the problem is to find a meaningful way of combining them. One simple and alluring solution to this problem would be to rank the cases in each index from the highest numerical value to the lowest in the expectation that towns of a similar type would fall into consistent positions in each scale. Such a method would be ideal for the computation of several statistical measures of the strength of relationship among the indices, and, in addition, if the towns proved to be in the same position on each index, it would allow any one of the measures to serve as a statistical key to town behavior. The differences among the natural groupings in the five indices, however, serve as warning that the method of parallel rankings would not yield significant results, and indeed much of the present study would be unnecessary if any one of the five single measures revealed the different types of town behavior in New England. Clearly the typology of towns requires a more complex analysis, and the full use of all available evidence.

More revealing than simple ranking is a procedure that exploits the groupings apparent in the several indices.[5] Looking first at the three measures of local political behavior, four distinct town patterns are distinguishable. According to the figures on average service and the concentration of terms, the towns fell into groups characterized respectively by long service and concentrated power, short service and an egalitarian

TABLE TWENTY-SEVEN

Indices of Town Types

Town	Town Founded	Pop. 1765-7	Leaders as % of Pop.	Terms per Leader	% of Terms by 5 Year Men	% Taxes Top 10%	Prominence Index	Commercial Index	Group
Amherst	1759	645	3.9	4.8	61.3	24.6	6.2	5.1	V
Andover	1650	2462	1.7	7.4	70.4	30.7*	6.9	15.3	III
Barnstable	1638	2146	1.0	10.7	80.8		33.1	8.0	II
Barrington	1717			9.4	80.0				III
Billerica	1656	1334	1.9	7.3	73.1	32.0	3.0	12.3	III
Boston	1630	15520	0.4	7.8	71.5	60.4	26.2	5646.0	I
Boxford	1685	841	5.5	4.2	46.6	33.9	4.7	12.7	IV
Braintree	1640	2445	1.5	8.2	69.2	59.1	11.9	15.7	III
Brookline	1705	338	6.8	9.7	76.8	33.3	56.2	38.4	III
Cambridge	1630	1582	2.0	8.3	76.1	50.1	47.4	30.1	II
Dedham	1636	1929	1.9	7.6	62.7	35.8	7.8	13.9	III
Dorchester	1630	1360	1.9	10.6	79.8	51.1	15.4	37.9	III
Duxbury	1636	1061	1.5	7.6	70.4		9.4	11.3	III
Fitchburg	1764	259	6.2	6.3	53.5	26.8	3.9	2.0	V
Grafton	1735	760	5.4	4.8	46.0		2.6	9.6	IV
Hadley	1661	573	9.8	6.3	65.9	35.1	14.1	8.1	II
Hanover	1727	c.1000	2.2	6.8	56.8		12.0	15.3	II
Hardwick	1739	1010	2.4	7.2	66.0	25.5†	7.9	6.3	III
Hatfield	1670	815	2.2	11.3	85.5		18.4	5.6	III
Leicester	1722	770	4.7	8.2	77.6		7.8	8.3	III
Lunenburg	1728	821	6.0	6.8	62.3	28.8	12.2	8.8	II
Manchester	1645	739	3.2	8.7	77.9	53.7	8.1	21.6	III
Medfield	1651	639	7.8	5.6	54.3	28.5	4.7	21.1	IV
Middleboro	1669	3438	1.1	7.1	77.4		3.2	6.9	II
Norton	1711	1942	1.6	7.5	69.0	40.8	9.3	9.5	II
Oakham	1759	270	8.1	5.0	61.2	34.3	0.0	2.1	V
Pelham	1743	371	12.4	4.3	39.1	28.5	0.0	4.4	IV
Salem	1628	4254				52.2	30.8	179.6	I
Shirley	1753	430	5.3	5.4	52.0	32.0	0.0	6.0	V

TABLE TWENTY-SEVEN: Continued

Town	Town Founded	Pop. 1765-7	Leaders as % of Pop.	Terms per Leader	% of Terms by 5 Year Men	% Taxes Top 10%	Prominence Index	Commercial Index	Group
Springfield	1638	2755	1.2	8.4	75.0	38.2	14.6	6.0	II
Sudbury	1639	1773	2.1	7.2	66.7	35.0	5.1	13.2	III
Swansea	1667	1799	1.9	6.4	65.0	51.5	8.3	16.8	III
Topsfield	1650	719	4.6	7.1	66.1	36.4	0.0	20.6	IV
Waltham	1738	663	3.5	7.4	66.1	34.7	9.1	19.0	III
Watertown	1630	693	4.8	7.4	67.9		15.9	47.6	II
Westminster	1759	468	3.6	5.8	65.0	37.0	2.1	2.4	V
Worcester	1722	1478	2.4	7.2	63.3	36.1	16.9	11.3	II
Biddeford	1717	753	2.4	7.4	83.5		8.3	8.4	III
Brunswick	1739	504	4.2	5.3	61.2	34.2	19.8	3.9	III
Falmouth	1719	3783		4.3	55.6	42.2	13.5	13.5	II
Gorham	1764	c.500	1.8	4.7	55.0	37.5	12.0	1.9	V
Newcastle	1754	454	5.7	5.0	43.0		2.2	4.5	V
Scarborough	1720	1272	1.9	5.6	66.5	43.6	4.7	8.5	III
Bedford	1750	362	11.0	4.2	24.8	27.9	2.8	141	IV
Canterbury	1750	503	5.8	4.2	52.4	30.4†	4.0	154	IV
Chester	1724	1189	2.9	4.0	38.0		1.7	225	IV
Concord	1732	752	2.7	5.9	58.8	25.2	6.7	159	III
Cornish	1767	133	11.3	3.8	44.3		0.0	35	V
Derryfield	1751	230	12.2	5.1	51.9	32.7*	4.4	133	V
Dover	1640	1614	2.4	7.4	72.3	34.3*	7.4	980	III
Dublin	1771			5.0	60.0	39.4*	0.0	37	V
Hampstead	1749	644	6.2	4.1	34.0		3.1	545	IV
Hampton	1640	866	5.5	4.5	41.1		6.2	431	IV
Hanover	1767	92	15.2	4.5	19.6		10.8		V
Londonderry	1719	2389	2.1	4.1	45.3	24.6†	1.3	392	IV
New Ipswich	1762		5.6	3.8	41.7	38.7*	5.0	250	V
Portsmouth	1640	4466	0.8	6.3	70.6	47.4†	21.5	3234	I
Weare	1764	268	9.3	3.2	44.7	23.2†	0.0	44	V

TABLE TWENTY-SEVEN:Continued II

Town	Town Founded	Pop. 1765-7	Leaders as % of Pop.	Terms per Leader	% of Terms by 5 Year Men	% Taxes Top 10%	Prominence Index	Commercial Index	Group
Exeter	1743	1634	2.8	8.6	74.7	47.0	2.4	2.6	III
Middletown	1743	830	5.8	7.8	78.2	47.4	7.2	15.3	III
Newport	1639	7980	0.7	7.6	86.0	55.2†	9.9	124.6	I
Providence	1636	3740	2.1	7.5	70.7	43.7†	14.2	67.7	II
Smithfield	1731	2405	1.7	6.8	77.3	42.7*	4.6	3.9	III
S. Kingstown	1723	2374	2.7	7.2	80.0	56.4†	15.2	7.8	II
Ashford	1716	1743	1.7	10.2	73.9		0.0	451	III
Bolton	1721	884	2.9	10.1	63.3	33.5*	0.0	512	III
Derby	1675	1445	3.0	4.7	62.3		4.3	506	IV
Enfield	1694	1205	2.0	11.2	81.0		7.5	551	III
Hartford	1636	5959		5.0	29.7		41.0	908	II
Kent	1739	1461	2.4	8.1	61.9	32.1*	4.0	305	IV
New Haven	1636	6690	0.8	5.9	59.1	27.7†	19.3	813	I
Newtown	1712	1741	3.8	5.0	45.9	31.4*	3.5	563	IV
Stonington	1660	4465	1.1	8.0	70.1		7.6	610	III
Woodbury	1670	4112	1.4	6.8	56.1	33.5*	9.7	618	II

Note: The symbols after figures in the Tax column refer to the specific types

of tax list. See Table Eleven.

distribution of power, and a frontier pattern of inconsistency. The small size of most egalitarian and frontier towns explains why the index measuring leaders as a percentage of population suggested a correlation between small size and broad participation. Moreover, the same index helps to refine the enormous category of towns with concentrated power by distinguishing between cities, which had tiny elites, and a group of towns which had slightly less restricted groups of leaders. On the basis of the three comprehensive measures of town behavior, towns fell into four apparent categories: frontier towns, egalitarian towns (often small), towns with restricted participation (often large), and finally cities.

Examination of the relative tax structures of the towns, although it confirms some known divisions, adds little further clarification to the typology; but inclusion of the index of prominence adds a fifth and final category. The well-defined groups of egalitarian and frontier towns remain unchanged, with the egalitarian towns ranking low in the prominence of their inhabitants, and with the frontier towns again demonstrating a pattern of inconsistency. The large group of towns with restricted elites, however, divides once again. A group of towns standing just above the egalitarian towns in prominence emerges as a distinct class of secondary or suburban towns containing a well-defined and numerically limited elite but producing few really distinguished leaders. By comparison the remainder of the towns with small elites all rank high in the prominence of their inhabitants, and are readily identifiable as leading towns in the colonies. Many of these towns are county seats, while the rest are of similar stature. Classes of major county towns and secondary or suburban towns complete the typology of towns.

The typology sketched here harmonizes more successfully with the previous analysis of town behavior in each of the indices than does a typology based on rigorous application of the ranking procedure, but because every type of town is not clearly present in each index, only the complicated reasoning in the preceding two paragraphs suggests the validity of the categories. As a check on the sort of synthetic analysis presented here, many scholars will wish to see a graphic presentation of the process of isolating categories or, alternatively, a statistical evaluation of the accuracy with which the five categories summarize variations within each index. Because graphic representations did not prove efficacious, statistical testing has been adopted as a method of checking the hypothesized typology of towns.

One way of verifying that the five categories are a useful way of organizing the data in the five indices is through analysis of variance, a statistical procedure that compares the variance from the mean of each subgroup of an index with the variance from the mean for all the cases in the index in order to determine whether or not the subgroups differ significantly from one another.* For the test the sample towns were assigned to the category that fitted their data best, and the frontier towns were excluded because the determining characteristic of such towns was that their newness made them behave inconsistently.[6] The results of analysis of variance showed that the four types of towns analyzed did differ substantially from one another in each of the five indices, and in each case the analysis showed that the variance was significant at or beyond the .01 level.† For four indices there was less than one possibility in a thousand that the statistical differences observed in the indices could occur if the groups of towns did not really differ from one another, and for the remaining index there was less than one possibility in a hundred that chance could explain the observed differences in a homogeneous population.

Statistical testing confirms that the proposed typology reflects real differences among the towns of colonial New England, but its importance in evaluating the system of classification should not be exaggerated. The goal of such a typology is to discover the major differences in town experience, clarify the relationship of towns to one another within the structure of society, and to provide a basis for understanding the effect of varying town behavior on the course of colonial history. Statistical analysis cannot determine whether the arrangement of towns furthers historical understanding; the role of statistical testing is limited, therefore, not to validating or invalidating the typology, but more strictly to deciding whether or not a body of data supports the typology in a strictly statistical sense.

A full understanding of the typology of towns and of its potential for explaining patterns of local behavior depends on a complete exposition of the characteristics of each type of town. The remainder of this chapter will attempt such an exposition. As each type of town is discussed, the text will explain more fully the behavior of the towns in the five indices that

---

*Blalock, *Social Statistics*, 242–53. Intuitively, the test can be understood by considering that for any mean (average), a related statistic exists that measures the dispersion of the individual cases around the mean. Analysis of variance proceeds by comparing the measured dispersion around a general mean with a combined measure of the dispersion around the subgroup means, to see whether the particular subgroups are homogeneous enough to reduce the total dispersion significantly. I am indebted to Professor Robert Zemsky, a commentator on the version of "Local Leadership and the Typology of New England Towns" (*Political Science Quarterly*, 86 [1971]: 586–608) that I read at the December 1970 convention of the American Historical Association, for pointing out to me the peculiar usefulness of analysis of variance for this purpose.

†The tests are summarized as follows:

Index	Number of Towns	Value of F	F at the .001 Level
Leaders as % of Population	57	8.24	approx. 6.25
Terms per Leader	59	11.70	approx. 6.20
Terms by 5-Year Men	59	18.16	approx. 6.20
Top 10% Taxpayers	43	5.87	approx. 4.31 (at .01 level)
Prominence	60	9.34	approx. 6.20

constitute the core of the typology. It will also discuss the position of the towns in measures such as the index of commercialization that are not consistent from colony to colony, and in measures like those relating to family continuity that can be calculated for only a limited number of towns.[7] Finally, the discussion will consider some of the implications of the observed patterns of town variation for more general aspects of individual and town behavior.

The first major type of town, of which Boston, Newport, Portsmouth, and, in the latter part of the period, New Haven were prime examples, was the city or urban center. In socioeconomic terms, these towns were highly developed, with a substantial concentration of wealth in the hands of the wealthiest inhabitants and a complex economy based on commerce and to a lesser extent on the presence of governmental agencies. Of the towns for which information on the distribution of wealth is available, Boston and Newport had the highest concentrations of property with more than 60 percent in the hands of the top tenth of the taxpaying population, while Portsmouth's concentration approached 50 percent. When a town became urban in character, the concentration of property rose accordingly. Providence, a sprawling agricultural town in the early part of the century, had a concentration of only about 30 percent, but as the town urbanized and the outlying farming districts seceded, the concentration rose to 40 percent by 1751 and to nearly 60 percent by 1773.[8] The cities were commercial centers, as is clear in the index of commercialization. Among the sample towns, Boston, Portsmouth, Newport, and Providence far outranked the other communities in their respective colonies. Only New Haven failed to generate high ratings in property concentration and commercialization, apparently because of the inclusion of four town-sized rural communities within the city's political bounds.[9]

The political structure in these towns was also highly developed. The group of town leaders was numerically large, although restricted in terms of population, and, in contrast to leaders in other types of towns, tended to specialize in offices. Boston, for example, had 180 leaders over the eighty-five years studied, far more than most towns, but the pool of active leaders never exceeded 1 percent of the town's population. Specialization explains the large number of Boston leaders. Forty of eighty-six representatives, or nearly half, never served a term as selectman, and a large number of the moderators were men of exceptional prominence who never served the town in its other major offices (see Table 2).[10] Power in the government of a city was concentrated, at least in the sense that leaders with five terms or more of service served about two-thirds of all terms, although neither the percentage of concentration nor the average length of service stood out from the general pattern for the major towns.

The political structure of the cities did, however, differ from that of the more stratified towns in the important area of mobility and family continuity in office. Most major towns had relatively stable populations, and were dominated by stable elites composed substantially of descendants of earlier leaders. In comparison, the populations of the cities were much less settled and continuity among elite families was a much less frequent occurrence.[11] A large majority of the urban leaders were new men, and the only person with their surname to hold major office. Urban town leaders were also less likely to begin their service in their twenties and early thirties, a pattern of behavior closely associated with family influence, apparently because men were expected to make their own way.[12]

One obvious reason for the unusual mobility of the city leaders was the prominence of merchants in politics at a time when commercial fortunes were notoriously speculative; but an equally important explanation can be found in the pattern of electoral politics in the urban setting. Boston and Portsmouth were both provincial capitals, and both followed the example set by London of electing independent and often opposition politicians to influential offices.[13] In Massachusetts, Boston representatives such as Elisha Cooke, James Allen, and Samuel Adams were longterm leaders of the opposition faction in the legislature, and Portsmouth legislators such as Henry Sherburne and Eleazar Russell filled the same positions in New Hampshire.[14] Voters in the cities were more sensitive to factional political ideologies than voters in the country towns, and were less willing to decide elections on the basis of family loyalties. Both Boston and Portsmouth systematically excluded Anglicans from the town leadership, presumably because of the strong association between the colonial churchmen and the prerogative faction in local politics.[15]

Beside having a distinctive pattern of town politics, the cities contained large numbers of provincial officials, including many of those at the highest levels. Many provincial officials held major town offices at some stage of their careers, but a substantial segment of the group did not. Boston produced 71 councillors, of whom only 37 were town leaders, and less than 40 percent of that town's 214 justices of the peace held one of the five major offices. City voters undoubtedly excluded some of the dignitaries because of their association with the Anglican church or because of their advocacy of prerogative-oriented policies. Many of the provincial elites, however, clearly held themselves above town politics, either because they were unwilling to devote time to town affairs, or because they did not want to expose themselves to the rough and tumble of the town meeting. Members of the Wentworth clique in New Hampshire, for example, had withdrawn from Portsmouth politics well before their conversion to Anglicanism disqualified them in the eyes of the voters. Such men either based their political positions on factors that were essentially external to the politics of their colony, such as contacts in the imperial bureaucracy in London and the economic resources of overseas trade, or relied on family status and personal prestige; or else were willing to accept a secondary role as supporters and dependents of the royal officials in the colony.

For a large number of provincial officials, city politics was an important source of power. Because of the size and strategic locations of the cities, those who could command the electoral support and financial resources of the urban centers were in an advantageous position to acquire colony-wide political power. In Massachusetts and New Hampshire the most powerful men in city politics became opposition leaders, but a more numerous group moved from the town level to a judiciously moderate or neutral posture in provincial politics. Massachusetts leaders who based their careers on substantial service in city politics ranged from Elisha Cooke and Samuel Adams to moderates such as Thomas Hubbard and Benjamin Lynde (of Salem), and finally to administration leaders like Thomas Hutchinson, who began his career with six terms as a Boston selectman and nine years as a representative.[16] At the level of justice of the peace, prominence in city affairs was one of the surest ways for a self-made man to obtain a commission. More than 60 percent of the justices appointed for Salem between 1700 and 1760, including virtually all the men who came from families of ordinary stature, received their commissions after serving several terms as selectman, and the same pattern prevailed for Bostonians such as Deacon Samuel Adams, father of the patriot, who became a justice on the strength of his service as selectman and his reputed influence in the popular political faction.

In Rhode Island and Connecticut the system of royal government and popular opposition did not exist, and city politicians advanced into colony-wide office by election. The support of an urban electorate was an apparent prerequisite for election to the Rhode Island governorship. That colony consistently chose Newport leaders for the office until Providence developed as a competing commercial and political center.[17] Then open partisan rivalry blossomed, with the Hopkins faction relying on large Providence pluralities in colony-wide elections and on the support of the Providence assembly delegation, and with the Ward faction receiving similar support from Newport. Connecticut politics were less urban oriented, and the city politicians gained their advantage from the fact that cities like New Haven were also administrative centers, so that their leaders were strategically located to fill the higher offices.

A second type of town, which might be called the "major county town," consisted of towns that were local social and economic centers, and often county seats, but that were not large enough to have a definite urban character. These towns were scattered all over New England; some of them, like Cambridge and South Kingstown, were near the coast, but others, such as Springfield and Worcester, were well inland. They had a distinctly stratified social structure, with 35 to 50 percent of the property in the hands of the wealthiest 10 percent of the taxpayers at one end of the spectrum, and a visible class of landless poor at the other end. In commercial terms they ranked far below the cities; but they consistently earned higher ratings than the surrounding towns in the index of commercialization, which suggests that they were local marketing and service centers.[18]

The internal political structure of a major county town was similar, but not identical to that of a city. As in the cities, a relatively limited group of leaders occupied the chief offices and compiled a record of high average service. The town leadership rarely comprised more than 3 percent of the total population, and the leaders usually served an average of six to ten years in major office. Power within the narrow elite group was also concentrated in a few hands, with those who served five years or more as selectman serving two-thirds or more of all the terms. In contrast to the open urban pattern, however, family continuity limited mobility in these towns.[19] One or two prominent families commonly headed the local elite, and members of such families served only in the highest local offices and treated some of those offices as private family preserves. Spectacular but not unrepresentative examples are the Leonard family, which served a fifth of all terms in major office in Norton; the Pynchon family, which served a quarter of the terms in Springfield; and the Partridge family, which served nearly a third of the terms in Hatfield. Members of such families frequently entered the town leadership soon after they attained their majority instead of waiting until middle age, like most ordinary leaders. Recruitment to the major offices not monopolized by the great families was open to new men, although the stability of most of the older country towns ensured that most of the leaders would come from established families.

Led by members of the prominent families, the local leaders in major county towns dominated the provincial offices available to inhabitants of their county. Analysis of the index of prominence reveals that county towns consistently earned a rating of 10 or more, and that on a per capita basis they produced as many prominent men as the more complex cities. Plotting the major county towns on a map suggests that a phenomenon very much like the central place system evident in the economic structure also existed in the political sphere. The operation of county government is an obvious explanation for the presence of politically prominent men in the county seats, but not all of the major county towns were county seats. Instead, the index of prominence reveals that most rural counties contained two, three, or four towns with roughly equivalent numbers of justices of the peace, judges, and councillors distributed so that the agents of central government were conveniently located in all parts of a colony. All of the judges and all of the councillors in Bristol County, Massachusetts, for example, were apportioned among the three leading towns of Norton, Taunton, and Dartmouth; and the County Court in Fairfield County, Connecticut, regularly consisted of judges from Fairfield, Stratford, Norwalk, and Stamford. Almost without exception the men in the major county towns who became provincial officials served as leaders of their town as well.

The monopolization of local positions in the provincial government by inhabitants of the major towns in a county, and the identity of the provincial officials as leaders in town affairs, suggest that the major county towns were important power bases for those who rose into the provincial hierarchy. In the cities some men were able to enter the provincial elite on the basis of their usefulness to the imperial bureaucracy or other circumstances essentially unrelated to the internal political system, but such power bases were available only in an urban environment. In the countryside, elite reputations depended on a man's ability to speak for the inhabitants of his area, and such reputations seemingly were created and maintained by establishing one's authority over a major town and its hinterland. Elite families, therefore, took an active role in local politics in virtually every major county town. A revealing exception was Cambridge, where because of the town's proximity to Boston a dual elite existed, one composed of local leaders who filled both town and county offices, and the other composed of the absentee West Indian sugar planters who lived in their great houses on "Tory Row" and enjoyed their honorary status as justices of the peace while taking no part in local politics.[20]

A strategic position in local politics was especially important during the formative years of the political structure in a county. When Worcester County was established, for example, the Chandler family quickly transferred its center of activities from stagnant Woodstock to Worcester, the growing county seat. Clear visioned men like William Jennison, an ordinary selectman in Sudbury, quickly joined them, to parley five years' service as a selectman and representative of Worcester into a justice's commission and a seat on the county Court of Pleas.[21] Some Worcester County leaders, such as Joseph Dwight of Brookfield and Timothy Ruggles of Hardwick, were prominent before they moved to new towns in Worcester, and others, such as ex-Bostonian Thomas Steele of Leicester, had obvious connections. Most county officials, however, like Jennison, Edward Hartwell of Lunenburg, and John Murray of Rutland, an Irish immigrant, made their way through the town hierarchy.[22] Whatever their origins, the county leaders provided continuous service to their towns as a cornerstone to the structure of power.

The interdependence of major county towns and their hinterlands was clearly revealed when political changes deprived a major town of its centralizing functions. Lunenburg, a budding major town during the mid-eighteenth century, was founded in 1728 as a central place for newly opened areas west of the Merrimac River and straddling the modern boundary between Massachusetts and New Hampshire. No central Massachusetts town lay north or west of Lunenburg, and during the decade after 1728 at least a dozen new townships were granted in that area.[23] The early leaders of Lunenburg included several men, such as Benjamin Bellows, the brother-in-law of Dunstable magnate Colonel Joseph Blanchard, and two grandsons of Major Simon Willard of Lancaster, who expected the town to offer substantial opportunities; and they were correct. By 1735 Josiah Willard and Edward Hartwell were justices of the peace, while John Grout had developed a thriving legal practice and most leaders had obtained substantial landholdings in the new towns. Just as quickly, Lunenburg acquired the internal hallmarks of a major town, with leaders serving an average of six terms between 1728 and 1749 and with five-term selectmen filling 65 percent of the terms in that office. The Lunenburg bubble burst in 1741, however, when a royal boundary commission awarded Lunenburg's northern hinterland to New Hampshire. As New Hampshire organized the towns under its jurisdiction in the late 1740s, Lunenburg leaders such as Bellows, Grout, and the Willards moved across the border to protect their interests, and the town declined in importance.[24] Edward Hartwell finished his career on the county court, and two local justices were appointed after 1750, but the position of major town in northern Worcester County went to Lancaster. In internal terms, the decline to secondary status meant shorter terms (5.6) for leaders and fewer selectmen terms served by five-year men (53 percent) after 1750, and an absence of marked concentration of property in the 1770 tax list. Without a hinterland and an elite to serve it, Lunenburg lost the internal characteristics of a major town.

In long-settled areas, long service in the affairs of a leading town became less crucial to the establishment and maintenance of local authority. By the eighteenth century the leading families in Connecticut and the Connecticut Valley of Massachusetts had established elaborate kinship networks, which enabled them to move easily from one town to another without weakening their power. The reputations of families like the Williamses, Wolcotts, Dwights, and Strongs were so well known and their status so clearly established that their members could move into new areas or relatively minor towns without losing their claim to high office. Members of the Williams family in such minor towns as Enfield and Sharon, Connecticut, for example, were men of importance. Even the new elite of Worcester County was moving toward the establishment of such kinship networks at the end of the colonial period. By the beginning of the Revolution, John Chandler of Worcester, a judge and councillor, was related by marriage to General Timothy Ruggles of Hardwick; John Murray, the mandamus councillor of Rutland; James Putnam of Worcester, the last royal attorney-general of Massachusetts; Timothy Paine, a councillor and son of a Bristol County judge; and Levi Willard, a member of the leading family of Lancaster.[25] The Worcester elite, in fact, consolidated power far beyond the accepted level, virtually excluded all new men from the higher offices, and provoked their own overthrow by the leaders below them at the beginning of the Revolution.

In a third distinct class were towns that functioned as suburbs to the cities or as secondary centers in the rural counties. Like the towns in the higher categories, these towns had a fully developed social structure, with between a third and a half of the property in the hands of the richest 10 percent and a substantial number of landless poor. Commercially, however, these towns ranked below the nearby city or county town, and often their index of commercialization was indistinguishable from the basic value for the surrounding towns.

As in the major county towns, a well-defined group of leaders occupied the principal offices with significant family continuity, a concentration of power in the hands of those who served the longest, and a high rate of average service. Secondary towns were virtually indistinguishable from the major towns in the average number of terms served by each leader, in the size of the leader pool in comparison with the total population, and in the proportion of terms served by men who held office for a total of five years or more. In contrast to the major towns, however, secondary towns usually had half a dozen families roughly equal in wealth and prestige at the top of local society. The members of these families were prosperous yeoman farmers, local tradesmen, or at most very minor gentry. Leaders' sons in the dominant families held town office in turn, but they served an apprenticeship in minor offices like that of the lesser leaders and rarely succeeded their fathers directly, as did the members of the single dominant family in the major county towns. No single family monopolized the chief positions in town government.

The limited social status of the town leaders in the secondary and suburban towns, the political equality of the leaders, and the relatively low position of the towns in the economic hierarchy all influenced their ranking in the index of prominence. Despite their size, social complexity, and relative wealth, secondary towns achieved prominence ratings of no more than ten, and were of debatable value as power bases. The towns were large and complex enough to require the service of justices of the peace, but at the same time they were so seriously overshadowed by the more important towns that their leaders were effectively excluded from the provincial elites. An occasional town leader received a justice's commission, but only in exceptional circumstances did an inhabitant of a secondary town achieve the rank of judge or councillor.

A further look at the careers of some town leaders from secondary towns of the suburban variety who reached the provincial elites will illustrate the limited avenues of mobility open to men in such towns. One avenue led from town office to the higher positions, but this progression was available primarily to men who had more than a town position to recommend them. Joseph Richards of Dedham began his career as a local selectman and ended it as a justice of the quorum and as a special justice of the Superior Court; but as his election to the town's top office at the age of thirty suggests, he had special advantages. Richards was a graduate of Harvard College and son-in-law successively of Joseph Belcher, the prominent local minister, and Judge

William Dudley, so that his social connections contributed as much to his career as did his local service. Similarly, Councillor Samuel Phillips, the only really prominent town leader from Andover, was a Harvard graduate (1734), a descendant of a distinguished line of New England ministers, and by marriage was related to the equally distinguished Barnard family.[26]

For most suburban townsmen, migration to the dominant city was virtually the only ladder into higher office. The only councillor from Dedham, for example, was Samuel Dexter, a son of the local minister, who moved into Boston as a young man, made a fortune as a merchant, and then retired in middle age to his native town.[27] Because he had maintained ties with Dedham, Dexter became a fully accepted town leader after his return, but town leadership was only incidentally related to his position in the elite. A somewhat similar relationship between town and leader developed when urban elite figures established residence in a country town in order to use the town's House seat to cut a figure in politics. Suburban towns would often agree to elect such a man as representative when no pressing issue of local significance was before the House, especially if he offered to turn his wages over to the town treasurer. Dorchester acquired the services of Nathaniel Hatch, a judge and mandamus councillor, and Needham those of William Bowdoin, brother of the future governor, by this method.[28] Men of that sort, however, characteristically took little interest in strictly local affairs, rarely serving in offices like selectman; and, in reality, both their position in the House of Representatives and in such higher offices as they acquired depended on their original status rather than on local service. Sometimes when a suburban town required the services of justices of the peace, men with political connections were able to obtain the offices without taking visible part in the corporate life of the town. Only one of six justices appointed for Dorchester after mid-century, for example, was a town leader, so that the well-established local elite was virtually excluded from even the lowest level of the provincial hierarchy. For most town leaders in secondary towns, offices above the town level were beyond reach and election to major town office was the culmination of a career.[29]

New England's small, self-contained farming villages composed a fourth type of town, a type characterized by a consistently egalitarian social order. Examples of village communities, which were scattered throughout the interior of the colonies, are Medfield, Boxford, Pelham, and Hampstead. In these towns the distribution of property was more equal than in the larger towns, with a fifth or less of the property in the hands of the wealthiest tenth of the inhabitants at the beginning of the century and no more than a third of the property belonging to the corresponding group at the end of the period. Commercial activities in village communities were of the most basic nature, and the towns consistently ranked low in the commercialization index for their area. The egalitarian social structures and agrarian economic systems were intimately related because most of the villages were small and relatively poor settlements, often in out-of-the-way locations or in unproductive hill regions, where natural resources were insufficient for either the accumulation of substantial wealth or the establishment of specialized activities. The towns, therefore, remained the exclusive domain of simple farming folk.

Because the village communities contained few wealthy men, few of the town leaders could afford to devote time to town business year after year, and the major offices were shared widely. Leaders made up four to ten percent of the population, a higher percentage than in the types of towns already described, and the average leader served no more than four or five terms. The distribution of power among the leaders was also much broader than in the more stratified towns, with leaders who served five years or more filling no more than half of the places. Furthermore, family continuity was not an important factor in the officeholding patterns of the village communities. Representatives of most well-established family groups (men with a common surname) became town leaders, and the townspeople demonstrated no significant preference for the sons of previous leaders or for members of particular family lines. There was also a slight tendency for the voters in some villages to be less rigorous in applying the traditional practice of continuing a prospective leader's apprenticeship until he reached middle age.[30] All in all, the political behavior of the village communities suggests that they were egalitarian societies in which men rarely achieved the economic or social distance necessary to set them apart as an elite, and in which local government never became complex enough to require the services of long-serving and carefully recruited leaders.

The limited development of elites was symptomatic of the low position of the villages in the hierarchy of political communities as well as of the nature of their internal government. The leaders in towns of this class were not the sort of men who would have contacts in high places, and their limited tenure in town office did not enable them to attract much attention or exert much influence outside their immediate neighborhood. Voters in isolated villages were precisely the groups of freeholders who were most apt to ignore their right of representation in the legislature, not because they did not care about colonial affairs, but because they were acutely aware that their leaders would not be able to exert enough influence to justify the expense.[31] The Connecticut Valley town of Enfield, for example, occasionally sent a representative to Boston, but when Enfield needed a spokesman before the General Court in 1706, the voters ignored their own leaders and attempted to persuade Joseph Parsons, Esq., of Springfield and Northampton to settle in the town and become their representative.[32]

Predictably enough, few men from the villages found their way into provincial office, and towns of this class all ranked low in the index of prominence. The appointment of an occasional justice of the peace was a great event in an egalitarian community, and the promotion of a justice to the quorum could be a cause for genuine consternation. When Henry Adams of Medfield heard of his pending promotion in 1773—occasioned, it would seem, by the governor's search for justices who were not actively involved in the political opposition—he wrote immediately to Samuel Dexter, the Dedham councillor, to ask whether the change would disqualify him from serving his neighbors as a country justice, and to find out what his duties at the General Sessions of the Peace would entail.[33] Twenty-six years' experience in the commission of the peace had given Adams little knowledge of the workings of the institution. Towns of the village type, isolated, self-contained, and governed with the participation and consent of the inhabitants, were preeminently the "Peaceable Kingdoms" that Michael Zuckerman has so ably described.[34]

Fifth and last in the typology were the newly settled, struggling, and unstable communities traditionally described as frontier towns. Properly speaking, the characteristics of this class describe, not a distinct type of town, but rather a stage of development through which all towns passed before taking their places in one of the first four categories. Exactly how much time a town needed to coalesce as a stable community, of course, depended on the circumstances of its settlement. Westminster, for example, where settlement had begun in the mid-1730s, remained a highly mobile frontier town on the eve of the Revolution, presumably because the absentee proprietors retained much of the property.[35] Kent, on the other hand, quickly developed into a stable community, as Charles Grant has demonstrated.[36] Few if any of the sample towns incorporated after 1750 had passed the frontier stage before the Revolution began, and since a large number of towns could be found at this stage of development at any time in the eighteenth century, it seems worthwhile to treat the frontier town as a distinct type.

During the first years of most new settlements, disorder and rapid change were the primary characteristics of the social and political order. For this reason, frontier towns presented patterns of inconsistency in index after index, with some measures pointing toward an egalitarian order and others suggesting a more stratified society. Such inconsistency rendered the indices for towns settled after 1750 unsuitable for statistical analysis and necessitated their exclusion from the calculation of analysis of variance. The failure of the frontier towns to follow consistent patterns, therefore, must be kept in mind in describing the characteristics of the type.

The most prevalent form of economic structure in new towns was an egalitarian pattern. In most frontier towns little stratification of property ownership had taken place, and the top 10 percent of the taxpayers typically owned little more than one quarter of the property. Even the wealthiest inhabitants had had little time to amass estates in the new town, and men with established fortunes rarely appeared in a town until it was pretty well settled. The tax records of a few towns revealed substantial stratification, with Westminster and Gorham providing the clearest examples. Both of those towns, however, had been partially settled for three decades when they finally achieved incorporated status, so that some men had had sufficient time to build large estates.[37] The level of commercialization in new towns was more consistent than the property structure; no frontier town surpassed the level of commercial activity attained by the least-developed established town in the vicinity.

Patterns of local officeholding were less clearly defined than the economic situation. In most cases no clear social or political hierarchy existed, and important decisions had to be approved by all inhabitants, not merely settled among the leaders. Men served as leaders on a trial basis, some to be replaced by more able newcomers and others to stay and be remembered as the town's fathers. Under these circumstances the average length of leadership service remained low, with few groups of town leaders averaging more than five years in office. On the other hand, men who served more than five terms often accounted for more than half of all the terms, because frontier towns were too thinly populated to permit their few settled inhabitants to remain out of office for long.

Availability of manpower influenced the age structure of the group of town leaders and the amount of family continuity among the leaders much as it affected the number of terms the leaders served. Family groups of fathers and grown sons were instrumental in settling many towns, and often both fathers and sons held several offices in the first years of a town's existence. Such families held office more because they were numerous and permanently committed to settlement than because they were especially prominent. When members of the Chase family won election to five of the seven top offices at Cornish's organizational meeting in 1767, they made up about 20 percent of the town's adult male population, and were the only large family in the town.[38]

Frontier towns, like the village communities they resembled more closely than any other type, were too small and underdeveloped to serve as an effective power base, and their inhabitants were too busy trying to carve farms out of the wilderness to seek an active role in provincial politics. As a result, most frontier communities produced few provincial officeholders and ranked low in the index of prominence. Newly settled towns, however, were inconsistent in the prominence of their inhabitants as well as in their internal structures, because the frontier condition was a stage of growth rather than a genuine type of town structure. Worcester was at once a frontier town and a county seat in the 1730s; and Hanover had a prominence rating second only to that of Portsmouth among the New Hampshire towns because, even as a raw frontier village, it was a terminus of the colony's highway network and the seat of Dartmouth College. Frontier towns differed in their social and political characteristics, not only because they were new and unstable, but because they were evolving into very different kinds of mature communities.

The social and political typology of towns outlined here has clear advantages over those developed previously. Traditionally, attempts to distinguish types of communities in the colonies have had a regional basis, and have usually offered a long-settled and highly commercialized coastal region, a later-settled and less commercialized inland agricultural area, and a western frontier zone as primary categories.[39] Such a classification system ostensibly suggests itself from the general age of settlement and the apparent economic character of each region, and then becomes a symbolic representation of the social and political order in each area. Central place studies, however, have demonstrated that economic systems rarely consist of homogeneous bands or regions; instead, an economic region comprises a network of producing areas and local trading centers, which in turn feed a hierarchy of larger commercial centers. Data presented in Chapter 3 have shown that, with some qualifications, such a hierarchy of economic places existed in eighteenth-century New England.

The particular virtue of the typology developed in these pages is that it groups towns by explicit measures of economic, social, and political behavior, instead of inferring social or political characteristics from economic evidence and generalizing about the nature of life in a town from data gathered in nearby communities. As a result, the differences among the towns of a region in size, social structure, political behavior, and elite formation become focal points for analysis of the relative weight of regional uniformities and hierarchical attributes in shaping patterns of community life.

What emerges from such an analysis is a persuasive case for placing primary emphasis on hierarchical factors, especially social and political ones, in weighing the similarities and differences in town life. Measures of internal political behavior and of social structure reflect the pattern of community life in the towns, and such measures reveal that towns varied from rigidly stratified communities to essentially egalitarian ones. These differences from town to town occurred in every part of New England, and groupings of towns according to their pattern of behavior transcended both regional and political boundaries. It was no accident that social relations and political life in Springfield and Hatfield resembled social relations and political life in Braintree and South Kingstown far more than they resembled the same facets of community behavior in less important Hampshire towns such as Amherst or Pelham. An appreciation of the place each town held in the overall structure of society is indispensable, not only for understanding how local leadership in the towns operated, but also for discovering how accurately the experience of any town or group of towns reflected the experience of New England society as a whole.

·8·

EPILOGUE

During the first three-quarters of the eighteenth century, the New England towns filled their chief offices with a special kind of public servant. Major officeholders were usually prosperous townsmen, were commonly in their middle age, were often church members, and had generally prepared for major responsibilities by serving the town capably in lesser offices. They varied substantially in family background and educational accomplishments, and ranged from men of purely local importance to men of colony- and even empire-wide prominence. Regardless of their overall prestige, however, the town officials of colonial New England were community leaders in a very real sense. One mark of their relationship to the community at large was the character of the electoral system. Leaders were elected without organized partisan political machinery, without even a formal nominating procedure, and even when questions of personal interest divided the leaders from the voters, the assembled electorate rarely failed to return proven leaders to major office.

That this political system had disappeared by the mid-nineteenth century scarcely needs stating. By 1830 Watertown's historian characterized the old system as "singular indeed," and three decades later Marlboro's lamented, "that in the choice of those officers, the people were more particular than they are at this day, when the powers of town officers are more limited and better defined. To be a Selectman in those days—to be regarded as one of the 'fathers of the town,' and a depository of almost unlimited power—was considered no small honor. The importance our fathers attached to this . . . is a lesson by which the present generation might profit."[1] In an era when clerkships, selectman's seats, and even lowly highway surveyorships were bitterly contested political plums, a transcendently respected community leadership was remote indeed.

Exactly how this monumental change came about has long intrigued historians, and most have suspected that the Revolution had something to do with it. A study of town leadership before the Revolution can not entirely solve the riddle, but by tracing the behavior of the towns through the Revolution, and by exploiting insights into the workings of the old system, such a study can suggest a tentative line of interpretation.

185

Whatever changes the coming of the Revolution brought to the political system in the colonies did not immediately alter either the pattern of leadership in the towns or the social composition of the local elites. One effect the crisis did have was to multiply the number of major offices in the gift of each town. Now to the traditional five offices were added an indefinite number of positions on committees of correspondence, which maintained contact with the Revolutionary government; on committees of inspection, which enforced the nonconsumption agreements; and on committees of safety, which dealt with various aspects of the military emergency. Also, delegates to the new Provincial Congresses were more numerous than the old representatives, and the war brought a vast expansion in the number of military commissions. In theory the creation of these new offices carried the potential for what historians once hailed as the "internal revolution"—the replacement of old elitist leaders by a younger, more radical, and above all more democratic group of men.[2]

As it happened, however, the history of the revolutionary committees is a very different one. From the outset and in almost every town the committees were headed by established town leaders. The early committees of correspondence in towns as disparate as Cambridge, Topsfield, and Enfield consisted entirely of experienced town leaders. Evidently the crisis inspired towns to turn to their senior statesmen. No member of Topsfield's committee was less than sixty years old, and the Enfield committeemen averaged fifty-four years (see Table 28).[3] The limited number of leaders available and the time-consuming nature of the new duties soon necessitated changes, and these followed two courses. First, new leaders were admitted to both the committees and to the traditional town offices, as would have happened in due course anyway. The new leaders were necessarily younger than the old ones, but most were precisely the sort of middle-aged men from leading families who ordinarily became leaders. Second, men who were not otherwise identifiable as town leaders assumed a minority role on the committees. The introduction of these new men did not represent a democratization of town government so much as a stretching of the town's limited leadership resources. During the Revolutionary era the turnover in the traditional leadership offices in many towns increased from about one new man a year to two or more new men as some of the leaders turned their attention to the newly important committee offices (see Table 6).[4] The regularity with which the towns retained a majority of leaders on committees indicates that their intent was to supplement rather than replace their leaders.[5]

Another indication of the continuity of town leadership as the towns prepared to revolt can be found in the membership rolls of the provincial congresses. In Rhode Island and Connecticut, of course, no royal authority intervened in colonial government, and the two colonies were able to establish their independence with the institutions and personnel of govern-

TABLE TWENTY-EIGHT

Town Leaders and the Revolution

Town	Committee[1]		# Leaders[2]	# Non-Leaders	#	Leaders Before	Tories Leaders After	Leaders Both
Amherst	C	1774	4 (3)	1	13	4	3	2
Amherst	C	1776	9 (1)	0				
Amherst	CIS	1777	7 (5)	0				
Barnstable	C	1774	4	3				
Barnstable	S	1775	1	4				
Barnstable	C	1777	3 (2)	2	?	1	1	2
Braintree	C	1773	4	1	13	1	0	0
Braintree	C	1775	7 (2)	2				
Brookline	C	1772	7	0				
Brookline	C	1776	3 (2)	0				
Brookline	C	1777	5 (1)	0				
Cambridge	C	1772	9	0				
Cambridge	C	1777	5 (5)	3	13	4	0	0
Hatfield					8	3	2	0
Leicester	CI	1778	5 (1)	2	1	0	0	0
Lunenburg	C	1773	7	0				
Lunenburg	CIS	1776	5 (1)	2	1	1	0	0
Manchester	C	1774	4	0				
Middleboro	C	1774	11 (3)	1	17	1	0	2
Topsfield	C	1773	3	0				
Topsfield	CIS	1776	1	2				
Watertown	C	1778	4 (1)	1				
Worcester	C	1773	2 (1)	1	52	14	3	1
Worcester	C	1774	4 (1)	3				
Worcester	I	1775	8 (5)	4				
Newcastle	CI	1775	7 (3)	2				
Bedford					1	0	0	0
Concord	S	1776	4	1	2	0	0	1
Chester					0	0	0	0
Canterbury					0	0	0	0
Derryfield	S	1775	5 (1)	0	0	0	0	0
Dublin					0	0	0	0
Hampstead					21	5	1	1
Hampton	C	1774	4	1	2	1	0	1
Hampton	S	1775	11 (2)	2				
Londonderry					15	6	0	0
Portsmouth					46	1	0	1
Weare					41	2	0	2
Exeter	I	1775	4	1				
S. Kingstown	C	1774	4	0				
S. Kingstown	I	1774	9	4				
Enfield	C	1774	7	0				
Enfield	I	1775	7 (4)	0				
Woodbury	C	1774	8	0				

1) "C","I", and"S"refer to Committees of Correspondence, Inspection, and Safety.
2) The figures in parentheses represent the number of men who became leaders after 1775.

ment virtually unchanged. In Massachusetts and New Hampshire, however, the presence of royal governors and officials obliged the patriot leaders to destroy the existing governments and replace them with ones more responsive to the popular will. In both colonies the new, provisional government consisted at first of a provincial congress, an institution modeled on the colonial houses of representatives, but admitting members from all towns regardless of their eligibility under the old system.

The ex-parte nature of the congresses, the enfranchisement of previously unrepresented areas, and the technical illegality of such assemblages all favored the selection of new, radical, and socially inferior men as delegates; but in spite of these influences, the men who assembled at Watertown and Exeter represented the traditional town elites. In terms of service the delegates were among the most established of town leaders.[6] Massachusetts congressmen averaged 9.7 years of prior town service and New Hampshire congressmen averaged 5.8 years, in each case more than the average for completed careers among the colony's town leaders. The Massachusetts Congress included Cushings, Winthrops, and Pynchons, and the New Hampshire body included Waldrons, Pickerings, and Sherburnes, all members of families of traditional importance. Some members were entirely new men who had never held town office, but such men made up only 21 percent of the total number. Moreover, the minority of new men came mainly from the few towns that suffered emigrations of loyalist leaders. Portsmouth, which lost most of its leaders through the emigration of the Wentworth faction and the simultaneous retirement of elderly popular leaders, accounted for a full quarter of the new Congressmen, and several major towns such as Worcester and Norton, where the dominant Chandler and Leonard families were respectively loyalist and neutral, sent most of the others. The few new men from towns that had normally tranquil politics, such as two young members of Springfield's Pynchon clan and Canterbury's temporarily political minister, can be attributed to ordinary leadership turnover. In most towns the Revolution caused little immediate change in the pattern of local leadership.

Town leadership could be continuous in New England because most town elites included few loyalists, and because where Toryism existed it was not a class phenomenon. As a result of the diligence of many towns in investigating and recording the conduct of persons suspected of disaffection, the incidence of loyalism can be studied with some precision. Of the four colonies New Hampshire provided the most comprehensive evidence, by requiring each town to report inhabitants who refused to sign the colony's Association Test Oath of 1776. Returns have survived for eleven of the fifteen sample towns, and these reveal an important loyalist problem only in Portsmouth, where forty-six men either refused to sign or were so "notoriously disaffected" that the oath was not administered (Table 28).[7] Four towns contained no nonsigners at all; Bedford contained one, a minister who considered taking the oath a violation of the separation of church and state; and several other towns contained numbers of men who objected to technical characteristics of the oath rather than to the Revolution. Many of these nonsigners were Quakers, and most of the non-Quakers expressed their willingness to fight for the new government. Because the few leaders on the list of nonsigners were often only technically disaffected, and because many communities were willing to forgive their leaders' temporary lapses, apparent Toryism did not necessarily end a leader's career. Seven of the twenty-two supposed Tories served as leaders again after 1776.

Figures for the other colonies are not as complete as those for New Hampshire, but they tell a similar story.[8] Few towns had serious loyalist problems and even fewer had problems with disaffected leaders. Braintree's Tories, for example, were primarily adherents of the local Anglican mission, and the only Tory leader, a son of an Anglican minister, represented the group in politics. Some towns with leaders of proven ability but doubtful loyalties adopted the practical expedient of replacing those leaders in sensitive offices but continuing to use their talents in other ways. When Springfield's John Worthington considered accepting appointment to the Mandamus Council in 1774, the town quickly replaced him as selectman and representative but continued to elect him to moderate town meetings when purely local subjects were under discussion. The sensitive offices of selectman, representative, and moderator of politically important meetings went to Springfield's patriot aristocrats, the Pynchons. Similarly, Hatfield removed Oliver Partridge, a neutral, from the board of selectmen but retained him as town clerk and town treasurer. In the absence of serious local divisions, towns were able to cope with the loyalism, or neutrality, of a few leaders without disturbing the social or political order.

Worcester was one of the few towns seriously divided by the Revolution, and even there division was only temporary. As early as 1758, John Adams recorded in his *Autobiography*, a faction in Worcester was discontented with the dominance of the Chandler family in town and county offices and wanted Adams to settle in the town as a nucleus for a competing electoral interest. As the Revolution approached, the unconcealed loyalism of the Chandlers provided the malcontents with an issue, and the anti-Chandler faction gained a majority on the Committee of Correspondence. The Committee blasted the Tea Act with a flaming resolution, and in response fifty-two members of the Chandler faction entered a protest in the town records questioning the legitimacy of the Committee and its proceedings.[9] In light of the events of 1774 this protest discredited its signers in the eyes of the town, and for a short time the patriot leaders, most of whom had been marginal officeholders during the Chandler hegemony, had free reign. Soon, however, the Chandler family emigrated and the town leadership closed ranks. Seven of the eighteen tory leaders were aged when they signed the protest and five others were Chandlers or Chandler sons-in-law. Of the remaining six men, four were back in town office by 1780. The internal revolution in Worcester eventually involved only a single family.

Scholars can probably agree that the Revolution caused no immediate change at the local level in New England, but at the county and colony levels a large body of literature asserts a contrary interpretation. Several authors have argued that the Revolution "democratized" American politics by transforming provincial governments dominated by wealthy, upper-class Easterners into state governments whose officials were less wealthy, less likely to have upper-class origins, and more likely to reflect the numerical strength of western voters.[10] The problems with such studies, however, are legion, and include both a dubious counter-hypothesis that the Revolution could have occurred without elite change combined with a failure to show that more aristocratic leaders were available in the Revolutionary context and were rejected, and a doubtful assumption that late-colonial elites were unchanging and unresponsive oligarchies. In other words, they fail to posit the exodus of English-oriented officials and to ask whether the replacements were genuinely new men or whether they were men who would have been likely candidates to fill the next vacancy under the old system.

To be fair, this kind of question is a very complicated one, requiring detailed knowledge of the relative status of potential officeholders, and it is made even more so by the fact that the Revolution brought about a geographical redistribution of offices so that after 1775 many more officials came from those newly settled regions where society was least stable and the relative claims of elite members hardest to determine. Under frontier conditions the appearance of new officeholders would not necessarily imply a decision to democratize politics. Full solutions to these problems are beyond the scope of a study concerned mostly with the towns in the colonial period, but information drawn from the towns suggests that the question of democratization of the state governments remains an open one. On the one hand, newcomers like Samuel Curtis of Worcester and Seth Washburn of Leicester, both of whom became Worcester County senators, were genuinely new men: neither of them had held high office before the Revolution, and neither had been especially prominent in his native town. But on the other hand, the same could have been said about the previous set of Worcester County leaders when they emerged less than two generations before: the Chandlers, Wilders, and Jennisons were all new men in their day.

Probably more typical than the strictly new men were leaders who were well established in lower levels of the political hierarchy before the Revolution and simply became logical candidates to fill new positions or ones that became vacant suddenly. The Gilmans and Pickerings of New Hampshire, for example, were families that had belonged to the second level of the provincial elite for generations and were therefore prime candidates to fill positions left vacant by the fleeing Wentworths. Less obvious but equally logical candidates were men like Matthew Thornton, the signer of the

Declaration of Independence, who began life as an Irish immigrant but had already become chief justice of the new Hillsborough County Court before the Revolution. Similarly situated was Timothy Walker, Jr., of Concord whom New Hampshire repeatedly elected to the Continental Congress. Walker's father was an immensely influential minister who had successfully defended Concord's dubious land title against the claims of the Wentworths and their grantees when sent to England as the town's agent, and only the hostility of the old Portsmouth clique had kept the Walkers out of high office before the Revolution.[11] From the standpoint of their local origins and their positions in local affairs, many leaders of the Revolutionary generation seem to have done no more than follow the normal path into higher office.

The democratization and politicization of local leadership, then, was not an immediate outgrowth of the Revolution, and its roots must be traced to deeper and more gradual changes. One contributing factor was the continuing formalization of the procedure for making community decisions discussed in Chapter 1. By 1775 the towns had worked out detailed rules to control the election of officials, the governance of town meetings, and the general conduct of town affairs. As procedures became more formal, the powers of each town officer became more tightly defined, and the town government became less capable of handling community problems in a flexible manner. The increasing frequency with which town meetings appointed temporary committees to handle unexpected problems supports this interpretation, as does the revolutionary generation's decision to establish committees of correspondence, inspection, and safety to deal with problems that men living a century before would have left to the selectmen. Selectmen, after all, had originally been charged with "managing the prudential affairs" of each town.[12]

In the final decades of the eighteenth century the major town offices became less clearly an embodiment of the community's leadership, and as that happened, they began to take on the character of political offices. Many towns reduced the number of selectmen from five or seven to three, and began to elect and reject candidates on the basis of their political associations.[13] A beginning of this process can be sensed in the increased numbers of very young selectmen elected in the 1780s (Table 17). If the largest increase had come during the previous decade, the enormous manpower requirements of the Revolution might have provided a suitable explanation, but the increase was most spectacular after 1780, when society was returning to normal. The trend in the 1780s becomes understandable in the context of the changing character of officeholding, because voters would be logically less concerned about the eminence and experience of the holder of a strictly circumscribed office than they would be about the qualifications of a leader with discretionary powers.

The relationship between leaders and their communities also changed because of the profound shift in the political culture brought about by the

Revolution. Before the Revolution leaders, particularly those with elite connections, had gained authority, not only through the confidence of the voters, but also through their position in a society that accorded deference to prominent men, a deference buttressed by the hierarchical bases of Anglo-colonial constitutional arrangements.[14] New England townspeople, however, understood both the political culture of deference, and the egalitarian consensual culture that governed relationships among ordinary persons, and determined the order of affairs in the less developed towns. When the Revolution destroyed the foundations of the hierarchical notion of social arrangements, therefore, deferential politics began to disappear. Political leaders ceased being regarded as social superiors and became explicitly servants of the people. In the egalitarian world of consensual politics and of the politics of conflict that succeeded consensualism as town office lost the aura of community leadership, selectmen could no longer be "the fathers of the town."

Appendix I

The Population of Towns

The following table presents two distinct kinds of population information. From the 1750s on, official census figures exist, and have been used. Except in the colony of Rhode Island, where official censuses were made as early as 1708, however, population figures for the period before 1750 consist of estimates based on the number of polls or taxpayers recorded in surviving tax lists. Exactly what number should be used as a multiplier to convert polls and taxpayers into estimates of population can be a topic of endless dispute. Evarts B. Greene and Virginia D. Harrington, in *American Population Before the Federal Census of 1790*, suggest that four be used in each case, and cite such authorities as Governor Francis Bernard and statistician Joseph B. Felt in support of their position. Inspection of a large number of New England tax lists, however, shows that the number of polls taxed was invariably larger than the number of taxpayers, because some men paid the tax for their dependent sons or hired men, as well as for themselves. I have adopted the multiplier 4 for polls and the multiplier 4.5 for taxpayers, on the pragmatic basis that both figures give close approximations of the real population when estimates based on tax lists from the late eighteenth century are compared with census figures. (The abbreviations TP and PL in the tables refer to taxpayers and polls, respectively.)

With the exception of the Rhode Island census of 1730, all of the censuses cited are summarized in Greene and Harrington, *American Population*, pp. 21–85. The missing Rhode Island census is in John Callendar, *An Historical Discourse on the Civil and Religious Affairs of the Colony of Rhode Island: Rhode Island Historical Society Collections* 4 (1838): 94. Unless otherwise noted, estimated populations are derived from tax lists cited in the Bibliography under the town in question.

TABLE A. I

Town	Late 1600s	1700-1724	1725-1749	1765	1776
MASSACHUSETTS					
Amherst	xxx	xxx	xxx	645	915
Andover		1720 261TP=1175	1740 357TP=1606	2462	2953
Barnstable				2146	---
Barrington	xxx			xxx	xxx
Billerica	1688 115PI=518[1]		1733 243TP=1094	1334	1500
Boston	1700=6700[2]	1722=10567[2]	1742=16382[2]	15520	2719
Boxford	1687 41TP=184	1711 119TP=536	1746 124TP=558	841	989
Braintree				2445	2871
Brookline	1693 40TP=180			338	502
Cambridge	1688 191PL=764	1708 260PI=1040[3]	1735 248TP=1116	1582	1596
Dedham		1710 218TP=981 1715 188TP=846	1740 310TP=1395	1929	1937
Dorchester				1360	1513
Duxbury				1061	1254
Fitchburg	xxx	xxx		259	643
Grafton	xxx	xxx	xxx	760	861
Hadley		1720 117TP=525	1731 15TP=684	573	681
Hanover	xxx	xxx		---	1105
Hardwick	xxx	xxx		1010	1393
Hatfield	xxx		1738 130TP=585	815	582
Leicester		xxx	1743 180TP=810	770	1005
Lunenburg		xxx		821	1265
Manchester	1696 50TP=225	1717 62TP=279		739	949
Medfield		1702 124TP=558		639	775
Middleboro				3438	4119
Norton		1711 67TP=302		1942	1329
Oakham	xxx	xxx	xxx	270	598
Pelham	xxx	xxx		371	729

A. I: Continued

Town	Late 1600s	1700-1724	1725-1749	1765	1776
Salem	1683 553TP=2489		xxx	4254	5337
Shirley	xxx			430	704
Springfield	1685 159TP=716		1738 376TP=1692	2755	1974
Sudbury		1722 121TP=1089[4]		1773	2160
Swansea				1799	---
Topsfield	1687 62TP=279	1724 79TP=356	1744 169TP=720	719	773
Waltham	xxx		1740 148TP=666	663	870
Watertown		1708 250PL=1000[3]	1730 145TP=1296[4]	693	1057
Westminster	xxx		xxx	468	1145
Worcester	xxx			1478	1925

MAINE

Town	Late 1600s	1700-1724	1725-1749	1765	1776
Biddeford	xxx			753	1006
Brunswick	xxx	xxx		504	867
Falmouth	xxx		1749=2346	3783	3026
Gorham	xxx	xxx	xxx		1471
Newcastle	xxx	xxx	xxx	454	656
Scarborough	xxx			1272	1817

NEW HAMPSHIRE

Town	Late 1600s	1700-1724	1725-1749	1767	1775
Bedford	xxx	xxx	xxx	362	495
Canterbury	xxx	xxx	xxx	503	723
Chester	xxx	xxx	1741 148PL=592[5]	1189	1599
Concord	xxx	xxx	1737 61TP=275	752	1052
Cornish	xxx	xxx	xxx	133	309
Derryfield	xxx	xxx	xxx	230	285
Dover	1681 121PL=484	xxx	1732 274TP=1233[6]	1614	1666
Dublin	xxx	xxx	xxx		305
Hampstead	xxx	xxx	xxx	644	768

A. I: Continued

Town	Late 1600s	1700-1724	1725-1749	1767	1775	1774
Hampton	1681 64PL=256		1732 257TP=1157[6]	866	862	
Hanover	xxx	xxx	xxx	92	434	
Londonderry	xxx		1732 160TP=720[6]	2389	2590	
New Ipswich		xxx	xxx		960	
Portsmouth	1681 120PL=480	1715 374TP=1638	1732 484TP=2178[6]	4466	4590	
Weare	xxx	xxx	xxx	268	837	

CONNECTICUT	Late 1600s	1700-1724	1725-1749	1756	1765[7]	1774
Ashford	xxx	1700 51TP=230	1732 70TP=315	1245	1743	2241
Bolton	xxx	1718 59TP=266	1728 62TP=279	766	884	1001
Derby				1000	1445	1889
Enfield		1700 307TP=1382		1050	1205	1360
Hartford		xxx	1744 64TP=288	3027	4029	5031
Kent	xxx	1700 330TP=1485	1745 833TP=3749	1000	1498	1996
New Haven		1702 376TP=1692		5085	6690	8295
Newtown	xxx	1700 128TP=576	1739 142TP=639	1253	1741	2229
Stonington				3153	4465	5777
Woodbury		1700 66TP=297	1736 196TP=882	2911	4112	5313

RHODE ISLAND	1708	1730	1748	1755	1765[7]	1774
Exeter	xxx	xxx	1174	1404	1634	1864
Middletown	xxx	xxx	680	778	830	881
Newport	2203	4640	5513	6753	7980	9208
Providence	1446	3916	3452	3159	3740	4321
Smithfield	xxx	xxx		1921	2465	2888
S. Kingstown	xxx	1523	1978	1913	2374	2835

[1] Greene and Harrington, American Population, p. 20.

[2] Ibid., p. 22.

[3] Ibid., p. 24.

[4] Estimates for Sudbury and Watertown doubled, because tax lists cover only one half of each town.

[5] Greene and Harrington, American Population, p. 75.

[6] Van Deventer, "Emergence of Provincial New Hampshire", p. 413.

[7] 1765 figures for Rhode Island and Connecticut obtained by interpolating between 1755/1756 and 1774 censuses.

Appendix II

Comparative Data on All New England Towns

The listing that follows presents information on the land area and index of commercialization (as presented in Chapter 3) for all towns in Massachusetts and New Hampshire that paid taxes in 1765 and 1767 respectively, and for all towns in Connecticut and Rhode Island that paid taxes in 1774. It also presents information on the residence patterns of justices of the peace or county court judges broken down into twenty-five-year periods. Although the substance of this study demonstrates that several other kinds of information on the structure and behavior of towns are necessary to fully understand their place in the hierarchy, the degree of commercialization and the political prominence of a town, as crudely measured by counting justices, provide some sense of how towns were distributed through the region. Note 21, Chapter 3, explains the derivation of the figures on land area and commercialization. Neither set of figures exists in any other location. Sources of information on justices of the peace are explained in Chapter 5. I have chosen to count the total number of commissions issued to residents of a town (both original commissions and renewals) rather than merely the number of men in commission for Massachusetts, Connecticut, and Rhode Island because the larger figures minimize the distortion caused by the fact that some justices remained in office for many years, while others retired or were dropped from commission within a short time.

TABLE A. II

	Commercial Index	Area (1000 acres)	County Court Service (years)		
			1698-1724	1725-49	1750-74
CONNECTICUT					
Hartford County					
Bolton	.512	21	x		
Chatham	.592	40	x	x	
Colchester	1.122	31			
E. Haddam	.770	36	x		
E. Windsor	.478	58	x	x	
Enfield[1]	.551	23	x	x	
Farmington	.613	110	38	14	0
Glastonbury	.508	38	1	18	4
Haddam	.541	29	1	0	0
Hartford	.908	54	59	37	36
Hebron	.604	37			
Middletown	.938	46	1	8	39
Simsbury	.470	75	3	0	7
Somers[1]	.566	17	x	x	
Stafford	.291	38	x		
Suffield[1]	.737	27	x	x	
Tolland	.568	25	0	0	10
Wethersfield	1.301	26	22	24	1
Willington	.427	21	x		
Windsor	.582	42	40	32	28
New Haven County					
Branford	.747	32	17	10	3
Derby	.505	39	18	17	0
Durham	.887	15	9	0	23
Guilford	.633	56	14	29	18
Milford	.975	30	36	37	31
New Haven	.813	89	72	26	41
Wallingford	.851	59	8	13	9
Waterbury	.453	88	0	5	0

A. 11: Continued

	Commercial Index	Area (1000 acres)	County Court Service (years)		
			1698-1724	1725-49	1750-74
New London County					
Groton	.561	48	0	10	18
Killingworth	.679	31	0	5	0
Lyme	.539	53	18	20	39
New London	.588	62	70	36	31
Norwich	1.025	67	21	32	38
Preston	.515	47	1	7	7
Saybrook	.546	50	40	24	6
Stonington	.610	62	25	10	0
Fairfield County					
Danbury	.717	42			
Fairfield	.879	58	84	49	31
Greenwich	.902	27			
New Fairfield	.451	29	x		
Newtown	.563	42			
Norwalk	.900	49	28	14	20
Redding	.674	21	x	x	20
Ridgefield	.817	22			
Stamford	.905	38	20	32	35
Stratford	.703	74	26	40	25
Windham County					
Ashford	.451	40			
Canterbury	.462	43	0	21	38
Coventry	.724	29			
Killingly	.365	72			
Lebanon	.855	48	8	36	46
Mansfield	.648	35	0	16	25
Plainfield	.541	27	2	21	0
Pomfret	.781	36	0	0	8
Voluntown	.315	43			
Union	.000	19	x		
Windham	.737	42	0	20	10
Woodstock[1]	.565	40			
Litchfield County					
Barkhamsted	.000	25	x	x	x
Canaan	.393	39	x		
Colebrook	.000	21	x	x	x

A. II: Continued

	Commercial Index	Area (1000 acres)	County Court Service (years)		
			1698-1724	1725-49	1750-74
Cornwall	.354	28	x		
Goshen	.444	27	x		
Hartland	.000	22	x	x	
Harwinton	.437	20	x		
Kent	.305	55	x		
Litchfield	.476	48	x	0	28
New Hartford	.389	24	x		
New Milford	.464	63	0	0	20
Norfolk	.000	29	x	x	
Salisbury	.408	39	x	0	5
Sharon	.460	39	x	0	23
Torrington	.254	25	x		
Winchester	.000	23	x	x	
Woodbury	.618	98	21	28	44

	Commercial Index	Area (1000 acres)	Number of J.P. Commissions		
			1692-1724	1725-49	1750-74
MASSACHUSETTS					
Suffolk County					
Bellingham	6.9	12	x	0	1
Boston	5646.0	1	59	138	191
Braintree	15.7	31	6	6	14
Brookline	38.4	4.4	2	10	7
Chelsea	20.5	6.5	x	2	1
Dedham	13.9	31	1	5	9
Dorchester	37.9	10	5	10	12
Hingham	23.8	21	6	4	9
Hull	30.0	1.6	0	1	3
Medfield	21.1	9.3	0	1	2
Medway	9.2	15	0	1	3
Milton	27.7	9.1	0	1	5
Needham	11.3	15	0	1	2
Roxbury	61.9	9.9	4	14	14
Stoughton	6.2	54	x	2	3
Walpole	10.5	14	x	0	1
Weymouth	22.4	11	3	2	4
Wrentham	7.7	49	0	4	2

A. II: Continued

	Commercial Index	Area (1000 acres)	Number of J.P. Commissions		
			1692-1724	1725-49	1750-74
Essex County					
Amesbury	5.1	18	1	5	9
Andover	15.3	41	4	2	4
Beverly	39.9	9.8	2	2	4
Boxford	12.7	15	0	1	2
Bradford	22.6	10	0	1	1
Danvers	20.7	20	x	x	1
Gloucester	28.7	21	3	5	14
Haverhill	25.3	19	4	6	7
Ipswich	23.1	40	16	26	11
Lynn	16.5	24	4	3	7
Manchester	21.6	4.9	0	1	2
Marblehead	293.2	2.8	9	18	23
Methuen	9.6	17	x	0	2
Middleton	15.6	9.2	x		
Newbury	28.4	25	13	25	13
Newburyport	99.7	5.7	x	x	16
Rowley	18.4	21	0	2	4
Salem	179.6	5.2	19	34	46
Salisbury	30.0	10	3	3	2
Topsfield	20.6	8.2			
Wenham	23.4	5.2	0	1	2
Middlesex County					
Acton	8.9	13	x		
Bedford	10.8	8.9	x		
Billerica	12.3	20	1	4	2
Cambridge	30.1	15	10	17	30
Charlestown	83.4	5.3	8	25	20
Chelmsford	10.6	20	2	4	6
Concord	14.2	21	6	5	6
Dracut	6.8	16			
Dunstable	5.3	22	3	3	6
Framingham	14.8	19	2	3	3
Groton	9.2	27	3	5	5
Holliston	8.9	14	x		
Hopkinton	7.8	21	0	2	6
Lexington	18.6	11	1	5	6
Lincoln	13.0	9.6	x	x	1
Littleton	12.3	13	0	1	3
Malden	20.2	8.8	0	3	1
Marlborough	18.4	20	2	2	2

A. II: Continued

	Commercial Index	Area (1000 acres)	Number of J.P. Commissions		
			1692-1724	1725-49	1750-74
Medford	39.0	5.4	3	4	11
Natick	7.2	10	x	x	
Newton	25.8	12	1	5	3
Pepperell	6.0	15	x	x	
Reading	14.9	22	4	10	3
Sherborn	12.0	11	1	1	3
Shirley	6.0	10	x	x	
Stoneham	17.2	4.3	x	1	0
Stow	7.8	18	0	3	2
Sudbury	13.2	28	4	4	4
Tewksbury	8.6	16	x		
Townsend	3.8	21	x		
Waltham	19.0	8.9	x	0	6
Watertown	47.6	3.8	4	3	6
Westford	9.6	20	x	2	2
Weston	16.5	11	1	2	4
Wilmington	11.6	11	x	2	1
Woburn	17.2	19	4	3	3
Hampshire County					
Amherst	5.1	18	x	x	3
Ashfield	.4	26	x	x	
Belchertown	1.5	36.7	x	x	1
Bernardston	.4	27	x	x	
Blandford	1.8	34	x		
Brimfield	5.8	23	0	2	3
Charlemont	.3	17	x	x	
Chesterfield	.2	24	x	x	
Colrain	1.4	28	x	x	
Deerfield	2.3	61	3	7	8
Granville	2.2	49	x	x	
Greenfield	2.3	23	x	x	
Greenwich	3.6	20	x	x	
Hadley	8.1	16	4	7	4
Hatfield	5.6	36	3	7	2
Monson	1.7	29	x	x	
Montague	2.8	21	x	x	
Murrayfield	0	42	x	x	
New Salem	2.7	24	x	x	
Northampton	6.0	49	9	13	13
Northfield	3.4	23	0	2	2
Palmer	4.4	21	x	x	
Pelham	4.4	21	x		

A. II: Continued

	Commercial Index	Area (1000 acres)	Number of J.P. Commissions		
			1692-1724	1725-49	1750-74
Shutesbury	1.8	20	x	x	
So. Hadley	4.5	30	x	x	
Southampton	3.7	19	x	x	
Springfield	6.0	93	6	13	13
Sunderland	3.3	24	x	1	1
Wales	4.3	19	x	x	
Ware	1.4	17	x	x	
Warwick	0.0	29	x	x	
Westfield	4.1	57	1	5	6
Wilbraham	3.1	27	x	x	

Plymouth County

Abington	10.5	17	0	1	3
Bridgewater	12.5	53	6	5	9
Duxbury	11.3	16	2	4	3
Halifax	8.7	11	x	1	4
Hanover	15.3	10	x	2	8
Kingston	11.3	12	1	2	4
Marshfield	13.3	18	5	9	8
Middleboro	6.9	70	1	3	6
Pembroke	9.3	25	1	3	3
Plymouth	4.9	66	7	18	20
Plympton	5.5	35	0	1	3
Rochester	7.0	43	1	3	5
Scituate	21.1	25	7	12	12
Wareham	2.6	24	x	1	0

Barnstable County

Barnstable	8.0	40	9	22	29
Chatham	14.1	10			
Eastham	9.7	18	11	13	6
Falmouth	5.9	29	0	3	2
Harwich	6.6	30	0	6	8
Mashpee	0.0	17	x	x	x
Provincetown	0.0	5.6	x		
Sandwich	5.1	54	4	8	10
Truro	8.2	14	1	4	2
Wellfleet	6.9	13	x	x	2
Yarmouth	8.3	30	6	11	4

A. II: Continued

	Commercial Index	Area (1000 acres)	Number of J.P. Commissions		
			1692-1724	1725-49	1750-74
Bristol County[3]					
Attleboro	9.4	30	0	2	1
Berkley	11.1	10	x		
Dartmouth	8.0	108	5	9	10
Dighton	14.0	14	2	9	2
Easton	6.8	19	x	2	1
Freetown	4.9	41	0	7	5
Norton	9.5	32	2	6	9
Raynham	7.8	13	x	1	4
Rehoboth	10.4	51	6	5	6
Swansea	16.8	20	3	7	4
Taunton	14.7	31	5	13	13
Dukes County					
Chilmark	6.6	22			
Edgartown	5.9	23			
Tisbury	4.5	22			
Nantucket County					
Sherburne	18.4	32	11	20	12
Worcester County					
Ashburnham	.9	32	x	x	
Athol	1.7	23	x	x	1
Barre	3.3	29	x	x	1
Bolton	6.9	23	x	0	2
Brookfield	5.9	45	1	6	7
Charlton	1.6	32	x	x	
Douglas	3.0	24	x	x	
Dudley	5.5	19	x	0	1
Fitchburg	2.0	18	x	x	
Grafton	9.6	14	x	2	0
Hardwick	6.3	21	x	0	5
Harvard	8.8	19	x	2	3
Holden	3.0	25	x		
Lancaster	7.6	48	0	12	13
Leicester	8.3	18	1	1	3
Leominster	5.5	19	x	0	2
Lunenburg	8.8	18	x	5	4
Mendon	8.3	35	1	3	5
New Braintree	6.3	13	x	x	

A. II: Continued

	Commercial Index	Area (1000 acres)	Number of J.P. Commissions		
			1692-1724	1725-49	1750-74
Oakham	2.1	14	x	x	
Oxford	7.0	23	0	2	4
Paxton	7.5	9.8	x	x	
Petersham	4.7	23	0	1	2
Princeton	1.6	23	x	x	1
Royalston	0.0	31	x	x	
Rutland	3.5	50	0	1	6
Shrewsbury	7.8	33	x	5	4
Southborough	14.2	9.9	x	3	2
Spencer	4.0	22	x	x	2
Sturbridge	3.6	33	x	0	2
Sutton	8.7	35	0	3	2
Templeton	0.7	35	x	x	
Upton	5.0	14	x	1	1
Uxbridge	6.0	31	x	1	2
Western	5.6	18	x	0	2
Westborough	8.6	26	0	4	4
Westminster	2.4	31	x	x	1
Winchendon	0.8	29	x	x	
Worcester	11.3	27	x	8	14

Berkshire County

Becket	0.3	38	x	x	
Egremont	5.0	12	x	x	
Gr. Barrington	3.3	29	x	1	8
Lanesborough	0.5	20	x	x	1
New Marlborough	1.8	31	x	x	1
Pittsfield	1.3	27	x	x	4
Richmond	0.3	26	x	x	x
Sandisfield	1.8	22	x	x	1
Sheffield	5.3	31	x	1	6
Stockbridge	1.3	27	x	3	5
Tyringham	1.3	39	x	x	1

York County (Maine)

Arundel	6.5	19	0	0	2
Berwick	8.2	46	3	1	3
Biddeford	8.4	16	1	4	7
Buxton (or #1)	1.3	23	x	x	
Kittery	29.8	16	7	13	21
Pepperrellboro	4.7	20	x	x	1
Wells	6.1	40	4	6	15
York	12.4	37	3	7	27

A. II: Continued

	Commercial Index	Area (1000 acres)	Number of J.P. Commissions		
			1692-1724	1725-49	1750-74
Cumberland County (Maine)					
Brunswick	3.9	28	x	2	7
Falmouth	13.5	51	2	8	34
Gorham	1.9	26	x	x	3
Harpswell	6.8	12	x	x	1
No. Yarmouth	1.8	67	0	3	10
Pearsontown	0				
Scarborough	8.5	31	x	1	9
Windham	.9	26	x	x	
Lincoln County (Maine)					
Georgetown	5.2	32	x	2	8
Newcastle	4.5	15	x	x	
Pownalborough	3.6	26	x	x	6
Topsham	1.8	23	x	x	
Woolwich	3.1	20	x	x	

	Commercial Index	Area (1000 acres)	Number of J.P. Commissions	
			1717	1768
NEW HAMPSHIRE				
Cheshire County				
Charlestown	150	30	x	
Claremont	41	24	x	
Cornish	35	23	x	
Dublin	37	27	x	
Gilsum	53	15	x	
Hinsdale	114	14	x	1
Keene	154	26	x	1
Nelson (or #6)	46	26	x	
Plainfield	32	25	x	
Rindge	92	24	x	
Swansea	107	28	x	
Walpole	104	28	x	1
Westmoreland	123	22	x	
Winchester	118	34	x	

A. II: Continued

	Commercial Index	Area (1000 acres)	Number of J.P. Commissions 1717	1768
Grafton County				
Haverhill	41	34	x	
Plymouth	94	16	x	
Hillsborough County				
Amherst	217	30	x	1
Bedford	141	21	x	1
Boscawen	65	32	x	
Derryfield	133	15	x	1
Dunbarton	102	21	x	1
Dunstable	263	19	x	
Goffstown	90	29	x	1
Hillsborough	22	27	x	
Hollis	558	12	x	2
Hopkinton	130	27	x	
Litchfield	41	8.5	x	
Lyndesborough	71	21	x	
Mason (or #1)	89	19	x	
Merrimac	237	19	x	
Mile-slip	90	5.0	x	
Monson	133	15	x	
New Boston	78	27	x	
New Ipswich	250	20	x	1
Nottingham-West	264	17	x	1
Peterborough	155	24	x	1
Peterborough-Slip	58	24	x	
Salisbury	59	29	x	
Weare	44	34	x	
Wilton	169	16	x	
Rockingham County				
Atkinson	578	6.8	x	1
Bow	94	16	x	
Brentwood	815	10	x	1
Candia	161	18	x	
Canterbury	154	26	x	1
Chester	225	49	x	2
Concord[2]	159	41	x	1
Deerfield	165	23	x	
E. Kingstown	677	6.2	x	

A. II: Continued

	Commercial Index	Area (1000 acres)	Number of J.P. Commissions	
			1717	1768
Epping	850	13	x	1
Epsom	74	19	x	
Exeter	1083	12	3	4
Greenland	952	6.3		1
Hampstead	545	11	x	1
Hampton	432	18	2	2
Hampton-Falls	955	11	x	1
Hawke	643	7.0	x	
Isles of Shoals	.2	.8		
Kensington	1071	7.0	x	
Kingston	622	12		2
Londonderry	392	44	x	3
Newcastle	2000	1.5	3	1
Newington	833	6.0	x	1
Newmarket	848	11	x	1
Newtown	755	5.3	x	1
Northampton	635	8.5	x	
Nottingham	130	43	x	
Pelham	288	16	x	
Pembroke	361	14	x	1
Plaistow	764	5.8	x	
Poplin	309	9.7	x	
Portsmouth	3234	10	9	18
Raymond	188	16	x	
Rye	641	7.8	x	1
Salem	438	16	x	
Sandown	447	8.5	x	
So. Hampton	447	9.4	x	1
Stratham	930	10	1	1
Windham	197	16	x	

Strafford County

	Commercial Index	Area (1000 acres)	1717	1768
Barrington	118	58	x	
Dover	980	15	2	5
Durham	667	15	x	4
Gilmanton	28	58	x	1
Lee	395	11	x	
Madbury	654	8.1	x	
Rochester	227	27	x	1
Sanbornton	20	50	x	
Somersworth	900	10	x	

A. II: Continued

	Commercial Index	Area (1000 acres)	County Court Service (years) 1729-49	1750-74
RHODE ISLAND				
Newport County				
Jamestown	12.9	6.2	1	6
Little Compton[3]	8.9	14		5
Middletown	15.3	8.5	6	28
New Shoreham	7.0	7.0		
Newport	124.6	5.1	43	54
Portsmouth	16.7	11	33	31
Tiverton[3]	5.5	26		1
Providence County				
Cranston	6.6	20	x	2
Cumberland	3.9	18	x	13
Glocester	1.7	73	0	24
Johnston	3.0	20	x	
No. Providence	4.7	9.8	x	
Providence	67.7	3.5	34	25
Scituate	2.1	69	13	20
Smithfield	3.9	50	4	36
Kings County				
Charlestown	3.5	26	15	18
Exeter	2.6	38	7	20
Hopkinton	3.3	28	x	
No. Kingstown	6.7	28	29	23
So. Kingstown	7.8	48	30	65
Richmond	2.6	27	x	
Westerly	5.8	19		
Bristol County				
Barrington[3]	8.4	5.3	x	15
Bristol[3]	17.1	6.3	8	58
Warren[3]	9.3	4.1	7	44
Kent County				
Coventry	2.3	40	0	13
E. Greenwich	9.5	10	10	53
Warwick	4.9	39	24	51
W. Greenwich	2.0	33	0	12

A. II: Continued

[1]Enfield, Somers, Suffield, and Woodstock were Massachusetts
towns until 1749, when, after a resurvey of the boundary line
between the colonies that showed them to be within the limits of
Connecticut's charter, they seceded and joined Connecticut. Under
Massachusetts, Woodstock had two justices' commissions before
1725 and three after that date, Suffield had two after 1725, and
Enfield had one after 1725.

[2]Concord was the only one of a large number of Massachusetts
towns awarded to New Hampshire to enjoy representation in the
commission of the peace. Concord had one justice, appointed
after 1725.

[3]Barrington, Bristol, Little Compton, and Tiverton were
Massachusetts towns until 1747, when a Royal Boundary Commission
awarded the four towns, with the part of Swansea nearest them,
to Rhode Island. Barrington and Swansea territory were incorporated
as Warren, and the name Barrington was not revived until Warren
was partitioned in 1771. Under Massachusetts, Bristol had eleven
justices before 1725 and twenty-five after that date, Barrington
had two justices after 1725, Little Compton had five justices
before and eleven after 1725, and Tiverton had one before and
four after 1725.

NOTES

Preface

1. See, especially, John Demos, *A Little Commonwealth, Family Life in Plymouth Colony* (New York, 1970); Charles S. Grant, *Democracy in the Connecticut Frontier Town of Kent* (New York, 1961); Philip J. Greven, Jr., *Four Generations: Population, Land, and Family in Colonial Andover, Massachusetts* (Ithaca, 1970); Kenneth A. Lockridge, *A New England Town: The First Hundred Years* (New York, 1970); and Sumner C. Powell, *Puritan Village: The Formation of a New England Town* (Middletown, Conn., 1963). The works cited in this and the following footnotes are but examples of an enormous literature.

2. Perry Miller, *The New England Mind from Colony to Province* (Cambridge, Mass., 1953); Richard L. Bushman, *From Puritan to Yankee: Character and the Social Order in Connecticut, 1690-1765* (Cambridge, Mass., 1967).

3. Robert E. Brown, *Middle-Class Democracy and the Revolution in Massachusetts, 1691-1780* (Ithaca, 1955); Michael Zuckerman, *Peaceable Kingdoms: New England Towns in the Eighteenth Century* (New York, 1970); Robert M. Zemsky, *Merchants, Farmers and River Gods* (Boston, 1971).

4. Hubert M. Blalock, Jr., *Social Statistics* (New York, 1960), 399-403.

5. There is one exception. The records of Smithfield, Rhode Island, have been lost in the century since the town historian extracted lists of officials.

6. Edwin S. Dethlefsen, "Colonial Gravestones and Demography," *American Journal of Physical Anthropology* 31 (1969): 321-34.

Chapter 1

1. The basic laws on town affairs, which were frequently amended as the century progressed, were: *Acts and Resolves of the Province of the Massachusetts-Bay*, vol. 1 (Boston, 1869), *1692-93*, chap. 28; *Acts and Laws of His Majesties Province of New Hampshire* (Portsmouth, 1761), pp. 29-34 (5 Geo. I), which is virtually a copy of the Massachusetts act; Sidney S. Rider, ed., *Acts and Laws of Her Majesties Colony of Rhode Island, 1705* (Providence, 1896), p. 35; *Public Records of the Colony of Connecticut*, J. Hammond Trumbull, ed., 2 (Hartford, 1852): 87, 224, 419; *Acts and Laws of His Majesties Colony of Connecticut in New England, 1702* (Hartford, 1901), pp. 111-12.

2. The town meeting described here is a composite one, based on a wide survey of town records, and does not follow any one town exactly. For another account of town meeting practice, which stresses the variety rather than the similarity of town meetings, see Michael Zuckerman, *Peaceable Kingdoms: The New England Towns in the Eighteenth Century* (New York, 1970), pp. 154-86.

3. See, especially, Swansea Town Records, 11 August 1749.

4. *Braintree Town Records*, p. 290 (7 March 1748/9); *Manchester Town Records*, 1: 166 (1726).

5. Of the town records surveyed systematically for information on order of election, the following conformed closely to the pattern described in the text: Amherst, Boston, Braintree,

Brookline, Cambridge, Dedham, Fitchburg, Lunenburg, Manchester, Springfield, Sudbury, Topsfield, Watertown, Worcester, Hanover (N.H.), Newcastle, Exeter, South Kingstown, Enfield, Kent, and Suffield. The towns of Lynn (Mass.), Concord, Derryfield, Londonderry, and Hartford elected no regular treasurer, and New Haven, Derby, and Tisbury (Mass.) elected their treasurers toward the end of the meeting. For sources not already cited, see Hezekiah S. Sheldon, *Documentary History of Suffield* (Springfield, 1879); *Records of the Town Meetings of Lynn 1691-1757*, vols. 1-5 (Lynn, 1949-1966); *Records of the Town of Tisbury, Mass.* (Boston, 1903).

6. *New Haven Town Records*, vol. 3, esp. pp. 158 (25 December 1699), 201 (20 December 1703), 286 (18 December 1710).

7. *Springfield Town Records*, vol. 1, esp. 12 March 1694/5 and 12 March 1699/1700. The custom of electing only the head of the Pynchon family moderator dated from the founding of the town, and was not violated until the town began electing moderators at every meeting in 1716.

8. Barnstable Town Records, 2: 1-15.

9. *Watertown Town Records*, 2: 209 (14 January 1712/13), 230 (15 February 1714/15); Medfield Town Records, 1 March 1707/8; see also *Cambridge Town Records*, II and *Derby Town Records*.

10. On Dedham, see Kenneth A. Lockridge and Alan Kreider, "The Evolution of Massachusetts Town Government 1640 to 1740," *William and Mary Quarterly*, 3d ser., 23 (1966): 553-59. Massachusetts law (*Acts and Resolves of Massachusetts*, vol. 1, *1692-93*, chap. 38) required that the selectmen preside at the election of representatives; and a look at almost any set of town records will confirm that they did so.

11. *Acts and Resolves*, vol. 2, *1715-16*, chap. 22.

12. A search of vol. 13, Massachusetts Archives (at the Statehouse, Boston, Massachusetts), which contains the files on internal town disputes referred to the General Court for the first quarter of the eighteenth century, revealed no cases of disorder in town meetings.

13. The following is a list of early towns and the dates they began electing moderators on a regular basis: Andover (before 1700), Barnstable (1715), Boston (before 1700), Boxford (1690), Braintree (1695), Brookline (1718), Cambridge (1715), Dedham (1714), Dorchester (1715), Hadley (1720), Hatfield (1719), Lynn (1715), Manchester (before 1700), Medfield (1708), Norton (1716), Salem (before 1700), Springfield (1716), Sudbury (1706), Swansea (1718), Topsfield (1714), Watertown (1716), Portsmouth (before 1700), Hampton (before 1700), Dover (1730), Kingstown (R.I.) (1696), Newport (before 1700), Ashford (1716), Enfield (1707), New Haven (see text), Hartford (after 1718).

14. *Acts and Laws of New Hampshire*, p. 75 (4 Geo. I).

15. *New Haven Town Records*, 3: 407 (22 December 1718), 622 (15 December 1739).

16. *Public Records of Connecticut*, 7: 244 (May 1729 session); John R. Bartlett, ed., *Rhode Island Colonial Records*, vols. 1-10 (Providence, 1855-67), 4: 425.

17. *Colonial Laws of Massachusetts Reprinted from the Edition of 1672* (Boston, 1887), pp. 40 (1636), 46 (1640). For a good account of voting procedures in colony elections, see Darrett B. Rutman, *Winthrop's Boston, Portrait of a Puritan Town 1630-1649* (Chapel Hill, N.C., 1965), pp. 169-171. The system of nominations and proxy voting was adopted by Connecticut (*Acts and Laws of Connecticut*, pp. 30-31), and the written or printed "prox" system became highly developed in Rhode Island (Howard M. Chapin, "Eighteenth Century Rhode Island Printed Proxies," *The American Collector*, 1 (Nov. 1925): 54-59. New Hampshire, of course, had no colony-wide elections after its separation from Massachusetts.

18. *Acts and Resolves of Massachusetts*, vol. 1, *1693-94*, chap. 14; Cortland F. Bishop, *History of Elections in the American Colonies* (New York, 1893).

19. *Boston Town Records*, 8: 58 (14 March 1708/9), 88 (10 March 1711/12); Portsmouth Town Records, 24 September 1711, 7 June 1714.

20. *Salem Town Records*, 3: 83, 104, 134. See also p. 19 below.

21. *Dedham Town Records*, 6: 261 (7 March 1725/6), 234 (26 August 1723). See also Edward M. Cook, Jr., "The Transformation of Dedham, Massachusetts, 1715-1750" (honors thesis, Harvard University, 1965), 46-52.

22. *Manchester Town Records*, 1: 98 (28 March 1701), 103 (2 March 1703), 107 (27 March 1705), 118 (26 March 1708), 132 (12 March 1716), 137 (26 March 1717), 142 (31 March 1718), 150 (27 March 1721).

23. Dorchester Town Records, vols. 1 and 2, esp. 2, 11 March 1717. The tabulations are copied in James Blake, *Annals of Dorchester* (Boston, 1846).

24. *Braintree Town Records*, p. 89 (4 March 1716/17).

25. Medfield Town Records, 4 March 1722/3; *Dedham Town Records*, 6: 234 (26 August 1723), 252 (1 March 1724/5), 261 (7 March 1725/6), 270 (6 March 1726/7), 281 (18 March 1727/8). The four towns were Barnstable (1715), Enfield (1714), Lynn (1723), and Swansea (1721). Several other towns made a point of altering the form of the election record from "chosen" to "Voted for and Chosen" at about this time, which may or may not be evidence of the date of their conversion. See, for example, *Watertown Town Records*, vol. 2, especially pp. 300 (4 March 1722/3) and 329 (7 March 1725/6).

26. For example, see *Braintree Town Records*, pp. 109 (2 March 1723/4), 167 (6 March 1732); Ashford Town Records, vol. 1, 1 Dec. 1729, 3 Sept. 1756. Portsmouth voted in 1729 "that the Selectmen Should be Chosen by Nomination for the year Ensuing but not to be made a President for the future" (Town Records, 25 March 1729).

27. This was the practice, for example, at the disputed Dedham election of 1728, described extensively in Edward M. Cook, Jr., "Social Behavior and Changing Values in Dedham, Massachusetts, 1700-1775," *William and Mary Quarterly*, 3d ser., 27 (1970): 554-56; and Kenneth A. Lockridge, *A New England Town: The First Hundred Years* (New York, 1970), pp. 110-115.

28. *Boston Town Records*, 8: 58 (14 March 1708/9); *Lynn Town Records*, vol. 4, 4 March 1733/4. The law governing town meetings specified that the elections be by "major vote of such assembly" (*Acts and Resolves of Massachusetts*, vol. 1, *1692-93*, chap. 28.

29. *Boston Town Records*, 12: 27 (12 March 1743).

30. *Braintree Town Records*, p. 353 (7 March 1757).

31. *Londonderry Town Records*, 1: 370 (18 January 1762); *Provincial Papers of New Hampshire*, vols. 1-40 (Manchester, Nashua, and Concord, 1867-1943), vol. 12, *Early Town Papers*, pp. 448-49. The mid-eighteenth century dispute over the adequacy of pluralities extended to other arenas as well. In 1748 Connecticut assemblymen challenged the election of the deputy governor by a plurality, and demanded a special election. Governor Law remonstrated that the requirement of a majority "was not the Understanding of this Government 'till very lately, nor of Neighboring Governments under like Circumstances," but he and the upper house were forced to acquiesce in a new election. Richard L. Bushman, *From Puritan to Yankee: Character and the Social Order in Connecticut, 1690-1765* (Cambridge, Mass., 1967), 239-40; *The Wolcott Papers: Correspondence and Documents During Roger Wolcott's Governorship of the Colony of Connecticut, Collections of the Connecticut Historical Society*, 16 (Hartford, 1916): 478-81.

32. *Braintree Town Records*, p. 290 (6 March 1748/9).

33. *Ibid.*; Medfield Town Records, 8 March 1730/1. Other towns to mention the procedure explicitly were Andover, Dedham, Grafton, Hadley, Manchester, Ashford, Kent, Bedford, Derryfield, and Portsmouth.

34. Andover Town Records, 1751-56; Grafton Town Records, 1753-84; Hadley Town Records, 1763-66; Medfield Town Records, 1737 and following; Bolton Town Records, 7 December 1778.

35. Lockridge and Kreider, "The Evolution of Massachusetts Town Government, 1640 to 1740": 549-74.

36. Both Massachusetts, under the first charter, and Connecticut elected their assistants by a system of nominations at a primary election, followed by an election in which the candidates were proposed one at a time, incumbents first, and the voters asked to decide on early candidates without being sure of the later alternatives. See the sources cited in note 17 above, and Charles S. Grant, *Democracy in the Connecticut Frontier Town of Kent* (New York, 1961), 122-27.

37. *Colonial Laws of Massachusetts*, p. 40.

38. Swansea Town Records, Proprietor's Book of Grants and Meetings, p. 115 (18 January 1720/1). One Cambridge town meeting handled the problem of judging voters' eligibility by collecting all the ballots offered, then adjourning while leaders "examine[d] into ye Qualifications of Such as have Voted," and certified the result. Cambridge Town Records, 13 March 1726/7, 20 March 1726/7.

39. Michael Zuckerman (*Peaceable Kingdoms*, pp. 177-86) argues, mistakenly I think, that the paper ballot in Massachusetts was a secret ballot, and cites as evidence a number of instances in which the tellers allowed, or were alleged to have allowed, voting frauds the town was unable to correct. He sees the secret ballot and the towns' helplessness to avert frauds through control mechanisms as manifestations of the lengths to which towns would go to avoid open conflict. It

should be noted, however, that he based his argument on the few cases in which the control mechanism worked so badly that the election had to be appealed to the General Court rather than on the majority of cases in which it succeeded. Even if Zuckerman's fraudulent elections were representative, however, they would not prove that the towns sacrificed honesty and control in the interest of superficial harmony, because in sending a formal, signed petition of protest to the General Court, the dissenters raised the public display of disagreement to a matter of colony-wide attention. The fraudulent abuse of voting procedures by partial or unscrupulous voters and tellers must be regarded as a fraud, and not as an expression of the public will.

40. David S. Lovejoy, *Rhode Island Politics and the American Revolution, 1760–1776* (Providence, 1958), pp. 1–30. Many of the lists of voters are in the "Freeman" file, Rhode Island Archives, Providence, R.I.

41. In 1745 the moderator of a Portsmouth meeting declined to order such a poll, explaining that "no Disorder had appeared to him in the meeting" and that the votes had all been "put in the box in as Regular orderly and unsuspected a manner as he Ever Saw Practised" (Portsmouth Town Records, 2 Dec. 1745). Derryfield, a deeply divided town, conducted at least four elections by polling; and Watertown, which was also divided, used the poll to settle several voting disputes. See *Derryfield Town Records*, vol. 1, 4 March 1754, 1 March 1773, 7 March 1774; *Watertown Town Records*, 3: 16–17 (3 March 1728/9), 246 (14 May 1742).

42. John Goffe to Gov. Benning Wentworth, 1 September 1766, quoted in *Derryfield Town Records*, 1: 370–72; Silas Carey's Deposition, East Greenwich folder, "Freemen" file, Rhode Island Archives.

43. The evidence here is intended to show that the voters had a clear understanding of who were and were not leaders and not to argue that the leaders were a cohesive "class" in any of the several meanings of that term. Evidence on the social and economic characteristics of leaders will be presented in later chapters.

44. See Chapter 2.

45. The towns were Barnstable, Boston, Duxbury, Hanover, Middleboro, Swansea, Portsmouth, Weare, Middletown, Newport, Providence, Smithfield, and South Kingstown. The cases of Boston, Portsmouth, and the Rhode Island towns will be discussed in the text. It is noticeable that all of the towns in the original Plymouth colony (Barnstable, Barrington, Duxbury, Hanover, Middleboro, Norton, and Swansea) ranked below the average of 85.2 percent selectmen, but whether this has any significance, and if so what, is not at all clear.

46. See Lovejoy, *Rhode Island Politics*. The behavior of the Rhode Island towns might also be explained by the fact that all four were relatively wealthy towns, in which a substantial number of men could be expected to seek major office. The fifth town, Exeter, was much poorer, and had much tighter officeholding patterns.

47. For example, Brookline elected Edward White (Harvard, 1712) clerk at the age of twenty-six, and Hatfield chose Oliver Partridge (Yale, 1730) at the age of twenty.

48. Massachusetts did not require the election of a treasurer until 1694 (*Acts and Resolves of Massachusetts*, vol. 1, *1693–94*, chap. 20; New Hampshire never required one, and in the other colonies they appeared under the general power to elect town officers (see note 1 above). Dedham began to elect treasurers in 1687 (*Dedham Town Records*, vol. 5), while Hadley and Hatfield did so only in 1725 and 1727. New Haven called its tax collector "treasurer" until 1750, and until 1734 treated the office as one to be thrust upon the leading men by turns, just as the office of constable rotated among lesser men. *New Haven Town Records*, vol. 3, esp. pp. 309 (17 December 1711) and 678 (18 December 1749).

49. *Salem Town Records*, 3: 83 (26 February 1682/3), 104 (8 March 1683/4), 134 (9 March 1684/5).

50. Service was determined by comparing the records with the lists of town officers in James Duncan Phillips, *Salem in the Seventeenth Century* (Boston, 1933), pp. 358–362.

51. *New Haven Town Records*, 3: 623 (10 December 1739).

52. Barnstable Town Records, 2: 15 (date uncertain).

53. Portsmouth Town Records, 21 January 1744.

54. *Acts and Resolves of Massachusetts*, vol. 3, *1748–49*, chap. 15.

55. Hadley Town Records, 25 March 1751. The last may have become a leader, too, but he was included in the new town of South Hadley, which separated from Hadley in 1753, and thus was unable to serve the old town.

56. Swansea Town Records, 29 March 1751, 22 May 1751, Aug 1751; Massachusetts Archives, 116: 135–36.

57. Massachusetts Archives, 116: 14–16. Zuckerman (*Peaceable Kingdoms*, p. 202) uses this petition as evidence of the large number of men eligible for selectmen in the "little village of Norton." Norton, however, had some 350 adult males in 1765, so that the 21 could not have amounted to 10% of the legally eligible population in 1751 by any stretch of the imagination.

58. *Brookline Town Records*, p. 126 (1 March 1724/5); p. 143 (1 March 1735/6), pp. 262–66 (17 March, 24 March, 26 May 1777).

59. A similar confrontation occurred in 1774 between the voters of Leicester, who wanted the selectmen to double as assessors, and the candidates, who refused to serve under those conditions. The town went through four unsuccessful elections before capitulating and electing three old selectmen and two new leaders (one of them a deacon) to the separate office of selectman. Leicester Town Records, 7 March 1774.

60. Sources on the Dedham precinct dispute are cited in note 27 above. On the minor officers, see pages 44–50, Chapter 2 below.

61. Ashford Town Records, 31 December 1716; Swansea Town Records, 31 March 1721. Similarly, when the New Hampshire Assembly voided the Londonderry election of 1737 and ordered a new one, eleven of the twelve men chosen in the two elections, which were won by first one and then the other of the contending factions, were established leaders. *Londonderry Town Records*, vol. 1, 5 March 1736/7; ibid., app., pp. 387–89.

Chapter 2

1. Robert E. Brown, *Middle-Class Democracy and the Revolution in Massachusetts, 1691–1780* (Ithaca, 1955), pp. 1–100; Lovejoy, *Rhode Island Politics*, pp. 1–17; Chilton Williamson, *American Suffrage from Property to Democracy: 1760–1860* (Princeton, 1960), 1–61.

2. On probate records see Kenneth A. Lockridge, "Letter to the Editor," *William and Mary Quarterly*, 3rd ser., 25 (1968): 516–17.

3. Zuckerman, *Peaceable Kingdoms*, pp. 190–200.

4. A few women did sign petitions and protests. See, for example, Andover Town Records, 12 October 1708, where Widow Hester Stevens was among forty-five dissenters from a town vote. Women also voted in some churches, especially among Baptists and New Lights. See, for example, Records of the First Baptist Church of Swansea, Brown University Archives, Providence, R.I.

5. Michael Zuckerman has discovered that an eighteen-year-old was permitted to vote in a Sheffield, Massachusetts, election because his father's death had made him the head of a substantial local family (*Peaceable Kingdoms*, p. 197), and undoubtedly the same impulse enfranchised a few minors elsewhere. Similarly, a minor was occasionally allowed to serve as a town officer, usually as a substitute for his father. For example, Londonderry accepted James Nesmith's underage son to serve in his place as constable (Londonderry Town Records, March 1764). Also, Hatfield elected Oliver Partridge, scion of the town's leading family and a college graduate (Yale, 1730), town clerk when he was three months short of his twentieth birthday (Hatfield Town Records, March 1732). For numbers used in dividing the population by age and sex, see Evarts B. Greene and Virginia D. Harrington, *American Population Before the Federal Census of 1790* (New York, 1932), p. xxiii; and Brown, *Middle-Class Democracy*, p. 49.

6. Another small percentage of the population, Indians and Negroes, must be added to the ranks of the nonparticipants. Indians, of course, did run their own towns of Natick, Stockbridge, Mashpee, and Gayhead in Massachusetts. According to various censuses, 3.1 percent of Massachusetts' population was nonwhite in 1765, as was 3.2 percent of Connecticut's in 1774, 8.7 percent of Rhode Island's in 1774, and less than 1 percent of New Hampshire's in 1775. See Josiah H. Benton, *Early Census-Making in Massachusetts* (Boston, 1905); John R. Bartlett, *The Census of the Inhabitants of the Colony of Rhode Island and Providence Plantations for 1774* (Providence, 1858); *Public Records of Connecticut*, 14: 485–491; *Collections of the New Hampshire Historical Society*, 1 (Concord, 1871): 231–35.

7. Information on the number of officers each year in several towns can be found in Table 8.

8. *Acts and Resolves of Massachusetts*, vol. 1, *1692–93*, chap. 38; ibid., *1693–94*, chap. 6; ibid., *1693–94*, chap. 7; *Acts and Laws of New Hampshire*, pp. 29–34 (5 Geo. I), p. 213 (4 Geo. I); *Acts and Laws of Rhode Island* (1767 ed.), p. 107; *Acts and Resolves of Rhode Island* (Newport,

1748), October 1747; *Public Records of Connecticut*, 2: 87 (May 1668), 419 (May 1687); Ibid., 3: 31-32 (May 1690); *Acts and Laws of Connecticut*, 17: 49-50. Some towns mended their highways by having the surveyors collect a tax and using the money to hire workers, but even so, their duties were mainly those of supervising the highway work.

9. *Acts and Resolves of Massachusetts*, vol. 1, *1692-93*, chap. 38; ibid., *1693-94*, chap 20; *Acts and Laws of New Hampshire*, p. 59 (2 Geo. I); *Acts and Laws of Connecticut*, pp. 111-112; *Acts and Laws of Rhode Island* (1705 ed.), p. 35; South Kingstown Town Records, 1742-85; Exeter Town Records, 1775.

10. The law in *Acts and Laws of Rhode Island* (1767 ed.), p. 107, provided wages of four shillings a day for fence viewers in that colony.

11. *Acts and Resolves of Massachusetts*, vol. 1, *1692-93*, chap. 17; ibid., *1692-93*, chap. 38; ibid., *1692-93*, chap. 30; ibid., *1710-11*, chap. 7; *Acts and Laws of New Hampshire*, pp. 29-34 (5 Geo. I), p. 182 (13 Wm. III); *Rhode Island Colonial Records*, 3: 395 (4 May 1698); *Acts and Laws of Rhode Island* (1719 ed.), p. 58 (25 February 1706); *Public Records of Connecticut*, 2: 87 (May 1668); *Acts and Laws of Rhode Island* (1730 ed.), pp. 41, 149-50.

12. *Acts and Resolves of Massachusetts*, vol. 1, *1693-94*, chap. 7; ibid., vol. 2, *1739-40*, chap. 3; ibid., vol. 4, *1760-61*, chap. 20; *Acts and Laws of New Hampshire*, 31 Geo. II; *Acts and Laws of Rhode Island* (1719 ed.), p. 111 (Oct. 1719); Samuel Whiting, *Connecticut Town-Officer* (Danbury, 1814), pp. 67-71; *Lunenburg Town Records*; *Hartford Town Records*; Portsmouth Town Records.

13. Vendue masters received 2 1/2 percent of the proceeds from their sales. *Acts and Laws of Rhode Island* (1719 ed.), p. 111 (October 1719). See also the ordinance in South Kingstown Town Records, 5 March 1727/8, establishing a fee of 1/2d. to pound keepers for each sheep impounded. In many towns men were willing to build and maintain pounds at their own expense, which suggests that pounding fees were widely enforced. See, for example, *New Haven Town Records*, pp. 284 (19 December 1709), 653 (16 December 1745), and 745 (28 December 1767).

14. *Acts and Resolves of Massachusetts*, vol. 1, *1693-94*, chap. 7; ibid., *1713-14*, chap. 16; ibid., vol. 2, *1720-21*, chap. 9; *Acts and Laws of New Hampshire*, p. 76 (4 Geo. I), p. 60 (4 Geo. I); *Public Records of Connecticut*, vol. 2 (May 1674). The Massachusetts and New Hampshire laws established specific fees for impounded strays, while Rhode Island town ordinances like the South Kingstown one cited in note 13 established similar fees. The humorous custom of electing newly married men to the office of hog reeve, mentioned in such town histories as Frank Smith, *History of Dedham, Massachusetts* (Dedham, 1936), p. 37, and Benjamin Chase, *History of Old Chester from 1719 to 1869* (Auburn, N.H., 1869), pp. 447-451, probably dated from a later period, when hogs were not so commonly allowed to forage at large, and the duties of the office were consequently not as important.

15. *Hartford Town Votes, passim*; Robert F. Seybolt, *Town Officials of Colonial Boston, 1634-1775* (Cambridge, 1939), *passim*. Boston's scavengers eventually evolved into honorary positions for gentlemen who supervised the actual work.

16. *Acts and Resolves of Massachusetts*, vol. 1, *1692-93*, chap. 38; ibid., vol. 3, *1756-57*, chap. 26; *Acts and Laws of New Hampshire*, pp. 29-34 (5 Geo. I); *Acts and Laws of Rhode Island* (1705 ed.), p. 103 (May 1702); ibid. (1719 ed.), pp. 36-38; ibid. (1730 ed.), p. 16; *Acts and Laws of Connecticut*, pp. 20-22, 37.

17. Sudbury Town Records, 1761-72. Nearly every young gentleman in Boston was elected constable; see Seybolt, *Town Officials of Colonial Boston*.

18. Data in Table 3 is based on *Dedham Town Records*, vols. 6 and 7, and on Cook, "Transformation of Dedham," app. B and app. F, with some corrections. In Windham, Connecticut, 486 men served 1,715 terms in the five minor offices of surveyor, constable, tithingman, lister, and grand juryman between 1755 and 1786; and the same men apparently served most of the 642 terms in seven other offices. The number of officeholders was equivalent to 71 percent of the 687 adult males recorded in the Connecticut census of 1774. See William F. Willingham, "Deference Democracy and Town Government in Windham, Connecticut, 1755-1786," *William and Mary Quarterly*, 3rd ser., 30 (1973): 401-422.

19. Those men whose ages are not known have been omitted from the calculations in this paragraph.

20. Data in the table is based on lists of town officers taken from the town records and on the tax lists for the year given in parentheses. Exact years for the officer samples are listed in Table 5.

21. Amherst, Andover (two samples), Brookline, Hadley (two samples), Dublin, Bolton (1720s).

22. Oakham, Concord, Derryfield (two samples).

23. Sudbury (two samples), Swansea, Watertown, Worcester, Portsmouth, Bolton (1750s), New Haven, Exeter, South Kingstown (two samples). The Sudbury (1730s) and Watertown tax lists covered only half of each town. Officials in the other half may have included a larger percentage of the taxpayers. Bolton was an exception to the statements about size, but it was only marginally below 40 percent in participation.

24. Distribution of Towns by Size, 1760-1775

Colony	Year	Over 1,200	Under 1,200	No Data
Massachusetts	1765	71	128	12
Connecticut	1774	61	15	
Rhode Island	1774	22	7	
New Hampshire	1773	10	126	
Totals		164 (36.3%)	276 (61.1%)	

25. Table 5 is based on a larger group of sample decades than Table 4. Once again, the lists of minor officers were drawn from the town records in each case, and the lists of major officers for each decade came from the data used in Tables 1 and 2.

26. A cutoff of 1,200 total population has been used to separate large and small towns. Populations after the 1750s are determined by census, earlier ones are estimated through available tax lists or extrapolated from the censuses (see Appendix I). In the first half of the century Andover, Dedham, and Sudbury, all marginal cases on the basis of estimates, have been counted as large towns.

27. Amherst (two samples), Barrington, Brookline (two samples), Fitchburg, Hadley (two samples), Lunenburg (two samples), Manchester (two samples), Medfield, Oakham, Topsfield (two samples), Newcastle, Concord, Derryfield (two samples), Dublin, Hampstead, Hanover, Ashford (1730s), Enfield (1720s).

28. The Rhode Island towns had very small pools of minor officers, so that an ordinary-sized pool of leaders looked large by comparison (see Table 4).

29. The population data is summarized in Appendix I.

30. This finding harmonizes with Daniel Scott Smith's observations on the shrinkage of elite members in proportion to population in P. M. G. Harris's data on colonial college graduates. See Smith, "Cyclical, Secular, and Structural Change in American Elite Composition," *Perspectives in American History*, 4 (1970): 363-72. Smith's article is a commentary on P. M. G. Harris, "The Social Origins of American Leaders: The Demographic Foundations," *Perspectives in American History*, 3 (1969): 159-346.

31. The breakdown by colonies was:

Massachusetts: 206 of 271 new leaders, or 76.0 percent
New Hampshire: 55 of 79 new leaders, or 69.6 percent
Rhode Island: 38 of 74 new leaders, or 51.4 percent
Connecticut: 75 of 99 new leaders, or 75.8 percent

The percentages for individual towns are in Table 8, part I.

32. Peter Oliver, *Origin and Progress of the American Rebellion*, ed. Douglass Adair and John A. Schutz (San Marino, 1963), pp. 39-41; Gerald R. Warden, *Boston, 1689-1775* (Boston, 1970).

33. Barnstable Town Records; John J. Waters, *The Otis Family in Provincial and Revolutionary Massachusetts* (Chapel Hill, N.C., 1969), 149-61.

34. *Brookline Town Records*, 1765-1769.

35. See above, pp. 26-27.

36. *Dedham Town Records*, 8: 98 (12 March 1743/4).

37. Barnstable Town Records, 9 March 1721. Captain Lothrop informed the meeting that he could not "axept of it considering ye office he sustains."

38. Barnstable Town Records, 12 March 1739/40, 14 March 1739/40.

39. The reputational method depends on questioning community members about their opinions of who are influential leaders, and the decisional method involves intensive study of the exact roles of specific leaders in making a single community decision. Social scientists prefer these two methods, while admitting that they have their drawbacks, and that they are

unworkable for historical studies. See Terry N. Clark, *Community Structure and Decision-Making: Comparative Analyses* (San Francisco, 1968), pp. 72-81.

40. The quotations are from Zuckerman, *Peaceable Kingdoms*, chap. 5, in which he shows that selectmen in fifteen towns served an average of 2.9 to 7.6 terms; Joel A. Cohen, "Democracy in Revolutionary Rhode Island: A Statistical Analysis," *Rhode Island History*, 29 (1970): 7; and George Levesque, "Coventry: The Colonial Years" (M.A. thesis, Brown Univ., 1969), p. 31.

41. The data on Coventry comes from Levesque, "Coventry," pp. 27-31; and data for Windham comes from Willingham, "Deference Democracy in Windham," pp. 401-22. The time period for each town can be found in Table 2, with the exception of Coventry (1741-66) and Windham (1755-86).

42. For a statistical discussion of the advantages of the average (technically, the arithmetic mean), see Hubert M. Blalock, Jr., *Social Statistics* (New York, 1960), pp. 57-60.

43. Boxford, Grafton, Medfield, Pelham, Chester, Hampstead, Hampton, Londonderry, Newtown.

44. Examples are Andover, Boston, Cambridge, Duxbury, Watertown, Dover, Portsmouth, Providence, Smithfield, Stonington, and New Haven.

45. Towns settled after 1750 comprise this group in Table 10.

46. See the towns listed in note 43 above.

Chapter 3

1. Bernard Barber, in *Social Stratification* (New York, 1957), pp. 1-50, describes political roles, military roles, religious roles, production roles, and professional roles as primary criteria for stratification, and wealth, family prestige, personal qualities, and voluntary community activities as secondary criteria.

2. On the Leonards see Clark, *History of the Town of Norton, Bristol County, Massachusetts* (Boston, 1859); on the Chandlers see William Lincoln, *History of Worcester, Massachusetts* (Worcester, 1837); and on the South Kingstown gentry see William Davis Miller, "The Narragansett Planters," *Proceedings of the American Antiquarian Society* 43 (1934): 49-115.

3. The figures for similar estates reported on valuation surveys like those concluded by Massachusetts in 1771 and 1784-86 varied enormously from town to town, and in Dedham's case the assessed values were as little as 5 percent of the values reported for the same property in probate inventories (Cook, "Social Behavior and Changing Values"). Changes in assessment procedures were numerous. For example, Massachusetts usually assessed land at "six years income of the yearly rents" (*Acts and Resolves of Massachusetts*, 3: 233), but the 1771 Assessment form called for a tabulation of "The Annual Worth of the Whole Real Estate without any Deduction for more than ordinary Annual Repairs" (ibid., 4: 156). Rhode Island assessed land at ten years' rent and trading stock at half its real value in 1744 (Rhode Island Reports, September 1744, at State Archives, Providence) but in 1767 her legislature rated land at twenty years' rent and trading stock at full value (*Acts and Resolves of Rhode Island*, June 1767, pp. 21-25). These fluctuations are a serious problem because most assessment records present only a lump sum value, rather than an itemized schedule. Connecticut's assessment formula included a high valuation on the poll (£18), high assessment of land and agricultural equipment, and a low valuation on all other forms of wealth. These factors, together with the reluctance of the colony to divide towns with as large and disparate populations as New Haven's effectively conceal most of the differences among the towns. See Jackson Turner Main, *The Social Structure of Revolutionary America* (Princeton, N.J., 1965), 293-94.

4. Analysis of probate inventories is an alternative method of establishing both absolute and relative wealth, but location and analysis of the probate records on the thousands of men involved in this study was ruled out by the magnitude of the task in comparison with the limited gain in precise information. Even when inventories are used they leave many questions unanswered because of the absence of probate records on many poorer men, and because some inventories recorded only movable property. Also, inventories recorded only property at death, which is a serious problem in view of the fact that tax records suggest that most men alienated large portions of their estates between the time when they were active in public affairs and the time the inventories were taken.

5. Little data exists for extending consideration of trends in property distribution back into the seventeenth century. Figures for Topsfield (26.7 percent owned by the top decile in 1668,

26.2 percent in 1687, and 26.7 percent in 1725), Medfield (19.2 percent in 1668 and 19.0 percent in 1697), Sherborn, Massachusetts (22.0 percent in 1686 and 24.0 percent in 1721), and Kenneth Lockridge's assertion that the distribution of property changed little in Dedham through the early years of the eighteenth century all suggest that the concentration of property was little greater in most towns in 1700 than it had been in the previous century. Such a conclusion is also logical in view of the fact that concentrations of no more than 20 or 25 percent of the property in the hands of the top 10 percent indicate about as egalitarian a distribution of wealth as can be expected anywhere. See *Essex Institute Collections* 30 (1897): 196; Abner Morse, *Genealogical Register of the Inhabitants and History of the Towns of Sherborn and Holliston* (Boston, 1856), pp. 271, 294–96; Medfield Town Records; Lockridge, *A New England Town*, pp. 73, 141–42.

6. See Main, *Social Structure of Revolutionary America*, pp. 7–44; James T. Lemon and Gary B. Nash, "The Distribution of Wealth in Eighteenth-Century America: A Century of Change in Chester County, Pennsylvania, 1693–1802," *Journal of Social History* 2 (1968–69): 1–24; James A. Henretta, "Economic Development and Social Structure in Colonial Boston," *William and Mary Quarterly*, 3rd ser., 22 (1965): 75–92.

7. Nathaniel Bouton, *History of Concord, from its First Grant in 1725 to the Organization of the City Government in 1853* . . . (Concord, 1856). Bouton asserted that the name "Concord" was a tribute to the unanimity with which the hand-picked Massachusetts settlers resisted the pretensions of the rival New Hampshire proprietors (p. 245).

8. Population statistics are summarized in Appendix I. The Massachusetts province tax of 1765 is in *Acts and Resolves of Massachusetts*, vol. 3, *1765–66*, chap. 18, pp. 620–29.

9. One is tempted to attribute this fact to the inheritance customs found by Philip Greven, which, by retaining property in a father's hands until old age and then prescribing for division only among those sons who could be amply provided for, tended to keep dependent sons off the tax rolls and to drive a steady stream of men out of town, thus keeping them from taking a place near the bottom of the list. Migration from Andover was higher than that from Dedham, but too little is known about inheritance patterns in Dedham or elsewhere for generalizations about the effect of inheritance on social structure to be made. See Philip J. Greven, Jr., *Four Generations: Population, Land, and Family in Colonial Andover, Massachusetts* (Ithaca, 1970); Cook, "Social Behavior and Changing Values," pp. 572–73. The high per capita tax paid by Medfield was an anomaly resulting from a temporary overassessment, and disappeared with the next province-wide reapportionment.

10. Data for Connecticut is both scarce, because so few tax lists have survived, and inconclusive, because the assessment procedures minimized differences (see note 3 above) and because poorer outlying areas were not set off as separate towns as they were settled. Wealth in the coastal parishes of New Haven, for example, was considerably more concentrated than in the inland Fourth ("North Haven") and Fifth ("Amity") Parishes, but neither the grand Lists of Estates in the colonial records, nor the censuses, provided breakdowns by parish.

11. See, for example, the rhapsody on self-sufficient farming in Percy W. Bidwell and John I. Falconer, *History of Agriculture in the Northern United States, 1620–1860* (New York, 1925), pp. 126–27. The best critique of the myth is Andrew H. Clark, "Suggestions for the Geographical Study of Agricultural Change in the United States, 1790–1840," *Agricultural History* 46 (1972): 165–72.

12. See, for example, Carl Bridenbaugh, *Cities in the Wilderness: The First Century of Urban Life in America, 1625–1742* (New York, 1938); Bernard Bailyn and Lotte Bailyn, *Massachusetts Shipping, 1697–1714* (Cambridge, Mass., 1959); Glenn Weaver, *Jonathan Trumbull, Connecticut's Merchant Magistrate, 1710–1785* (Hartford, 1956).

13. Main, *Social Structure of Revolutionary America*, pp. 7–43.

14. Rivers were, of course, the principal avenues of communication in Maine but that region was too little settled to constitute a major exception.

15. Samuel Clough, *Kalendarium Nov-Anglicanum or an Almanac for 1705* (Boston, 1705); Nathaniel Whittemore, *The Farmer's Almanac for 1716* (Boston, 1716).

16. Nathan Bowen, *New England Diary or Almanack for 1727* (Boston, 1727); Thomas Prince, *The Vade Mecum for America* (Boston, 1732).

17. Roger Sherman, *An Astronomical Diary or Almanack for 1755* (Boston, 1755); Nathaniel Ames, *An Astronomical Diary or Almanack for 1760* (Boston, 1760); Benjamin West, *The New-England Almanack* (Providence, 1764); John Anderson, *The Rhode Island Almanack* (Newport, 1772); John Mein and John Fleeming, *Massachusetts Register* (Boston, 1766); Benjamin Edes and John Gill, *North American Almanack and Massachusetts Register* (Boston, 1770).

18. Walter Christaller, *Central Places in Southern Germany*, Carlisle W. Baskin, trans. (Englewood Cliffs, N.J., 1967), pp. 14-23. See also the bibliographical footnotes in James T. Lemon, "Urbanization and the Development of Eighteenth Century Southeastern Pennsylvania and Adjacent Delaware," *William and Mary Quarterly*, 3rd ser., 24 (1967): 503n.

19. Christaller specifically warns that population is not a true index of the importance of a central place (*Central Places in Southern Germany*, pp. 17-18), but both he and Lemon associate population sizes with towns of various orders.

20. The resulting index does not measure the real value of a town's land, because the taxes included assessments on the value of personal property and commercial wealth, but it is peculiarly sensitive to the amount of commercial development in the town precisely because it does include taxes on those classes of property. The values for each colony must be considered separately.

21. See Appendix II, where the index for all towns in New England is given. Figures for the sample towns are summarized in Table 27. I have divided the colony taxes for Massachusetts and New Hampshire cited in note 8 and p. 74, the Rhode Island tax of 1771 (in *Acts and Resolves of Rhode Island*, October 1774 [Newport, 1774], p. 119), and the Connecticut Grand List of 1774 (in *Public Records of Connecticut*, 14: 384-86) by town areas in acres, as of the 1760s and 1770s, reconstructed substantially from the following sources: Eliphalet and Phineas Merrill, *Gazetteer of the State of New-Hampshire* (Exeter, 1817); Commonwealth of Massachusetts, *Historical Data Relating to Counties, Cities, and Towns in Massachusetts*, prepared by Kevin H. White, Secretary of the Commonwealth (Boston, 1966); *Massachusetts Board of Harbor and Land Commissioners, Annual Report for the Year 1915* (Boston, 1915); John C. Pease and John M. Niles, *Gazetteer of Rhode Island and Connecticut* (Hartford, 1834); Rhode Island Development Council, *Rhode Island Towns and Cities: Community Facts* (mimeo, 1957); Moses Greenleaf, *Survey of the State of Maine* (Portland, 1829), pp. 402-18.

22. Because of death, geographical mobility, and other reasons, about 13 percent of the leaders in the decades studied did not appear on the tax lists used.

23. Overall 29.8 percent of the men in the top deciles of the ninety-five lists were leaders. The twenty-two cases in which a majority served were Amherst (1771), Boxford (1687), Fitchburg, Hadley (all three lists), Manchester (1696), Norton (1711), Oakham, Pelham, Bedford (both lists), Canterbury, Concord (1737), Derryfield (1775), Dublin, New Ipswich (1763), Providence (1705), Bolton (1753), Derby (both lists), Kent (1744), Newtown (both lists), Woodbury (1736). The only three cases in which top-decile leaders constituted a majority of both the men in that decile and the whole leadership were Canterbury, Bolton (1753), and Newtown (1767). These were probably fortuitous instances, as Bolton's top decile had provided only two leaders in the previous list, and Newtown changed its leaders so often that it clearly was not very selective.

24. Manchester and New Ipswich each took all of its leaders from the top quarter of the list in one decade, but not in others.

25. Barber, *Social Stratification*, pp. 41-42.

26. The records of South Kingstown and Exeter, Rhode Island, provide particularly good examples of the delays involved in paying accounts because their financial records are very detailed. Both towns repeatedly voted to pay leaders interest on accounts that had remained unpaid for as long as five or six years. See for example, Exeter Town Records, 17 April 1765; South Kingstown Town Records, December 1755, June 1764, June 1765, 5 March 1766, 26 August 1766, December 1766.

27. Watertown imposed such conditions on its representatives from 1751 to 1755 (*Watertown Town Records*, 5: 95, 109, 127, 165), and Cambridge did so from 1750 to 1757, although they dropped the practice in 1758 because the preferred candidate, Andrew Boardman, was reluctant to meet such terms (Cambridge Town Records, May 14, 1750-May 15, 1758). In Dedham the men who were representatives in 1756 and 1757 through 1759 gave the town £15 (Old Tenor) each year, and Samuel Dexter, the representative in 1765 and 1766, gave £6-13-4 (Lawful Money). The regularity of the gifts suggests that they were expected, although one was not mentioned in the records at all (the reference is in a private diary), and the others are carefully treated as free gifts, given some time after election. *Dedham Town Records*, 7: 261 (21 May 1759), 333 (12 Aug. 1765), 349 (12 Aug. 1766); "Diary of John Whiting," *New England Historical and Genealogical Register* 68 (1909): 188. See also *Boston Town Records*, 14: 176 (15 May 1750).

28. Northampton Town Records, 1674, cited in James P. Walsh, "Solomon Stoddard's Open Communion: A Re-examination," *New England Quarterly* 43 (1970): 101.

29. Some historians, notably Clifford K. Shipton, have argued that local office was in effect a special form of taxation on the rich and the able.

30. For an exposition of the country ideology, see J. G. A. Pocock, "Machiavelli, Harrington, and English Political Ideologies in the Eighteenth Century," *William and Mary Quarterly*, 3rd ser., 22 (1965): 549-83; and for its application to New England, see T. H. Breen, *The Character of the Good Ruler: Puritan Political Ideas in New England 1630-1730* (New Haven, 1970). Working largely from antigovernment tracts, Breen stresses the anticorruption aspect of liberty, but it is clear that when New Englanders turned to local affairs, they were anxious that voters and local officials be free from the influence of the other inhabitants. See esp. Zuckerman, *Peaceable Kingdoms*, pp. 196-98. The desire to have elected officials who were free to serve the public good as they conceived it also had important, although largely unexplored, roots in the puritan doctrine of magistracy.

31. *Provincial Papers of New Hampshire*, 37 (1939): *Probate Records of the Province of New Hampshire, 1760-1763*, pp. 324-5; ibid., 38 (1940): *Probate Records, 1764-1767*, 153, Cook, "Social Behavior and Changing Values," pp. 575-76. These sources confirm the finding of Norman H. Dawes ("Titles of Prestige in Seventeenth Century New England," *William and Mary Quarterly*, 3rd ser., 6[1949]: 69-83) that titles like "gentleman" and "mister" quickly lost their precise meaning in America. Considerable precision remained in the use of terms like "esquire" for officials with commissions of the peace or of higher rank. Little clarity is gained by accepting all self-styled "gentlemen" as a "squirearchy," as does Carl Bridenbaugh in "The New England Town: A Way of Life," *Proceedings of the American Antiquarian Society* 56 (1946): 22-24, on the strength of the doubtful assertions of the anonymous author of *American Husbandry*.

32. William M. Sargent, comp., *Maine Wills, 1640-1760* (Portland, 1887), contains the following occupational information for leaders in the six sample towns:

Occupation	No. of Decedents	Occupation	No. of Decedents
Esquire	6	Trader	1
Gentlemen	7	Mariner	2
Yeoman	5	Shipwright	1

33. The following shows the average service in major town office of the men mentioned by occupational groups in footnote 32 and on p. 87.

Colony	Esquires	Gentlemen	Merchants	Yeomen	Other Trades	All Town Ldrs
New Hampshire	9.7	6.6	18.3	5.4	5.5	4.9
Maine	7.7	6.3	—	2.3	3.3	4.5

34. Biographical data on the town leaders is too limited to support detailed study of why some men at the middle or bottom of the list were able to afford to serve as leaders when others presumably were not. Clearly, some such leaders were older men who had turned the management of their farm or business over to their sons, although still enjoying an adequate income, and other leaders were sons of wealthy men who were not entirely independent of their fathers. But others were men who had no apparent access to much property, and must have been able to spare time from their own affairs because they had no families to support, or because they maintained an exceptionally low standard of living.

35. See Clark, *Community Structure and Decision Making*, pp. 72-86, and the discussion on page 51 above.

36. Francis G. Wallett, ed., "The Diary of Francis Parkman, 1729-1738," *Proceedings of the American Antiquarian Society* 71 (1961): 408; James MacSparran, *Letter Book and Abstract of Out Services, 1743-51*, ed. Daniel Goodwin (Boston, 1899), p. 34. MacSparran's neighbor Jeffry Watson, a wealthy Narragansett planter and an assistant of the Colony of Rhode Island, was a gentleman of leisure, but he cheerfully mended fences and stacked hay on occasion. Matthew Patten, a justice of the peace in Bedford, New Hampshire, was even more regularly engaged in physical labor. See Jeffry Watson's Diary, transcript at Rhode Island Historical Society, and *Diary of Matthew Patten of Bedford, N.H., 1754-1788* (Concord, 1903).

37. Book of Records of the North Precinct of Braintree, 1709–1766, transcript at Massachusetts Historical Society, p. 52; *Lunenburg Town Records*, p. 96; Thomas W. Bicknell, *History of Barrington, Rhode Island* (Providence, R.I.), p. 268; *Amherst Town Records*, p. 11; *Dedham Town Records*, 6: 141 (2 April 1715) and 205 (31 October 1720).

38. Samuel Sewall, "Dairy of Samuel Sewall" (vol. 2, 1700–14), *Collections of the Massachusetts Historical Society*, 5th ser., 6 (Boston, 1879): 144–47; Henry W. Cunningham, ed., "Winchester Genealogy," *New England Historical and Genealogical Register* 78 (1924): 7–28. See also the account in Breen, *The Character of the Good Ruler*, pp. 229–31, which points out the ideological bias of Dudley's views but unfortunately assumes that Winchester and his companion were thorough proletarians.

39. For a general account of seating, see Robert J. Dinkin, "Seating the Meeting House in Early Massachusetts," *New England Quarterly* 43 (1970): 450–64. Dinkin argues that wealth became increasingly important as a seating rule in the eighteenth century and points out that some towns began to abandon the custom at about the time of the Revolution.

40. Bolton Town Records, 14 December 1730, 20 January 1730/31. For other examples of seating at the discretion of the committee, see *Boxford Town Records*, 20 January 1700/1, 9 March 1702/3; *Dedham Town Records*, 6, 127 (11 March 1714), 176 (13 May 1718).

41. *Watertown Town Records*, vol. 4, 13 March 1726/7, 10 April 1727, 10 June 1728, 5 March 1728/9, 21 April 1729, 5 May 1729, 17 June 1729. The neighboring town of Brookline explicitly placed prestige ahead of money when it voted to sell its pews, but only to men nominated by a committee and individually approved by the town. *Brookline Town Records*, pp. 105 (12 March 1716), 112 (29 April 1718), 146 (16 May 1737), 226 (5 March 1770).

42. *Watertown Town Records*, 4: 62 (13 March 1731/32), and 90–91 (24 April 1732), which is a detailed seating list. Dates of birth are taken from Henry Bond, *Genealogies of the Families and Descendents of the Early Settlers of Watertown, Massachusetts* (Boston, 1855), and the data on wealth from the 1730 tax list in the Massachusetts Historical Society.

43. Alfred M. Copeland, *History of the Town of Murrayfield* (Springfield, 1892), pp. 81–89.

44. Dinkin ("Seating in the Meeting House," pp. 458–59) and Michael Zuckerman (*Peaceable Kingdoms*, pp. 217–18) both argue that towns customarily reseated every three or four years, but such frequent changes were almost entirely limited to towns that were growing rapidly, as was the case with Amherst and Weston, the prime examples. Towns like Watertown and Lunenburg gave the appearance of rapid change by prolonging a single reseating operation for five or six years, while the town meeting repeatedly altered the seating rules. See the Watertown sources cited in notes 41 and 42 above and *Lunenburg Town Records*, pp. 68–91 (8 February 1730/1–1 March 1735/6) and 144–155 (18 December 1750–25 May 1752).

45. See page 86, above.

46. Zuckerman, *Peaceable Kingdoms*, 217–19.

Chapter 4

1. John Adams, "A Defense of the Constitutions of Government of the United States of America," in Charles Francis Adams, ed., *The Works of John Adams* (Boston, 1851), 4: 392–93.

2. Brown, *Middle-Class Democracy*; Zuckerman, *Peaceable Kingdoms*, p. 189.

3. With the exception of Fitchburg and Oakham, which were settled very late, only towns with two reasonably spaced tax lists were considered so that the number of names found in the tax lists would be representative of the town's population over the century; where more than two lists have been used in other parts of the study, the following selection has been made for this table: Andover, 1720, 1760; Billerica, 1733, 1771; Boxford, 1687, 1774; Dedham, 1710, 1735; Hadley, 1720, 1771; Manchester, 1717, 1769; Topsfield, 1725, 1765; Concord, 1737, 1776; Kent, 1744, 1771; New Haven, 1720, 1766; and Woodbury, 1736, 1765.

4. See Chapter 7.

5. Only towns incorporated before 1730 have been considered. The towns in Table 14 are representative in the sense of including all major types (except first-generation towns), rather than in the sense of providing a proportional microcosm of New England.

6. The fourteen leaders' sons in these families served an average of 12.8 terms in major office, nearly double the average for the whole leadership.

7. Shipton, *Sibley's Harvard Graduates*, 6: 553–55.

8. The eleven families were the Abbotts, Barkers, Chandlers, Farnums, Fosters, Fryes, Holts, Johnsons, Lovejoys, Osgoods, and Stevens, and together they included 48 percent of the taxpayers. Selection is based on tax lists of 1720, 1740, and 1760, and on Greven, *Four Generations*, p. 216.

9. The seven families included 21.5 percent of the taxpayers on the 1730 and 1774 lists.

10. The three Boardmans served 27.6 percent of the leadership terms in Cambridge and the three Chandlers served 23.9 percent in Worcester.

11. Sir Lewis Namier, *The Structure of Politics at the Accession of George III*, 2d ed. (London, 1957), pp. 1-7; Sumner Chilton Powell, *Puritan Village: The Formation of a New England Town* (New York, 1965), pp. 29-44, 51-73; Lockridge and Kreider, "Massachusetts Town Government," pp. 549-50; Zuckerman, *Peaceable Kingdoms*, p. 187.

12. Information on the percentage of town officers serving as selectmen can be found in Tables 1 and 2, and the discussion of their data in Chapter 1. The standard for inclusion in Table 15 was that the birth date for two-thirds of a town's leaders be known. Exceptions have been made for Boston and Newport, because of their obvious importance, and for Londonderry, because it presents the best data of any of the towns settled by Scotch-Irish immigrants. The overall average age at first service is an average of the town figures, not of individual cases.

13. Portsmouth constitutes the most important exception to the rule that low averages occurred in small towns, for reasons discussed on page 109, below.

14. See Chapter 2, page 53, for a discussion of the limitations of the "mean" or "average."

15. South Kingstown and Dublin are exceptional cases, in the first instance because of the unusually large group of provincially prominent families in the town, and in the second because of the town's small population and recent settlement.

16. Summary figures for the fifteen towns as a group showed 15.5 percent of new leaders aged under thirty-five, 62.5 percent aged between thirty-five and fifty, and 22 percent aged over fifty, although no pretense is made that the group of towns was exactly representative of New England as a whole.

17. The fifty-one towns are identified in Table 16.

18. Lockridge and Kreider, "Massachusetts Town Government," pp. 567-70. See also Chapter 1, above.

19. The ten towns are Amherst, Boxford, Grafton, Hadley, Medfield, Topsfield, Hampstead, Hampton, Londonderry, and Derby. Hadley and Amherst are marginal cases, because their long union as a large, populous, and important town left each town with mixed egalitarian and elitist tendencies when they became separate and homogeneous communities in 1759.

20. Hardwick, Oakham, Shirley, Westminister, Gorham, Cornish, Dublin, New Ipswich, and Weare.

21. Consecutive five-year averages, beginning with 1700-04 are as follows:
Dorchester: 53.6, 46.2, 50.7, 53.8, 53.5, 44.9, 48.0, 51.9, 53.8, 52.8, 44.2, 46.4, 49.1, 48.4, 47.0, 50.2, 48.9.
Hatfield: 48.8, 44.0, 45.7, 50.6, 54.0, 53.6, 44.0, 48.3, 43.3, 50.0, 48.5, 52.9, 53.4, 51.3, 49.5, 55.3, 52.1.
S. Kingstown (from 1723): 49.5, 45.3, 48.0, 44.4, 49.5, 42.1, 38.7, 44.9, 45.1, 47.7, 54.9, 48.5, 52.6.
Stonington: 49.2, 50.3, 48.1, 48.5, 47.1, 48.4, 50.6, 44.1, 44.0, 46.4, 49.6, 52.3, 51.6, 47.4, 45.5, 46.7, 51.2.

22. Blake, *Annals of Dorchester*, 69.

23. Lockridge and Kreider, "Massachusetts Town Government," pp. 568-569. Of the pre-1690 selectmen listed in Herman Mann, *Historical Annals of Dedham from its Settlement to 1847* (Dedham, 1847), pp. 80-81, only one man, William Avery (1645-1708), served more than one term after that year, and he was evidently the only man of his age group to have served before 1690.

24. Of fifteen out-precinct leaders identifiable from petitions and from the records of the 1728 riot, five were born between 1655 and 1670, and another seven were born between 1680 and 1695. For details of the precinct dispute, which was far more complex than the present context makes clear, see Cook, "Social Behavior and Changing Values," pp. 546-80, and Lockridge, *A New England Town*, 93-118. The sudden changes in the age structure of Dedham's leadership are graphically displayed in Cook, "Transformation of Dedham," Appendix E. Equally sudden changes took place in the leadership of other towns. At Billerica, for example, a whole set of leaders born before 1730 was simultaneously and permanently dismissed in 1785.

25. The rationale for selecting these particular indicators of prominence will be discussed further in Chapter 7.

26. The figures cited in the text have been corrected by excluding men who moved into a sample town after their fortieth birthday, and hence could not have served earlier. Of the seventy-four towns listed in Table 26, Falmouth, Salem, and Hartford are excluded because the sources for officeholding give only length of tenure, not exact years of service, and Boston and Portsmouth are excluded for reasons that will be explained in the text.

27. The figures for Newport, which are rather incomplete because of the absence of vital statistics for several prominent men, did not differ enough from those for other Rhode Island towns to warrant special treatment.

28. Harris, "Social Origins of American Leaders," p. 188.

29. Shipton, *Sibley's Harvard Graduates*, 8: 490–98.

30. The stated proportions of prominent men really constitute minimum values, because they depend on two generations of officeholding in New England. Additionally, some men brought high status with them from England or another colony, while others achieved it without holding public office.

31. For a summary of that debate see John B. Kirby, "Early American Politics—The Search for Ideology: An Historical Analysis and Critique of the Concept of 'Deference'," *Journal of Politics*, 32 (1970): 808–38.

32. Zuckerman, *Peaceable Kingdoms*, p. 189.

33. *Springfield Town Records*, esp. 13 March 1683/4; *Proceedings at the Centennial Celebration of the Incorporation of the Town of Longmeadow, October 17th, 1883, with numerous Historical Appendices* (Longmeadow, Mass., 1884), p. 151.

34. Jere R. Daniell, "Politics in New Hampshire Under Governor Benning Wentworth, 1741–1767," *William and Mary Quarterly*, 3d ser., 23 (1966): 76–105; and the sketches in Shipton, *Sibley's Harvard Graduates*, for Benning Wentworth (6: 113–30), Nathaniel Rogers (6: 213–14), and Henry Sherburne (8: 490–98).

35. Lovejoy, *Rhode Island Politics and the American Revolution*, pp. 1–68; Mack E. Thompson, "The Ward-Hopkins Controversy and the American Revolution in Rhode Island: an Interpretation," *William and Mary Quarterly*, 3d ser., 16 (1959): 363–75.

36. Robert Redfield, *Peasant Society and Culture* (Chicago, 1967), pp. 40–43.

37. Zuckerman, *Peaceable Kingdoms*.

38. For a brief statement of the traditional view of the relationship between society and the British constitution, see Bernard Bailyn, *The Origins of American Politics* (New York, 1968), 19–23.

39. Adams, *Works*, 4: 392–93.

Chapter 5

1. See Robert Emmett Wall, Jr., "The Massachusetts Bay Colony Franchise in 1647," *William and Mary Quarterly*, 3d. ser., 27 (1970): 136–44; and Timothy H. Breen, "Who Governs: The Town Franchise in Seventeenth Century Massachusetts," *William and Mary Quarterly*, 3d. ser., 27 (1970): 460–74, which cite earlier works.

2. About half of the thirty-two towns lack only records for small, short-lived, remote, or dissenting churches. Sixteen churches beside the forty-two mentioned in the text have surviving lists of church officials, such as deacons and elders.

3. Approximate Numbers of Churches in New England

Date	Congregational	Anglican	Baptist	Presbyterian	Quaker
1700	124	2	10	0	10
1775	554	74	101	16	55

These estimates derive mainly from the following sources: Harold Field Worthley, *An Inventory of the Records of the Particular (Congregational) Churches of Massachusetts Gathered 1620–1805* (Cambridge, Mass., 1970); Edes and Gill, *North American Almanack*; Robert F. Lawrence, *The New Hampshire Churches* (Claremont, N.H., 1856); Connecticut

Historical Society, *List of Congregational Ecclesiastical Societies Established in Connecticut Before 1818* (Hartford, 1918); Henry A. Hazen, "Ministry and Churches of New Hampshire," *Congregational Quarterly* 27 (1875): 545-74; Isaac Backus, *A History of New England with Particular Reference to the Denomination of Christians Called Baptists*, 2 vols. (Newton, Mass., 1871), 2: 306-10; William G. McLoughlin, *New England Dissent, 1630-1833*, 2 vols. (Cambridge, Mass., 1971), 1: 279-80; Bruce E. Steiner, "New England Anglicanism: A Genteel Faith?" *William and Mary Quarterly*, 3d. ser., 27 (1970): 122-35; Henry J. Cadbury, "A Map of 1782 Showing Friends Meetings in New England," *Quaker History* 52 (1963): 1-3. The exact number of churches at any time is uncertain because many churches had at best a shadowy existence for long periods of time, while others were arguably branches of, or temporary schisms in, larger churches. Churches of the lesser sects tended to have small memberships. McLoughlin (*New England Dissent*, 1: 121) estimates that as late as 1735 dissenters from the Standing Order made up no more than 4 percent of the New England population.

4. *Acts and Resolves of Massachusetts*, vol. 1, *1692-93*, chap. 26; Ibid., *1692-93*, chap. 46; Susan M. Reed, *Church and State in Massachusetts, 1691-1740* (Urbana, Ill., 1914), pp. 24-30, 86-189; Charles B. Kinney, Jr., *Church & State: The Struggle for Separation in New Hampshire, 1630-1900* (New York, 1955), pp. 36-38, 54-56; *Rhode Island Colonial Records*, 2: 5-6.

5. See Edmund S. Morgan, *Visible Saints: The History of a Puritan Idea* (New York, 1963); and Robert G. Pope, *The Half-Way Covenant: Church Membership in Puritan New England* (Princeton, N.J., 1969).

6. The Andover and Medfield records begin with lists of the active members in the 1690s, and the Dedham records are incomplete after 1672. I have not attempted to supplement leaders identified in church records by consulting the lists of freemen.

7. See Breen, "Who Governs," pp. 466-67; Wall, "Bay Colony Franchise," 136-44; and Lockridge and Kreider, "Massachusetts Town Government," pp. 566-70. Wall shows that about half of the identifiable adult males in Massachusetts were freemen in 1647, at a time when all freemen were church members but many church members avoided becoming freemen.

8. See the discussion of leadership service in Chapter 2. Lockridge and Kreider ("Massachusetts Town Government," p. 574) discuss a similar trend in Dedham and Watertown.

9. At an early stage in the research it was anticipated that systematic differences might exist in recruitment from the churches in a town, and particularly that first church membership might be especially closely associated with leadership. Final calculations showed, however, that members of first churches averaged precisely the same number of terms as members of junior churches, and that although differences in prominence did exist among members of churches within a town, they occurred without any discernible pattern. The anticipated differences did occur among deacons, and are discussed below.

10. This point is discussed further in Chapter 7.

11. The towns of Amherst, Falmouth, Leicester, Providence, Smithfield, and South Kingstown are omitted from the discussion because church records give exact dates of church membership in very few cases. Differences among groups of towns occurred in the figures on prior membership, as well as in more general measures. In particular, several cities seem to have had an informal religious qualification. Boston, Portsmouth, and New Haven all were cities where Congregational majorities regarded Anglicans and other dissenters with suspicion, and all showed the greatest favor to men who began their careers as orthodox church members, electing them to longer terms than either nonmembers or men who joined later in life. The only other city in the sample, Newport, was an exception that proved the rule, because no single religious group was politically dominant or threatening in the town, and the voters showed no preference for church members in elections. The country towns showed less interest in making membership a qualification or in electing early members to long terms, and differed from one another mainly in the general variation in length of service among large and small towns.

12. Philip J. Greven, Jr., "Youth, Maturity, and Religious Conversion: A Note on the Ages of Converts in Andover, Massachusetts, 1711-1749," *Essex Institute Historical Collections* 108 (1972): 119-34; J. M. Bumsted, "Religion, Finance, and Democracy in Massachusetts: The Town of Norton as a Case Study," *Journal of American History* 57 (1971): 817-31; Gerald F. Moran, "Conditions of Religious Conversion in the First Society of Norwich, Connecticut, 1718-1744," *Journal of Social History*, 5 (1972): 331-43; James P. Walsh, "The Great Awakening in the First Congregational Church of Woodbury, Connecticut," *William and Mary Quarterly*, 3d. ser., 28 (1971): 543-62.

13. Two additional selectmen appear in the statistics in Table 23 because they became deacons after first election to high office, while their presumably early dates of admission are missing from the records.

14. See esp. pp. 42–50, 80–86, and 98–102.

15. Richard D. Brown, "The Emergence of Urban Society in Rural Massachusetts, 1760–1820," *Journal of American History* 61 (1974): 29–51.

16. Fifty-four percent of the deacons whose ages are known were chosen between the ages of forty and fifty-four, 24 percent were over fifty-five years of age, and the remaining 22 percent were under forty. By comparison, 62.5 percent of the town leaders were first elected to office between their thirty-fifth and fiftieth birthdays. See page 103, above.

17. Towns with multiple parishes and the dates of their division were Boston (no parish system, four Congregational churches), Scituate (1642), Salem (1672), Cambridge (1691), Newbury (1695), Plymouth (1695), Springfield (1696), and Watertown (1697) in Massachusetts; and Hartford (1669 and 1696), Stratford (1691), Windsor (1696), and Haddam (1700) in Connecticut. Sources for the tabulations are listed in footnote 3 above. Rhode Island towns, which had no parish system, are excluded from the tabulation.

18. Scholars have made extensive studies of the causes and consequences of intratown divisions in the eighteenth century. See esp. Bushman, *Puritan to Yankee*; Lockridge, *A New England Town*; and Cook, "Social Behavior and Changing Values," all of which focus on this theme.

19. Sample towns known to have had apportionment plans, with approximate initial dates and a "T" to indicate tacit plans discovered through study of officeholders' residence patterns, were Ashford (1755), Hartford (1697), New Haven (1762), Woodbury (1780s), Barnstable (1737), Braintree (1723), Dedham (1735T), Dorchester (1719), Hadley (1735T), Springfield (T, date uncertain), Swansea (1774), Dover (1702T), Hampton (1718T), and Portsmouth (1705).

20. Excluding the minister's salary, which was fixed by contract, parish budgets could amount to as little as ten shillings a year, enough to pay only for routine record keeping. See Clapboardtrees Parish Records (Dedham Third Precinct) at Dedham Historical Society, Dedham, Massachusetts.

21. The only indication of formal nominations comes from a list headed "Nomination For Town Office For the Year 1787" on the inside cover of the record book of Roxbury Parish, Woodbury, Connecticut. Scattered sources such as the comments on Braintree politics in John Adams's *Diary* (discussed below, pp. 140–41), and the records cited in the discussion of how meetings nominated officers (Chapter 1) suggest that formal nomination lists were exceptional rather than common.

22. Reed, *Church and State in Massachusetts*; Cadbury, "A Map of 1782"; Records of the New England Yearly Meeting of Friends, on deposit at Rhode Island Historical Society Library, Providence.

23. Backus, *History of New England*; McLoughlin, *New England Dissent*, esp. 1: 279–80; and local sources.

24. Bruce E. Steiner, "Anglican Officeholding in Pre-Revolutionary Connecticut; The Parameters of New England Community," *William and Mary Quarterly*, 3d. ser., 31 (1974): 369–406.

25. A handful of non-Irish Presbyterian churches appeared after the Great Awakening when dissident, usually New Light, groups adopted Presbyterian forms to gain the status of legitimate churches in the eyes of the Standing Order.

26. Chase (*History of Old Chester*, p. 26) reports that intermarriage between the Irish and the original New England settlers remained taboo in that town as late as the 1760s, an assertion that fully accords with other evidence of the degree to which each group preserved its identity while living in close and amicable proximity.

27. Dissenting churches in the remaining towns were small, short-lived, composed of members from out of town, or left no satisfactory records, so they are better excluded from calculations than counted as churches providing no leaders.

28. Swansea contained no Congregational church. Its Baptist founders had preceded their certification of the First Baptist Church as the official town church by signing an agreement never to attempt to collect ecclesiastical taxes in the town, or to exploit the official status of the church in other ways, and that "foundation settlement" was repeatedly reaffirmed in the eighteenth century.

29. Additional statistics for towns in the 1700-49 and 1750-84 samples were Barrington, one Baptist selectman, 15 terms; Newtown, ten Anglicans, 2.7 terms; Gorham, five Baptists, 2.8 terms; and Weare, five Baptists, 2.2 terms, and four Quakers, 2.0 terms.

30. William G. McLoughlin, the Baptists' foremost modern historian, has argued that eighteenth-century Baptists suffered "clear social prejudice," were "socially ostracized, abused, and ridiculed," were "seldom elected to town office (except perhaps as 'hogreeves'),"and were relegated to a town's outskirts "where the ne'er-do-wells and scapegraces lived." ("Massive Civil Disobedience as a Baptist Tactic in 1773)" *American Quarterly*, 21 (1969): 712-13. The case for Baptist persecution seems exaggerated in the context of data now available, and rests on a misunderstanding of how New England towns functioned and why they decided issues as they did.

31. *Town Records of Dudley, Massachusetts* (Pawtucket, R.I., 1893-94), 2: 9-22.

32. McLoughlin, *New England Dissent*, 1, 466-7; Greenville Baptist Church, *Exercises on the 150th Anniversary of its Formation* (Worcester, Mass., 1889), pp. 22-56; L. Kinvin Wroth and Hiller B. Zobel, eds., *The Legal Papers of John Adams* (Cambridge, Mass., 1965) 2: 32-47; Emory Washburn, *History of Leicester* (Boston, 1860), p. 111. The presence of several Baptists among the pewholders in the First (Congregational) Parish meetinghouse built in 1771 confirms the conciliatory nature of the official town church.

33. William S. Tilden, *History of the Baptist Church in Medfield, Mass.* (Boston, 1877), pp. 4-13; Shipton, *Sibley's Harvard Graduates*, 11: 71-75; McLoughlin, "Massive Civil Disobedience," pp. 712-13; Medfield Town Records, 5 March 1749/50, 14 January 1771, 2 March 1772; *Boston News-Letter*, September 30, 1773.

34. The selection of individual dissenters as leaders in Medfield followed the town's custom of electing many townsmen to office, but individual dissenters of suitable stature and ability attained office in towns that were more restrictive. Watertown, for example, had only a handful of Anglican dissenters who attended church in Boston, but elected two of them to major offices.

35. William A. Benedict, *History of the Town of Sutton, Massachusetts* (Worcester, Mass., 1878), p. 796.

36. Several of the Connecticut parishes that were most successful in electing town officers pointedly dispensed with the Anglican system of conducting parish affairs through wardens and vestrymen, and held parish meetings and elected parish committees exactly as Congregational parishes did. (Trinity Church Records, Newtown, vol. 1 (1764-1792), at the Connecticut State Library.) See also Steiner, "Anglican Officeholding," pp. 402-406, which explores in detail the process by which Connecticut towns admitted their Anglican inhabitants to office. Paradoxically, the revolutionary crisis facilitated the entry of Anglicans into office on a large scale by providing an opportunity for individuals to demonstrate their loyalty to the American cause and disassociate themselves from generalized fears that all Anglicans were subversive. Anglican officeholding in country towns increased markedly in the 1760s, and gained ground in cities where Anglicans had been virtually excluded after 1776. See ibid., 372-74.

37. William Stevens Perry, ed., *Historical Collections Relating to the American Colonial Church*, vol. 3, *Massachusetts* (n.p., 1873), pp. 72, 84, 92, 206, 209, 220, 221, 326, 492, 565; Shipton, *Sibley's Harvard Graduates*, 6: 382-85; ibid., 11: 97-107.

38. Adams, *Diary*, 1: 301-305.

Chapter 6

1. Jeremy Belknap, *The History of New-Hampshire*, 3 vols. (Philadelphia, 1784-92), remains the standard narrative history. William Henry Fry, *New Hampshire as a Royal Province* (New York, 1908), pp. 66-126, 422-472, provides detail on the institutional structure, and Jere R. Daniell, *Experiment in Republicanism: New Hampshire Politics and the American Revolution, 1741-1794* (Cambridge, Mass., 1970), pp. 3-73 analyzes the politics of the colony.

2. The list of councillors is in Belknap, *History of New-Hampshire*, 2: 370-72. Councillors and other provincial officials living in the sample towns were identified through the sources listed for each town; while references in *Provincial Papers of New Hampshire*, especially vol. 3 through 8, provided information on most of the others.

3. Only 6 of 17 Portsmouth councillors appointed after Benning Wentworth became governor in 1741 were town leaders. See also Daniell, *Experiment*, pp. 18, 66; Jackson Turner Main, *The Upper House in Revolutionary America, 1763-1788* (Madison, Wis., 1967), 60-67.

4. New Hampshire had an Inferior Court of Common Pleas with colony-wide jurisdiction until the division into counties, but its personnel did not differ significantly from that of the Superior Court in social and geographical background. After 1769, judges in the western counties came from towns such as Hollis, Amherst, and Charlestown, which were the largest and wealthiest towns in their region. See the lists of officials in *Register of New Hampshire and Almanack for 1768*; Daniel Fowle, *Civil, Military, and Ecclesiastical Register of the Province of New Hampshire, 1772* (Portsmouth, N.H., 1771); and *New Hampshire: The Official Succession for Two Centuries* (Concord, N.H., 1879).

5. David E. Van Deventer, "The Emergence of Provincial New Hampshire, 1623-1741" (Ph.D. diss., Case-Western Reserve University, 1969) analyzes early New Hampshire society and its leadership. (To be published by the Johns Hopkins University Press in 1976.)

6. Commission of the Justices of the Peace, 1717, at New Hampshire Historical Society; *Register, 1768*; Fowle, *Register*, 1772.

7. Daniell, *Experiment*, pp. 22-33.

8. Belknap, *History of New-Hampshire*, quoted in Daniell, *Experiment*, p. 17.

9. On Patten's life-style see Patten, *Diary*, *passim*. For Clough see James Otis Lyford, *History of the Town of Canterbury, 1727-1912* (Concord, N.H., 1912), p. 43, and the town records. Justices are fully tabulated in Appendix II.

10. Chapter 3, pp. 78-79, and Appendix II.

11. *Acts and Resolves of Massachusetts*, vol. 1, Charter, p. 12.

12. For example, see Main, *The Upper House*, p. 69.

13. Councillors have been tabulated from the rosters in William H. Whitmore, *The Massachusetts Civil List for the Colonial and Provincial Periods, 1630-1774* (Albany, N.Y., 1870), pp. 45-63. The identification of individuals follows the procedures outlined in the note on genealogy in the bibliography.

14. Robert J. Taylor, *Western Massachusetts in the Revolution* (Providence, 1954), pp. 11-26; Shipton, *Sibley's Harvard Graduates* for John Stoddard (5: 96-118) and Israel Williams (8: 301-333).

15. Examples are Samuel Danforth (ibid., 6: 80-86), Thomas Hubbard (ibid., 6: 490-95), and Timothy Lindall (ibid., 4: 245-48).

16. During the same period, the Connecticut Upper House, a byword for stability, averaged slightly more than one new man a year in a body less than half as large, so that the rates for the two colonies are quite comparable. Average service in Massachusetts was 9.4 years, and in Connecticut it was 11.7 years.

17. Whitmore, *Massachusetts Civil List*, pp. 64-65. In 1703, shortly after he had polarized the factions by expelling all of his opponents from appointive office, Governor Dudley "negatived" Elisha Cooke and four supporters; and in 1741 Governor Belcher vetoed thirteen paper-money partisans.

18. John M. Murrin, "The Legal Transformation: The Bench and Bar of Eighteenth Century Massachusetts," in Stanley N. Katz, ed., *Colonial America: Essays in Politics and Social Development* (Boston, 1971), pp. 423-25. The roster of judges is in Whitmore, *Massachusetts Civil List*, pp. 68-70.

19. Ibid., pp. 434-37; John J. Waters and John A. Schutz, "Patterns of Massachusetts Colonial Politics: The Writs of Assistance and the Rivalry between the Otis and Hutchinson Families," *William and Mary Quarterly*, 3d ser., 24 (1967): 543-63; Hugh F. Bell, "A Personal Challenge: The Otis-Hutchinson Currency Controversy, 1761-1762," *Essex Institute Historical Collections* 106 (1970): 297-323. Waters, *The Otis Family*, supports the general contentions about Massachusetts county elites made in this chapter.

20. Whitmore, *Massachusetts Civil List*, pp. 77-123. Much biographical detail on the judges is available in Emory Washburn, *Sketches of the Judicial History of Massachusetts* (Boston, 1840), pp. 241-400.

21. The Records of the General Sessions of the Peace for Suffolk County, 4 vols. (1703-1731), at the office of the Clerk of the Supreme Judicial Court for Suffolk County, Suffolk County Courthouse, Boston, Mass.; and Franklin B. Rice, ed., "Records of the Court of General

Sessions of the Peace For the County of Worcester," *Collections of the Worcester Society of Antiquity* 5 (1883): 1-190. Both illustrate the dominance of the justices of the quorum.

22. See the lists of justices in Whitmore, *Massachusetts Civil List*, pp. 126-52. The exact number of quorum members cannot be known. Whitmore's list of justices of the quorum is clearly not complete, because no quorum appears in many of the mid-century general recommissioning lists, although many of the quorum justices can be identified tentatively by their position in the list. Whitmore's source, the Records of the Council in the Massachusetts Archives, listed justices in order of seniority at recommissioning time, quorum first, and then ordinary justices beginning with the most senior man. There were, however, enough errors in ordering to prevent accurate tabulation of the missing quorum members.

23. The percentage is a minimum figure because judges who were councillors served as justices ex officio and so were not listed in the commission, and because allowance must be made for the incompleteness of the quorum lists.

24. See Appendix II. The county distributions are as follows:

	1692-1724	1725-1749	1750-1774
Barnstable	2	4	3
Bristol	1	7	4
Essex	4	4	9
Hampshire	1	5	3
Middlesex	2	3	3
Plymouth	2	3	5
Suffolk	1	4	7
Worcester	—	2	3

25. Waters and Schutz, "Patterns of Massachusetts Politics," pp. 543-57; John A. Schutz, *William Shirley: King's Governor of Massachusetts* (Chapel Hill, 1961), pp. 44-80. An indication of the role of the county leaders can be found in the furor over the appointment of Charles Phelps to the Hampshire bench in Shipton, *Sibley's Harvard Graduates*, 8: 313.

26. Lucius R. Paige, *History of Cambridge, Massachusetts, 1630-1877* (Boston, 1877), pp. 167-69.

27. Francis G. Wallett, "The Massachusetts Council, 1766-1774: The Transformation of a Conservative Institution," *William and Mary Quarterly*, 3d ser., 6 (1949): 605-27.

28. Shipton, *Sibley's Harvard Graduates*, 14: 625-26; Nina M. Tiffany and Susan I. Lesley, eds., *Letters of James Murray, Loyalist* (Boston, 1901).

29. Charles S. Grant, *Democracy in the Connecticut Frontier Town of Kent* (New York, 1961), pp. 122-27; Main, *The Upper House*, 81. Lists of nominees and magistrates are to be found in the records of each October and May session of the Assembly respectively (*Public Records of Connecticut*, vol. 2-15, *passim*). I have used the term "magistrates" to include the elected governor and deputy governor, as well as the assistants, in my discussion of Connecticut and Rhode Island.

30. County populations (from Greene and Harrington, *American Population*, pp. 56-61):

	1708 (Polls)	1756 (White Inhabitants)	1774 (White Inhabitants)
Hartford	1549	35,714	50,675
New Haven	949	17,944	25,896
New London	1165	22,015	31,542
Fairfield	788	19,849	28,936
Windham	267	19,670	27,494
Litchfield	—	11,773	26,905

31. Twenty-three of the twenty-five magistrates who lived in sample towns were active town leaders, and a twenty-fourth, John Sherman of Woodbury, was active during a period for which the town records are lost.

32. Dwight Loomis and J. Gilbert Calhoun, *The Judicial and Civil History of Connecticut* (Boston, 1895), pp. 124-40. The judges came from nineteen towns, with Hartford, New Haven,

New London, Fairfield, Milford, Windsor, and Stratford each supplying two or more. Seven of the eight judges in sample towns were town leaders.

33. Loomis and Calhoun, *Judicial and Civil History*, 130. The county court in its eighteenth-century form was established in 1698, and the tabulations of judges and justices, assembled from the volumes of the *Public Records of Connecticut*, begin with that year.

34. Loomis and Calhoun, *Judicial and Civil History*, pp. 155-56; *Public Records of Connecticut*, 4: 324; ibid., 5: 242, 429.

35. For detailed figures, see Appendix II.

36. See the lists of assistants in *Rhode Island Colonial Records*, vols. 2-10. Most of the earlier assistants are identified in J. O. Austin, *Genealogical Dictionary of Rhode Island* (Baltimore, reprint, 1969).

37. Greene and Harrington, *American Population*, pp. 64-65.

38. Patrick T. Conley, "Rhode Island Constitutional Development, 1636-1775: A Survey," *Rhode Island History* 27: 60-63, 82-85.

39. *Rhode Island Colonial Records*, 3: 477-78. This regularized the traditional distinction between "the Island" and "the Main" in the organization of the militia and the colony administration.

40. *Rhode Island Colonial Records*, 3: 55; Conley, "Constitutional Development," p. 84n.

41. Ibid., pp. 87-88; Lovejoy, *Rhode Island Politics*, pp. 7-9, 23-24.

42. Main, *The Upper House*, pp. 86-89. As was the case in Massachusetts and New Hampshire, city magistrates were less certain to be town leaders. Fifty of the fifty-four assistants from the country towns were leaders, but only thirty-eight of the fifty-two Newport magistrates served the town.

43. Conley, "Constitutional Development," pp. 85-86; Lovejoy, *Rhode Island Politics*, pp. 93-96.

44. The judges and justices of the peace are listed in Joseph J. Smith, *Civil and Military List of Rhode Island, 1647-1800* (Providence, 1900).

45. Conley, "Constitutional Development," pp. 85-86.

46. Lovejoy, *Rhode Island Politics*, pp. 60-62.

47. Ibid., pp. 94-95.

48. See Appendix II.

49. See Chapter 4, p. 114, above.

Chapter 7

1. Chapter 2, pp. 37-42, and Table 7.

2. Chapter 2, pp. 60-62, and Table 9.

3. Chapter 2, pp. 53-60, and Table 10.

4. Chapter 3, pp. 65-71, and Table 11; Chapter 6, pages 159-63, and Table 26.

5. For convenience, the salient features of Tables 7, 9, 10, 11, and 26, as well as Appendix II, have been drawn together in Table 27.

6. The group to which each town was assigned is shown in Table 27. The five groups represent cities, major county towns, secondary and suburban towns, village communities, and frontier towns, respectively. In cases where towns behaved according to criteria for more than one type of town, they have been assigned to the group indicated in the largest number of indices.

7. The Index of Commercialization (Appendix II) is discussed in Chapter 3, and family continuity is discussed in Chapter 4.

8. The rise of Providence as a commercial city can be traced in James B. Hedges, *The Browns of Providence Plantations: The Colonial Years* (Cambridge, Mass., 1952). Providence included the northern half of Rhode Island until 1731, when the northern and western three-quarters of its territory became the separate towns of Smithfield, Glocester, and Scituate. Cranston, Johnston, and North Providence seceded in 1754, 1759, and 1765 respectively, so that by 1770 the corporate boundaries of the town approximated the limits of its built-up area. The progressive concentration of property in Boston is traced in Henretta, "Economic Development

and Social Structure," pp. 75-92; and in Allan Kulikoff, "The Progress of Inequality in Revolutionary Boston," *William and Mary Quarterly*, 3d. ser., 27 (1971): 375-412.

9. The communities were the parishes of Amity (or Woodbridge), East Haven, North Haven, and West Haven, which became separate towns in 1784, 1785, 1786, and 1822, respectively. The problem of New Haven is discussed in Chapter 3, p. 64, n.3 and page 74, n.10.

10. Only 50 percent of the Boston moderators served as selectmen.

11. See Chapter 4, pp. 98-102.

12. See Chapter 4, pp. 111-14.

13. Lucy S. Sutherland, "The City of London in Eighteenth Century Politics," in Richard Pares and A. J. P. Taylor, eds., *Essays Presented to Sir Lewis Namier* (London, 1956), pp. 49-74.

14. For Boston see Warden, *Boston: 1689-1775*; for Portsmouth compare the lists of representatives scattered through *Provincial Papers*, vols. 3-8, with the account of politics in Belknap, *History of New-Hampshire*, and with the biographical sketches in Shipton, *Sibley's Harvard Graduates* for such men as Henry Sherburne (8: 490-98), Benning Wentworth (6: 113-30), and Nathaniel Rogers (6: 213-14).

15. In both cases the assertion that Anglicans were excluded derives from an examination of the religious affiliations of the town leaders. See pp. 124-27. Boston's politics also differed from the normal town pattern in that occasionally leaders were preselected in a nominating caucus. See G. B. Warden, "The Caucus and Democracy in Colonial Boston," *New England Quarterly*, 43 (1970): 19-45; and the more analytical Alan and Katherine Day, "Another Look at the Boston 'Caucus,' " *Journal of American Studies 5 (1971): 19-42*.

16. On Hubbard and Lynde, see Shipton, *Sibley's Harvard Graduates*, vol. 6 (1718 and 1721); for the others see Warden, *Boston, 1689-1775*, esp. pp. 103-26.

17. Seven of the eleven Rhode Island governors from 1700 to 1775 were Newport residents, two were Providence men, and a tenth, Samuel Ward, was a Newporter transplanted to Westerly.

18. See the discussion of central-place theory in Chapter 3.

19. See Chapter 4.

20. Paige, *History of Cambridge*, pp. 167-69.

21. Lincoln, *History of Worcester*, pp. 58, 274-8, 356-9; Shipton, *Sibley's Harvard Graduates*, 6: 389.

22. Ibid., 7: 56-66 (Dwight); ibid., 9: 199-223 (Ruggles); ibid., 8: 783-85 (Steele). For Murray, see Lorenzo Sabine, *Biographical Sketches of Loyalists in the American Revolution* (Boston, 1864), 2: 115.

23. New towns granted above Lunenburg in these years included Townsend (1732), Ashburnham (1735), Winchendon (1735), Templeton (1734), Westminster (1728), New Ipswich (1735), Rindge (1736), Richmond (1735), Peterborough (1737), Amherst (1734), and, more distantly, Swansey (1734), Winchester (1733), and Keene (1734). Only the first five towns remained in Massachusetts after 1741, and most were speculative "Canada" or "Narragansett" townships. See Roy Hidemichi Akagi, *The Town Proprietors of the New England Colonies* (Philadelphia, 1924), 190-96.

24. Bellows became a New Hampshire justice of the peace and judge of the Cheshire Inferior Court when it was organized in 1769, while Josiah Willard, Jr., was a justice and the Cheshire sheriff.

25. Shipton, *Sibley's Harvard Graduates*, 7: 621-23 (John Williams of Sharon), and 9: 235-40 (Elijah Williams of Deerfield and Enfield); George Chandler, *Descendants of William and Annis Chandler* (Worcester, 1893), pp. 115-35, 222-52.

26. Shipton, *Sibley's Harvard Graduates*, 6: 553-55; ibid., 9: 431-36.

27. Lawrence Shaw Mayo, "Samuel Dexter," *Dictionary of American Biography*, 5 (New York, 1930): 280.

28. Dorchester Town Records, 1758-1761; George Kuhn Clarke, *History of Needham, Massachusetts, 1711-1911* (Cambridge, Mass., 1912), p. 183.

29. Many great figures in colonial politics as well as their less prominent associates often bought estates in the suburbs, but, significantly, the more prominent men used their estates exclusively as country retreats and took no part in local affairs. Governors Belcher and Hutchinson, as well as Treasurer William Foye, had estates in Milton, and Lieutenant Governor Andrew Oliver had one in Dorchester; but as far as can be determined none of them

bothered to attend a town meeting. See Albert K. Teele, *History of Milton, 1640–1887* (Boston, 1887), pp. 109–40, 221–35; Shipton, *Sibley's Harvard Graduates*, 7: 385.

30. See Chapter 4, pp. 108–9.

31. For evidence of the lack of influence of representatives from remote or obscure towns, see Robert Zemsky, "Power, Influence, and Status: Leadership Patterns in the Massachusetts Assembly, 1740–1755," *William and Mary Quarterly*, 3d. ser., 26 (1969): 506–10, 518.

32. Francis Olcott Allen, *History of Enfield, Connecticut* (Lancaster, Pa., 1900), 1: 305.

33. Dexter to Adams, October 13, 1773, Adams-Morse Papers, Massachusetts Historical Society, Boston.

34. I do not wish to imply that the desire to govern by consensus existed only in village communities. Clearly the impulse occurred in some form and to some extent in every New England town. But consensus as Zuckerman has explained it could only dominate in the villages because only they approximated the conditions of social and political equality and the insularity he has described as the hallmarks of his towns.

35. William Sweetzer Heywood, *History of Westminster, Massachusetts* (Lowell, 1893), pp. 53–141; Akagi, *Town Proprietors*, pp. 95–100, 141.

36. Grant, *Democracy in Kent*, pp. 55–65, 128–73.

37. Heywood, *History of Westminster*, pp. 53–93; Hugh D. McLellan, *History of Gorham, Maine* (Portland, 1903), pp. 93–100.

38. William H. Child, *History of the Town of Cornish, New Hampshire* (Concord, c. 1910), p. 4.

39. This arrangement of homogeneous zones, in reality a legacy of the Turnerian concern for the moving frontier, is more often implicitly assumed than explicitly developed. See, for example, Bidwell and Falconer, *History of Agriculture*, pp. 69–144. My discovery of the usefulness of a nonregional approach is not original, as the extended examination of the problem in H. Roy Merrens, "Historical Geography and Early American History," *William and Mary Quarterly*, 3d. ser., 22 (1965): 530–48, indicates. Still, it is worth noting that two of the most sophisticated recent works to consider the spatial dimension, Jackson Main's *Social Structure of Revolutionary America* (esp. pp. 7–43), and Robert Zemsky's *Merchants, Farmers and River Gods* (Boston, 1971), use essentially regional models.

Chapter 8

1. Convers Francis, *An Historical Sketch of Watertown* (Cambridge, Mass., 1830), p. 78, cited in Zuckerman, *Peaceable Kingdoms*, p. 149; Charles Hudson, *History of the Town of Marlborough* (Boston, 1862), p. 279.

2. A classic statement is J. Franklin Jameson, *The American Revolution Considered as a Social Movement* (paperback edition, Boston, 1956). See esp. p. 15.

3. The Topsfield committeemen (May, 1773) were born in 1710, 1713, and 1716; the Enfield committeemen (April, 1774) were born in 1701, 1713, 1718, 1719, 1730, and 1731.

4. The rates can be inferred by comparing the number of men serving in the period 1750–74 and the number serving 1775–84. The arithmetic, however, is not precise, because some leaders served during more than one period.

5. Brown, *Middle-Class Democracy*, pp. 334–39, presents information on the continuity of leadership in Andover and Hatfield by stressing that the members of the committees were men of substantial property. Twenty of the thirty Andover men mentioned, and all five of the Hatfield men, were established town leaders.

6. Prior Town Service of Provincial Congressmen

Years Service	Massachusetts	New Hampshire
0	17	11
1–5	34	12
6–10	14	6
11–15	6	4
16 and above	20	4
Average Service	9.7 years	5.8 years

I am indebted to L. Kinvin Wroth, editor of the Massachusetts Revolutionary Bicentennial Commission's edition of the Journals of that colony's Provincial Congress, for allowing me to see the official list of members. The names of members of the New Hampshire Congress are in *Provincial Papers of New Hampshire*, 7: 452, 468, 690.

7. The returns are in *State Papers of New Hampshire*, 8: 204-296. Kenneth Scott, in "Tory Associators of Portsmouth," *William and Mary Quarterly*, 3d. ser. 17 (1960): 507-15, presents a slightly different but essentially similar list.

8. Figures for Massachusetts Tories may be found in Edward Carpenter, *History of the Town of Amherst, Massachusetts* (Amherst, 1896), pp. 82-87; Francis T. Bowles, "The Loyalty of Barnstable in the Revolution," *Publications of the Colonial Society of Massachusetts* 25 (1922-24): 265-348; *Braintree Town Records*, 481 (22 May 1777); Paige, *History of Cambridge*, 168-69; Hatfield Town Records, 12 June 1775; Thomas Weston, *History of Middleborough, Massachusetts* (Boston, 1906), 153; *Worcester Town Records*, 4: 232-3. According to Joel A. Cohen, "Rhode Island Loyalism and the American Revolution," *Rhode Island History* 27 (1968): 97-112, loyalists were not numerous in Rhode Island. A Test Oath in 1776 revealed only 17 Tories among the leaders of 6 towns.

9. Lyman H. Butterfield, ed., *The Adams Papers*, vol. 3, *Diary and Autobiography of John Adams* (Cambridge, Mass., 1961), 268-270; *Worcester Town Records*, 4: 232-33.

10. Examples are Merrill Jensen, *The Articles of Confederation* (Madison, 1940); James K. Martin, *Men in Rebellion: Higher Governmental Leaders and the Coming of the American Revolution* (New Brunswick, 1973); and Main, *Upper Houses*.

11. Shipton, *Sibley's Harvard Graduates*, 14: 107-10.

12. *Acts and Resolves of Massachusetts*, vol. 1, *1692-93*, chap. 28.

13. A frequently cited observation is that of William Bentley of Salem, who wrote in his diary on March 12, 1796, that "electioneering goes on in our own state and in New Hampshire. It extends itself in Boston to the petty offices of the town" (*The Diary of William Bentley, D.D.* [Salem, 1907], 2: 174).

14. Chapter 4, pp. 114-18.

BIBLIOGRAPHY

Sources for Individual Towns

CONNECTICUT TOWNS

Ashford

Settled about 1710, recognized as a town in 1716.

Ashford Town Records, 1700–1785. At Town Clerk's Office, Ashford.

"The Old Paper Book," transcribed 1770.

Vol. 1, 1729–1804 (copy). (Volume 1 [original] is at Connecticut State Library, Hartford.)

Ashford Church of Christ. Records, 1718–1834. At Connecticut State Library.

West Ashford Baptist Church. Records, 1765–1863. At Connecticut State Library.

Bolton

Settled about 1720 and incorporated as a town in that year. The town was subdivided into northern and southern precincts in 1760.

Bolton Town Records, 1720–85. At Town Clerk's Office, Bolton.

Town Meeting Records, 1700–85.

List of Rateable Estates, 1732.

List of Polls and Rateable Estates, 24 September 1753.

List of the Town of Bolton, 1774.

Vital Records of Bolton to 1854 and Vernon to 1852. Hartford, 1909.

Talcott, Mary K., ed. "Bolton Church Records." *New England Historical and Genealogical Register* 52 (1898): 180–85, 307–11, 408–20; 53 (1899): 447–49; 56 (1902): 162–67, 347–56.

———. "Vernon Church Records." *New England Historical and Genealogical Register* 58 (1904): 193–98, 400–03; 59 (1905): 95–101, 208–14, 412–16; 60 (1906): 73–81, 199–202.

Derby

Incorporated as a town in 1675 and settled about the same time. Parishes of Derby, proper, and Oxford were organized in 1741.

Town Records of Derby, Connecticut, 1655–1710. Derby, 1901.

Orcutt, Samuel. *History of the Old Town of Derby, Connecticut, 1642–1880.* Springfield, 1880. Contains Grand List of 1718.

Sharpe, W. C. *History of Oxford.* Part I. Seymour, Conn., 1885.

————. *Oxford: Sketches and Records.* Part II. Seymour, Conn., 1910. Contains Commoners' List of 1728.

The 150th Anniversary of the Founding of St. James' Parish, Birmingham (Derby), *Connecticut, 1741–1891*. Privately published, 1891.

Hutchfield, Norman. *History of St. Peter's Church in Oxford, Connecticut.* Oxford, 1958.

Jacobus, Donald L. "Records of St. James' Church, Derby, Conn., 1740–1796." *New England Historical and Genealogical Register* 76 (1922): 130–153, 170–174.

Enfield

Organized as a town by Massachusetts in 1683, in territory later found to lie within Connecticut's chartered boundaries. Enfield seceded from Massachusetts and joined Connecticut in 1749. An eastern portion of the town received incorporation in 1734 as the town of Somers, and the rest of the town was subdivided into precincts in 1770.

Allen, Francis Olcott. *History of Enfield, Connecticut.* 3 vols. Lancaster, Pa., 1900. Includes town records.

Hartford

Settled and incorporated as a town in 1636. Joint capital of Connecticut.

Hartford Town Votes, 1636–1716. Collections of the Connecticut Historical Society, vol. 6 (1897).

Daniells, Bruce C. "Large Town Power Structures in Eighteenth-Century Connecticut: An Analysis of Political Leadership in Hartford, Norwich, and Fairfield." Ph.D. dissertation, University of Connecticut, 1970.

Kent

Settled and incorporated in 1739. Separate precincts were organized in eastern and southern sections in 1750 and 1753 respectively.

Kent Town Records, 1739–85. At Town Clerk's Office, Kent.
    Land Records, vols. 1–5, 7, contain town meeting and tax records.
    Town Meeting Book, 1781–85.

Atwater, Francis. *History of Kent, Connecticut.* Meriden, Conn., 1897.

Grant, Charles S. *Democracy in the Connecticut Frontier Town of Kent.* New York, 1961.

Kent First Church Records, vol. 1, 1741–1823. At Town Clerk's Office, Kent.

First Congregational Church in New Preston, Records, 1757–1845. At Connecticut State Library.

Warren Church of Christ Records, 1756–1931. At Connecticut State Library.

East Greenwich Society Records. At Connecticut State Library.

New Haven

Settled in 1638, as capital of New Haven Colony. After the merger of Connecticut and New Haven, the town became joint capital of the colony. Separate precincts were organized in the outlying sections of East Haven in 1680, West Haven in 1715, North Haven in 1716, Amity in 1738, and Mount Carmel in 1756. A schismatic poll-parish, White Haven, was organized in New Haven, proper, in 1759.

Powers, Zara Jones, ed. *New Haven Town Records, 1684-1769: New Haven Colony Historical Society, Ancient Town Records*, vol. 3. New Haven, 1962. Includes Commons Division List of 1702.

Atwater, Edward E., ed. *History of the City of New Haven to the Present Time by an Association of Writers*. New York, 1887.

Osterweis, Rollin G. *Three Centuries of New Haven, 1638-1938*. New Haven, 1953.

New Haven Grand List of 1745. At New Haven Colony Historical Society, New Haven.

New Haven Grand List of 1766. At New Haven Colony Historical Society.

Dexter, Franklin B. *Historical Catalogue of the First Church of Christ in New Haven, 1639-1914*. New Haven, 1914.

Eversull, Harry K. *Evolution of An Old New England Church: Being the History of the Old Stone Church in East Haven*. East Haven, Conn., 1924.

Manual of the Congregational Church in North Haven, 1718-1871. New Haven, 1871.

Manual of the Congregational Church in Woodbridge. Woodbridge, Conn., 1874.

Manual of the First Church of Christ in New Haven. New Haven, 1886.

Manual of the North Church in New Haven, 1742-1867. New Haven, 1867.

Stiles, Ezra. *Extracts from the Itineraries and other Miscellanies*. Edited by Franklin B. Dexter. New Haven, 1916. Contains a religious census of New Haven, 1762, and a list of church members in Mount Carmel Parish, 1768.

Bethany Society Records, 1762-1808. At Connecticut State Library.

Jacobus, Donald L. "Churchmen of 1738 Under Rev. Jonathan Arnold of West Haven, Connecticut," *American Genealogist* 34 (1958): 246-51.

————. "Families of Ancient New Haven." *New Haven Genealogical Magazine*, vols. 1-8 (1922-32).

Dexter, Franklin B. "Notes on some of the New Haven Loyalists including those graduated at Yale." *New Haven Historical Society Papers 9* (1918): 29-45.

Newtown
Settled about 1700 and incorporated as a town in 1711.

Hurd, Duane Hamilton. *History of Fairfield County, Connecticut*. Philadelphia, 1881.

Johnson, Jane E. *Newtown's History and Historian*. Newtown, 1917. Contains Grand Lists of 1739 and 1767.

Newtown First Church Records. At Connecticut State Library. Admissions, 1752-73, in vol. 5.

Trinity Church Records, Newtown, 1764-1921. At Connecticut State Library. Society Meetings, 1764-1792, in vol. 1.

Stonington
Settled and incorporated by Massachusetts in 1658 and relinquished to Connecticut soon after.

Wheeler, Richard Anson. *History of the Town of Stonington, Connecticut*. New London, 1900.

————. *History of the First Congregational Church, Stonington, Conn., 1674-1874*. Norwich, Conn., 1875.

Records of the Church of Christ in North Stonington, 1727-1800. At Connecticut State Library.

Woodbury

Settled and incorporated in 1670. Outlying parishes were established at Southbury (1731), Bethlehem (1739), Judea or Washington (1742), Roxbury (1743), and South Britain (1769).

Woodbury Town Records. At Town's Clerk's Office, Woodbury.
    Town Meeting Records, 1731–85.
    Tax List Books I and II, 1731–1800.
    (Records before 1731 were burned in the 18th century.)
Cothren, William. *History of Ancient Woodbury, Connecticut.* 2 vols. Waterbury and Woodbury, 1854–79.
Woodbury First Church Records, 1670–1829. At Connecticut State Library. (Copy at Woodbury Town Clerk's Office.)
Bethlehem Congregational Church Records, 1738–1829. At Connecticut State Library.
Catalogue of the First Congregational Church in Washington, Conn. Litchfield, Conn., 1875.
Confession of Faith and Covenant of the First Congregational Church in Woodbury, Conn. Hartford, 1850.
Fay, Charles E. *Historical Sketch: Roxbury Congregational Church.* Roxbury, Conn., 1944.
Manual of the Congregational Church in South Britain, Connecticut. New Haven, 1885.
Roxbury Congregational Church Records. At Connecticut State Library.
    Vol. 1, 1742–95.
    Vol. 2, 1797–1888.
Sharpe, W.C. *South Britain: Sketches and Records.* Seymour, Conn., 1898.
Southbury Congregational Church Records. At Connecticut State Library. Vol. 4, Members Living in 1813.
St. Paul's, Woodbury, Society Records, 1784–98. At Connecticut State Library.
Walsh, James P. "The Great Awakening in the First Congregational Church of Woodbury, Connecticut." *William and Mary Quarterly,* 3d. ser., 27 (1971): 543–62.

MASSACHUSETTS TOWNS

Amherst

Settled about 1700, organized as the Third or East Precinct of Hadley in 1734, and incorporated as a district (equivalent to a town) in 1759.

Carpenter, Edward. *History of the Town of Amherst, Massachusetts.* Amherst, 1896. Includes town records, precinct records, and the valuation list of 1759.
Amherst Province Tax, 1771. In Massachusetts Archives 130: 243, The Statehouse, Boston.
Manual of the Second Congregational Church, Amherst, Massachusetts. Amherst, 1924.
For genealogical information see Judd, *History of Hadley,* under Hadley.

Andover

Settled and recognized as a town in 1646. The town was divided into northern and southern precincts in 1707.

Andover Town Records, 1700-1785. Microfilm copy at Andover Public Library, Andover.

Town Meeting Records, 1700-1785.

Town and County Tax Lists, 1717-68. Contains Province Tax Lists of 1720, 1740, and 1760.

Vital Records of Andover, Massachusetts to the End of the Year 1849. 2 vols. Topsfield, Mass., 1912.

Greven, Philip J., Jr. *Four Generations: Land, Population, and Family in Colonial Andover, Massachusetts.* Ithaca, 1970.

———. "Youth, Maturity, and Religious Conversion: A Note on the Ages of Converts in Andover, Massachusetts, 1711-1749." *Essex Institute Historical Collections* 108 (1972): 119-34.

Historical Manual of the South Church in Andover, Massachusetts. Andover, 1859.

Records of the North (First) Church in Andover. At Merrimac Valley Textile Museum, North Andover.

Barnstable

Settled and recognized as a town by Plymouth Colony in 1638; divided into eastern and western precincts in 1717. Barnstable became the county seat when Barnstable County was organized in 1685.

Barnstable Town Records, 1640-1783. Transcript at New England Historical and Genealogical Society, Boston.

Vol. 1, 1640-1712.

Vol. 2, 1713-1764.

Vol. 3, 1764-1783.

Commons Division List of 1702 in 1: 236-38.

Freeman, Frederick. History of Cape Cod: Annals of the Thirteen Towns of Barnstable County. 2 vols. Boston, 1862-69.

Trayser, D.G., ed. *Barnstable: Three Centuries of a Cape Cod Town.* Hyannis, Mass., 1939.

Articles of Faith and Covenant of the Congregational Church of West Barnstable. Sandwich, Mass., 1917.

Records of the East Parish Congregational Church of Barnstable, Massachusetts, 1717-1801. Microfilm copy at the Congregational Library, Boston.

Bowles, Francis T. "The Loyalty of Barnstable in the Revolution." *Publications of the Colonial Society of Massachusetts* 25 (1922-24): 265-348.

Barrington

Settled about 1667 as part of Swansea; organized as a town in 1717 at the behest of Congregationalists dissenting from Swansea's Baptist establishment. Most of Barrington was annexed to Rhode Island in 1747 as part of the boundary settlement between the two colonies. Barrington in Rhode Island became part of Warren until 1770, when the town was reincorporated with its original name.

Bicknell, Thomas W. *History of Barrington, Rhode Island.* Providence, 1898.

Billerica

Settled and recognized as a town in 1654. Major sections of Billerica were included in the new towns of Bedford, Wilmington, and Tewksbury, incorporated in 1729, 1730, and 1734, respectively.

Hazen, Henry A. *History of Billerica, Massachusetts, with a Genealogical Register.* Boston, 1883. Contains Minister's Rate Lists of 1733 and 1755. Billerica Province Tax, 1771. At Massachusetts Archives, vol. 131.

Boston

Established as a town and as the colonial capital in 1630. Brookline and Chelsea were incorporated from outlying areas in 1705 and 1739.

Boston Records Commission. *Reports of the Boston Records Commissioners,* vols. 1–31 (1876–1904).

Seybolt, Robert F. *Town Officials of Colonial Boston, 1634–1775.* Cambridge, Massachusetts, 1939.

Warden, Gerald R. *Boston, 1689–1775.* Boston, 1970.

——. "The Caucus and Democracy in Colonial Boston." *New England Quarterly* 43 (1970): 19–45.

Winsor, Justin, ed. *Memorial History of Boston,* vol. 2. Boston, 1881.

Day, Alan and Katherine. "Another Look at the Boston 'Caucus'." *Journal of American Studies* 5 (1971): 19–42.

Henretta, James A. "Economic Development and Social Structure in Colonial Boston." *William and Mary Quarterly,* 3d. ser., 22 (1965): 75–92.

Babcock, Mary K., ed. "Christ Church, Boston, Records." *New England Historical and Genealogical Register* 99 (1945): 25–28, 117–22, 204–9, 279–85.

Foote, Henry Wilder. *Annals of Kings Chapel.* Boston, 1896.

Fuller, Arthur B. *Historical Discourse Delivered in the New North Church.* Boston, 1854.

Historical Catalogue of the Old South Church. Boston, 1883.

Hollis Street Church Records, 1732–1885. Transcript at the New England Historical and Genealogical Society Library.

The Manifesto Church: Records of the Church in Brattle Square, Boston, 1699–1872. Boston, 1902.

New South Church: Births, Marriages, Deaths, and Admissions to Communion, 1719–1811. At Boston City Registrar, City Hall, Boston.

Pierce, Richard D., ed. "Records of the First Church in Boston, 1630–1868." *Publications of the Colonial Society of Massachusetts,* vols. 39, 40, 41. Boston, 1961.

"Records of the West Church, Boston, Massachusetts." *New England Historical and Genealogical Register* 93 (1939): 250–63.

Robbins, Chandler. *History of the Second Church or Old North in Boston.* Boston, 1852.

Trinity Church in the City of Boston, Massachusetts, 1733–1933. Boston, 1933.

Wood, Nathan E. *History of the First Baptist Church of Boston, 1665–1899.* Philadelphia, 1899.

Wyman, Thomas B., Jr., ed. "New Brick Church, Boston, List of Persons Connected Therewith from 1722–1775." *New England Historical and Genealogical Register* 18 (1864): 237–40, 337–44; 19 (1865): 230–35, 320–24.

Boxford

Settled in the seventeenth century as a part of Rowley; incorporated as a town in 1685. A second precinct was organized in 1735, including the northwest part of Boxford and a section of Andover.

"Boxford Town Records, 1685-1706." *Essex Institute Historical Collections* 36 (1900): 41-103.
Perley, Sidney. *History of Boxford*. Boxford, 1880.
Boxford Parish Rate List, February, 1745/6. At Town Clerk's Office, Boxford.
Boxford Single Rate List for the Province Tax of 1761. At Town Clerk's Office, Boxford.
Boxford Single Rate List for the Province Tax of 1774. At Town Clerk's Office, Boxford.
Perley, Sidney, comp. "Boxford Tax Lists, 1711-1744." *Essex Institute Historical Collections* 57 (1921): 242-48.
————. "First Known Tax Rate of Boxford, 1687." *Essex Institute Historical Collections* 56 (1920): 297.
Manual of the Second Congregational Church of Boxford. West Boxford, 1922.
Parkhurst, Winifrid. *History of the First Congregational Church in Boxford, Mass., 1702-1952*. Topsfield, Mass., 1952.

Braintree
Recognized as a town in 1640 from a part of Boston called "Mount Wollaston." Northern and southern precincts were organized in 1708, and a third precinct was added in 1728.
Bates, Samuel A., ed. *Records of the Town of Braintree*. Randolph, Mass., 1886.
Records of the North Precinct of Braintree, 1709-66. Transcript at Massachusetts Historical Society, Boston.
Province Tax List for the North Precinct of Braintree, 1774. In Joseph Palmer Papers, at Massachusetts Historical Society.
Braintree First Church Records. Photostat at New England Historical Genealogical Society Library.
Vol. 1, 1671-1775.
Vol. 2, 1775-1856.
A Church Manual with Brief Historical Notes of the First Congregational Church in Braintree. Boston, 1860.
Jackson, Edward E., ed. "Records of the First Church at Braintree, Mass., 1672-1708." *New England Historical and Genealogical Register* 59 (1905): 87-91, 153-59, 269-75, 360-65.
Manual of the First Congregational Church in Randolph. Randolph, Mass., 1862.
Perry, William Stevens, ed. *Historical Collections Relating to the American Colonial Church (Episcopal)*, vol. 3, *Massachusetts*. N.p., 1873.
Sprague, Waldo C. Quincy, Mass. Records: Church Records, 1672-1850. 5 vols. At New England Historical and Genealogical Society Library.
Wilson, D. M. *The 'Chappel of Ease' and the Church of Statesmen: The First Church of Christ in Quincy*. Cambridge, Mass., 1890.
Diary of John Marshall of Braintree, 1689-1711. At Massachusetts Historical Society.
Shipton, Nathaniel N. "General Joseph Palmer (1716-1788): Massachusetts Patriot." Master's thesis, Clark University.

Brookline
Settled during the 1630s as the "Muddy River" section of Boston, incorporated as a town in 1705.

Muddy River and Brookline Records, vol. 1. Boston, 1875.

Bolton, Charles Knowles. *History of a Favored Town*. Brookline, 1897.

Curtis, John Gould. *History of the Town of Brookline, Mass.* Boston, 1933.

Brookline Valuation List, 1771. At Massachusetts Archives 130: 424.

"Muddy River Country [Rate List] 1693." *Report of the Record Commissioners of the City of Boston, Containing Miscellaneous Papers* 10 (1886): 135.

Cambridge

Settled and recognized as a town in 1630, established as county seat of Middlesex County in 1643. Part of Cambridge became the town of Lexington in 1713, a western portion of the town became a second precinct in 1732, and a southern section ("Little Cambridge") became a third precinct in 1779.

Records of the Town of Cambridge, Massachusetts, 1630–1703, vol. 2. Cambridge, 1901.

Cambridge Town Records, 1700–1785. At City Clerk's Office, Cambridge.

Book B, 1704–1788.

Notebook of Andrew Boardman III (Town Clerk 1731-69), marked "City of Cambridge, Records 1731-1779."

Paige, Lucius R. *History of Cambridge, Massachusetts, 1630–1877*. Boston, 1877. Contains Valuation List of 1688.

Cutter, Benjamin, and Cutter, William. *History of Arlington, Massachusetts*. Boston, 1880.

Parker, Charles S. *History of Arlington Past and Present*. Arlington, 1907.

Cambridge First Parish Province Tax, 1770. At Massachusetts Archives 130: 430.

Sharples, Stephen P., ed. *Records of the Church of Christ at Cambridge in New England, 1630–1830*. Boston, 1906.

Dedham

Settled the recognized as a town in 1636. Needham, Bellingham, and Walpole were taken from Dedham and incorporated in 1711, 1719, and 1724, respectively. Three precincts were organized in Dedham during the early 1730s and a fourth was organized in 1748.

Hill, Don Gleason, ed. *Early Records of Dedham, Massachusetts*, vols. 1-5. Dedham, 1886-1899.

Tuttle, Julius, ed. *Early Records of Dedham, Massachusetts, 1707–1736*, vol. 6. Dedham, 1936. Includes Province Tax Lists of 1710 and 1735.

Fisher, Nathaniel, ed. *Early Records of Dedham, Massachusetts, 1737–1766*, vol. 7. Dedham, 1969.

Cook, Edward M., Jr. "Social Behavior and Changing Values in Dedham, Massachusetts, 1700-1775." *William and Mary Quarterly*, 3d. ser., 27 (1970): 546-80.

―――. "The Transformation of Dedham, Massachusetts, 1715-1750." Honors thesis, Harvard University, 1965.

Lockridge, Kenneth A. *A New England Town: The First Hundred Years*. New York, 1970.

Mann, Herman. *Historical Annals of Dedham from its Settlement to 1847*. Dedham, 1847.

Smith, Frank. *History of Dedham, Massachusetts*. Dedham, 1936.

Dedham Valuation List of 1771. At Massachusetts Archives 132: 214.

Whiting, John F., ed. "The Diary of John Whiting." *New England Historical and Genealogical Register* 62 (1909): 185–92, 261–65.

Dorchester

Dorchester was settled and recognized as a town in 1630. A southern portion of the town known as the "New Grant" became a second precinct in 1715 and the town of Stoughton in 1726.

Dorchester Town Records, 1700–1785. At City Clerk's Office, Boston City Hall, Boston. (Microfilm copies at Boston Public Library.) Vols. 1–3.

Boston Records Commissioners. *Dorchester Births, Marriages and Deaths to 1825: Report of the Records Commissioners*, vol. 21 (1890).

Blake, James. *Annals of the Town of Dorchester to 1750.* Boston, 1846.

History of the Town of Dorchester, Massachusetts, by a Committee of the Dorchester Antiquarian and Historical Society. Boston, 1859.

Dorchester Province Tax of 1771. At Massachusetts Archives 130: 597.

Dorchester Assessors. *The Taxable Valuation of the Real and Personal Estates . . . in the Town of Dorchester for 1869.* Boston, 1869. An appendix contains historical information.

Records of the First Church at Dorchester, 1636–1734. Boston, 1891.

Clapp, David. *The Ancient Proprietors of Jones Hill, Dorchester.* Boston, 1883.

Boston Cemetery Department. *Annual Report of the Cemetery Department of the City of Boston for Fiscal Year 1904–5 and a Historical Sketch of the First Burying Ground in Dorchester.* Boston, 1905.

Endicott, Frederic, ed. *Record of Births, Marriages, and Deaths and Intentions of Marriage in the Town of Stoughton, 1727–1800, and in the Town of Canton, 1797–1845, Preceded by the Records of the South Precinct of Dorchester, 1715–1727.* Canton, Mass., 1896.

Duxbury

Settled before 1637 and recognized as a town by Plymouth Colony in that year.

Records of the Town of Duxbury from 1642–1770. Plymouth, 1893.

Winsor, Justin. *History of the Town of Duxbury, Massachusetts, with a Genealogical Register.* Boston, 1849.

Fitchburg

Incorporated as a town in 1764 from a recently settled part of Lunenburg.

Davis, Walter A., ed. *Old Records of the Town of Fitchburg, Massachusetts, 1764–1789*, vol. 1. Fitchburg, 1898.

Fitchburg Valuation List of 1771. At Massachusetts Archives 131: 262.

Grafton

Incorporated as a town in 1735, replacing the almost extinct Praying Indian Plantation of Hassanamisco.

Grafton Town Records, 1735–99. At Town Clerk's Office, Grafton.

Vol. 1, 1735–76.

Vol. 2, 1753–78.

Vol. 3, 1779–99.

Hassanamisco Proprietors' Book, 1728–1800.

Pierce, Frederick Clifton. *History of Grafton, Massachusetts.* Worcester, Mass., 1879.

Grafton Congregational Church Records, 1774–99. At Town Clerk's Office, Grafton.

Hadley

Settled in 1659 and incorporated as a town in 1661. Hadley was divided twice in the eighteenth century, in 1753 when South Hadley became a town and in 1759 when Amherst gained incorporation.

Hadley Town Records, 1680–1785. At Town Clerk's Office, Hadley.

Judd, Sylvester. *History of Hadley, Massachusetts, Including the Early History of Hatfield, South Hadley, Amherst, and Granby.* Northampton, 1863. Includes Commons Division lists of 1720 and 1731.

Hadley Province Tax list of 1771. At Massachusetts Archives 130: 736.

Manual of the First Church in Hadley. Northampton, 1855.

Hanover

Incorporated in 1727 from parts of Scituate and Abington.

Dwelley, Jedediah, and Simmons, John F. *History of the Town of Hanover, with Family Genealogies.* Hanover, 1910.

Hanover Town Records, 1727–1799. At the Town Clerk's Office, Hanover.

Briggs, Vernon L. *History and Records of the First Congregational Church, Hanover, Massachusetts, 1727–1865.* Boston, 1895.

Perry, William Stevens, ed. See listing under Braintree (Mass.)

Hardwick

Settled about 1735 and incorporated in 1739.

Paige, Lucius R. *History of Hardwick, Massachusetts, with a Genealogical Register.* Boston, 1883. Contains Tax List of 1776.

Hatfield

Incorporated in 1670 from the part of Hadley west of the Connecticut River. Whately and Williamsburg were taken from Hatfield and incorporated as towns in 1771.

Hatfield Town Records, 1700–85. At Town Clerk's Office, Hatfield. Books 1–3. Book 2 contains the Hatfield Province Tax List of 1738.

Wells, Daniel White, and Wells, Reuben Field. *History of Hatfield, Massachusetts.* Springfield, Mass., 1910.

Leicester

Incorporated in 1714 but not settled enough to function until 1722.

Leicester Town Records, 1722–85. At the Town Hall, Leicester. Town Meeting Books contain Tax Lists for 1728 to 1743 and several lists of Baptist and Quaker dissenters.

Washburn, Emory. *Historical Sketches of the Town of Leicester, Massachusetts during the First Century of its Settlement.* Boston, 1860.

Greenville Baptist Church in Leicester, Massachusetts. Exercises on the 150th Anniversary of its Formation. Worcester, 1889.

Smithfield, Rhode Island, Monthly Meeting of Friends. Minutes, 1718-1857. At Rhode Island Historical Society Library, Providence. Leicester Quakers belonged to the Meeting.

Lunenburg
Incorporated as a town in 1728. Fitchburg was set off in 1764.

Davis, Walter A., ed. *Early Records of the Town of Lunenburg, Massachusetts, 1728-1763*. Fitchburg, Mass., 1896.

Lunenburg Town Records, 1728-85. At Town Clerk's Office, Lunenburg.

Cunningham, George A. "History of the Town of Lunenburg in Massachusetts." Typescript at Town Clerk's Office, Lunenburg.

Crandall, Ruth, comp. Microfilm Edition of the Tax and Valuation Lists of Massachusetts Towns Before 1776. The Charles Warren Center for Studies in American History, Cambridge, Massachusetts, 1971. Reel 17 contains Lunenburg Province Tax Lists for 1762 and 1770.

Lunenburg Church Records, 1733-1805. At Town Clerk's Office, Lunenburg.

Manchester
Established as a town in 1645, originally a part of Salem.

Town Records of Manchester, 1636-1785. 2 vols. Salem, Mass. 1889-91. Includes the Meeting House Tax List of 1696, the Province Tax List of 1717, and the Town Tax List of 1769.

Lamson, D.F. *History of the Town of Manchester, 1645-1895*. N.p., 1895.

Vital Records of Manchester, Massachusetts to 1849. Salem, 1903.

Medfield
Incorporated as a town in 1651. The town of Medway separated from Medfield in 1713.

Medfield Town Records, 1651-1786. At Town Clerk's Office, Medfield. Includes Valuation List of 1668 and a Commons Division list of 1689/1697.

Tilden, William S. *History of the Town of Medfield, Massachusetts, 1650-1886*. Boston, 1886.

Medfield Valuation List of 1771. At Massachusetts Archives 133: 171-74.

Records of the First Congregational (Unitarian) Church of Medfield, 1693-1770. At the Church, Medfield.

Tilden, William S. *History of the Baptist Church in Medfield, Massachusetts*. Boston, 1887.

Middleborough
Established as a town by Plymouth Colony in 1669. Parts of Middleborough were annexed to Plympton and Halifax in 1734. The town split into three precincts at the time of the Great Awakening.

Weston, Thomas. *History of Middleborough, Massachusetts*. Boston, 1906.

Middleborough Town Records, 1747-1800. At Town Clerk's Office, Middleborough. The records for 1700-1747 have disappeared in recent years.

Norton
Settled about 1700 as a part of Taunton, and incorporated as a town in 1711. Parts of Norton became towns as Easton and Mansfield in 1725 and 1770.

Clark, George F. *History of the Town of Norton, Bristol County, Massachusetts.* Boston, 1859. Contains the Tax List of 1711.

Norton Valuation List of 1771. At Massachusetts Archives, vol. 133.

Petition of the Town of Norton, 1751. At Massachusetts Archives 116: 14–15.

Bumsted, John M. "Religion, Finance, and Democracy in Massachusetts: The Town of Norton as a Case Study." *Journal of American History* 57 (1971): 817–31.

Oakham

Settled about 1740, organized as the autonomous precinct of Rutland West Wing in 1759, and incorporated as a district in 1762. Oakham began as a Scots-Irish settlement, but the Irish were largely supplanted by native New Englanders by 1775.

Wright, H. B., and Harvey, E. D. *The Settlement and Story of Oakham, Massachusetts.* 2 vols. New Haven, c. 1947.

Oakham Valuation List of 1771. At Massachusetts Archives 132: 250.

Pelham

Incorporated in 1743, Pelham was a Scots-Irish town.

Parmenter, C. O. *History of Pelham, Massachusetts.* Amherst, Mass., 1898.

Pelham Valuation List of 1771. At Massachusetts Archives 131: 276.

Salem

Settled before 1630 and recognized as a town in that year. The second and third precincts of Salem, organized in the seventeenth century, became the District of Danvers in 1752.

Salem Town Records, 1628–1691. 3 vols. Salem, 1868–1934.

Perley, Sidney. *History of Salem, Massachusetts, 1626–1716.* 3 vols. Salem, 1924–28. Volume 3 contains the Country Rate of 1683.

Crandall, Ruth, comp. See listing under Lunenburg. Reel 9 contains the Salem Province Tax List of 1764.

Baum, Margaret. "Religion and Social Structure in Salem from 1730 to 1820." Paper read at the Conference on Essex County History, Essex Institute, Salem, June 30, 1971.

The First Centenary of the North Church in Salem. Salem, 1873.

Phillips, James Duncan. *Salem in the Seventeenth Century.* Boston, 1933.

———. *Salem in the Eighteenth Century.* Boston, 1937.

Tapley, Harriet Silvester. "St. Peter's Church in Salem Before the Revolution." *Essex Institute Historical Collections* 80 (1944): 229–60, 334–67; 81 (1945): 66–82.

Shirley

Settled about 1720 as a part of Groton and incorporated as a district in 1753.

Chandler, Seth. *History of the Town of Shirley From its Earliest Settlement to A.D. 1882.* Shirley, 1883.

Shirley Province Tax List of 1771. At Massachusetts Archives 131: 461.

Springfield

Recognized as a town in 1641. Eighteenth-century Springfield included as many as six precincts. West Springfield (1696), Agawam (1737), and Holyoke (1750) became the town of West Springfield in 1774; Longmeadow Precinct (1714) became a town in 1783; and Springfield Mountain Precinct (1740) became the town of Wilbraham in 1762.

Springfield Town Records, 1735–85. At City Clerk's Office, Springfield City Hall.

Burt, Henry M. *The First Century of the History of Springfield, 1636–1736.* 2 vols. Springfield, 1898–99. Includes town records for 1636–1736.

Green, Mason A. *Springfield: 1636–1886, History of a Town and a City.* Springfield, 1888.

Springfield Valuation List of 1771. At Massachusetts Archives 134: 141.

Springfield Valuation List, c. 1685. At City Collector's Office, Springfield City Hall.

Ellis, Theodore W., comp. *Manual of the First Church of Springfield.* Springfield, 1885.

Lewis, Ella May, copyist. "Baptisms, Marriages, and Deaths, 1736–1809, First Church of Springfield, Massachusetts." Mimeographed, 1938.

Proceedings at the Centennial of the Incorporation of the Town of Longmeadow, October 17, 1883, with numerous Historical Appendices and a Town Genealogy. Longmeadow, Mass., 1884.

Sudbury

Settled in 1639 and recognized as a town in 1640. Sudbury divided into eastern and western precincts in 1721.

Sudbury Town Records, 1700–1785. At Town Clerk's Office, Sudbury, Books 4–6.

Sudbury West Side Province Tax List, November 1722. Microfilm at Goodenow Library, Sudbury.

Sudbury Province Tax List, 1771. At Massachusetts Archives 131: 512.

Records of the First (West) Church of Sudbury. Microfilm at Goodenow Library, Sudbury.

Swansea

Settled in 1667 by a Baptist congregation from Wales, and accepted as a town by Plymouth Colony in 1668. The western portion, Barrington, became a town in 1717. Swansea was unique in Massachusetts as a town with two Baptist churches, both recognized as members of the Standing Order. Shawomet territory (now Somerset) was administered by Swansea during the eighteenth century.

Swansea Town Records, 1700–85. At Town Clerk's Office, Swansea.

    Proprietors' Book: Grants and Meetings, 1663–1769.

    Proprietors' Records, 1670–1718.

    Town Meetings, 1667–1793.

Swansea Valuation List, 1771. At Massachusetts Archives, vol. 134.

Records of the First Baptist Church of Swansea. In Brown University Archives, Providence, R.I.

Topsfield

Recognized as a town in 1650.

Town Records of Topsfield, Massachusetts, 1659–1778. 2 vols. Topsfield, 1917–20.

Dow, George Francis. *History of Topsfield.* Topsfield, 1940.

Crandall, Ruth, comp. See listing under Lunenburg (Mass.). Reel 6 contains Topsfield Single Lists of 1744 and 1765.

"Taxes Under Governor Andros: Topsfield Town Rate, 1687," *New England Historical and Genealogical Register* 35 (1885): 34–35.

"Topsfield Bill of Estate Made Between 1723 and 1725." *Essex Institute Historical Collections* 33 (1897): 194–96.

Records of the First Church in Topsfield: Historical Collections of the Topsfield Historical Society, vol. 14 (1909).

Waltham

A part of Watertown until its incorporation in 1738. The Watertown church split in an acrimonious dispute during the 1690s, and the territory of the western faction became a precinct in 1720.

Waltham, Board of Aldermen. *Record of the West Precinct of Watertown, 1720–1737/8*. Waltham, 1913.

Bond, Henry. *Genealogies of the Families and Descendents of the Early Settlers of Watertown, Massachusetts*. Boston, 1855.

Crandall, Ruth, comp. See listing under Lunenburg. Reel 25 contains the Waltham Province Taxlist of 1740.

Waltham Valuation List, 1771. At Massachusetts Archives 131: 635–38.

Watertown

Established as a town in 1630. The towns of Weston and Waltham were taken from Watertown in 1713 and 1738 respectively, and a part of Watertown was annexed to Cambridge in 1754.

Watertown Records, vols. 2–6. Watertown and Newton, Mass., 1900–1928. Contains town meeting, parish, and church records.

Bond, Henry. See listing under Waltham (Mass.).

Constable Perry's Rate [Watertown East Precinct], February 1729/30. At Massachusetts Historical Society.

Westminster

Granted to veterans of King Philip's War in 1729 as Narragansett Township no. 2. Settlement began in 1737 and the plantation was incorporated as a district in 1759.

Heywood, William Sweetzer. *History of Westminster, Massachusetts (First Named Narragansett No. 2), 1728–1893*. Lowell, Mass., 1893.

Westminster Valuation List, December 1759. At Massachusetts Historical Society.

Worcester

Settlement began in 1684 but was soon abandoned because of the Indian danger. The town was reoccupied about 1720, and began to function in 1722. It became the county seat of newly organized Worcester County in 1731.

"Early Records of the Town of Worcester, 1722–1784." *Collections of the Worcester Society of Antiquity*, vols. 2 and 4. Worcester, 1881–82.

Hurd, Duane Hamilton. *History of Worcester County with Biographical Sketches of its Prominent Men*. 4 vols. Philadelphia, 1889.

Lincoln, William. *History of Worcester, Massachusetts*. Worcester, 1837.

Nutt, Charles. *History of Worcester and Its People*. New York, 1919.

Worcester Valuation List, 1771. At Massachusetts Archives 134: 250.

Biddeford (Maine)
Settled in 1653 as Saco, but abandoned during the Indian wars of the 1690s. The town was reestablished as Biddeford in 1717. An eastern section of the town became the town of *Pepperrellborough in 1762.*
Folsom, George. *History of Saco and Biddeford.* Saco, 1830.
Owen, Daniel E. *Old Times in Saco.* Saco, 1891.
Ridlon, G. T. *Saco Valley Settlements and Families.* Reprint. Rutland, Vt., 1969.
"Records of the First Church of Christ in Biddeford." *Maine Historical and Genealogical Recorder* 5 (1888): 202–206.

Brunswick (Maine)
Settled but twice abandoned in the seventeenth century and in the 1720s. Resettled about 1730 and incorporated in 1738. The town was half Yankee and half Scots-Irish.
Wheeler, George A., and Wheeler, Henry W. *History of Brunswick, Topsham, and Harpswell, Maine.* Boston, 1878.
Brunswick Valuation List, 1771. At Massachusetts Archives 130: 165.

Falmouth (Maine)
Settled but twice abandoned in the 17th century. Resettled in 1713 and incorporated in 1719. Outlying precincts were established at Cape Elizabeth in 1733, at New Casco in 1753, and at Stroudwater in 1765. Cape Elizabeth became a town in 1765, and the commercial center of Falmouth became the new town of Portland in 1786.
Willis, William. *History of Portland from its First Settlement.* Part II, *1700–1833.* Portland, Me., 1833.
Jordan, William B., Jr. *History of Cape Elizabeth, Maine.* Portland, Me., 1965.
Falmouth Valuation List, 1761. At Massachusetts Archives, vol. 130.
Willis, William, ed. Journals of the Reverend Thomas Smith and the Reverend Samuel Deane. Portland, Me., 1849.
King, Marquis F., comp. *Baptisms and Admissions from the Records of the First Church in Falmouth, now Portland, Maine.* Portland, 1898.
Perkins, John Carroll. "Some Old Papers Recently Found in the Stone Tower of the First Parish Church of Portland." *Collections and Proceedings of the Maine Historical Society,* 2d ser., 6 (1895): 7–36.

Gorham (Maine)
Settled about 1736 and incorporated in 1764.
McLellan, Hugh D. *History of Gorham, Maine.* Portland, Me., 1903.
Gorham Valuation List, 1770. At Massachusetts Archives, 130: 688.

Newcastle (Maine)
Part of the Sheepscot settlement of the 17th century destroyed by Indians in 1676, resettled as "New Dartmouth" about 1683, and destroyed again during the next decade. Settled a third time about 1730 and incorporated in 1754.
Early Records of Newcastle, Maine from June 24, 1756 to January 6, 1779. Damariscotta, Me., 1914.
Cushman, David Quimby. *History of Ancient Sheepscot and Newcastle with Genealogies.* Bath, Me., 1882.

Scarborough (Maine)

Settled during the 1630s and incorporated in 1658 but abandoned during the Indian wars. The town was reestablished in 1720.

Libbey, Dorothy S. *Scarborough Becomes a Town*. Portland, Me., 1955.

Southgate, William S. *History of Scarborough, 1633-1785*. Portland, Me., 1853.

Scarborough Valuation List, 1771. At Massachusetts Archives, 134: 122.

"Scarborough Church Records." *Maine Historical and Genealogical Recorder* 1 (1894): 54; 4 (1897): 256-59.

NEW HAMPSHIRE TOWNS

Bedford

Granted by Massachusetts to veterans of King Philip's War in 1732 as Souhegan-East, or Narragansett no. 5, and confirmed by New Hampshire in 1750. Scots-Irish settlers from Londonderry began to occupy the town in 1737, and it was incorporated in 1750.

Bedford Town Records, 1770-1800. At New Hampshire Historical Society, Concord. Contains Tax List of 1770.

History of Bedford, New Hampshire, from 1737 . . . by the Town. Concord, 1903. Contains Town Tax List of 1750.

Woodbury, Peter P., et al., comp. *History of Bedford, New Hampshire, being Statistics compiled on the Occasion of the One Hundredth Anniversary*. Boston, 1851.

Canterbury

Granted to men from Dover in 1727 and settled soon after. The town was incorporated in 1750, and the town of Northfield was taken from it in 1780.

Canterbury Town Records, 1774-1800. At New Hampshire Historical Society. Contains Tax List of 1782.

Lyford, James Otis. *History of the Town of Canterbury, 1727-1912*. 2 vols. Concord, N.H., 1912.

Chester

Settled about 1723 but governed by absentee proprietors until 1728. In 1740 the town divided into two parishes, one Congregational and the other Presbyterian.

Chase, Benjamin. *History of Old Chester from 1719 to 1769*. Auburn, N.H., 1869.

Chase, John Carroll. *History of Chester, New Hampshire, including Auburn: A Supplement to the History of Old Chester*. Derry, N.H., 1926.

Records of the Presbyterian Parish in Chester, 1738-1842. At New Hampshire Historical Society.

Concord

Granted by Massachusetts to men from Andover and Haverhill and settled in 1727. Incorporated as Rumford in 1734. Rumford served as a test case for Massachusetts' claim to the territory west of the Merrimac River. After New Hampshire acquired title to the territory, it refused to reincorporate Rumford, maintaining that it was a part of an almost coterminous New Hampshire township called Bow, and allowing its governmental authority to lapse in 1748. The proprietors of Bow then attempted to assert title, but the Rumford settlers appealed to England and won confirmation of their land titles. New Hampshire incorporated the settlement as the parish of "Concord" in 1765, but the parish functioned as an independent town.

Concord [N.H.] Town Records, 1732–1820. Concord, 1894. Includes Assessment List of 1757.

Bouton, Nathaniel. History of Concord from its First Grant in 1725 to the Organization of the City Government in 1853. Concord, 1856.

Rumford Tax List of 1737. At New Hampshire Historical Society.

Concord Tax List of 1776. At New Hampshire Historical Society.

Walker, Joseph B., ed. "Diaries of Rev. Timothy Walker of Concord, 1730–1782." Collections of the New Hampshire Historical Society 9 (1889): 123–91.

Cornish
Settled in 1765 and incorporated in 1768.

Child, William H. History of the Town of Cornish, New Hampshire. Concord, c. 1910.

"Church Records and Marriage Records at Cornish, N.H., 1768–1805." New England Historical and Genealogical Register 72 (1918): 279–86.

Derryfield
Settled in 1722 as an offshoot of the Londonderry settlement and incorporated in 1751. The town changed its name to Manchester after 1800.

Early Records of Derryfield, 1751–1800, vols. 1–2. Manchester Historical Association Collections, vols. 8–9. Manchester, 1906. Includes Town Tax List of 1758 and Province Tax List of 1775.

Clarke, John B. Manchester: A Brief Record of Its Past. Manchester, N.H., 1875.

Dover
Settled before 1640 as one of the original four New Hampshire towns. Parishes of Newington (1713), Durham (1716), Somersworth (1729), and Madbury (1754), became towns in 1713, 1754, and 1755.

Quint, Alonzo H. The First Parish in Dover, New Hampshire. Dover, 1884.

Scales, John. History of Dover, New Hampshire. Dover, 1923.

Stackpole, Everett S. History of the Town of Durham. 2 vols. Durham, n.d.

Wadleigh, George H. Notable Events in the History of Dover, New Hampshire, 1623–1865. Dover, 1913.

"Vital Records of Dover." Collections of the Dover, New Hampshire, Historical Society, vol. 1 (1894).

"The Counterpin [Tax List] of Dover Parish, 1741." Provincial Papers of New Hampshire 23 (1894): 697–700.

"Dover Part for the Year 1753 Parish Rates." Provincial Papers of New Hampshire 11 (1882): 518–22.

"Church Records of Newington, N.H." New England Historical and Genealogical Register 22 (1868): 297–302, 447–51.

Manual of the First Church, Dover, N.H. Dover, 1893.

"A Record of Marriages, Deaths, Etc., As Made By the Rev. Hugh Adams of Durham, N.H." New England Historical and Genealogical Register 23 (1869): 297–99; 24 (1870): 27.

Dublin
Granted in 1749, settled in 1762, and incorporated in 1771.
Dublin Town Records, 1771–1800. At New Hampshire Historical Society.
Leonard, Levi W. *History of Dublin, New Hampshire*. Dublin, 1919. Contains Tax
List of 1771.

Hampstead
Incorporated as a town in 1749 from a section of the Massachusetts town of Haver-
hill cut off by the new boundary line.
Hampstead Town Records, 1749–1785. At New Hampshire Historical Society.
Noyes, Harriette E. *Memorial of the Town of Hampstead, New Hampshire*. 2 vols.
Boston, 1899–1903.

Hampton
One of the original four New Hampshire towns, incorporated in 1639. Parishes of
Hampton-Falls (1709) and North Hampton (1738) became towns in 1718 and 1745
respectively.
Hampton. Miscellaneous Town Papers. At New Hampshire Historical Society.
Dow, Joseph. *History of the Town of Hampton*. 2 vols. Salem, Mass., 1883.
Ross, John A. *History and Manual of the Congregational Church in Hampton, New
Hampshire*. Hampton, 1902.
Seabrook-Hampton Monthly Meeting of Friends. Minutes, 1700–1757. At Rhode
Island Historical Society Library.

Hanover
The town government was organized in 1761 as a proprietorship at Mansfield,
Connecticut, and transferred to Hanover in 1767, upon which the town was incor-
porated. Hanover became the seat of Dartmouth College in 1769.
Records of the Town of Hanover, New Hampshire, 1761–1818. Hanover, 1905.
Chase, Frederick. *History of Dartmouth College and the Town of Hanover, New
Hampshire*, vol. 1. Cambridge, Mass., 1891.
Lord, John King. *History of the Town of Hanover, New Hampshire*. Hanover, 1928.

Londonderry
Settled and incorporated in 1719 by Scots-Irish immigrants, the town was the center
of Irish settlement in colonial New England. It divided into two parishes in 1739.
*Londonderry Town Meeting Records, 1719–1762: Early Records of Londonderry,
Windham, and Derry*, vol. 1: *Manchester Historical Association Collections*,
vol. 5 (1908).
Londonderry Town Records, 1763–1785. At New Hampshire Historical Society.
Parker, Edward L. *History of Londonderry*. Boston, 1851.
Willey, George F. *Willey's Book of Nutfield*. Derry Depot, N.H., 1895.

New Ipswich
Granted by Massachusetts in 1735 and settled as early as 1738. The town was incorporated in 1762.
Chandler, Charles H. *History of New Ipswich, New Hampshire, 1735–1914*. Fitchburg, Mass., 1914.

Kidder, Frederick, and Gould, Augustus. *History of New Ipswich*. Boston, 1852. Contains Minister's Tax List of 1763 and Town Tax List of 1774.

Lee, Sarah Fiske. "Records of the Church at New Ipswich, New Hampshire, 1764–1773." *New England Historical and Genealogical Register* 71 (1917): 357–60.

Portsmouth

One of the original four towns and the capital of New Hampshire. The town of Greenland was set off in 1705.

Portsmouth Town Records, 1700–1785. W.P.A. Typescript at New Hampshire State Library, Concord.

"Portsmouth Town Officials." *New Hampshire Genealogical Record* 2 (1904): 97–105.

Brewster, Charles W. *Rambles About Portsmouth: Sketches of Persons, Localities, and Incidents of Two Centuries*. Portsmouth, 1859.

Portsmouth Town Records: Tax Records. Microfilm copy at New Hampshire State Library. Contains Province Tax List of 1715 and Province Tax List of 1758.

Gooding, Albert, ed. "Records of the South Church of Portsmouth, New Hampshire." *New England Historical and Genealogical Register* 81 (1927): 419–53; 82 (1928): 25–53.

Hovey, H. E. *History of Saint John's Church, Portsmouth*. Portsmouth, 1896.

Parish Register of King's Chapel, Portsmouth, 1738–83. Transcript at New Hampshire Historical Society.

Records of the First (North) Church of Portsmouth. 2 vols. Transcript at New Hampshire Historical Society.

"North Church Records of Portsmouth." *New Hampshire Genealogical Record* 3 (1905): 49–56.

Records of the Third Church of Portsmouth, 1758–1831. At New Hampshire Historical Society.

Scott, Kenneth. "Tory Associators of Portsmouth." *William and Mary Quarterly*, 3d. ser., 17 (1960): 507–515.

Weare

Granted to veterans of Phips' Canada expedition of 1690 in 1735 and regranted by New Hampshire in 1749. Incorporated in 1764.

Little, William. *History of Weare, New Hampshire, 1735-1888*. Lowell, Mass., 1888. Contains Tax List of 1764.

RHODE ISLAND TOWNS

Exeter

A part of North Kingstown, Exeter was incorporated in 1743.

Exeter Town Records, 1743–85. At Town Clerk's Office, Exeter.

Exeter Town Tax List for 1763. Exeter Papers, at Rhode Island Historical Society Library.

Exeter Colony Tax List for 1774. Exeter Papers, at Rhode Island Historical Society Library.

Middletown
Middletown was incorporated from the rural part of Newport in 1743.
Middletown Town Records, 1743–76, 1780–85. At Town Clerk's Office, Middletown.
    No records were kept from 1776 to 1780 while the town was occupied by British
    troops.
Middletown State Tax List for 1783. In Rhode Island State Archives, Statehouse,
    Providence.

Newport
Established 1639. The rural part of the town became Middletown in 1743, and
    Newport became a city in 1784.
Newport Town Meeting Records, 1702–1735, 1750–76, 1780–81. At Newport His-
    torical Society, Newport. No records were kept from 1776 to 1780 while the town
    was occupied by British troops. The earlier records were damaged severely in
    1780 when a British ship foundered while attempting to remove them to New
    York, and are illegible in many places.
Newport Colony Tax List of 1760. At Rhode Island State Archives.
Newport Town Tax List of 1782. At Newport Historical Society.
First Baptist Church Record Book, 1725. At Newport Historical Society.
Second Baptist Church, Six Principal, Records. At Newport Historical Society.
Seventh Day Baptist Church Records, 1708–1817. At Newport Historical Society.
First Congregational Church Records. At Newport Historical Society.
    Rates of Pews in the Congregational Meeting House.
    Marriages and Baptisms.
First and Second Congregational Church Records. Typescript at Newport Historical
    Society.
Second Congregational Church Records. At Newport Historical Society.
    Record Book, 1725–72.
    Records, 1728.
    Records and Accounts, 1733–1834.
Newport Monthly Meeting of Friends Records. At Newport Historical Society.
    Births and Deaths to 1800.
Hammett, Charles E., Jr. "Sketch of the History of the Congregational Churches of
    Newport." Typescript (1891) at Newport Historical Society.
Mason, George Champlin. *Annals of Trinity Church, Newport, Rhode Island,
    1698–1821.* 2 vols. Newport, 1890.
Stiles, Ezra. See listing under New Haven (Conn.). Contains a religious census of
    Newport for 1760.

Providence
One of the original four towns in Rhode Island, settled in 1636. Six towns were
incorporated from Providence lands during the eighteenth century: Glocester
(1731), Scituate (1731), Smithfield (1731), Cranston (1754), Johnston (1759), and
North Providence (1765).
Providence Town Records, 1700–1785. At City Clerk's Office, Providence.
Staples, William R. *Annals of the Town of Providence from its First Settlement to
    the Organization of the City Government in June 1822.* Providence, 1843.
Providence Town Tax List, 1705. At Rhode Island Historical Society Library.
Providence Colony Tax List, 1751. At Rhode Island Historical Society Library.

Providence Colony Tax List, 1773. At Rhode Island Historical Society Library.

Act of Incorporation of the Benevolent Congregational Society in the Town of Providence. Providence, 1771.

Hall, Edward B. *Discourses Comprising a History of the First Congregational Church in Providence.* Providence, 1836.

King, Henry Melville, comp. *Historical Catalogue of the Members of the First Baptist Church.* Providence, 1908.

Sprague, Waldo C. See Listing under Braintree (Mass.). Contains data on Providence Anglicans.

Vose, James G. *Commemorative Discourses Preached in the Beneficient Congregational Church.* Providence, 1869.

Smithfield

Incorporated from a part of Providence in 1731.

Steere, Thomas. *History of the Town of Smithfield, Rhode Island.* Providence, 1881.

Smithfield Colony Tax List of 1760. At Rhode Island State Archives.

Smithfield Monthly Meeting of Friends. Minutes, 1718–1857. At Rhode Island Historical Society Library.

South Kingstown

Settled in the 1660s and incorporated in 1723 from the old town of Kingstown. South Kingstown was the county seat of Kings County and the heart of the "Narragansett country."

South Kingstown Town Records, 1723–85. At Town Clerk's Office, Wakefield, Rhode Island.

Town Meeting Records, Books 1 and 2.

Tax List Books 1 and 2. Includes the Town Tax List for 1730 and the Colony Tax List for 1774.

Miller, William Davis. "The Narragansett Planters." *Proceedings of the American Antiquarian Society* 43 (1934): 49–115.

"Taxes under Governor Andros, #10." *New England Historical and Genealogical Register* 35 (1881): 124–27. Kingstown Tax List for 1687.

South Kingstown Monthly Meeting of Friends. Minutes, 1743–89. At Rhode Island Historical Society Library.

South Kingstown Monthly Meeting of Friends. List of Members, 1782. In Monthly Meeting Papers, Box 37, Rhode Island Historical Society Library.

Stiles, Ezra. See listing under New Haven (Conn.). Contains a religious census of South Kingstown for 1760.

Biographical and Genealogical Sources

A NOTE ON GENEALOGY

No attempt has been made in this study to specify the sources used in tracing genealogical data on some 5,000 individuals; indeed, to do so would require far more space and time than the increase in information would repay. In general, the procedure followed was to begin with the sources cited in this bibliography for the town in question, to proceed to sources such as genealogical collections and compilations of vital records, and finally to turn to family genealogies. Many town histories, including some whose titles do not so indicate, contain extensive genealogical registers, and the vital records are available for many towns in published form. Where town sources fail, much information is available in broader compilations, in the form of colony-wide genealogical collections, and compilations of vital records for units above the town level. A last resort, used extensively in this study, involves the examination of individual family genealogies. Many of these are accurate, but some are remarkably naïve, attempting to trace the family to Adam and Eve or to equally remote ancestors, and all must be used with caution. Individual genealogies have not been listed in this bibliography, but much of the work with individual family sources was done at the Rhode Island Historical Society Library, and that institution's collection constitutes a reasonable basis for pinpointing specific sources.

BIOGRAPHICAL AND GENEALOGICAL COMPILATIONS

Alexander, Samuel D. *Princeton College during the Eighteenth Century.* New York, 1872.

Arnold, James N. *Vital Records of Rhode Island.* 17 vols. Providence, 1883.

Austin, John O. *Genealogical Dictionary of Rhode Island.* Reprint. Baltimore, 1969.

Bowen, Clarence Winthrop. *History of Woodstock, Connecticut.* 8 vols. Norwood, Massachusetts, 1923–35. Volumes 2–8 contain extensive genealogical information on eastern Connecticut.

Dexter, Franklin B. *Biographical Sketches of the Graduates of Yale College with Annals of the College History,* vols. 1–6. New York, 1885–1912.

Essex Institute Historical Collections, vols. 1–89 (1859–1953).

New England Historical and Genealogical Register, vols. 1–124 (1847–1971).

Noyes, Sybil, et al. *Genealogical Dictionary of Maine and New Hampshire.* Portland, Me., 1928–39.

Roberts, Oliver Ayers. *History of the Military Company of Massachusetts Now Called the Ancient and Honorable Artillery Company of Massachusetts.* 4 vols. Boston, 1895–1901.

Savage, James. *Genealogical Dictionary of the First Settlers of New England.* 4 vols. Boston, 1860.

Shipton, Clifford K. *Sibley's Harvard Graduates,* vols. 4–16. Boston, 1933–1972.

Sibley, John Langdon. *Biographical Sketches of Graduates of Harvard University,* vols. 1–3. Cambridge, Mass., 1873–85.

University of Pennsylvania: Biographical Catalogue of the Matriculates of the College, 1749–1893. Philadelphia, 1894.

General Works

PUBLIC RECORDS

Connecticut

Acts and Laws of His Majesties Colony of Connecticut in New England, 1702. Hartford, 1901.

Hoadly, Charles J., and Labaree, Leonard W., eds. *Public Records of the State of Connecticut*, vols. 1-7. Hartford, 1894-1948.
Trumbull, J. Hammond, and Hoadly, Charles J., eds. *Public Records of the Colony of Connecticut*, vols. 1-15. Hartford, 1850-90.
State of Connecticut: Register and Manual, 1934. Hartford, 1934.

Massachusetts
Acts and Resolves of the Province of the Massachusetts-Bay. 21 vols. Boston, 1869-1922.
Colonial Laws of Massachusetts Reprinted from the Edition of 1672. Boston, 1887.
Journal of the House of Representatives of Massachusetts. 42 vols. Boston, 1919-1970.
Massachusetts Board of Harbor and Land Commissioners. *Annual Report for the Year 1915.* Boston, 1915.
Massachusetts Secretary of State (Kevin H. White). *Historical Data Relating to Counties, Cities, and Towns in Massachusetts.* Boston, 1966.
Whitmore, William. *The Massachusetts Civil List for the Colonial and Provincial Periods, 1630-1774.* Albany, 1870.
Records of the General Sessions of the Peace for Suffolk County, 1703-1731. 4 vols. At the Office of the Clerk of the Supreme Judicial Court for Suffolk County, Suffolk County Courthouse, Boston.
Rice, Franklin B., ed. "Records of the Court of General Sessions of the Peace For the County of Worcester." *Collections of the Worcester Society of Antiquity 5 (1883): 1-190.*
Town Records of Dudley, Massachusetts. Pawtucket, R.I., 1893-94.
Green, Samuel A., ed. *Early Records of Groton, Massachusetts, 1662-1707.* Groton, 1880.
Records of the Town Meetings of Lynn, 1691-1757. 5 vols. Lynn, Mass., 1949-66.
Nourse, Henry S., ed. *Early Records of Lancaster, Massachusetts, 1643-1725.* Lancaster, 1884.
Sargent, William Mitchell, comp. *Maine Wills, 1640-1760.* Portland, Me., 1887.
Records of the Town of Tisbury, Massachusetts. Boston, 1903.

New Hampshire
Acts and Laws of His Majesties Province of New Hampshire in New England . . . to October 16, 1759. Portsmouth, 1761.
New Hampshire: The Official Succession for Two Centuries. Concord, 1879.
Provincial Papers of New Hampshire, vols. 1-40. Manchester, Nashua, and Concord, N.H., 1867-1943.
Province of New Hampshire: Commission of the Justices of the Peace, 1717. At New Hampshire Historical Society.

Rhode Island
Acts and Resolves of Rhode Island, 1747-1785. Newport and Providence, 1747-85.
Bartlett, John R., ed. *Rhode Island Colonial Records*, vols. 1-10. Providence, 1855-67.

Rider, Sidney S., ed. *Acts and Laws of Her Majesties Colony of Rhode Island, 1705.* Providence, 1896.

Smith, Joseph Jenckes. *Civil and Military List of Rhode Island, 1647–1800.* Providence, 1900.

ALMANACS AND NEWSPAPERS

Ames, Nathaniel. *An Astronomical Diary or Almanack for 1760.* Boston, 1760.

Anderson, John. *The Rhode Island Almanack.* Newport, 1772.

Bowen, Nathan. *New England Diary or Almanack for 1727.* Boston, 1727.

Clough, Samuel. *Kalendarium Nov-Anglicanum or an Almanac for 1705.* Boston, 1705.

Edes, Benjamin, and Gill, John. *North American Almanack and Massachusetts Register.* Boston, 1770.

Mein, John, and Fleeming, John. *Massachusetts Register.* Boston, 1766.

Prince, Thomas. *The Vade Mecum for America.* Boston, 1732.

Register of New Hampshire and Almanac for 1768. N.p., n.d.

Sherman, Roger. *An Astronomical Diary or Almanack for 1755.* Boston, 1755.

West, Benjamin. *The New-England Almanack.* Providence, 1764.

Whittemore, Nathaniel. *The Farmer's Almanac for 1716.* Boston, 1716.

Boston *News-Letter*, 30 September 1773. Microcard Edition.

Newport *Mercury*, June 1763–June 1780. At Rhode Island Historical Society Library.

SECONDARY SOURCES

Adams, John. *Defense of the Constitutions of Government of the United States of America,* edited by Charles Francis Adams. *The Works of John Adams,* vol. 4. Boston, 1851.

————. *The Diary and Autobiography of John Adams,* edited by Lyman Butterfield. *The Adams Papers,* vols. 1–4. Cambridge, Mass., 1961.

————. *The Legal Papers of John Adams.* vol. 2, edited by L. Kinvin Wroth and Hiller B. Zobel. Cambridge, Mass., 1965.

Akagi, Roy Hidemichi. *The Town Proprietors of the New England Colonies.* Philadelphia, 1924.

Backus, Isaac. *A History of New England with Particular Reference to the Denomination of Christians called Baptists.* 2 vols. Newton, Mass., 1871.

Bailyn, Bernard. *The Origins of American Politics.* New York, 1968.

Bailyn, Bernard, and Bailyn, Lotte. *Massachusetts Shipping, 1697–1714.* Cambridge, Mass., 1959.

Barber, Bernard. *Social Stratification.* New York, 1957.

Batchelder, Calvin R. *A History of the Eastern Diocese.* 2 vols. Claremont, N.H., and Boston, 1876–1910.

Belknap, Jeremy. *History of New-Hampshire.* 3 vols. Philadelphia, 1784–92.

Bell, Hugh F. " 'A Personal Challenge': The Otis-Hutchinson Currency Controversy, 1761–1762." *Essex Institute Historical Collections* 106 (1970): 297–323.

Bentley, William. *Diary of William Bentley,* vol. 2. Salem, 1907.

Benton, Josiah Henry. *Early Census-Making in Massachusetts*. Boston, 1905.

Bidwell, Percy W., and Falconer, John I. *History of Agriculture in the Northern United States, 1620-1860*. New York, 1925.

Bishop, Cortland F. *History of Elections in the American Colonies*. New York, 1893.

Blalock, Hubert M., Jr. *Social Statistics*. New York, 1960.

Bouton, Nathaniel. See listings under Concord (N.H.).

Breen, Timothy H. *The Character of the Good Ruler: Puritan Political Ideas in New England, 1630-1730*. New Haven, 1970.

————. "Who Governs: The Town Franchise in Seventeenth Century Massachusetts." *William and Mary Quarterly*, 3d. ser., 27 (1970): 460-74.

Bridenbaugh, Carl. *Cities in the Wilderness: The First Century of Urban Life in America, 1625-1742*. New York, 1938.

————. "The New England Town: A Way of Life." *American Antiquarian Society Proceedings* 56 (1946): 19-48.

Brown, Richard D. "The Emergence of Urban Society in Rural Massachusetts, 1760-1820." *Journal of American History* 61 (1974): 29-51.

Brown, Robert E. *Middle-Class Democracy and the Revolution in Massachusetts, 1691-1780*. Ithaca, 1955.

Bumsted, John M. See listing under Norton (Mass.).

Bushman, Richard L. *From Puritan to Yankee: Character and the Social Order in Connecticut, 1690-1765*. Cambridge, Mass., 1967.

Cadbury, Henry J. "A Map of 1782 Showing Friends Meetings in New England." *Quaker History* 52 (1963): 1-3.

Callendar, John. "An Historical Discourse on the Civil and Religious Affairs of the Colony of Rhode Island." *Rhode Island Historical Society Collections*, vol. 4 (1838).

Chapin, Howard M. "Eighteenth Century Rhode Island Printed Proxies." *The American Collector* 1 (November 1925): 54-59.

Christaller, Walter. *Central Places in Southern Germany*. Translated by Carlisle W. Baskin. Englewood Cliffs, N.J., 1967.

Clark, Andrew H. "Suggestions for the Geographical Study of Agricultural Change in the United States, 1790-1840." *Agricultural History* 46 (1972): 155-72.

Clark, Charles E. *The Eastern Parts: The Settlement of Northern New England, 1610-1763*. New York, 1970.

Clark, Terry N., ed. *Community Structure and Decision Making: Comparative Analyses*. San Francisco, 1968.

Clarke, George Kuhn. *History of Needham, Massachusetts, 1711-1911*. Cambridge, Mass., c. 1912.

Cohen, Joel A. "Democracy in Revolutionary Rhode Island: A Statistical Analysis." *Rhode Island History* 29 (1970): 3-16.

————. "Rhode Island Loyalism and the American Revolution." *Rhode Island History* 27 (1968): 97-112.

Conley, Patrick T. "Rhode Island Constitutional Development, 1636-1775: A Survey." *Rhode Island History* 27 (1968): 49-62, 74-94.

Connecticut Historical Society. *List of Congregational Ecclesiastical Societies Established in Connecticut Before 1818*. Hartford, 1918.

Cook, Edward M., Jr. "Local Leadership and the Typology of New England Towns, 1700-1785." *Political Science Quarterly* 86 (1971): 586-608.

————. See also listings under Dedham (Mass.).

Copeland, Alfred M. *History of the Town of Murrayfield, 1760-1783.* Springfield, Mass., 1892.

Daniell, Jere R. *Experiment in Republicanism: New Hampshire Politics and the American Revolution, 1741-1794.* Cambridge, Mass., 1970.

Dawes, Norman H. "Titles of Prestige in Seventeenth-Century New England." *William and Mary Quarterly*, 3d. ser., 6 (1949): 69-83.

Demos, John. *A Little Commonwealth: Family Life in Plymouth Colony.* New York, 1970.

Dethlefsen, Edwin S. "Colonial Gravestones and Demography." *American Journal of Physical Anthropology* 31 (1969): 321-34.

Dinkin, Robert J. "Seating the Meetinghouse in Early Massachusetts." *New England Quarterly* 43 (1970): 450-64.

Estes, David F. *History of Holden, Massachusetts.* Worcester, Mass., 1894.

Felt, Joseph B. "Statistics of Population in Massachusetts." *American Statistical Association Collections* 1 (1847): 121-216.

Field, David. *Statistical Account of the County of Middlesex [Connecticut].* Middletown, 1819.

Fowle, Daniel. *Civil, Military, and Ecclesiastical Register of the Province of New Hampshire, 1772.* Portsmouth, 1771.

Fry, William Henry. *New Hampshire as a Royal Province.* New York, 1908.

Grant, Charles S. See listing under Kent (Conn.).

Greene, Evarts B., and Harrington, Virginia D. *American Population Before the Federal Census of 1790.* New York, 1932.

Greenleaf, Moses. *A Survey of the State of Maine in Reference to its Geographical Features, Statistics, and Political Economy.* Portland, Me., 1829.

Greven, Philip J., Jr. See listing under Andover (Mass.).

Harris, P. M. G. "The Social Origins of American Leaders: Their Demographic Foundations." *Perspectives in American History* 3 (1969): 159-346.

Hazen, Henry A. "The Ministry and Churches of New Hampshire." *Congregational Quarterly* 17 (1875): 545-74.

Hedges, James B. *The Browns of Providence Plantations: The Colonial Years.* Cambridge, Mass., 1952.

Henretta, James A. See listing under Boston (Mass.).

Hudson, Charles. *History of the Town of Marlborough.* Boston, 1862.

Hutchinson, Thomas. *The History of the Colony and Province of Massachusetts-Bay.* Edited by Lawrence Shaw Mayo. Cambridge, Mass., 1936.

Jameson, J. Franklin. *The American Revolution Considered as a Social Movement.* Paperback. Boston, 1956.

Kirby, John B. "Early American Politics—The Search for Ideology: An Historiographical Analysis and Critique of the Concept of 'Deference'." *Journal of Politics* 32 (1970): 808-838.

Kinney, Charles B., Jr. *Church & State: The Struggle for Separation in New Hampshire, 1630-1900.* New York, 1955.

Kulikoff, Allan. "The Progress of Inequality in Revolutionary Boston." *William and Mary Quarterly*, 3d. ser., 28 (1971): 375-412.

Lawrence, Robert F. *The New Hampshire Churches.* Claremont, New Hampshire, 1856.

Lemon, James T. "Urbanization and the Development of Eighteenth Century Southeastern Pennsylvania and Adjacent Delaware." *William and Mary Quarterly*, 3d. ser., 24 (1967): 501–542.

Lemon, James T., and Nash, Gary B. "The Distribution of Wealth in Eighteenth Century America: A Century of Change in Chester County, Pennsylvania." *Journal of Social History* 2 (1968-9), 1-24.

Levesque, George. "Coventry: The Colonial Years." Master's Thesis, Brown University, 1969.

Lockridge, Kenneth A. "Letter to the Editor." *William and Mary Quarterly*, 3d. ser., 25 (1968): 516-17.

————. See listings under Dedham (Mass.).

Lockridge, Kenneth A., and Kreider, Alan. "The Evolution of Massachusetts Town Government 1640-1740." *William and Mary Quarterly*, 3d. ser., 23 (1966): 549-74.

Loomis, Dwight, and Calhoun, J. Gilbert. *The Judicial and Civil History of Connecticut.* Boston, 1895.

Lovejoy, David S. *Rhode Island Politics and the American Revolution, 1760-1776.* Providence, 1958.

MacSparren, James. *A Letterbook and Abstract of Out Services Written during the Years 1743-1751.* Edited by Daniel Goodwin. Boston, 1899.

Main, Jackson T. *The Social Structure of Revolutionary America.* Princeton, N.J., 1965.

————. *The Upper House in Revolutionary America, 1763-1788.* Madison, Wisc., 1967.

McLoughlin, William G. "Massive Civil Disobedience as a Baptist Tactic in 1773." *American Quarterly*, 21 (1969): 710-27.

————. *New England Dissent, 1630-1833.* 2 vols. Cambridge, Mass., 1971.

Merrens, H. Roy. "Historical Geography and Early American History." *William and Mary Quarterly*, 3d ser., 22 (1965): 529-48.

Merrill, Eliphalet, and Merrill, Phineas. *Gazetteer of the State of New-Hampshire.* Exeter, N.H., 1817.

Miller, Perry. *The New England Mind From Colony to Province.* Cambridge, Mass., 1953.

Miller, William Davis. See listing under South Kingstown (R.I.).

Moran, Gerald F. "Conditions of Religious Conversion in the First Society of Norwich, Connecticut, 1718-1744." *Journal of Social History* 5 (1972): 331-43.

Morgan, Edmund S. *Visible Saints: The History of a Puritan Idea.* New York, 1963.

Morse, Abner. *Genealogical Register of the Inhabitants and History of the Towns of Sherborn and Holliston.* Boston, 1856.

Murrin, John M. "The Legal Transformation: The Bench and Bar in Eighteenth Century Massachusetts." In *Colonial America: Essays in Politics and Social Development,* edited by Stanley N. Katz, pp. 415-49. Boston, 1971.

Namier, Lewis. *The Structure of Politics at the Accession of George III.* 2d ed. London, 1961.

Newcomer, Lee Nathaniel. *The Embattled Farmers: A Massachusetts Countryside in the American Revolution.* New York, 1953.

Oliver, Peter. *Origin and Progress of the American Rebellion.* Edited by Douglass Adair and John A. Schutz. San Marino, Calif., 1963.

Patten, Matthew. *The Diary of Matthew Patten of Bedford, New Hampshire, 1754–1788.* Concord, N.H., 1903.

Pease, John C., and Niles, John M. *Gazetteer of Rhode Island and Connecticut.* Hartford, 1819.

Pocock, John G. A. "Machiavelli, Harrington, and English Political Ideologies in the Eighteenth Century." *William and Mary Quarterly,* 3d. ser., 22 (1965): 549–83.

Pope, Robert G. *The Half-Way Covenant: Church Membership in Puritan New England.* Princeton, N.J., 1969.

Powell, Sumner Chilton. *Puritan Village: The Formation of a New England Town.* Paperback edition. New York, 1965.

Rutman, Darrett B. *Winthrop's Boston: Portrait of a Puritan Town 1630–1649.* Chapel Hill, 1965.

Reed, Susan M. *Church and State in Massachusetts, 1691–1740.* Urbana, Ill., 1914.

Schutz, John A. *William Shirley: King's Governor of Massachusetts.* Chapel Hill, N.C., 1961.

Sewall, Samuel. "Diary of Samuel Sewall." *Collections of the Massachusetts Historical Society,* 5th ser., 6 (Boston, 1879): 144–47.

Sheldon, Hezekiah Spencer. *Documentary History of Suffield in the Colony and Province of the Massachusetts-Bay in New England, 1660–1749.* Springfield, Mass., 1879.

Shipton, Clifford K. See listing under Biographical and Genealogical Sources.

Sly, John Fairfield. *Town Government in Massachusetts 1620–1930.* Cambridge, Mass., 1930.

Smith, Daniel Scott. "Cyclical, Secular, and Structural Change in American Elite Composition." *Perspectives in American History* 4 (1970): 363–72.

Steiner, Bruce E. "Anglican Officeholding in Pre-Revolutionary Connecticut: The Parameters of New England Community." *William and Mary Quarterly,* 3d. ser., 31 (1974): 369–406.

––––––. "New England Anglicanism: A Genteel Faith?" *William and Mary Quarterly,* 3d. ser., 27 (1970): 122–35.

Sutherland, Lucy S. "The City of London in Eighteenth-Century Politics." In *Essays Presented to Sir Lewis Namier,* edited by Richard Pares and A. J. P. Taylor, pp. 49–74. London, 1956.

Taylor, Robert. *Western Massachusetts in the Revolution.* Providence, 1954.

Teele, Albert K. *History of Milton, 1640–1887.* Boston, 1887.

Tiffany, Nina M., and Lesley, Susan I., eds. *Letters of James Murray, Loyalist.* Boston, 1901.

Van Deventer, David E. *Emergence of Provincial New Hampshire 1623–1741.* Ph.D. dissertation. Case-Western Reserve University, 1969. (To be published by the Johns Hopkins University Press in 1976.)

Wall, Robert Emmett, Jr. "The Massachusetts Bay Colony Franchise in 1647." *William and Mary Quarterly,* 3d. ser., 27 (1970): 136–44.

Wallett, Francis G. "The Massachusetts Council, 1766–1774: The Transformation of a Conservative Institution." *William and Mary Quarterly,* 3d. ser., 6 (1949): 605–27.

––––––, ed. "The Diary of Francis Parkman, 1729–1738. *Proceedings of the American Antiquarian Society* 71 (1961): 361–448.

Walsh, James P. "Solomon Stoddard's Open Communion: A Re-examination." *New England Quarterly* 42 (1970): 97–114.

Warden, Gerald R. See listings under Boston (Mass.).

Washburn, Emory. *Sketches of the Judicial History of Massachusetts.* Boston, 1840.

Waters, John J. *The Otis Family in Provincial and Revolutionary Massachusetts.* Chapel Hill, N.C., 1968.

Waters, John J., and Schutz, John A. "Patterns of Massachusetts Colonial Politics: The Writs of Assistance and the Rivalry between the Otis and Hutchinson Families." *William and Mary Quarterly,* 3d. ser., 24 (1967): 543–67.

Watson, Jeffry. Jeffry Watson's Diary. Transcript at Rhode Island Historical Society Library.

Weaver, Glenn. *Jonathan Trumbull, Connecticut's Merchant Magistrate.* Hartford, 1956.

Whiting, Samuel. *The Connecticut Town Officer.* Danbury, Conn., 1814.

Williamson, Chilton. *American Suffrage from Property to Democracy: 1760–1860.* Princeton, N.J., 1960.

Willingham, William F. "Deference Democracy and Town Government in Windham, Connecticut, 1755–1786." *William and Mary Quarterly,* 3d. ser., 30 (1973): 401–22.

Worthley, Harold Field. *An Inventory of the Records of the Particular (Congregational) Churches of Massachusetts Gathered 1620–1805.* Cambridge, Mass., 1970.

Zemsky, Robert M. *Merchants, Farmers, and River Gods.* Boston, 1971.

————. "Power, Influence, and Status: Leadership Patterns in the Massachusetts Assembly, 1740–1755." *William and Mary Quarterly,* 3d ser., 26 (1969): 502–20.

Zuckerman, Michael. *Peaceable Kingdoms: The New England Towns in the Eighteenth Century.* New York, 1970.

INDEX

Library of Congress Cataloging in Publication Data

Cook, Edward M   1944–
    The fathers of the towns.

    (Johns Hopkins University studies in historical and
political science; 94th ser., no. 2)
    Bibliography: pp. 237–65
    1. Municipal officials and employees—New England—
History. 2. Municipal government—New England—History.
I. Title. II. Series: Johns Hopkins University.
Studies in historical and political science; 94th ser.,
no. 2.
JS431.C66   301.15′53′0974   75-36937
ISBN 0-8018-1741-2